Coming Home?

Coming Home?

Refugees, Migrants, and Those Who Stayed Behind

Edited by
Lynellyn D. Long and Ellen Oxfeld

PENN

University of Pennsylvania Press

Philadelphia

10   9   8   7   6   5   4   3   2   1

Published by
University of Pennsylvania Press
Philadelphia, Pennsylvania 19104-4011

Library of Congress Cataloging-in-Publication Data

Coming home? : refugees, migants, and those who stayed behind / edited by
Lynellyn D. Long and Ellen Oxfeld.
    p. cm.
  ISBN 0-8122-3751-X (cloth : alk. paper)—ISBN 0-8122-1858-2 (pbk. : alk.
paper)
  Includes bibliographcal references and index.
  1. Return migration—case studies. I. Long, Lynellyn. II. Oxfeld, Ellen, 1953-
JV6032 .C66   2004
304.8—dc 22   2003061825

In memory of Beatrice Hackett for her work and scholarship on return

Contents

Introduction: An Ethnography of Return   1
Ellen Oxfeld and Lynellyn D. Long

PART I   Imagined Return

1. Illusions of Home in the Story of a Rwandan Refugee's Return   19
John Janzen

2. Contemplating Repatriation to Eritrea   34
Lucia Ann McSpadden

3. Filipina Depictions of Migrant Life for Their Kin at Home   49
Jane A. Margold

PART II   Provisional Return

4. Viet Kieu on a Fast Track Back?   65
Lynellyn D. Long

5. Chinese Villagers and the Moral Dilemmas of Return Visits   90
Ellen Oxfeld

6. Changing Filipina Identities and Ambivalent Returns   104
Nicole Constable

PART III   Repatriated Return

7. Returning German Jews and Questions of Identity   127
John Borneman

8. Repatriation and Social Class in Nicaragua   150
James Phillips

9. Refugee Returns to Sarajevo and Their Challenge to Contemporary
Narratives of Mobility   170
Anders H. Stefansson

10. The Making of a Good Citizen in an Ethiopian Returnee
Settlement   187
Laura Hammond

11. West Indian Migrants and Their Rediscovery of Barbados   206
George Gmelch

Notes   225

Bibliography   237

List of Contributors   263

Index   267

Acknowledgments   277

Introduction:
An Ethnography of Return

Ellen Oxfeld and Lynellyn D. Long

> Someday, when my daughter has grown enough to understand and remember, we will take a trip to Russia. We will go to my village, where nobody lives anymore, where empty windows are nailed down. We will find my house, and I will show her a real Russian stove, with hundreds of tiny fingerprints on it. We will find our *banya* on the bank of the river. We will clean this now cold little hut and sit there for a long time, inhaling the smell of old birch leaves. With the beginning of twilight we will take off our clothes and swim under the moon in the river of my childhood. A flock of birds will timidly take wing from our loud squealing. They will circle above, surprised by the sound of human joy, so long forgotten in this abandoned, neglected place.
> —A thirty-eight-year-old Russian, Burlington, Vermont, 1999

People often remember a place from their past to which they want to return and share with future generations. However, for some, returning home is problematic and, given existing social, economic and political conditions, the return may be neither possible nor desirable. Historically, many immigrants, refugees, and exiles have been unable to return home.[1] Yet, surprisingly in recent times, many people find they can return home again and they are doing so—to visit, to live temporarily, or to reestablish a long-term residence.

In the past decade alone, the world witnessed the unprecedented return of millions of displaced persons, refugees, and migrants to their former homes.[2] According to the United Nations High Commission for Refugees (UNHCR), beginning in the 1990s and continuing to the present time, there was a steady rise in the number of refugee returns. In 1998 alone, UNHCR estimated that 3.5 million out of 22.5 million refugees and internally displaced persons returned to their homelands. Most recently, there have been major return movements in the Balkans, East Timor, Rwanda, and Guatemala. In 2000, between Bosnia-Herzegovina and Croatia, for example, cross border returns of different ethnic minority groups outnumbered the previous five years, although the potential for a renewed outbreak of hostilities in Bosnia-Herzegovina remained high.

Voluntary mass repatriations are only part of the story. Throughout the world, immigrants and refugees are choosing to go home again and expending their own resources to re-establish themselves in a former home even after having left many years earlier. Irish immigrants from Boston are returning home to raise families in Northern Ireland (Mooney 1997; Barry 1997), Koreans from Los Angeles returned to South Korea after civil riots targeted their businesses (Kang 1997), and Puerto Ricans from the United States mainland retire to the island after years of work away. A quiet, steady stream of refugees and migrants are returning of their own accord to Vietnam, China, the Philippines, Barbados, Ireland, the Balkans, and many other countries. Contrary to widespread perceptions that people want to settle in their new homes, especially in wealthy Western countries, many refugees and migrants want to return eventually, and they lead their lives in the new home always hoping and/or planning for that eventuality. For example, of the 30 million people admitted to the United States between 1900 and 1980, some 10 million (one-third) returned home again (Stalker 2001: 114). Despite common experiences of uprooting, dislocation, and mobility in part characteristic of globalization, the idea of being rooted still has its own appeal. Indeed, at present, those who live outside the country of their birth comprise only 3 percent of the world's population (Stalker 2001: 11).

In this volume, we address return movements and how they affect both the communities to which people return, as well as the returnees themselves. Despite ample evidence of returns worldwide, quantifying return has always been problematic.[3] Circular migrations, the inability of governments to get precise data, and the many ways in which humans migrate make it impossible to assemble a completely accurate picture. Nonetheless, both contemporary and historical dimensions of this phenomenon have been assessed through a variety of techniques. These include the use of census data, surveys, immigration records, biographies and life histories, city directories, church registries, retrospective interviews, and estimates based on monetary remittances and return savings (Sills 2000/2001). For instance, from government, shipping, business, religious, and labor records, as well as the accounts of journalists and travelers, the historian Wyman has estimated that in the late 1800s and early 1900s a quarter to a third of all immigrants returned from the U.S. to resettle again in Europe permanently, totalling as many as four million returnees (Wyman 1993: 6). And, from a combination of Census and Immigration and Naturalization Service (INS) data, Brjas and Bratsberg estimated that 21.5 percent of all legal immigrants who arrived in the United States between 1970 and 1974 had left by 1980 (1996: 169).[4] Presumably, most of these immigrants returned home. More recently, from interview and survey data, Reyes (1997) found that 50 percent of immigrants surveyed in 7,500 households in Mexico and the U.S. returned to Mexico within two years (cited in Sills 2000/2001: 5).

These studies demonstrate that return is an integral part of the migration experience. With increased flexibility in the flow of capital and trade goods, which may undermine the local subsistence base, migration has assumed increasing importance as an economic and social strategy for families. But, often returns make further migration possible, since the returnees provide knowledge of and networks in the host country (Massey 1987: 1399).

Numbers alone do not justify the critical importance of returns to contemporary issues of globalization, national and ethnic identities, human rights, and transnationalism. Returns have important political, social, economic and cultural consequences. For governments and local communities alike, returns of ethnic minorities to war torn societies or of diaspora groups to long awaited homelands have significant political consequences (Koser 2000)[5] leading to new balances of power and political arrangements. Returnees may also strain existing resources and relationships within local communities. Often returning migrants engage in building new houses and conspicuous consumption (Gmelch 1980). Although these activities may stimulate growth in the construction trade, such returns do not necessarily lead to new economic growth, investment, or innovation as is often argued by government authorities (in both sending and receiving countries) to justify the rapid return of refugees.

Nonetheless, return of certain professional groups appropriately timed may have positive economic effects on redeveloping poor and/or war-torn economies (Koser 2000; Gmelch 1980 and this volume; International Organization for Migration 2001). Many governments and even local communities encourage returns—especially with accompanying remittances, investment, and certain categories of skilled labor—to stimulate economic growth as a means to counter dependency on foreign capital and humanitarian assistance. In response to terrorist threats, many Western governments are also evicting immigrants (especially young labor migrants from the Middle East, North Africa, and Central Asia). Yet, many of these immigrants are leading productive lives in their host communities and filling key positions in the construction, information, and service sectors.

The contemporary phenomena of returns are not immune to the underlying processes and pressures of globalization. The compression of time and space, as well as an increasing velocity of global capital flows affect local economies and propel new labor movements (Harvey 1990). Ties to home and host often co-exist (Basch 1994). Transnational networks become important survival strategies and create identities that transcend national borders and boundaries (Brettel 2000; Ong 1993; Oxfeld 1993).

However, return as an analytic category differs from notions such as globalization and transnationalism, which are universal categories. Return, in contrast, is situated in particular events and experiences. While responding to larger universal processes, returns reflect particular historical, social, and personal contexts. Specifically, the concept of return allows us to analyze these larger processes in terms of people's own systems of meaning and experiences and to discern the particular human consequences of these larger forces in everyday lives and actions. Return is a category that people themselves use, embellish, and understand.

Return is also an important analytic category because each return has important political, social, economic and cultural consequences—not only for those who return but also for the sending and receiving communities. As others (Gmelch 1980; Brettel 2000; Ong 1993) who have analyzed returns observe, diaspora communities continue their cultural, physical, and economic ties to an ancestral or current homeland and such ties become part of return processes.

Of particular relevance to this analysis is exactly what connects or reconnects people to their earlier communities as they contemplate a possible or actual return. Also important are the conditions necessary for people to decide to return voluntarily (or to accept an assisted return), and when and on what basis they then decide to return. A fuller analysis also considers what happens to people in the sending and receiving communities afterward, whether the return is only for temporary periods or permanent. Finally, there are the effects on processes of globalization and transnational identities. Returns are a growing worldwide phenomenon that transform not only particular communities, but also global ways of relating and interacting with one another.

Defining Return

The contributors to this volume provide a series of ethnographic case studies to develop a comparative analysis of return. Return ranges temporally from short visits to permanent repatriation, spatially from one's original place of origin to a reconstructed homeland (a particular site in the home country where one has never actually lived), and legally from voluntary to coerced movements. This definition of return also includes the processes leading to returns. As such, return encompasses but is broader than return migration, which does not always include temporary visits or the preparations for return.

Some returns described in this volume take place after only a few years of exile, others after several decades. Several authors portray the experiences of refugees who earlier fled war and violence, others address the returns of labor migrants, who left primarily for economic reasons. The geographic locales include Ethiopia, Eritrea, Rwanda, Nicaragua, Barbados, the Balkans, Germany, China, Vietnam, and the Philippines. Many scholars limit their analyses of return to the initial act of return (see for example, Bovenkerk 1974: 5), yet return may also be a habitual, circular, or periodic movement, as in the case of Filipina guest workers in Hong Kong. Likewise, some Viet Kieu (overseas Vietnamese) re-open businesses in Vietnam but maintain economic ties and homes in the West.

The authors confine the analysis of return to those people who are actually returning or contemplating a return to a physical place of residence. Virtual returns, connections facilitated by computer networks and other types of media (referred to by Appadurai as "mediascapes" [1996: 33]), for example, warrant separate analysis. Focusing on those uprooted within their own lifetimes also excludes consideration of the eschatological return of Jews to Israel, a homeland where they have never lived before, or of African Americans to ancestral lands. While these ancestral and historical returns are important phenomena, they differ quite profoundly from the experience of returning to a place where one once lived or to another physical setting in one's homeland. Such returns raise concerns about the continuity of ethnic identities and boundaries across generations that are worthy of attention in their own right.

The notion of homeland (as part of the analysis of return) does not imply that going home is necessarily desirable or natural. Suggesting that culture is rooted in particular geographic places would imply that uprooted refugees or migrants somehow lose their culture (Malkki 1997). People do not necessarily return to the same specific locale from which they left, and even if they do, that place may be so profoundly changed that its physical, spatial, and geographic attributes have little relevance. Thus, this analysis does not naturalize homelands in the discussions of return. Nevertheless, national boundaries and the role of states in constructing homelands are critical to understanding return, and the cases in this volume all involve return across national boundaries, though we recognize that such boundaries are themselves contingent and historically defined.

These case studies also explicitly address the cultural ambiguities and complexities of returning without assuming immutable ethnic identities or boundaries. Several authors examine the changing, transnational networks and identities resulting from interactions between those who return and those who stay behind. Potential returnees may simultaneously identify with and be estranged from former homelands. Home may eventually come to mean the new abode (Hackett 1997), or returnees may feel like outsiders in both places (see Long, this volume; Turki 1994). In addition, the distinction between returnees and those left behind often masks underlying historical, gender, class, and ethnic affinities or differences (see McSpadden and Phillips, this volume).

Return in the Literature

Diaspora literature is an excellent starting point for analyzing different experiences of return. Those who write about diaspora commonly agree that homeland plays a central role in diaspora consciousness (Cohen 1997). Even if the homeland exists only in memory, the idea of return is critical for many dispersed communities (Safron 1991), and it extends beyond those who personally remember the home country. A homeland has meaning even when people are ambivalent about it rather than identifying with a particular place (Clifford 1994: 305), or when the diaspora in question, such as the Afro-Caribbean, does not have a single center (Clifford 1994).

Migration literature, in contrast to diaspora literature, is less focused on ideologies of home. Migration literature traditionally depicts different kinds of spatial movements involved in returning. Migrants engage in circular or repeat migration patterns while maintaining ties in both sending and receiving countries (Skeldon

1997). Refugees and migrants may be compelled to return either within their home area or to another area within their country of origin (Koser 2000; King 1986, cited in Sills 2000/2001). Thus, refugee and migration studies often consider the push and pull factors and degree of volition that force or compel migrants and refugees to return, and they divide returns by cause into forced, planned, and spontaneous movements (Koser 2000; Long 2000). In most analyses of return, migration specialists go beyond geographical typologies to consider temporal criteria such as occasional, periodic, seasonal, temporary, or permanent returns (Koser 2000).

Many studies address the effects of return on both receiving and sending communities, and how returns may strengthen or weaken existing ties and relationships (Gmelch 1980, 1992; King 1986 cited in Sills 2000/2001; Watson 1977, Ong 1999). The roles of family, kinship ties, and property are often noted in the kinds and timing of various returns (King 1986; Massey 1987; Dustman 2001). Returns reflect transnational connections and identities and "the fluidity with which ideas, objects, capital and people move across borders and boundaries" (Basch etal, 1994: 27). Some ethnic groups adopt flexible citizenship strategies and maintain ties and relationships across transnational borders and boundaries (Ong 1993; Oxfeld 1993).

Transnational movements and repeat or circular migrations reinforce cultural hybridity (see Appaduri 1990, 1996; Trinh 1991; Ong 1993; White 1997). Not surprisingly, people negotiate the multiple spaces and movements by forming complex and at times, seemingly contradictory identities. How people negotiate this ambiguity across space and time is extensively explored in numerous fictional accounts (Narayan 1967; Ghosh 1988; Mukherjee 1989; Kingston 1989; Jen 1991), as well as in memoirs that speak specifically to the dilemmas of exile (Said 1987, 1994, 1999; Alvarez 1992; Ahmed 1999; and Rushdie 1991).

The authors in this volume analyze return first and foremost as a situated concept. A particular return necessarily receives its meaning from the returning individuals' experiences and points of view. Various accounts of return in the migration, refugee, diaspora, and exile literatures depict one or more overlapping or consecutive series of experiences. These involve both the processes and consequences of return across time and space and reflect various transnational ties, identities, concepts of homeland, and degrees of volition on the part of returnees. From these accounts, the authors consider returns (not just the physical act of transport but also the process over time) as *imagined, provisional,* and *repatriated.* These three aspects of the return experience need not be exclusive or sequential but permit comparative analyses, for example, of the return experiences of different economic groups. Many exiles can only imagine the possibility of return; others first imagine and later are able to return. Likewise, while a return may initially consist of a temporary (provisional) visit, it may later become permanent.[7] Yet a provisional return may also illuminate the reasons why permanent return is impossible or undesirable. Furthermore, returns have their own histories. Often the act of returning engenders other consequences that affect subsequent returns.

The sections that follow address the categories of experience that organize the accounts in this volume.

Imagined Return

Most people imagine returning first. They anticipate, plan, long for, and/or fear the return, but the physical act itself remains a future possibility. Thus, returning is imagined before deemed feasible or unlikely. Many people spend their whole lives imagining the return but are never able or willing to enact it. Nonetheless, the possibility frames how they relate to their countries of origin and settlement. For instance, refugees from the former Yugoslavia contemplate returning (Huseby-Darvas 1997), but ethnically mixed marriages may also endanger them in an environment marked by continuing conflict and an emphasis on ethnic purity. Many refugees simply are not allowed to return, or to return with the intention of settling down, by the current political regime in their homelands.

Imagining return is often an emotionally charged experience, becoming more so as it is imminent. In order to return, people analyze the potential consequences (such as the degree of danger, financial viability, and reception) and confront strong emotions. For example, a Croatian refugee imprisoned in a Serbian prisoner of war camp insisted that he wanted to return home (Povzranovic 1998). However, once he realized that he could actually do so, he started losing consciousness and sleeping hours at a time.

In imagining one's return, the returnee will not necessarily romanticize the past but often pragmatically explores various options and likely outcomes of different decisions. Refugees from Eritrea who want to participate in the building of a new homeland weigh this desire against political insecurity and limited educational and career options, especially for women (see McSpadden, this volume). The material expectations of receiving communities often initially discourage some people (particularly those without the means) from returning (Oxfeld, MacSpadden, Gmelch, and Constable, this volume). People may wish to wait until they have the financial means to lavish gifts on their home communities. Both sides may seek to maintain face and justify the time away with reference to appropriate remittances, for the returnee's change in material status redounds to the home community.

Sometimes the return may be dangerous and people imagining the return weigh the risks. Bugingo, a Rwandan refugee, faced extreme danger and potential imprisonment in returning (Janzen, this volume). Although not directly implicated in the genocide, he knew that he could be arrested or killed upon return. Ultimately, he weighed his fears of returning against the deprivations of remaining indefinitely in the Congolese refugee camps. Similarly, displaced and impoverished Nicaraguan peasants (Phillips, this volume) find life harsh in the Honduran refugee camps, where they are separated from their economic livelihood, farming, and supportive local social ties.

Historical, social, and personal memories provide critical material for imagining a future return. Exiles may need to construct new narratives about their earlier lives in order to return. Local and international authorities expected ethnic Croats, Hungarians, and Slovenes to return and live peacefully again amongst Serbian neighbors who supported the aggression in their villages (see Povzranovic 1998; Long, personal observation 2001). To overcome a resistance among Croatian minorities to return to Eastern Slavonia, international and local authorities developed a new folkloric festival tradition, advocating an alternate, idealized history of the region.

While memories of trauma and horror must be effaced, confronted, or overcome, such intense experiences also compel returns years later. The Pomeranians who fled the eastern parts of Germany in the wake of the advancing Soviet army at the end of World War II, initially felt profoundly uprooted (Hackett 1997). To deal with the loss, they romanticized versions of home and formed organizations devoted to remembering.

The imagined return may influence whether and under what circumstances an eventual return occurs. Hutu camp and town refugees in Tanzania, for example, constructed very different images and trajectories of return (Malkki 1995a). Town refugees analyzed the political changes of the regime in Burundi that would make their return possible. They assessed the practical implications, such as the economic security of their families. Camp refugees, on the other hand, linked return to a political movement of "reclaiming the nation" and considered their residence in Tanzania as a temporary stage preceding a millenialist return (Malkki 1995a: 193), a return that could only remain imaginary.

Those imagining a return may use photographs and other objects to memorialize the past and to develop symbolic architecture for a future return. Filipinas in Hong Kong provide an idealized photographic presentation of their life in preparation for a triumphal return at some later date (Margold, this volume). Instead of being saved for the future, photographs may also replace an actual return (Slyomovics 1998). Some Palestinians journey to Israel to find their previous homes. Others, deterred by imagining the painfulness of seeing their houses occupied by others and the finality of dispossession, stay behind. Instead, "friends acting as surrogates may travel to the villages in order to photograph them for those unable or unwilling to make the journey" (Slyomovics 1998: 16).

Gender considerations play a role in the imagined returns of Filipina maids in Hong Kong. Familial obligations provide equally compelling cases for staying in Hong Kong and earning more money or returning home to spouses and children. Tensions back home and the relative freedom of life away from daily familial scrutiny may also cause women to delay their return and to sign on for another multi-year contract (Constable, this volume). Women in particular often appreciate the expanded educational, social, and employment opportunities and freedom to redefine their social roles in the new place and may be very ambivalent about returning to former roles (as shown in MacSpadden's study of Eritrians). However, continuing to imagine a possible return makes the decision to stay socially acceptable.

The home communities (those who remained behind) also imagine the return. For these local communities, imagined homecomings may be initially used to confirm the local community members' own decisions not to leave and their maintenance of a particular way of life. They may view their communities as ancestral centers and expect returnees to celebrate their return by throwing banquets, giving gifts, and making ancestral offerings (for example, when overseas Vietnamese or Chinese return).

Provisional Return

The act of imagining a return is integrally related to the possibility and circumstances of an actual return. While many refugees and displaced are forced to repatriate permanently, there are numerous examples of voluntary, provisional returns.

People provisionally return to their previous homes to visit relatives, invest in businesses, donate philanthropically, celebrate rituals and festivals, or make religious pilgrimages. Nicaraguans from the new global business class (in contrast to rural peasants who must permanently repatriate) have the option of returning for a part of every year, while retaining residence outside Nicaragua for the remaining part (Phillips, this volume). Others may return provisionally as part of a pattern of seasonal migration. Emigres who do not return, but who vote in local elections (Verdery 1998) are returning in one aspect as well. Such returns are initially acts of political participation but may eventually lead to permanent repatriation.

As such, provisional returns give people a chance to decide if they want to return on a long-term basis. For instance, during the years of 1999 through January 2002, 4,684 voluntary repatriations occurred between Bosnia-Herzegovina and Croatia. But during the same period almost double that many individuals participated in "Go and See Visits." These were organized by international agencies to help people decide whether they wanted to repatriate permanently.[8]

Provisional returns to homelands also may be understood as modern day pilgrimages to affirm or redefine religious and other cultural traditions, and to counter the universalizing influences of the global economy. Yet such provisional returns, by strengthening transnational identities, also reflect the very forces they oppose in their own mobility and flexibility. Before or following a provisional return, people may apply for permanent citizenship and a passport in their host or asylum country. This has been common among Hong Kong Chinese returning from Canada (*Migration Dialogue*, February 1995, cited by Sills 2000/2001), and among some Bosnians returning to Sarajevo (Steffansson, this volume).

These returns are also used to overcome the initial fears and hesitations surrounding the act of leaving in the first place. In recent years, for instance, many Israeli Jews have returned to the lands of their birth. Partly pilgrimage, partly tourism, Moroccan Israelis on one such trip were critical of the Jews who remained behind and relived the feelings of insecurity that lead them to emigrate (Levy 1997). Finding their birthplace altered, they constructed a new narrative about the past.

A provisional return visit may emphasize the impossibility or undesirability of permanent return. Recent Palestinian accounts of returning to Israel (before the current *intifada*) accentuate many refugees' dispossession and are necessarily provisional (see Slyomovics 1998: 14). Israelis tell of Palestinians suddenly appearing on their doorsteps, looking around, asking questions, and disappearing (Rubinstein 1991). For the Arab returnees, this is no "homecoming" but a grotesque distortion (Rubinstein 1991: 62). Likewise, Edward Said recounts how in returning to his birthplace, Jerusalem, he confronted the difficult reality of Israel's existence and the dismemberment of neighborhoods he once knew. "I found myself repeating to myself that I did have a right to be here, that I was a native," he observes (Said 1994: 177).

Several memoirs of intellectuals moving between post-colonial societies and North America or Western Europe contain references to return (Ondaatje 1982; Mukherjee and Blaise 1995). In these encounters, the return visit often prompts a reevaluation or even confrontation with past cultural practices and traditions (see Turki 1994). Contemporary Viet Kieu (overseas Vietnamese) returning to work in Saigon or Hanoi report how they see coming back as a way of confronting past memories, becoming reconciled with their parents' silences and reconnecting (especially at Tet) with ancestral rites and traditions (Long, this volume).

As the act of returning unfolds, the specific experiences often contrast with the returnee's original dreams. Barbadian returning parents report difficult reunions with children who do not recognize them. A society that initially seems beautiful and relaxed gradually appears narrow and old-fashioned. Further, returnees face jealousy and complex social expectations. As one returnee observes, "If you come back with money, they are jealous. If you come back with nothing, they ridicule you." (Gmelch, this volume). Given these difficulties, some returnees travel back and forth and/or return only during certain periods. Even though Pomeranians from Eastern Germany initially expected to return permanently they contrasted their former homes in the East with their comfortable and settled existence in the West. By provisionally returning, they could accept their new lives in the West and view their former homeland as a place for occasional vacation visits. One Pomeranian observed, "What we [once] looked down upon in East Germany as old-fashioned—is now being touted by tour businesses as nostalgic—see Germany as it used to be!" (Hackett 1997)

A provisional return often confirms the home community's expectations. When people eventually return home, they may carry with them photographs and other memorabilia to signify their success in the other culture (Margold, this volume). Chinese villagers in the home village assume their kin want to return to their ancestral lands (Oxfeld, this volume).[9] Likewise, the Vietnamese view the returning Viet Kieu as legitimating the current political, post-Doi Moi (renovation) transition although the returnees articulate their vision of return in very different terms (Long, this volume).

But the return of overseas relatives may also create new social divisions amongst the home community. Chinese villagers welcome their visiting relatives, and see their return as a necessary reconnection with their ancestors (Oxfeld, this volume). At the same time, return distinguishes those with active links to family members overseas and access to wealth, from those with no such connections. Because return may introduce new social divisions, some villagers are apprehensive about the role of visiting kin in their community.

Repatriated Return

Refugees are going home. But to what? For many people, the trauma of being driven from one's home will now be matched by the shock of returning to a home that does not exist. (Levy 1999)

Of all the aspects of return, long-term repatriation, especially involuntary or forced, receives the most attention (see Van Hear 1998 for an overview). However, since the term repatriation often refers only to organized and assisted returns,[10] we therefore use repatriated return rather than repatriation as an organizing principle. Repatriated return includes both organized *and* individual returns, as well as returns that are both forced *and* voluntary. What is common to all cases of repatriated return is resettlement in the home country with a long-term commitment, usually with resumption of citizenship status. Repatriated returnees may view their resettlement as permanent. Nevertheless, such permanency is a commitment rather than an assured reality, since there are no guarantees of permanency.

Repatriated return includes but is not limited to involuntary repatriations. Such involuntary repatriations may be the outcome or consequences of war (e.g., the flight of over 400,000 Palestinians from Kuwait at the end of the Gulf War). Others reflect internal inter-ethnic discrimination and strife. In 1954, for example Operation Wetback led to the massive deportation of Mexicans from the United States. Likewise, in the early 1980s, some two million Ghanaians were expelled from Nigeria. Sometimes, people born in the host countries are expelled or forcibly repatriated to places they have never lived in or barely remember. This circumstance applies to many Palestinian expellees during the Gulf War (Van Hear 1998) and in the United States, to adopted children from another culture who violate U.S. law. Such involuntary repatriations raise a host of legal and political issues that change the meaning of return.

Mass forced repatriations are not homecomings or the natural outcome of a refugee cycle (Koser and Black 1999b; Akol 1994; Allen 1996b; Allen and Morsink 1994; Bascom 1994; Harrell-Bond 1989; Simon and Preston 1992; Stepputat 1999). In a forced repatriation, people may be allowed to return only to their former nation-states, not to their former home (Koser and Black 1999). In such situations, they often replace refugee status with that of internally displaced

(Koser and Black 1999b: 7–8). Even if allowed to return home, such returns radically change the social fabric, and returnees may return to a different social or class status (Stepputat 1999; Phillips, this volume).

As Hammond tells us, "Many returnees . . . do not see the object of repatriation as the 'rebuilding' or 'reconstruction' of their lives. Likewise, they often do not aspire to reclothe themselves in the culture of the past or to rejoin the community that they left" (1999: 235). They may merely return to the same physical place, and in some cases may even settle in "a place to which they do not even have ancestral or kinship ties" (Hammond 1999: 235).

As such, the idea of a repatriated return may be limited to re-establishing one's national, ethnic or kinship affiliations and networks rather than returning to one's original geographic home. For example, many Viet Kieu are returning to Hanoi rather than to Saigon, where they once lived. As soon as they decide to reestablish permanent ties, they often find themselves enmeshed in an ethnic Viet or Kinh identity and series of kinship networks and obligations that they can more easily avoid in the U.S., Europe, or Australia—and/or with a provisional return. Because Vietnam's political system has also changed, those who come back to live must also re-nationalize themselves in contemporary socialist, Doi Moi terms. Nevertheless, they remain cultural outsiders in the local community.

There are variant responses to repatriated returns but the degree of choice and reason for return are obviously critical. German Jews who returned to West Germany contrast with those who returned to the East (Bornemann, this volume). Unlike the West German returnees who described return as the result of chance life experiences, those who returned to the East described it as a commitment to building a new anti-fascist socialist society in Germany. Likewise, Barbadian emigrants articulated "identification with the Caribbean and lack of interest in assimilation" (Gmelch, this volume). In the Nicaraguan, Rwandan, and Bosnian accounts in this volume, some refugees view return as the best option among difficult alternatives. In Sarajevo, those returnees who were expelled from their host countries generally felt more estranged than those who had returned through their own volition. In part, this was because those who returned voluntarily did so only after knowing that they had some economic prospects awaiting them (Stefansson, this volume).

Returnees often transform their homelands, but they may also be unable or unwilling to challenge ongoing cultural and social practices (King and Strachan 1980; Watson 1975; Saloutos 1956). Many immigrants returning to Europe from the U.S. at the beginning of the twentieth century were regarded with suspicion or envy upon return (Wyman 1993; King and Strachan 1980). Their economic impact was limited to building new houses (King and Strachan 1980; Gmelch 1980). At the same time, social changes are often cited among both the returnees and those left behind. For example, returnees learned new skills in union and political organizing. Thus, a number of political leaders in new states and or new democracies in the early twentieth century were returnees (Wyman 1993: 206).

Southern Italians, who came to the United States between 1900 and 1924 altered attitudes of subservience to wealthy landowners when they returned home (Cerase 1974, cited in Sills 2000/2001).

Repatriated returns involve creating and negotiating new relationships (including class and social relations) as well as reestablishing earlier ties. Not surprisingly, connections between permanent returnees and the home communities are often complex. Issues of land title, property rights, political orientation and religious and cultural beliefs and practices are only a few of many areas in which returnees and their home communities may conflict, or undergo transformation (Phillips, Gmelch, and Hammond, this volume).

In Sarajevo, returnees sometimes had to overcome accusations of betrayal and cowardice by those who had stayed behind (Stefansson, this volume). In Guatemala, tensions erupted between returnees and those who had stayed behind, surviving torture and violence at the hands of the military. While the returnees had faced traumatic flights and endured difficult conditions in Mexican refugee camps, they had escaped the daily control of the army and environment of terror, and consequently had a more activist and participatory vision of how they wanted to change society at the grassroots level. The two groups disputed over land, property, and social organization (Taylor 1999).

The notion that time does not stand still is echoed over and over again in people's experiences of return, especially repatriated return (Gmelch, Hammond, Stefansson, and Borneman, this volume). Returnees to Sarajevo remarked that the city felt like an "alien place" marked by "physical destruction—economic decline" and "cultural deterioration" (Steffansson, this volume). However, African-Americans who returned from northern cities to their rural homes in the south transformed the places to which they returned rather than reaffirming traditional cultural practices (Stack 1996). Although they did not cross a national border, these "repatriated returnees" also saw their return as a long term rather than a provisional commitment. As one returnee recounted, "You have to create another place in that place you left behind" (Stack 1996: 199).

Conclusions

Whether imagined, provisional, repatriated, or some combination thereof, returns take place over space and time and develop their own histories and trajectories. Returnees reconnect with family, ancestors, friends, and their communities and confront past memories. They often reclaim houses and political rights, though such claims may be contested. While return is a way to reconcile and heal past conflict, it also gives rise to new tensions and boundaries, sometimes fueling ethnic hatreds. The state may welcome the returnees as deterritorialized subjects, feel threatened, or restrict their freedom of action and movement.

Returnees, whether engaged in imagined, provisional, or repatriated returns, reconstruct their homelands both figuratively and in practice. Examples from this volume range from donations to and investments in the local economy in China, to new land use patterns in Ethiopia, to introduction of new work methods, technologies, and ways of thinking in Vietnam and Barbados.

State policies are critical to determining whether a return is only imagined or becomes physically possible and under what conditions. States construct the legal, social, and political parameters and interpretations of return. In both contemporary Vietnam and China, the governments have established more flexible rules for overseas populations than they allowed during their orthodox Communist periods. At the same time, government policies and pronouncements suggest that state officials are nervous about the ideological orientation or cultural values of returnees, and place certain restrictions on their activities (Oxfeld and Long, this volume). In Ethiopia, the state prescribes standards of good citizenship to which returnees are expected to conform. Returning Tigreans help in laying pipelines and vote even when gravely ill in order to demonstrate their civic loyalty despite their time abroad (Hammond, this volume).

States often desire the returnees' remittances, investments, skills, and knowledge and consequently encourage returns. Alternatively, and even concurrently, states may view the returnees, as untrustworthy and potential political and economic competitors or threats. By imagining a return, the returnee may also betray his or her foreignness in the new host society. Thus, returnees expose boundaries and issues of political and social incorporation.

Economic and social class relations (as well as gender) further limit the possibilities and kinds of return. Nicaraguan peasants in the camps had different options than the upper class Nicaraguans who fled the country and created new identities as members of a transnational business elite. The peasants, unable to access land title and credit, felt uprooted from their original peasant ties (Phillips, this volume). Those who stayed behind may thus have gained at the expense of those who left. For example, they may occupy returnees' houses or property, take over their business, and appropriate their assets. If the returnees' claims are not considered, these actions establish new relationships and patterns of conflict. Permanent reconciliation may no longer be possible when people are unwilling to redress such claims (Janzen, this volume).

Returnees confront how much they themselves have changed while abroad (Gmelch, this volume). Coming to terms with the receiving community compels returnees to reconsider who they were and what they have become. Such reflections become central tropes for some Viet Kieu in Hanoi and Saigon (Long, this volume). Likewise, returning German Jews espoused multifaceted identities. Those who defined themselves and their return through dedication to an antifascist ideal in East Germany were compelled to reevaluate their identities upon German reunification (Borneman, this volume).

Historical conditions shape prevailing beliefs about the possibility and desirability of a return. Certain returns are privileged and politically attractive. For example, initially Viet Kieu returning from the Eastern bloc countries had easier access to visas and citizenship privileges than those returning from the West.

Later, with new economic ties to the West, those privileges were extended. Evaluations of returns change over time given larger political and economic events and as returnees interact with and bring new resources to their communities.

Returns not only reflect historical contexts, but also generate their own histories. They cannot be analyzed as singular acts in time or space. In Rwanda, exodus and return have responded to, but also helped create, political imbalances leading to further flight and return in a series of continuous population movements since the colonial period (Newbury 1998). The most recent return of hundreds of thousands of people from Congolese and Tanzanian refugee camps (Janzen, this volume) is further complicated by the fact that some returnees are victims while others are perpetrators (a situation also characteristic of return movements in the Balkans). Such unresolved conflicts may generate future discord and instability.

While many returnees begin with an idealized image of return, those past images are modified by new experiences, and returns require managing one's own expectations. Both returnees and "homelands" are altered during the time apart and the return itself forces further alterations. Edward Said observes, "as any displaced and dispossessed person can testify, there is no such thing as a genuine, uncomplicated return to one's home" (Said 1999). The accounts in this volume demonstrate that each return creates its own logic, contradictions, and possibilities for the future. And in each return the meaning of home is created anew.

Part I
Imagined Return

Chapter 1
Illusions of Home in the Story of a Rwandan Refugee's Return

John Janzen

Longing for Home

In his story "The Other Shore: Chronicle of an Ordinary African Refugee,"[1] Burundian writer Katihabwa Sabastien describes a fictional—but very true to Central African life—landscape in which two ethnic peoples are arbitrarily manipulated by politicians and militants into opposing identities and political parties. The protagonist, part of the targeted category at odds with the regime in power, is forced to flee with his family to a neighboring country where they join a refugee camp. Often he goes to the river that divides his refuge from his own homeland. The story's title, "The Other Shore," depicts the natural sign of the border between countries as well as the emotional distance from and longing for everything that home means. He attends school in the country of his refuge; in his contacts and in further travels and studies he meets many of his compatriots. He even encounters traveling politicians who represent the despot whose manipulations have caused his exile. Yet none of this can satisfy the sentiment of longing for home at the center of his mind and soul, a sentiment that pervades his thoughts and being every waking hour, as a bigger than life place and metaphor. Katihabwa suggests that this larger than life image of home that grows in refugees is driven by, and seemingly inversely proportional to, the disintegration of the refugee family's coherence as a community.

This chapter presents and evaluates a very similar real-life story of a Rwandan refugee named Bugingo.[2] He was one of the Rwandans who frequented the guesthouse in Bukavu where I stayed in late 1994 while working with a nongovernmental organization (NGO) following the Rwandan war and genocide.[3] With pen and notebook I took down his words as he spoke to me for several hours that first time in December 1994. Over the next two weeks he came several times to talk and to sort out his life before me. Each time his voice was full of fear, and his narrative concentrated on his "persecutors." He had been a soldier in the pre-genocide Rwandan Armed Forces (Forces Armies Rwandaises, referred to after the genocide and war as the "ex-FAR")[4] but had been dismissed in 1991 following a series of confrontations with his commanders on a variety of charges, including desertion and, he feared, accusations of collaboration with the enemy (the Rwandan Patriotic Front, RPF), who formed the backbone of the post-genocide Rwandan government.[5]

Along with most Hutu refugees in Eastern Congo, Bugingo was fearful of the consequences of returning home. Rumors abounded in the camps that the new government imprisoned all who returned, or worse. Stories circulated about returnees having disappeared. In Bugingo's case the fear of return was offset by the equal fear he felt of staying in Congo because he believed his former persecutors were out to threaten, rob, and even kill him as they had tried before the war. In our first encounter he appeared paralyzed by fear.

Two and a half years later, in mid-1996, Bugingo finally took the initiative to return to Rwanda. His last letter to us from Zaire/Congo[6] alluded to the turmoil surrounding the clashes between ex-FAR and Zairian soldiers with militia of local Congolese "Rwandans" in North and in South Kivu, the eastern province of Zaire. These were Tutsi communities that had settled in these areas at earlier times. As the months went on into 1996, the opposing parties of Rwanda within the Kivu of eastern Zaire polarized Zairian society. Under pressure of Rwandan Hutu forces the local Zairian government ordered the historic Zairian Tutsi to leave the country and return to Rwanda, "their" home. Instead of complying, they mounted an offensive campaign to create a safe zone for themselves, insisting they were Zairian citizens. The first group to do this were the Banyamulenge, the people of Mulenge, in south Kivu. Not only were they successful in defeating some Rwandan Hutu militia who occupied Kivu, they attracted Zairian opposition parties, who saw the possibility to launch a Congolese rebellion. The new government of Rwanda and its allies in Uganda and Burundi quickly extended their support to the Banyamulenge fighters, together constituting what became the Alliance of Democratic Forces for the Liberation of Congo-Zaire (ADFLC). The ADFLC moved on Bukavu in October and November 1996 and in December attacked the large refugee camps around Goma in north Kivu. Many refugees who had for two years been held hostage by Hutu forces of the former government in exile, were able to return home. Just after New Year, 1997, they were shown on Western television trudging across the Rwandan border at Gisenyi. Others, particularly the ex-Rwandan army, the militia, and their sympathizers fled westward, deeper into the forests of Eastern Zaire, where they were pursued by the ADFLC and the Rwandan Patriotic Army. Tens of thousands of Rwandans and many Zairian/Congolese lost their lives in battles or from disease or starvation.

Bugingo had returned to Rwanda in July 1996, well ahead of the two million Rwandan refugees. But his homecoming was bittersweet. As soon as he crossed into Rwanda he was arrested and imprisoned. He was released in April 1997, only to be re-arrested and imprisoned for another two years, finally to be released in August 1999.

This chapter focuses on selections from Bugingo's longer narrative of exile (Janzen and Janzen 2000: 21–35) and discusses some of the circumstances of his story, strategies for returning home and perspectives that have emerged in the course of time since those initial encounters. Bugingo's story is largely representative of those Rwandan Hutu who returned home within several years after the events of 1994. He is one of nearly three million mostly Hutu Rwandans who fled their country in 1994 at the close of the genocide and war. Of these, over two million returned. Because Bugingo spoke to me so passionately in late 1994 about his tortured situation, full of both longing for home and fear to return home, his story offers a perspective on the refugee experience and challenges of returning home.

Narrative of Exile, Narrative of Life

Many of the stories of war I heard in Rwanda, Burundi, and Zaire in late 1994 and early 1995 had a consistent plot. They often began with an account of the personal encounter with war, where they had been or what they had been doing when the war reached them. This included telling of family and lineage members killed, along with the names or identities of the killers, where known. Then the story moved on to the flight, the search for, and location of refuge, followed by uncertainty and continuing fear (Janzen and Janzen 2000: 6). This pattern was consistent for persons of all persuasions and identities; Hutu, Tutsi, Twa, professionals and peasants alike. The targeted Tutsi and dissenting Hutu classes who survived inside Rwanda told a story of having temporarily fled their homes, or hidden during the worst of the fighting in their area, to return home when it was all over. Surprising to me was the fact that even those with whom I spoke in the camps in Congo who had been in the Habyarimana government, who had organized, or who had participated in the killing, told similar stories (Janzen and Janzen 2000: 54–58).

Bugingo's story, which is featured in this chapter, more or less followed this pattern. He eventually covered his experience during the outbreak of the war. But perhaps because the course of events was so painful to him, with vivid memories of the three times he was nearly executed, he could only relate where he was at the outbreak later on, after I had talked several times. When it came, it was poignant and powerful.

Then the war broke out. It was April 1994. My brother was in Kigali. We lived near the airport and worked for the French. He went with the French to the Protected Zone. I stayed. The neighbors tried to implicate me in the killing and the pillaging. I told them I was not at all interested in this since leaving the military. So I found a ride to Butare with a vehicle. I went to the theology faculty where I had a friend. Suddenly [the war broke out in Butare] and [my tormentors] knew I was there. I was nearly killed four times. They asked me, "Why are you here?" I told them I was a teacher.

"But your card says you're a farmer. You're an old soldier."

"This man is suspect," they said to each other. "Cut off his head."

So they took me to the communal pit. They wanted to take my money, so I gave it all to them and they freed me.

I returned to my friend from the theology faculty, and we went to a Belgian unit of Doctors Without Borders. We were arrested by the military. There were lots of questions and orders.

"If he's an ex-soldier, kill him."

"If he's a teacher, kill him."

"If he's a cultivator, . . ." My friend vanished and I was alone. Christ saved me. I went to the president of the court and presented them my ID card. There were more questions. A professor in Butare from my commune saved me from this situation. But there was more harassment, and I was again rescued by him. We fled together to Gikongoro and Cyngugu and then to Bukavu [in Zaire]. I found refuge with an Anglican bishop in Bukavu behind the college. (24)

Bugingo's story of the war was really the story of his life. Looking back at what I wrote at the very beginning from this trembling man seated before me, I am still puzzled by it. His account of how he had been affected by the war began with him telling the story of his life. The underlying connection between the two offers us a kind of challenge to understand the refugee experience. I return to it in the conclusion.

Bugingo's "story of life" began with his rejection for training in the priesthood, despite his good school marks. This was the first of a series of disappointments that opened Bugingo's lengthy testimony to me, whose leitmotif, upon reflection, was a series of injustices upon him. Here was that enigmatic opening.

You could enter the priesthood if you felt called. I opted for both exams. When the results were to be announced, we all went to the parish. I was third in the results. We went with our parents to the priest. But he didn't encourage anyone at this time. Then the hierarchy spoke in church. Later, the students were interviewed. My parents were not Christian, my father was polygamous. When I was asked if my parents were Christian, I explained. Then a new list was posted, and I was excluded from those who could continue their studies. On the official exam, not one had passed. I tried to find out what the priest and the teachers were doing in this. It turned out that only the students with Christian parents were passed. (21)

From this disappointment in education Bugingo's testimony moved on to other aspects of his life, including his entry into, and ultimate dismissal from, the Rwandan Armed Forces (FAR) on the eve of the 1994 war, and his failed marriage. Excerpts from the lengthy sections of the narrative will have to suffice here.

A friend encouraged me to become a soldier. I was tempted and got the necessary certificate from a friend; that is, we created a false ID. I was accepted and entered. They knew of this falsification, but they let me continue anyway. The commander simply demanded good work. So I worked at this for 10 years. I studied sport, combat, karate with Koreans, so I could apply to the Presidential Guard. After this I returned to my unit in the Bugesera, near Gashora, the military camp of the Gako Training Center. They learned I had karate training and invited me to teach them in the evenings. I was very isolated, they had time. (22)

At this point in his narrative Bugingo relate a series of misunderstandings or confrontations between himself and various commanders.

In Gako camp there was a commander of the commando training who was mean and beat his men and oppressed them. I didn't know any of this and didn't want to meddle. He told me to stop the karate training to only a few, he wanted all the men to learn it. I understood nothing of his and their intrigues. For some reason the commander began to see me as his enemy or rival, but I continued to train the few, not understanding the commander's motives. Each time he wanted to punish me, the officers protected me. I was perplexed at all this. Maybe I was naive. In any case the commander was replaced by another. When he arrived, it appeared that he had been banished to this camp. Again, I was singled out for punishment by him. (22)

As these episodes of intrigue and threatened sanction continue, Bugingo becomes increasingly concerned about his record and his identity. This concern takes the concrete form of anxiety over his ID cards, his photographs, and the official papers he needs to move from one camp to another, and from one position to another in the Rwandan military.

Meanwhile, I applied to train as a military teacher and was accepted. But I first wanted my papers . The commander refused. They put my things in a jeep headed to go to Kigali. But I wanted first to clarify my status. I went to the commanders. They sent me with a letter to my old commander. But he refused, accusing me of having intrigued against him. So I left for Kigali and told my new commander about all this, calling into question the old commander.
So I followed the course in military education. The new commander, he too began to harass me. . . . When the course was completed, I went to the adjutant chief to seek to remove this punishment from my record. They agreed, but they kept punishing me, again, to humiliate me. . . . I was sent to a unit in the northeast of the country, at Mutara, where the army sent soldiers who had a reputation for lacking discipline, whom they monitored closely with a surveillance sheet and a photograph. It was intimidating and humiliating. (22)

Bugingo's frustrations in the army joined in his mind with the possible causes of difficulty in his marriage. He told of one commander who was involved in smuggling contraband at the Ugandan border and who had wanted him to join him with prostitutes in a brothel. Bugingo refused because of his marriage. But his life in the army and his marriage both took turns for the worse. A defining moment in his military career—and in the country—came when he was sent to defend the northern border of Rwanda during the October 1990 invasion by the Rwandan Patriotic Front from Uganda. Bugingo still lacked proper identity papers.

I was sent to the front where there were no administrative services. We under-officers were to wear red armbands. . . . I was under-officer of a unit with artillery support behind us. "You approach," we were told. The officer accused me of being afraid. It was night. The RPF enemy attacked. Our soldiers began to flee because the officers were gone. Where was the commander? Major? "Did you order them to flee?" He said, "Stay with the twelve soldiers," and he left and didn't return. In fact, they all left, some 30 kilometers back from the front. We were alone. There was another attack the next morning. Some were killed; the rest o f us fled. We found the commander and the others. They had reported that I was missing, or dead. We regrouped. The chef d'état major and others passed by in a jeep headed for Kigali. Our unit also went to Kigali, but they told me to stay behind and hold the front. The leaders fled. "You, the under officers, you stay, we'll leave." I stayed, the others left. There was another attack. I fled on foot, and more retreating. I fled into a banana grove where I removed my officer's uniform and officer's shirt. I took my weapon apart, and left it there.

All of a sudden I saw another comrade, and we continued together. We heard a vehicle approach. We used a password to identify ourselves, but they didn't reply. Were they the enemy? They asked us to surrender and demanded to see our identity cards. I tried to explain. My colleague defended me, backing up my story. They appeared to believe me, but they wouldn't say who they were. I took them to my weapon to back up my story. They said not to touch the weapons; they couldn't make them work, but they took them anyway. We were then accused of being deserters and were taken to the commander. He turned out to be the one who had taken me to the prostitutes. He had also fled. He took me to Kigali in a jeep.

We were interrogated about the events, and the transcription they made was accurate. After two or three days we were taken to another camp in Kigali and put in a cell where we were given an interrogation in the form of Q. and A. and asked us to sign. I contested his version of things, but I signed not to have further troubles. They needed a pretext to explain the events and to have scapegoats. (23)

After six months in military prison in April 1991, Bugingo was freed by committee action and dismissed from the army. At this time he needed to come to terms with his marriage.

Life in the home became impossible. The woman accused me of not being like others and wished me death or imprisonment. She went out every night between 8 and 11 p.m.; she took money and other goods; she caused two wounds to my sexual organs; she began a tale of venereal disease and obliged me to have myself examined in a medical laboratory; she continually tried, without success, to get me involved in sorcery. She left a packet of poison on the table and later tried to deny it. I finally noticed that she was not the only one in on the act, given that all this was reinforced by Colonel N., who was the commander of the military camp, who did his best to erase the traces of this story of poison . . . when I began my request for divorce, the persecutions increased and all civil and judicial authorities, backed up by the military authorities, reinforced her with their protection. (2)

The chaos, confusion, and suspicion in Bugingo's personal life, whatever their imagined or real cause, were mirrored by the upheaval in national public life in late 1991 and 1992, resulting from the combined economic crisis and the introduction of multiple political parties. The Rwandan regime, formerly a single party state, felt itself under siege just as the northern tier of communes was now occupied by the Rwandan Patriotic Front. As opponents joined the newly legal opposition parties, elements in the government took measures to maintain control. This is the moment when all communal mayors who had chosen an opposition party were replaced by party faithful. Youth wings of the parties close to power were converted to militia, such as the notorious Interahamwe, who would in 1994 become the shock troops of the genocide. For Bugingo, who demanded to have his name cleared and injustices righted, this moment represented something else. He was dismissed from the army for desertion, by commanders who had themselves fled the front at the moment of attack. But the utter despair of his testimony may also have mirrored the bankruptcy of the Rwandan regime and the society in 1991:

My wife wrote a letter, to which I added some lines, asking to get to court. The divorce was granted, and I was expelled from the army. Now I was without anything.—I returned to my "colline natal" [rural home community].

 I went to the mayor for a paper requesting to get my things . . . I obtained a new identity card with "cultivator" on it. (23)

For someone who had tried so hard to find his way in education, in the priesthood, and in the military to have to return to his rural home to be reclassified as a peasant must have been the ultimate humiliation. He took the first pretext he could find to escape this setting and to move to Kigali where his brother lived. His testimony reveals his continuing despair. "I had no papers with me. I went to find papers in another commune. I was now completely adrift [déraciné]" (24).

These were the circumstances of Bugingo's personal life in April 1994, when the war broke out, and he was drawn into the tragic events as he recounted them at the opening of this chapter that led to his flight to Zaire as a refugee. Yet these circumstances also led him to observe the irony in his status, that "I was [already] a refugee in my own country before the war" (21).

Story and Context

The reader of this chapter will by now see how relatively small was the opening string of episodes of the war within Bugingo's much longer account of his troubled life. It is hardly possible here to explore adequately whether the circumstances of his personal life were representative of more widespread conditions in Rwandan society. According to Newbury, Bugingo was one of many young adults whose aspirations were blocked or shattered at a time when in Rwandan society "amorphous power was the major ticket to success" (David Newbury, quoted in Janzen and Janzen 2000: 21). Bugingo was part of that historical layer of exile who were associated with the genocide, although only a small 5 percent of the two million who fled Rwanda in 1994 were instigators or active perpetrators of the genocide of Tutsi and opposition Hutu. Yet the path of his flight had not left him unscathed.

In many Rwandan communities the war and genocide produced a limited number of types of actions that I characterize as "emotional-moral profiles" (Janzen 1999). Bugingo was certainly not an instigator of the massacres; he tried to avoid any involvement in the politics of the war. He was not killed, although he barely escaped several attempts on his life. He did not intervene to rescue the threatened, as some did. He was a survivor of assault. But he also fell within the group of Hutu who were expected to participate, and by his reluctance to participate he incurred the wrath of the perpetrators. He also succumbed to some degree of complicity in the massacres in Butare, where he had fled to save his life. His emotional-moral profile was that of one who against his will became an accessory of genocide in order to save his life, and this made him a member of one of the most troubled groups of all. They experienced simultaneous and often overwhelming sentiments of trauma and guilt.

Story and Tone of Voice

This terrible combination of trauma and guilt, it is now clear with hindsight, accounted for Bugingo's trembling, frightened, agitated, anxious manner during our first conversations. Especially as his story recounted the Butare episodes, his trembling increased, his voice became agitated, and he began sobbing. The overwhelming emotion he expressed was, however, of fear, both of being forced to go into the refugee camps, and of being forced to return to Rwanda. The camps were the sites of, and often controlled by, the former Rwandan military and the militia, amongst whom were his persecutors. Because he had succumbed to some kind of involvement in the massacres in Butare, he feared returning to Rwanda, where he knew he might be imprisoned or, worse, executed, because someone might recognize him there and would testify against him.

Other moral-emotional experiences may be identified with other voices.[7] Survivors of significant assault, such as Tutsi survivors of genocidal massacres of their entire families, often told their stories in a flat voice detached from affect, a tone we associate with deep and overwhelming trauma. Ideologically motivated perpetrators of genocide, in contrast, often spoke of their war experiences in a somewhat agitated, defensive and self-justificatory manner that frequently blamed the victims for their own deaths as a class, within a war. They denied that there had been genocide. The most remarkable voices were those of individuals, whether they had experienced aggression or not, who acted out of some reservoir of courage to rescue targeted victims, or survivors of other families. Their voices were amazingly—to us—ebullient and radiant, thankful for what they had been able to do during the war.[8] They rejoiced at how they had stood up for humanity and for their beliefs. Thus, it is not really possible to speak of a homogeneous kind of national trauma.

Story and Truth

Bugingo's fears—both his fear of his persecutors in the refugee camps in Zaire and his fear of returning to Rwanda—seemed to be real enough that relief agencies working under the United Nations High Commission for Refugees permitted as many as 20,000 Rwandans, who felt similarly threatened, to remain in various accommodations in Bukavu city under the rubric of the refugee's right to protection from forcible removal or danger to life.

Over the course of time, however, the fields of threat shifted for Bugingo, just as his ability and willingness to articulate his circumstances changed. He formulated a story and a memory of what happened in his own life, and in those fateful days in Butare. In the weeks and months that followed our initial conversations, Bugingo articulated additional dimensions of his life and experience in Butare.

After we left eastern Zaire, Bugingo wrote a number of lengthy letters to agencies and individuals describing his circumstances, including his life story and involvement in the war, particularly the Butare moment. These provide as it were three layers of his narrative, each one of course written for the particular interlocutor, but each one getting closer to his ability to state openly what in fact happened. A limited review of these writings permits us to see this progression of his story, his building up of the truth of his memory.

In a petition in March 22, 1995 to High Commissioner Sagako Ogata, of the UNHCR, for permission to remain in Bukavu, he writes:

Madam President, I the undersigned, Bugingo, Rwandan refugee in Zaire, sheltered at the Anglican Bishopric in Bukavu for eight months, have the honor to address myself to your highness, in order to ask you to kindly bear witness to my great indulgence in finding a permanent solution to my security and my future.

I am an ex-soldier and I served in the army from October 1975 until 1990. But on 23 October 1990 I was imprisoned without trial for six months and then discharged without reason. I was released on 15 April 1991.

Imprisoned soldiers in that period of the war were commonly considered accomplices of the political adversary of the regime in place. But in the detention dossier, as with most of the other soldiers, I was branded a deserter.

Here is the truth of this affair as far as I know it. It all began in 1980 when I was a young sergeant and military instructor in the Bugesera Military Camp of Gako. (27)

Here Bugingo goes over much the same ground as in his story as told to me, combining the intrigues of the military command with those of his former wife and her accomplices. He believes he was framed so that he could be made a scapegoat for the failed military operation against the RPF in 1990, and as punishment for having demanded to clear his name of false charges. He adds that he was put under house arrest and surveillance in his home commune. He continued to fear entrapment. This was the state of affairs when the war broke out in April 1994.

When the war broke out, he writes Ms. Ogaka, he was suspected by militia of having been involved with Belgian units of Doctors Without Borders, known antagonists of the regime. He was also held in suspicion by the militia and military officials for teaching at a college in Kigali known for its association with the RPF. At a roadblock during the massacres, his papers were searched and English language material was discovered. Specifically he writes of his moments in Butare during the genocide there.

In May 1994, I escaped arbitrary execution three times and was two to three steps away from ending in the communal pit. Each time it was the intervention of a member of a militia who saved my life. (28)

He adds to his list of evidence for the plot to harm him the fact that he was robbed in late December, 1994, in Bukavu, and all his personal effects were stolen, probably for the purpose of going through them and the photographs as evidence for further reconnaissance of me.

Believe me, Madam, that this recital of my misfortunes is not the whole story but that my fear of going into the refugee camps is well founded and is based on the annoying experience of earlier harassment. You would do me a great service in saving me from having to go live in the camps. (27–28)

Although one wonders whether this letter reached Ms. Ogata, it achieved the immediate purpose of securing permission to remain in Bukavu city. He also received $U.S. 60 for his material needs.

In July of that year Bugingo wrote two letters (July 6 and 16, 1995) regarding his circumstances and the possibility of his repatriation to an Anglican missionary woman in Kigali whom he had known before the war. In particular he sought someone to mediate with authorities some assurance of safe passage. In the first letter he merely reestablished the acquaintance, telling her news of himself and identifying the topic of his interests. In the second letter he explained in greater detail the reasons for his anxiety, including his encounter with death in Butare and the appearance of complicity.

It is now quite a while that I continue with the support of the UNHCR of Bukavu attempts to obtain my repatriation. They are ready to facilitate the movement of all persons who wish to return to Rwanda, but the gossip circulates everywhere that each and every person who returns to Rwanda goes either to prison or to transit camps where a selection is made of the victims to be executed by implicating them in the genocide; whereas those who are acknowledged to be innocent are sent to their country homes of origin. This may be true, it may be false, but my greatest preoccupation is that they add that someone who was at the barricades during this war crisis, he cannot escape the accusation of being implicated in the genocide. This seems monstrous to me, given that even some victims of the genocide succumbed after months to this dirty work, hoping to buy their freedom through obedience. Personally, I refused in Kigali despite the pressure, but at Butare after more than a month in which I experienced all the threats of execution, I ended by helping to save my skin. Happily my conscience is free of a single drop of bloodshed. The dirty work was nearly finished. We only stood guard. (30)

To this friend and confidant Bugingo finally acknowledges what occurred. He refuses to take responsibility for his actions at the barricades. He explains his actions in terms of threats of execution and his desire to "save my skin."

Several days later (July 20, 1995) Bugingo wrote to the President of the International Court of Rwanda to explore the possibility of protection for repatriation. He also offers the possibility of exposing harassment against him before the court. Finally he addresses the Butare episodes in this elliptical sentence that refers to the UNHCR report he encloses:

It outlines the multiple menaces of execution I experienced and witnesses to the traumas that awaited me if I would persist in refusing to participate in rounds of duty at the barricades. (31)

In a thoroughgoing work on Burundian Hutu refugees living in Tanzania, Liisa Malkki has collected and evaluated many stories of personal experiences, and has studied the construction of memory of home and of the conflict that sent these refugees fleeing, as well as the language in which the memories are couched. She has used the notion of "mytho-histories" (Malkki 1994) to describe the constructions of reality that often reveal strong stereotypes of the other, of home, and of the history of conflict. Such mytho-histories certainly pervaded the accounts of refugeed Rwandan officials with whom I spoke in the camps, who denied that there had been a genocide and who justified their actions as self-defense before an invasion. But Bugingo's painful acknowledgment of his complicity at the barricades in Butare, and his fear of, and persistent refusal to join, the camps that were largely under the control of the militias, the FAR, and the administrators of the genocide government, meant that he confronted his own actions quite deliberately in order to be able to go home. Thus, in a general sense, the memory that is constructed of the experience that sent one into exile becomes the foundation upon which the hope for a return home is imagined and upon which strategies are built.

Strategies for, and Obstacles to, Returning

Bugingo tried to build a bridge of trusted individuals to assure his safe passage home. In addition to Madame Sogako Ogata of the UNHCR, head of the Rwanda War Crimes Tribunal, and Anglican missionary Margaret Court, Bugingo also sent or tried to send letters to colleagues and officials at the college in Kigali where he had worked. In response to a news item I gave him about an army chaplain who had returned from Goma, Congo with soldiers of the FAR who wished to be repatriated and reintegrated into the new Rwandan army, Bugingo wrote a letter of inquiry exploring this option for himself. This very same chaplain had encouraged Bugingo to join the Rwandan army years earlier, and was someone he knew very well. He called this coincidence an irony, and it produced one of the first moments of levity in Bugingo's otherwise somber tone. He noted that he was not sure if this cast his life more in the tragic or the comic direction, since this was the same chaplain who had tried to mediate his marriage. This familiarity among Rwandans was both a blessing and a curse for Bugingo and others. While it was easy to find acquaintances in the camps and at home, one also could not hide from one's enemies or hide one's actions from the authorities inside Rwanda.

In the absence of functioning mail or telephone between Zaire and Rwanda, neutral outsiders such as the members of my agency in Bukavu became important contacts in a society in which many people knew each other but before whom many were fearful of revealing their experiences and plans. Thus many of Bugingo's letters destined for Rwanda were posted via the Anglican office in Bukavu to Kenya, where they were stamped and mailed to me in the United States for forwarding to a destination inside Rwanda.

The obstacles to effective communication between Zaire and Rwanda were not merely of a physical or technical nature having to do with the absence of post offices and mail distribution routes. They were also, and perhaps primarily, of an ideological nature that reflected the gulf dividing the old Rwanda—of the unfinished genocide, the partisans of the Hutu revolution and power clique—from the new Rwanda—the Patriotic Front, the returned Tutsi. The divide between the two sides of Rwandan society was like an emotional and ideological canyon filled with suspicion and paranoia. For someone like Bugingo, and many others who wished simply to cross over, this ideological divide was a significant obstacle. One risked being destroyed by one side or the other, and one didn't know which it would be. Strangers and outsiders were drawn into the many schemes of those who wished or needed to cross the gulf. Even members of my agency, traveling between Rwanda controlled by the RPF, and eastern Zaire, controlled by the MRND, the militias, and the Hutu Power cliques, sensed the palpable divide of hate, fear and paranoia between the two sides.

Going Home

Looking back at our correspondence, Bugingo's hesitancy to return home was overcome by the greater fear of the danger that was looming in Zaire. In his last letter to us from Zaire, in April, 1996, Bugingo reported attacks by FAR and Rwandan militia, as well as by the Zairian army, on groups of ethnic Rwandan Zairians in north Kivu—eventually all lumped under the label "Banyamulenge" and called "Tutsi."

Some of the camp's refugees in Zaire are now under Zairian soldiers' control; they have already surrounded them. Troubles are stirred up in Masisi, northwards Kivu region, some Kinyarwanda speaking citizens are sneaked away from Zaire and have got shelter in northwest Rwanda as forcibly repatriated. These very people and Rwandese authorities declare their citizenship to be Zairian, and that the fact of speaking Kinyarwanda is not enough to justify what they are suffering. Probably Zairian soldiers and former Rwandese militiamen are just using this way in order to loot their belongings. They say to be all born in Zaire, some of them a long time before 1959. (34)

In the south Kivu, Kinyarwanda speaking Zairians came to be called Banyamulenge—the people of Mulenge, a name that the international press soon picked up and used for all Kivu Kinyarwanda speakers not of the current wave of refugees. Although they had not been party to the Rwandan conflict, they now came to be identified as Tutsi and thus allied with the RPF in Rwanda. The Zairian army and Kivu administration, heavily influenced, even controlled, by the Rwandan genocide forces, began to put pressure on the Banyamulenge. Ultimately, in 1996, the Zairian/Kivu governor ordered their expulsion from Zaire. The Banyamulenge, or the Zairian Tutsi of Kivu, protested that they were Zairian citizens, and instead of packing their belongings to return to Rwanda, they armed themselves, organized into militias, and began their defense. They thus formed the nucleus of what would become the Alliance of Democratic Forces for the Liberation of Congo Zaire (ADFLC/Z) that would drive the FAR and Interahamwe militia from the border areas in Kivu.

Bugingo must have seen the imminence of this military conflict and the danger he faced if he stayed in Bukavu. So, he crossed the border in July, 1996, and walked right into imprisonment in Rwanda, as he wrote to us in April, 1997.

I wish you a very happy new year 1997 even if this comes too late. I haven't sent you any letter for a very long time. I judged better to write one as soon as I got back home. Unfortunately, trouble was [sic] on my way back. I was arrested just before I made a second step on Rwandese ground. I was imprisoned, allegedly because I was a former soldier regardless of being dismissed since 1990. I was the only one among other prisoners.

I was released from jail on January 18 and sent back to my home place on 2 March 1997. So I spent eight months on my way. It is very bad news that my father died while I was in prison and I couldn't know it until I reached my home. (34)

Despite his imprisonment, Bugingo was fortunate. Had he stayed in Bukavu, he might very well have been killed by the ADFLC/Z who did not stop to ask the identity of individuals in their way, and were determined to break up anything that looked like resistance. Furthermore, they were intent on either destroying the ex-FAR and Interahamwe or driving them west away from the border area. Many RPF soldiers participated in this military action. The ADFLC/Z armies not only broke up the camps, they released thousands of refugees from their hostage-like status, and these streamed back into Rwanda around New Year 1997. They also pursued without mercy those who fled westward, on the grounds that they were *génocidaires*. Many of these died and were buried in mass graves between Goma and Kisangani.

The Teeth of Justice, or Just Teeth?

Bugingo survived, but as many that returned from the camps in Zaire, he was treated as an accomplice of the genocide, as he describes in his next letter of August 27, 1999, two years later.

This opportunity to send you a message is welcome, it'll certainly tell you what happened with me since two years of silence. It was not long after I got your letter of June 5th, 1997, just on July 11th, [that] I was re-arrested and imprisoned, instead of understanding in spite of a great and courteous display I made of my document of identification. I was driven in prison where I've spent two years and 9 days . . .

This last experience was the worst I have ever lived inasmuch as death was more active in our cell than anywhere else. The only similarity with other situation is that they never told me why I had to be detained, until we were all asked to confess our crime and to apologize. Some of us were responsible of some crime so, they conferred them and wrote apologetical letters. Then all of us, except three people only, were set free at a number of 232 people in all. Afterward we have had three weeks in a solidarity camp and were set free on August 13th 1999. There in solidarity camp we were told that all problems are mistakes due to confusion that gets its power from evil deeds that go along with war evil activities. . . .

I am sending you this letter on my way to my elder brother home . . . many people are stunned to see I am still alive and I have hard time to tell them all I have lived. The most valuable of this is that people's faith grows stronger and stronger. (35)

Bugingo's account reflects the struggle of the Rwandan authorities to bring justice to the more than one hundred thousand still imprisoned suspects of the genocide. It is not clear whether he was considered by the Rwandan authorities to be in one of four categories in the Organic Law of August 30, 1996 on crimes against humanity.[9] That he was released after a "confession" and reeducation in a solidarity camp suggests he may have been in the category of those held to have been accomplices. But he continued to consider himself innocent. He suggests that he is shown here to have been held among those unjustly accused, or perhaps accomplices who did not initiate action.

But another sentiment, besides that of growing faith in the presence of death in the Rwandan prisons, emerges in Bugingo's next letter of October 15, 1999, and perhaps it was already part of his conviction that he was unjustly accused and imprisoned. He offers his understanding of why he was rearrested.

Please be helpful in this situation and protect me from this evil abusive plans. The only wrong I have done is to decline the offer [a job] they proposed me after my first releasement, since it consisted of being involved in criminal and political activities—you know, accusing falsely someone and have him condemned injustly. (35)

Conclusion

Through Bugingo's account here one has a glimpse of how the Rwandan government is coming to terms with the more than one hundred thousand imprisoned suspects of the genocide. One can also see how difficult it is to return to being just an ordinary citizen without being involved in political machinations.

This chapter opened with Burundian author Katihabwa Sebastian's proposition that the image of home that grows in refugees is driven by, and seemingly inversely proportional to, the disintegration of the refugee's immediate social surroundings. In other words, the desperation to visualize home compensates for the chaos of the refugee experience. In Katihabwa's story "The Other Shore" the protagonists experience loss of dignity and inability to maintain their status as a family because family members are forced into temptations, accommodations, and compromises with surrounding society in order to survive. Katihabwa presents this as a kind of moral disintegration that compromises their identity. His analysis of violence in Burundian society is similarly grounded in the gradual erosion of the moral fabric of society, which he speaks of as "deculturation," the loss of a way of life and a culture.[10]

Katihabwa's protagonist in "An Ordinary African Refugee" decides, like Bugingo, to return home, regardless of the consequences. Although he eludes the border guards and safely reaches his home community where an uncle welcomes him in his old home, like Bugingo he is eventually arrested and imprisoned. Katihabwa's story ends with a popular uprising against the corrupt regime that used the vilification of ethnic identity to retain power.

Katihabwa's hypothesis about the strength of the sentiment of home is to an extent borne out in Bugingo's case. The strength of imagined home is rooted not in romantic visions but in a sense of injustice, of a personal story of the unfairness of life, that same thread that led him to say that he had already been a refugee in his own country before the war. His immediate family situation was not ideal, although it was by no means as desperate as the stories of some—especially Tutsi—who had lost all family members. Later, when Bugingo reached his rural home he mourned for his father who had died during his first imprisonment. But his sense of loss of home was more existential than physical. It arose in exile, from the suspected sorcery that cost him his marriage. It now arose from the double imprisonment he faced at the hands of the new authorities, who were no different from the old authorities who had imprisoned him for deeds he did not commit. Another returned refugee—a Tutsi—whose father, a Hutu, was imprisoned for no apparent reason upon return, felt "disgusted with life" (Janzen and Janzen 2000: 38–39). Yet from other returnees, who were middle-class merchants and teachers, one heard that the new life was tolerable, that the dangers were diminishing. The role of the state in manipulating ordinary citizens contributed in all these cases, as well as in Katihabwa's fictional account, to the alienation of refugees from fulfilling their sense of home.[11]

For Bugingo, and thousands more, the point seems to be that one cannot really go home again, even if one can regain one's physical home. That home for which he longed, and which he imagined was waiting for him, had been shattered long ago. Perhaps one should conclude that home, for these refugees, is not so much an illusion, but that it is an elusive, receding mirage of hope on a future horizon.

Chapter 2
Contemplating Repatriation to Eritrea

Lucia Ann McSpadden

In May 1991, after a brutal thirty-year war, the Eritrean liberation struggle with Ethiopia ended, allowing Eritrean refugees the possibility of returning to a peaceful but impoverished homeland. Research with Eritrean refugees in North America, Sweden, and Eritrea reveals that the willingness to return is shaped by an analysis of what will enhance social and economic power and status. The sense of belonging is negotiated and transnationally expressed in dual citizenship, homes in two countries, educational decisions, gift-giving, visiting, and paying taxes in two countries. Current and desired future identities are integrated within the different social contexts of Eritrea and the resettlement countries. Belonging and empowerment are derived in access to political, economic and social resources, and are differentially constructed by women and by men. The presumed linkage between these refugees and their homeland is problematic and should be understood in terms of the processual nature of negotiating identity, situating belonging, and reconstructing social space.

As the longest standing armed conflict in Africa, the struggle caused over a quarter of Eritrea's population to flee. The majority of the refugees, as many as a half million persons at a given time, sought asylum in Sudan, where some have lived for over twenty years. A small number, undistinguished from Ethiopians by host countries, were granted resettlement in the west—the United States, Canada, Sweden, and Germany.[1] The men and women resettled represent for the most part the educated strata of Eritrean society.[2] Those resettled were more likely to be men.[3] By 1997, both women and men had been resettled from two to fifteen years and had resided outside Eritrea even longer.

In this chapter, I analyze the decision-making of 44 Eritrean women and men originally resettled in Canada (8), the United States (25), Germany (2), and southern Sweden (9), as they confront the possibility of returning permanently to a liberated, peaceful, and independent Eritrea.[4] Of these, seven were living in Eritrea at the time of the 1995 interviews. The interviews were conducted over several studies carried out in 1983–98. Although the data are derived from different places and periods of time, several consistent themes emerged about refugees' decisions to return. As I will show, when the refugee experience is examined temporally, concepts of home and community are problematic and need to be analyzed rather than taken for granted.

In the discussion that follows, I first sketch the current political and economic context of contemporary Eritrea to which the refugees contemplate returning as well as some of the relevant aspects of their resettlement experiences. Next I discuss the various issues and concerns that refugees themselves articulate about their return. Finally, I speculate on how different conceptions of home and place shift over time and affect the possibility of returns.

The Political Economic Context of Return

The fall of the Mengistu regime in Ethiopia and the subsequent retreat of the Ethiopian army from Eritrea in May 1991 brought the thirty-year war between Eritrea and Ethiopia to an end. Following a 1993 global referendum initiated by the winning guerrilla army, the Eritrean People's Liberation Front (EPLF), the international community recognized Eritrea as an independent, sovereign nation.

The reconstruction of Eritrea after thirty years of village-to-village trench warfare continues to be daunting. Eritrea is one of the poorest countries in Africa. As the War-Torn Societies project of the United Nations Research Institute for Social Development reports, "Eritrea is one of the lowest per capita users of commercial energy. . . . Out of 7,000 kilometres of road, only seven to eight per cent is paved or gravel covered . . . the present telecommunication system reaches only about 0.49 per cent of the population and is concentrated in urban areas" (UNRISD 1996: 3).

Given the devastation, about 80 percent of the population is on food aid. The infrastructure—roads, hospitals, mosques, churches, and schools—has been destroyed or is unusable; the land has been deforested; and landmines remain a major problem (Gebremedhin 1995). Housing in urban areas is basically unavailable.[5] The University of Asmara was stripped clean by the retreating Ethiopian army. Employment in the private sector is limited; most jobs are with a government that in 1995 laid off 10,000 persons in an effort to downsize and consolidate administration.

Diaspora literature often analyzes the balance between force and choice in migration.[6] For refugees, including Eritrean refugees, force—due to fear, persecution, and threats to life—is dominant. After liberation, choice becomes a real possibility. Politically, the government of Eritrea is formed from the liberation fighters and hence does not represent the government from which the refugees fled. There is, therefore, the possibility of repatriation to a country at peace. In facing the possibility of return, refugees resettled in the West compare life in the country of resettlement to the likely shape of life in Eritrea. Unlike the decision to flee, the decision to return does not need to be made in haste. As the next section will show, the specific political economic context of the resettlement country may also influence these decisions and their timing.

The Resettlement Context

Experiences within resettlement are predictably influential in the decision-making processes. In considering whether or not to return, some issues appear to be especially salient for the Eritreans. As Africans, they must confront the personal prejudices and structural racism embedded within the western societies of resettlement. The historical, structural, and cultural factors affecting the incorporation and marginalization of "people of color" generally, and refugees in particular, in these countries are significantly different and affect the resulting social places of the Eritreans.

Most Eritreans have heard of the historical oppression of blacks, especially in the United States, but are not prepared to encounter it themselves. Thus refugees were shocked when North Americans classified Eritreans in the same social category as African Americans. Every Eritrean I initially interviewed rejected this association. From the perspective of the Eritreans, their history as Eritreans is unrelated to the experiences of blacks in North America. The Eritreans separated themselves from the perceived devalued social position and lower economic class of blacks. Many of the Eritreans in the United States stated that they were afraid to associate with blacks because of the risk of "losing my future." Clearly they perceived how racial identity and class connected in North America. Such comments were typically expressed in conjunction with the desire to get a higher education and a "good job" (McSpadden 1989: 186–88). Moussa reports that some Eritrean and Ethiopians in Canada also began to call themselves "brown" to distinguish themselves from other black communities (Moussa 1993: 229).

Eritreans in Sweden are one of the largest African groups in a country that has had a long involvement in Africa. The Church of Sweden, the state church, has had mission work in Africa for decades. The government of Sweden supported development work in East Africa and anti-apartheid efforts in South Africa. Eritrea is one of Sweden's twenty "Program Lands," countries that are preferentially allocated development funds. Ethnically, Eritreans are more often categorized as Africans than as blacks by Swedes; they are consistently considered "non-Swedes" even if born in Sweden.

The response of the Eritreans in the face of the oppression and discrimination that blacks in Western countries face is to assert being Eritrean. They reject equating being black with being inferior and emphasize their pride in Eritrea's successful struggle for liberation against the most powerful army in Africa. Their insistence on their Eritrean identity also reveals their commitment to a political cause, the liberation of Eritrea. Resettled Eritreans are often angry when they encounter the ignorance of persons of Europe and North America about the Horn of Africa and the events that caused these Eritreans to flee.

Being a refugee ("I am forced to be here")—as distinct from being an immigrant ("I choose to be here")—also becomes salient in class-related identity construction in resettlement (McSpadden and Moussa 1996: 217). With a pride in being Eritrean, these refugees emphasize social mobility through education, along with increased social status conferred by family position or high status employment. Eritreans struggled both financially and with their self-respect as they found themselves forced into low-paying, entry-level jobs in order to survive. In response, "they asserted the uniqueness of being a refugee, an . . . Eritrean and an African," or, as one observed, "I would not be working at this job if I were not a refugee. I am well-educated" (cited in McSpadden and Moussa 1994: 212).

In these situations asserting one's identity as a refugee—in contrast to an immigrant or an indigenous black—is a positive defensive response. Paradoxically, such identity assertion is maintained at the same time as Eritreans struggle to gain the skills, knowledge, and socio-economic resources that would enable them to move more successfully toward their personal goals. These new assets, in turn, facilitate their integration into the resettlement society and distance them from the constraints of being "refugees" and, over time, also distance them from Eritrea itself.

Profile of Resettled Eritreans Interviewed

The 44 Eritreans interviewed included 5 married and 4 single women, 16 married and 19 single men. Eight of the women were in Canada; one was in Asmara, Eritrea. Some had no dependents living with them. A few were divorced, and some were single mothers. A few, both men and women, who were single when they were interviewed in 1983–88 later had brothers and sisters with them. One man married in the interim. Among the married men, one was resettled with his wife and child; the others had their wives join them later from various asylum locations.

At the time of their flight the women ranged in age from fourteen to thirty-four and the men from seventeen to thirty-two. At the time of interviews the women's ages ranged from twenty-three to forty-six and the men's from twenty to forty-two. The past social status of their families in Eritrea varied: wealthy land owner, bus driver, farmer, civil servant, mechanic, businesswoman/man (for example, barber), soldier, professional. All had lost members of their family in the war. One woman said that she had no one left in her family in Eritrea. One man had lost 20 relatives. Several of the women and men had been imprisoned and tortured prior to their flight. In some instances their homes or villages no longer existed. Most families were scattered. The majority had come into resettlement in North America and Europe after three to four years of asylum in Sudan. Some came from Italy; others came through Kenya, Djibouti, Uganda, and Spain.

In the United States and Sweden all the men were working at least part-time. Most combined school with part-time employment. Two married men had full-time professional employment. One was an accountant; the other, having just completed medical training, was working at two professional jobs and beginning to pay back student loans. In Canada all but one woman were employed outside the home in 1991 and 1992. When they first arrived in Canada, most of the women were employed in predominantly female, low-paying jobs (e,g., hotel housekeeper, waitress, and factory worker). The women are now mainly employed in computer related jobs and as cashiers. Some hold professional and management positions. Some of the younger women, in their twenties, are going to school. In Eritrea, one woman, originally resettled in Oakland, California, ran a small coffee shop. Two of the married men were employed by the Eritrean government and two by the University of Asmara. The single young man was a high school student.

Determinants of Return

As refugees, the Eritreans, having been forced to flee, longed to return. The political struggle of Eritrea against Ethiopia claimed their loyalty and their hope for the future. In interviews prior to liberation in 1991, Eritreans unequivocally asserted that they would return as soon as their country was liberated. However, by the time this was achieved, many found that the decision was not so clear and that they had to consider several factors in their decision to return or not. The most salient factors that the resettled refugees expressed were educational opportunities, employment, familial responsibilities and obligations, gender and marriage relations, and political and social security.

Along with these various factors, resettled Eritreans often tried to develop a timeline for return. Many initially returned to Eritrea to visit but not to stay. Their plans often incorporated a series of specific steps to be taken over time rather than an immediate and all-encompassing plan to return. One way to handle the complexities of the decision was to develop separate short-term, mid-term, and long-term plans with an expectation in the long term to return. As Berhane, a twenty-six-year-old male student, explained, "Ten years in my calculation. I will get my education—that will take two years. I will work eight to ten years, pay my debts, collect some money. Then I may go back. Not now, but in ten years."[7]

Tewolde, a forty-eight-year-old married accountant who had recently returned from visiting family in Eritrea, lamented the lack of current opportunities for him in Eritrea but hoped to return in the future,

The country is broken down. There is nothing there for me to do. Eritrea is rebuilding; so much has been destroyed. They don't need an accountant, at least right now. Maybe later they will. [My wife] can work there; they always need nurses. But they don't need accountants. The jobs are for the people who stayed during the struggle. We will just go for a visit, but not to stay. When the country is rebuilt and there is more money, they will need accountants. Then I will see about going back, but not now.

Education

Eritreans traditionally place and continue to place a very high value on education. In recent years the perceived importance of formal schooling as the pathway to high status, government employment, increased privilege, and community respect has increased. Western education is a contemporary, sought-after means to personal and family achievement in a chiefly status-by-ascription society (Levine

1965; Giorgis 1984; Cichon 1986; McSpadden 1989; Tebeje 1989; Moussa 1993).[8] These benefits from education, especially college-level education, are believed to accrue not only to the individual but to the family and the nation. Becoming well-educated is part of one's family and civic responsibility. Yet, males have also traditionally had more access to education at all levels than females in Eritrea (McSpadden 1999: 247–48).

Most refugees specifically compared Eritrea and the West with regard to educational opportunities. Except for a few who were already in professional positions, all men saw education as their highest priority. Abu Baker explained,

education is the most important thing. If I have good schooling, I can get a job. I will visit for the summer and come back to school here. After I graduate from college, I will work three or four years and get some money. Then I will go back, *maybe*. You have to have money to build something to start out. Then I can help my family and help myself.

For both men and women there was concern about the ability to continue their own education or to educate their children, siblings, or other relatives. Tadesse stated that there is,

a lot of opportunity here. . . . Most people [are] thinking about school to get education here. Besides education we have to work or have financial aid . . . so the government [helps us] to go to school. . . . My kids are going to school. That is the first thing. Our kids will have more opportunity for education here. . . . My wife is thinking about going to ——— College. . . . I hope she will . . . [she] really wants to do something.

The resettled refugees were also well aware of the challenges Eritrea faces in rebuilding its educational infrastructure. They judged educational opportunities and governmental financial support to be significantly superior in the West. One man said,

America is better than my country. Everything, education in America is better than everything in my country. A lot of opportunity here. It depends on what you want to do, can get a doctorate, whatever. Every Friday I go to the Eritrean group; we watch VCR. Most people, [are] thinking about school to get education here. Besides education we have to work or have financial aid . . . so the government [helps us] to go to school.

Education for Eritreans was not for its own sake. Reflecting their cultural values, most men saw it as the means of getting access to the job market, earning more money and increasing social power. For those who had not been able to get an education in Eritrea, resettlement in the west had brought an undreamed of possibility. Almost 100 percent of the Eritreans linked getting an education with having a good job. For the men this was linked to becoming a responsible adult, to "not being a beggar," a linkage that is especially salient given that many Eritrean males experienced a severe loss of status in resettlement especially related to employment. All the men linked having a good job with achieving a good life and seemed almost desperate in that pursuit. Social power was considered contingent upon one's socioeconomic position coupled with the ability to help one's family both in resettlement and in Eritrea. One man observed,

It is a hard decision. [One has to] to have something in hand—education or money. But those people here who haven't had this opportunity, can't go back. . . . I was amazed how people treated me [during his recent visit to Eritrea]. I was gone nine years. I was so happy to see people. My family was so happy to see me. I must go to my country as "a refreshment." I have money, and I can invite people for tea. People are very poor. Money has power. Also education has power.

As Moussa (1993) observes, in Eritrean society education is also a source of power for Eritrean women, giving them opportunities to delay marriage as well as to gain increased autonomy.[9] Although many of the single women delayed pursuing their own education after resettlement in the West because of family responsibilities, once those responsibilities were met, they put considerable effort into education. With an education they could be self-supporting and, thus, escape some of the gender role expectations of Eritrean culture. A professional or technical education protected, if not ensured, their rights as women (McSpadden and Moussa 1996: 230).

Women interviewed by Moussa expressed varying viewpoints about children's education and returning to Eritrea. Some of those in Canada said that their children would get a better and a free education in Canada, including university study, and therefore they would not return to Eritrea. Others agreed, but stated that they themselves would return to Eritrea after their children had finished high school, again a deferred return. For some it was critical that they return to Eritrea when their children were ready to go to school. This last perspective was stated strongly by one woman.

I definitely want to take my children back when they are young so that they can be socialized in our culture . . . it is a very good culture. . . . That is why we have been able to survive and succeed here. . . . We know we are Eritreans and we are proud of it . . . I prefer to take them when they are young. Later on they can come to Canada if they want to come to University.

Children's education was a special concern in refugees' decisions about returning, and they considered the situation of children with them in resettlement and young relatives in Eritrea, "I am thinking of bringing my niece in Eritrea here to go to school. Also my brother has a daughter who is still in school. It is very hard to get to college. There is only one in Asmara."

The issue of children's schooling was often compounded by language differences. Several Eritreans said that their school-age children were fluent in a western language (English, Swedish, German) and would not be able to manage school in Tigrinya. For that reason, going back to Eritrea was not feasible. One man who had resettled in Germany had returned with the intention of establishing a German language school so his children could also return.

It is likely, as many of the women discerned, that the children would face difficulties in adjusting to life in Eritrea. They had been raised in another culture. A school student in Eritrea bluntly stated such feelings. He had been sent by his mother in New York City to live with his aunt in Asmara for the last year of high school. His mother wanted him to connect to his family and establish roots in Eritrea. Having trouble with his return plane reservation, he exploded angrily in a perfect New York City street dialect, "I have to get out of this fucking country! It is killing me! They are all fucking creeps. If I don't get out of here, I'll go crazy!"

Although education was one of the most important factors the Eritreans assessed when deciding about return, men emphasized the increased social status and increased income associated with a higher degree, whereas women also emphasized the need to use education to protect their rights as women.

Family Responsibilities

Responsibility toward their families both in the country of resettlement and in Eritrea was a central issue in many people's decisions. Several people expressed grief and pain at leaving parents and/or younger relatives in Eritrea. For men, especially, this was coupled with the responsibility to care for parents and siblings. Mulatu was the sole surviving male in his family; his father, brothers, and uncles had been killed. His mother insisted that he flee so he would not be killed as well. However, Mulatu went into a deep depression after resettlement in California castigating himself for leaving his mother. "It is my responsibility to take care of her; there are no other men in the family. What will happen to her? What if she gets sick? I have done the wrong thing; I should not have left. I am a bad person!"

Their education and jobs—if they had employment—enabled some refugees to provide for their families in both locations. "I send money to home and to my sister in Greece whenever I can. . . . It is not easy. It is almost expected to send money and to support our family" (Matsuoka and Sorenson 1999: 225).

Many individual Eritreans also struggled with the various benefits for their children versus longing for one's homeland. Making a decision about returning can be a conflicted experience. Ruth expressed it poignantly,

Even if I have my family here. . . . I feel I am in somebody else's land. . . . I guess it is because I grew up in Eritrea. . . . I want to be called Eritrean. I want my children to feel Eritrean . . . even if I am accepted here. . . . I sometimes feel it is not fair. . . . The children say they wish they had grandparents . . . they wish they could go there" [to Eritrea]. (Moussa 1993: 250–51)

Some Eritreans decided not to return because they could not bring money or gifts back to their families in Eritrea. Although there was clearly a cultural expectation of gift-bringing, the refugee experience itself added another level of meaning. One man said that his family had sacrificed so much; he, too, had "lost years of his life" (he had been in asylum in Sudan for four years prior to resettlement). He had not been able to take care of his mother as he should have. Realizing that he could not go back unless he had achieved a good education and had earned enough to return with gifts and money, he stated, "All the sacrifices have to be worthwhile." When I said that surely his parents would rather have him back without gifts than not see him, he said that was true for his parents. However, his other relatives would expect gifts.

For some Eritreans the need to bring back gifts or money is related to the financial condition of the family in Eritrea. One woman in Canada stated,

I have nothing to take back (funds or financial resources to buy gifts) with me to start all over again. I can't depend on my family because they are poor and they expect me to help them. At least here I can get Family Allowance until I find work. My child can go to a good school. I get medical insurance. Even though my family in Eritrea can't understand why I am not sending them money, I don't have to explain it to them every day. (McSpadden and Moussa 1996: 233–34)

Some Eritreans said they could help their families better financially by working in the West and sending money or by setting up a small business operation in Eritrea which they could fund from the West while relatives in Eritrea managed the business. Eritreans in Sweden, organized into a more or less formal organization, pooled funds for several years in order to buy larger pieces of property in Eritrea when that is legally allowed.[10] They intended to live in Sweden and manage the property through family networks while they themselves traveled back and forth. An added complexity is the recent decision of the Eritrean government to designate all land as government rather than private land, and thereby prohibiting individuals from purchasing and/or owning land (Pool 1997).[11] How the government will implement this is not yet apparent.

Returning even for visits makes the changes in familial relationships and expectations apparent. One man, who walked for a week to return to his village for a visit, recounted that his mother and sister did not understand that he had to leave again after two weeks. They expected him to stay at least six months and were bewildered when he tried to explain about his job and limited vacation time. Another said that his relatives thought that he must be rich because he was living in the United States. They kept asking him to send them money and electronic items. He told me that this was preventing him from returning since he was not, in fact, rich at all. He had been working two jobs until he became ill from overwork and was now only working part-time.

Those who returned to Eritrea for visits reported extremely positive experiences of homecoming and emotional reunions with their remaining family members. They spoke of "sleeping by the side of the road in peace" or "walking alone at night and not being afraid." However, they still returned to the West after the visit.

Employment

Work is the key aspect of a social place in the Eritrean cultural context, especially for men. Jobs were a key factor in their return decisions. They made direct comparisons between the possibilities for them in Eritrea and in the resettlement country. One of the professional men who decided to go back to the United States after his visit to Eritrea explained:

Part of my life is here, my family. Especially my work is here . . . they are trying to build the country, the economy. It is a very young country—it is not a good time for me. *Your home is where you work.* . . . People who live there have more opportunity to get a job than those who come back from . . . another country. I don't even know what kind of job I could look for over there. I don't think I would take *any* kind of job. I would work in a hospital or own my own business. That takes a lot of money. *I have to take a job according to my experience or my training.* (emphasis added)

Several men spoke of earning enough money so they could go back to Eritrea to start their own business. They stated clearly that this would require many years in the United States.

Political issues provide an important influence in such assessments. Most indicated that any jobs available would and should be for people who had remained in Eritrea during the liberation struggle, and government officials in Eritrea concurred. Affiliation with the EPLF appears necessary for government jobs. The German government-financed Return of Talent Programme, however, is structured to assist returnees in establishing small businesses, thus circumventing or mitigating these restraints (Black, Koser, and Walsh, 1997).

Interestingly, a woman in Asmara had done just what the men talked about. She saved money during resettlement in California and eventually operated a small juice bar/cafe in Asmara. She said she enjoyed the small cafes of Berkeley so very much and wanted to replicate one in ambiance and food in Eritrea. At the same time she could be an independent businesswoman. She implied that she was combining positive aspects of the United States and Eritrea. Nevertheless, she eventually returned to the Bay Area. A medical doctor from Germany used the funds from the German government's Return of Talent Programme to build a simple clinic.

The difficulty of finding employment is revealed in the reports of the Eritrean government's program for the demobilization of former combatants. Although these former veterans have first priority for employment in Eritrea, jobs are scarce for both men and women. The government notes that the problems confronting female former combatants are especially difficult. Among other issues, the lack of child care makes it different for single mothers to find employment (GDI 1995; Amanuel Mehreteab 1995: 5). (Married women also suffer from lack of child care, but they get more help from extended family.)

Marital Status and Gender Relations

The majority of the resettled Eritreans are young and single, which makes the issue of marriage and building a family relevant. In earlier interviews the men often discussed the difficulty of getting married during resettlement since there were comparatively few single Eritrean women. Now that Eritrea is liberated, transnational linkages for marriage are possible. By living in the West for the foreseeable future, men obtain comparative power in realizing their frequently stated desire to marry a "traditional [and submissive] Eritrean woman." The traditional social inequality of women and men is reinforced or even strengthened if the men have gained valued social benefits, e.g., higher education and/or a high status job, during resettlement. Bereket asserted that it

is not hard to find a woman if I return as an educated person from America. That is why it is easy there. . . . Some say it is like buying a woman. When you have some education and money, the women approach you. . . . But the man is doing the selecting so you know what the situation is.

One man stated that 60 to 70 percent of the single Eritrean men he knew were going to Eritrea for a visit with the intention of selecting a wife. Going to Eritrea to find a wife was not just because of a lack of Eritrean women in resettlement but also because women in resettlement have gained more independence and, therefore, eschewed traditional social relationships with Eritrean men. One woman told Moussa (1993: 234),

You can make your choices. . . . I can say I am competing with men [professionally] and I can make progress [towards my goals.]. . . . In [my country] women are dominated by men and we have to expect it. Here we can do work like men.

Women control the relationships by keeping themselves somewhat socially aloof or by reframing the conditions for relationships in non-traditional terms. As one man noted "Women here [in the United States] are strong like men [independent]. They would not come to us easily." Matsuoka and Sorenson (1999) reported that Eritrean husbands in Canada blamed Western feminism for the women's lack of appropriate submission to male authority. One man is quoted as saying, "The main problem is with the women. The women get educated and now they are not following our culture. They want to be equal to the men" (1999: 235).

As Moussa (1996) found in her interviews with women, some women are concerned about returning because they may lose certain perceived rights. One woman asserted, "there are no laws yet about pay equity and against wife abuse, assault and rape. . . . I would find it difficult to live without [guaranteed] basic human rights."

Women's rights were, for these women, very much tied to the creation of a democratic Eritrea which would allow for the rights of its citizens to express their opinions, enjoy employment equity and shared responsibilities in the family, as well as the right to an education and access to basic health services (McSpadden and Moussa 1996: 228).

Yet Eritrean women resettled in the West report that they experience greater freedom and rights in the home and in the work place. They resist a return to subordination and fear that the Eritrean men, even when they exhibit more sex-role flexibility in resettlement, for example, sharing in housework and childcare, have not really changed their gendered values. They wondered if these gains would be lost (much as they were lost for women in the Algerian, Cuban, and Mozambican struggles). As one woman asked, " 'Are women going to return to the kitchen?' " (McSpadden and Moussa 1996: 228). Although women and men fought side by side in the field during the liberation struggle, and the Eritrean government states a commitment to gender equity, women are afraid that there will be a reversion to the traditional patriarchal ways now that the war is over.

Priorities may conflict within a family, as is clearly seen in the painful choices available to the men who return to Eritrea. Their loyalties to Eritrea and desire to participate in its reconstruction conflict with the need of their wives to protect the rights they have gained in resettlement and the desire of parents to provide good education for their children. One woman, by insisting on educating their children in Canada, said she was "killing her husband," who wanted to return.

In Eritrea, former combatants frequently spoke of a high divorce rate among their ranks in spring 1995. A number of married former combatants reported to me that the housing shortage forced many to live with parents. Consistently they reported that their parents, disapproving strongly of the former combatants' egalitarian marital relationships, put strong pressure upon the women to assume traditional gender roles. Men reported that it was almost impossible to counter this pressure as long as the couple lived with parents.

Security and Citizenship

Being refugees rather than immigrants influences Eritreans' desire to return. What caused them to flee has ceased to exist: the liberation struggle was successful. From a political perspective nothing prevents them from returning.

However, being a refugee also means having a keen awareness of the unpredictability of political events. All persons interviewed insisted that whether or not they returned to Eritrea, they would maintain dual citizenship. Being Eritrean was basic to their identity, but being a citizen of a Western country provided political security. One young man said "If things turn bad in Eritrea and my family is in danger, I can bring [my relatives] here." Eritrean women in Canada said that maintaining Canadian citizenship provided them with rights and opportunities and, above all, protected them from again experiencing the powerlessness of being stateless. A woman reflected, "Who knows what will happen in the future? . . . Who knows, we may have to flee our country again. Or it may happen to our children."

Having Western citizenship provides opportunities for families back in Eritrea. Being a "permanent resident alien" or, preferably, a citizen of the United States, Canada, or Sweden provides the status whereby the Eritreans can bring close relatives to join them under the immigration quotas or student visas. One man, who had been able as a permanent resident alien to bring his two younger brothers from Sudan to the United States, stated, "[being] here is like insurance. If I'm not here, I couldn't bring my brothers here. What would they do? Maybe they would be dead. They would not be in school" (in Eritrea).

They may also recognize that employment possibilities are enhanced by citizenship in a Western country. A young man in college asserted, "I will get United States citizenship. If I get citizenship, I can work overseas. I can go to Saudi Arabia or Europe. This country is a powerful nation, therefore, it is good to be an American—for education purposes or for a job."

The Decision to Return

Wanting to return yet wanting to stay: weighing the differing factors is clearly a painful experience for the Eritreans. Where the choice is unambiguous, circumstances often limit or dictate the response; for example, in Eritrea, even if all wish to return there simply may not be jobs for the adults or appropriate schooling for children. In such a situation, the values of Eritrea and the West are congruent, but there are significant resources in the resettlement countries.

Zetter (1988; 100–101) argues that the refugee experience, "may simultaneously create a parallel structure of 'new' and powerful agendas." These new agendas often become relevant to refugees' decisions about whether or not to return. The causes that precipitated flight may be replaced by new "causes" when repatriation is considered. Malkki (1992) in her study of Hutu refugees in exile, questions the taken-for-granted territorial connection between people (refugees) and place (homeland). She reports that the refugees living in camps linked their identity and their desired community to their homeland; they were outsiders who needed to go home. However, those who had developed small businesses in urban areas "borrowed from the social context of the township" and no longer considered themselves refugees (Malkki 1992). Effectively, the resettlement country became their new home.

As research among Latin American exiles in Europe has shown, a "critical integration" allows the exile to critique one's country of origin while finding the spaces and relationships in the country of asylum or resettlement that are congruent with one's values and ideology. Likewise, the idea of a "transcultural identity," points to exiles having multiple identities, often feeling they can belong to two countries and cultures.[12]

Bennett (1991) constructs a developmental model based on self-reflectivity. "One's self is both a cultural product and a producer of the meanings that constitute cultural patterns . . . people consciously select and integrate culturally disparate aspects of their identities." (1991: 38). In this development the individual is being challenged to integrate multiple frames of reference in which he/she is "always in the process of becoming *a part of* and *apart from* a given cultural context" (38).

Resettled refugees attempt to shape realities in accordance with early socialization, their particular refugee experience, and expectations for the future. This view implicitly challenges the linear and unitary portrayal of the refugee experience as adaptation, integration, and assimilation (Berry 1992: 69–85), as well as the refugee as an ideal-type posited by many refugee researchers and practitioners.

Certainly home, understood as a social place that provides safety, dignity, valued resources, power, and belonging, is not, for these Eritreans, automatically linked to the territory of one's birth nor even of one's allegiance. However, home is not completely identified with the country of resettlement. It is a process of balancing *a part of* and *apart from*. In fact, the western country may be more valued in instrumental terms of social resources, opportunities, and protection, while Eritrea is more valued as the source of one's identity, history, and values. Both can provide belonging and social power, albeit differently construed.

With the need to belong, to develop or strengthen powerful social places, the Eritreans are balancing values and social responsibilities in two cultures. They are negotiating multiple and sometimes conflicting expectations within themselves and between two social spaces. As one Eritrean woman said, "We are caught between two worlds." For most, remaining in the west seems to be the choice, however, there are intense contradictions embedded in this choice.

National identity strengthened by the political framework of liberation evokes strong emotions. However, this identification is overridden by pressing economic issues and educational goals. Opportunity structures are assessed and compared within the world view, values, and social status/class concerns of Eritrean culture evaluated in terms of the advantages presented by resettlement in the west.

Some concerns are gendered. Women are concerned about retaining certain rights which they have achieved in resettlement in the West, while men are more likely to focus on the education needed for jobs leading to higher status. Educational opportunities strongly weight the decision toward staying in the west. In important ways the need to contribute to one's family and to one's society—Eritrea—also weights the decision towards constructing a social place in the west.

If home is basically belonging, the Eritreans are in a transnational process that is constantly reshaping and shifting under their feet. Home is no longer clearly linked to nation and territory. Home is also where one can carry forward life hopes and plans, can protect one's rights and social status, and care for family. Essential qualities shaping identity are differently stressed in resettlement than they are in one's native land. "Who am I?" in this context and "Who do I want to be?" are questions that weave their way through all these issues of choice and possibility considered by the Eritreans.

Belonging is finally painfully ambiguous in spite of the powerful social place that residing in the West provides. Negussie vividly portrays the dilemma. "I will want to go back to Eritrea in 10 years. There is no psychological happiness here. We don't belong to blacks or to the whites. I will be a minimum 10 years here. Everyone will apply for citizenship here. When we reach a certain age, like 45, we can live in our own country. *I can get American citizenship, and I will always say, I am an Eritrean*" (emphasis added).

Appendix: Interview Methods

The research reported in this paper is part of longitudinal and comparative research begun in 1983 and continuing to the present. Some of the work has been done in cooperation with my colleague, Helene Moussa, who has focused extensively on research with Ethiopian and Eritrean women in Canada.

The early research (1988–91) was developed from two independent streams with Ethiopian and Eritrean refugees (McSpadden 1989, 1991, 1993; Moussa 1992, 1993). Both employed a life history approach. For that stage of the research Moussa interviewed 16 Ethiopian and Eritrean women of whom approximately half were Eritrean. In addition she interviewed a few Eritrean women in Switzerland. I initially interviewed 110 Ethiopian and Eritrean men. For the purposes of the research design the responses of 59 men were compared. Of these 21 were Eritrean. I also administered two research instruments to the final cohort of men. These two research studies, carried out from 1982 to 1991, were done prior to the end of the armed struggle by Eritrea to achieve liberation from Ethiopia, a liberation which was achieved in May 1991.

The second stage of the research, carried out in 1992 and 1993, was explicitly a comparative gendered analysis regarding repatriation decisions of Eritrean women and men in resettlement at the time immediately after liberation. A sample of Eritrean men (11) was chosen from the original research population. The same Eritrean women were interviewed in both the first and second stages of the research. The results of this second stage are reported more fully in McSpadden and Moussa (1996).

The third stage of the research was carried from 1995 to 1998 out by McSpadden in Sweden and Eritrea. Both men and women were interviewed.

In all aspects of the research, interviews were done one-to-one in homes, offices, or restaurants in Stockholm and Uppsala, Sweden, Toronto, Canada, Seattle, Washington, Reno, Nevada, and the San Francisco Bay Area of northern California. In Asmara, Eritrea, interviewing was done in homes, hotels, and government offices.

The refugees were identified in various ways: through resettlement staff, church volunteers, personal contacts of my colleague and myself in our community volunteer work, and other Eritrean refugees. The longitudinal nature of the research and the consistency of the responses throughout the various aspects of the study give confidence to the analysis.

Chapter 3
Filipina Depictions of Migrant Life for Their Kin at Home

Jane A. Margold

This chapter examines the expressive production of Filipina domestic workers in Hong Kong. The women's self-representations, in the form of posed photographs and videotapes, are seen as a form of autobiography, intended for consumption by kin and neighbors in the Philippines. As highly selective accounts of the Filipinas' sojourn overseas, the photos and tapes edit out the indignities endured by low-wage workers in an unwelcoming host society. They portray their subjects as beautifully groomed, cosmopolitan women, pausing for a moment in Hong Kong's upscale malls or participating in beauty contests sponsored by fellow Filipinos. These cultural expressions reflect and affirm a future-oriented kinship system, noted elsewhere among highly migratory Southeast Asian island groups. They are imaginative resources that rehearse the new, higher-status identities the Filipinas are likely to enjoy upon return to their homeland. They are a link with home and kin and a promise of a better life for generations to come.

Diaspora, once understood as the enforced movement of persecuted or enslaved peoples, has come to be linked with the more voluntary, temporary dislocations of particular groups. Through expanded possibilities of communication and transport, migrants now remain integrated into social, economic and cultural circuits connecting their homelands with their countries of work. Yet, even if displaced people's imagination of their place of origin is continually refreshed by these increased opportunities for return, their memories are also constrained by a lack of contact with the homeland's daily life. The process of defamiliarization is intensified as the diasporic community discovers how its natal country and culture are regarded—or disregarded and devalued—by populations in the country of work. Cultural reframings of self and home become at once a necessity and an opportunity, as the displaced, newly visible as a distinct population in their place of settlement, see themselves refracted in their host's eyes.

Diaspora as defamiliarization challenges us to understand the structuring elements that cushion the migrant from the shock of the new. As the host society's unwelcoming scrutiny compels the migrants into a disturbing awareness of their

social repositioning, what are the stabilizing influences that remain? More generally, my interest is in how the overseas experience is received selectively by Asian
women migrants taking service jobs at low levels of the global labor hierarchy.
What do the women provisionally retrieve from the diasporic encounter? What do
they ignore, avoid or render inconsequential, as a means of protecting themselves
from the unreceptive host society? And who is the audience for their reconstructions of their experience abroad?

   The argument I lay out here considers kinship and the apparatus of the senses
as powerful connectors that bind the migrant to home while enabling her to re-
assess and rework her identity. Following Janet Carsten (1995), I briefly point to
the significance of a "downward-looking" (or future-oriented) kinship system to
Filipina migrants, who, like the Malay villagers studied by Carsten, attach far less
value to ties to deceased ancestors than to the acquisition of kin relationships in
the present and future. To Carsten, a downward-looking kinship system, which is
sometimes negatively labeled "structural or genealogical amnesia" (Carsten
1995), may also be understood more positively as a means by which a highly mobile people reduce the importance of differences of origin and recast themselves
as a coherent group. Among new settlers, forgetting becomes a creative act, facilitating the formation of new kin ties based on present and anticipated relationships.

   Among people who remain displaced, a downward-looking kinship system has
a similar degree of utility. What might preferably be termed *onward-looking* kin relations hold out the promise to the migrant mother that her past of modest origins and present reality of distasteful work will recede to a remote corner of
memory when her children are afforded social mobility through her overseas
earnings. For the Filipinas in Hong Kong, who largely take jobs as domestic workers in the city's private households, the primary expressed goal of migration is to
improve the finances of their natal and marital families. Kin in the Philippines are
the recipients of the $U.S. 7 billion dollars that overseas workers remit annually.[1]
It is for parents, siblings, and husbands—and particularly for their actual and future children—that the Filipina migrants speak alternately of self-abnegation and
the potential reconstruction of self. Taking on the low-status but relatively well-
paid job of domestic worker is conventionally discussed in terms of "sacrificing"
oneself to the needs of the family. But self-sacrifice and individual ambition are
not necessarily seen as dissonant. Especially for younger unmarried women, overseas work is equally an opportunity for "achieving something" in life, for "developing" oneself, as the migrants say. Migration for the sake of the family can be
reconciled with the seemingly contradictory aim of migration as self-realization
because devotion to the family is a deep cultural motif, lending itself to multiple
understandings. For those who do not wish to migrate, protecting the family from
the breakups and other social costs of separation may be invoked as a reason to
stay at home. But for aspiring migrants, the family may conversely be cited as the
motivation for and the ultimate beneficiaries of a sojourn overseas. Thus, as
Aguilar (1999) usefully observes, women migrants "may appear to be faithfully

conforming with the expected gender roles of altruistic mother and dutiful daughter" (1999: 111) while setting off on a quest for self-expansion that will enhance their control over their own lives (113).

Migration as "a journey of achievement" is equally a powerful cultural theme, as Aguilar and others point out (1999: 102; Margold 1995, citing Buaken 1948 and Siegel 1969). In an article explicitly comparing the overseas contract worker to a pilgrim whose journey entails "a period of sacrifice, ascetic self-denial and the abandonment of worldly comfort and pleasures," Aguilar argues that the migrant, like the pilgrim, must display "the determination to persevere through (the journey's) trials" (1999: 103) until the migrant worker/pilgrim's successful return to the homeland, community and family (105). Yet, the time period between self-denial and its eventual rewards may be more fluid than Aguilar suggests. The migrant worker need not actually return home to experience the sense of accomplishment and the altered, elevated self that is the end-goal of the pilgrim. An imagined return may suffice to provide some pleasurable moments during routine or unpleasant work. In Hong Kong, moreover, legally mandated days off and holidays yield opportunities for meeting people and attending events not available at home. As they socialize with their friends during their Saturday or Sunday off, the women migrants may try on an expanded, transformed self, circulating new possibilities of identity to members of their own overseas community and to the host society.

Recording Selective Aspects of the Diasporic Experience

The Filipinas' efforts at self-realization are chronicled in the photographic self-portraits, videotapes, and other memorabilia they collect and mail home. These material, sensory remembrances form a selective archive of the diasporic experience. As such, they can tell us what is bracketed and what is registered of the daily flow of images, social encounters, and happenings that are part of the migrants' overseas lives. Photographic self-portraits, videotapes and other "souvenirs," as the Filipinas term them, can be considered a poesis, a experimental making of something that was previously experientially and culturally unmarked (Serematakis 1996). But at the same time, they are prosaic objects that are passed around to friends in the Filipino community of Hong Kong, sent home in letters and saved explicitly by migrants who are parents or anticipating parenthood as a visual autobiography for the generations to come.

During fieldwork in Hong Kong and in the Philippine rural north, I found that it was rare, even in the most modest household, for families not to possess several albums filled with photographs of migrant kin. These were produced soon after the conversation turned to going overseas to work ("panag-abroad," in Ilokano, the lingua franca of the north). Particularly when the migrant was still overseas, the photographs invoked his or her presence, allaying family anxieties and bearing witness to the household's continuing bonds (Sontag 1989: 8). The portraits of the absent family member became a focal point for telling a visitor proudly of the other material objects that had been sent home or paid for as a concrete result of the migrant's work—a new cement-block house with glass windows and corrugated tin roof, the latest electronic equipment, gold earrings and watches, and other costly goods. At a minimum, a small table or bookcase would be purchased locally with the migrant's remittances, so that one or two albums could be accessed easily. Photographs and the array of solid, tangible material paraphernalia seemed to furnish certain evidence of the migrant's existence. The photographs, in particular, bestowed a kind of immortality on the absent family member and bespoke a hope of future reunion (Sontag 1989: 11).

For the migrants, the photographic portraits presumed confidence not only in the continuity of the dispersed household but in the rootedness of the kin and neighbors who remained in the Philippines. In Hong Kong, as I noticed how many dozen snapshots were taken by my Filipina friends on every weekend outing, I often asked where this abundance of keepsakes would be stored. The women answered confidently that grandmothers, parents, aunts, husbands, or neighbors in the Philippines would easily find space. Through these links, the photographs and videotapes recorded a journey of social and personal development that spoke not only to the migrant herself, but also to the recipients of her remembrances. In this way, a spectral audience of kin operated as an important constituent of the diasporic experience.[2] But the Filipinas' sojourn abroad was also shaped by the women's perceptions of the attitudes displayed toward foreign domestic workers by the local people they encountered daily while shopping, running errands for employers and taking care of their children. Thus, in what follows, I consider Hong Kong society's encroachments upon the Filipina migrant's sense of herself. I then discuss the ways in which diasporic memory-making is also a dialogue between the migrant and a set of imagined audiences, the most important of which are the kin and community to which she will return.

Hong Kong as an Ambivalent Host

Diasporas, it should be emphasized, do not merely operate at the level of challenging an individual's understanding of who she is and to what she belongs. Diasporas also call into question the sovereignty of sending and receiving states. For the sending nation, an exodus such as that of more than three million Filipinos weakens state legitimacy, displaying its inability to provide for its own citizens. For the host nation, the massing of a foreign ethnic collectivity within its borders raises continuing problems of political self-definition. Questions arise as to who is to be viewed as an integral part of the host community and who is to be excluded. In what ways is the diasporic other regarded as distinct? And how will her alien traits be monitored?

In contemporary Hong Kong, the dilemmas of hosting non-nationals have been heightened and complicated by the ambiguities that remain unresolved with respect to the status of the city's locally born residents. On the whole, it is widely acknowledged that the Hong Kong Special Administrative Region (SAR) has remained a place where basic civil freedoms have been respected. Political parties critical of the Chinese central government were allowed to run for election in 1998. Growing crowds have attended commemorations of the anniversary of the Tienanmen massacre each year, without fear of violent confrontation or repression. And the SAR's internal affairs have been allowed to precede largely without interference (Ching 1999). Yet, at the same time that freedom of speech, assembly and movement have been maintained, the limits of SAR independence have also begun to become apparent. In May 1999, the SAR government challenged the authority of its own highest court by asking China's legislature to intervene in a ruling that would have extended the right to settle in Hong Kong to children of mainland immigrants. The move was a controversial one, arousing concern that the rule of law in Hong Kong had been undermined and a precedent had been set for treating the SAR as an extension of China rather than a separate entity. Anxieties about political autonomy have been accompanied by local criticism of the SAR authorities' slowness to address the effects of the regional economic crisis. At the turn of the twenty-first century, the highest unemployment rate ever recorded in Hong Kong, as well as widespread wage reductions and pay freezes, made workers more aware of the precariousness of their own jobs and concerned about the local economy's capacity for recovery.

Amid these shifts in the political-economic landscape of Hong Kong, a bitter social debate has continued over the status of foreign domestic workers, the majority of whom are Filipinas. These women have become a highly visible community in Hong Kong over a markedly short period of time. According to Immigration department figures, the numbers of Filipino migrants to the city doubled in the early to mid-1990s, to an estimated 130,000 by 1996 (Choo 1996: 5–6). By 1999, 80 percent of the 170,000 foreign domestic workers in Hong Kong were Filipinas (*Migration News* 1999). Within the same time span, the migration of other Southeast Asian and South Asian women also increased dramatically. But as a result of their sheer numbers, it has been Filipinas who have become most closely associated with household work. One indicator is the common use of the Cantonese term *ban-mui* ("Philippine girl") for any brown-skinned woman seen on the street. The term is a disdainful one that collapses the diverse identities of Hong Kong's non-Chinese Asian women into a single national and racial entity, while denying them full civil standing. "Philippine girl" downgrades the high levels of education achieved by many Filipinas, even as their fluency in English is marketed and exploited.[3] The "Philippine girl" appeals equally to upwardly mobile parents who want a maid who can clean, cook *and* tutor their children in English, and to merchants who illegally employ their domestic workers as saleswomen because "the Filipinas speak with and smile so easily at the customers," as one shop owner told me.

As Constable (1996a) observes, the terms for the domestic worker, *ban-mui*, or the equally blunt *gungyahn* (servant/worker) have none of the quasi-familial overlay that softened the master/servant relation in earlier years, when wealthy Chinese households employed the *muijai* (little maid or younger sister) or a more respected domestic worker who was addressed as *mahjeh* or *yok-jeh* (big sister or mother). While today children are usually told to use such kinship terms for their foreign caretaker as "auntie," school-age children are likely to refer to her in her absence, as "ngoh ge gungyahn" (my servant) making no pretense of a familial tie.

The naming of the inferior translates easily into acts of abuse, as an expanding literature on Asian women's migration has documented (Tadiar 1997; Cheng 1996; Anderson 1993; Javate de Dios 1996/7). Instances of physical violence are thought to be fewer in Hong Kong than elsewhere because labor protections are extensive (Cheng 1996). Hong Kong has a more progressive legal system for protecting migrant domestic workers than other major destinations such as Singapore, Taiwan, and the Arab Gulf countries. An Employment Ordinance sets their terms of employment and working conditions in a standard contract that specifies employers' obligations in relation to pay, food, rest days, holidays, annual leave, and conditions for termination. Migrants are also allowed to form unions, which they have done. Several nongovernmental organizations in Hong Kong advocate as well for the domestic worker. Within this relatively protective context, physical abuse does occur, but infrequently enough that NGO personnel and other activists consider the major problems to be verbal insults, lack of pay, insufficient food, and long working hours. Yet outright bodily assault is not the only way in which the domestic worker's psyche can be violated. Hong Kong is unique in having a 1,000-member employers' association whose primary aim is to "protect" the interests of households that hire foreign women as domestic workers. The Hong Kong Employers of Overseas Domestic Helpers Association promotes the notion that employers' difficulties have been overlooked by local advocates for the Filipinas. A reverse rhetoric of human rights keeps alive the idea that Hong Kong employers are often victims of false accusations by their employees. By a logic that ignores the vastly unequal power relation between master and maid, employers are seen as injured by the domestic worker's disloyalty and driven to desperation by the prospect of her desertion. Abandoned, the wife may have to concentrate her energies on performing the household labor, depriving the family of the dual income and middle-class life style that are now seen by many in Hong Kong as their entitlement.

"It is now a fact that Hong Kong's laissez-faire attitude toward foreign maids has led to widespread abuses by them," the head of the Employers' Association has written to the local media.[4] Employers who are "victims" of their domestic workers' "malpractices" are like "sitting ducks waiting for their ex-helpers to shoot them." These employers are "devastated" by "stress and mental anguish," and "the time and money wasted" in recruiting and training the foreign helper. More recently, following a June 1998 amendment to Hong Kong's Labor Ordinance, which made it illegal to fire foreign domestic workers who became pregnant after five or more weeks on the job, the Employers Association complained that the pregnancy rate was increasing among these women workers.[5]

The employers' group reflects a prevalent, exaggerated view of the Filipinas as an increasingly militant and expressive nuisance. The theme of excess is the dominant motif in the media depictions of the domestic workers' periodic marches for higher wages and better treatment. While activists constitute a tiny percentage of a population of women who are more inclined to pray and cry in private than to protest in the streets, the Hong Kong media capture those few who carry posters and wear sandwich boards demanding justice in Tagalog, English and Chinese. The women activists' protest is grounded in an NGO-heightened awareness of the global political-economic factors that disadvantage the Filipina and other overseas workers from the less affluent Asian countries. To a Hong Kong audience, however, the signs, posters, hats, chants, and sight of the women protesting publicly are a signal that the foreign domestic worker is no longer contained within the boundaries of reason. She has overstepped, becoming an "invading horde," a "social menace," an "eyesore," as letters to the editor of the English-language dailies argue heatedly.

In the Chinese media, ads for maids are suffused with fantasies of constraint. The *ban-mui* promised by the ads is "highly obedient" and "easily trained." She knows how to "eat/swallow bitterness" or endure silently, avoiding the "black face" or unhappy countenance that the Filipinas say is sometimes sufficient cause for being fired. In some ads, the representational breakthrough is that the domestic worker dematerializes entirely, leaving no personal trace.[6] It is only the result of her ministrations that need be portrayed. Thus, one ad for domestic workers displays a set of beaming parents, relaxing in a park with their two small children, above a subtitle that states that the family is "enjoying a warm period," presumably because all the unpleasant household chores have been assigned the absent maid.

The dream of what Gaw (1991) has termed "the superior servant" is rooted in a widespread nostalgia for the Chinese amahs or paid domestic workers of the past, according to one persuasive argument. Constable (1997a) accounts for the mounting criticism of the Filipina domestic workers by noting that the Chinese amah is recalled as a devoted caretaker who, unlike the Filipina, served one family most of her life, in the hope that she in turn could rely on their care in her old age. However, as Constable observes, memories have faded since the 1970s, when the amah—a vanishing commodity as new factory jobs absorbed the female working classes in Hong Kong—came to realize her increased value and was suddenly seen by her employers as bossy, unscrupulous, and money-grubbing. Twenty or more years later, similar stereotypes circulate about Hong Kong's non-Chinese domestic workers. The Filipinas in particular are perceived as aggressive, ungrateful, apathetic about their jobs, and ready to seize any better opportunity. In a popular play, *Amah Drama*, which was staged in Hong Kong in 1996, a Filipina domestic worker was portrayed as not merely seducing the British expatriate husband and taking over her employers' house, but as manipulating the man into giving her the money to buy a restaurant-bar at home. Her new boyfriend relocates to the Philippines with her, only to have the tables turned. As a foreigner, his co-ownership of the bar is officially declared invalid. He then has little choice but to work as a busboy for his former servant. Out of guilt, he sends remittances to his former wife and dolefully tries to save enough money to go home.

In Hong Kong, the Filipina domestic worker has commonly been perceived as a low-status foreigner who merits some protection but should generally recede into the background. Toward this end, a sign was posted in a prestigious apartment building barring maids from using the main elevator. Beneath it was a another sign that banned dogs as well from the same elevator. To the dismayed Philippine consulate, which filed a diplomatic protest, what was suggested was that the domestic workers were akin to beasts.[7] In a second incident, the Royal Hong Kong Jockey Club also sought to render the domestic worker invisible when she entered the traditional playing grounds of the colonial elite. She was only to be allowed in the club house when accompanied by her employer or escorting a member's child. Club members "applauded" the policy, claiming that the maids "crowded" the premises and were "annoying" and perhaps capable of stealing (O'Neill 1993: 46).

Such accusations made it difficult to set aside recreation centers where the domestic workers could have their own space for meeting. When specific neighborhood schools were considered, residents protested, expressing concerns about "hygiene" and "safety," as if the Filipinas were singlehandedly responsible for the noise, litter, traffic, illegal vending, and congestion that made chaos of the central district, where the women met en masse every Saturday and Sunday.[8] The assessment of social menace had little to do with rationality, as one newspaper cartoon attempted to demonstrate. Behind a sign reading "Central Government Offices," the cartoon had one bureaucrat warning another: "No, you fool, the campaign's against AIDS, not Maids," as the two planned out a new program of public education.

The implications are telling. The Filipina and other foreign Asian domestic workers were perceived as a social problem, potentially contaminating the city.[9] Linking AIDS with maids associated the domestic workers with a careless sexuality, which required efforts at containment. They were a threat, best confined where their persons would not be intrusive. Such stereotypes were not universally accepted, of course. The domestic workers had their defenders in many employers and in NGOs, which pointed out the crucial economic role the foreign women played as suppliers of the labor needed for social reproduction.[10] Yet, the host society's dominant view of the Filipinas ranged from unsympathetic to openly hostile. Outrage was expressed in the letters columns of the English-language media that the Filipina workers had the freedom to "chat outside supermarkets" or line up at the bank and post office on weekdays, when they should have been performing their chores at home. Although the women had no choice about the work their employers illegally assigned them, the migrants were popularly held responsible and criticized for "selling hamburgers in fast-food restaurants," "doing the cleaning in commercial buildings," and "rendering photocopying services in photocopying stores," thereby illegally taking jobs from local people."[11]

Filipina Performances

Returning to the theme of how the Filipinas regarded the criticisms that circulated about them, what is most striking about the photographs and videotapes that the women keep and send home is the absence of references to the nature of their daily work. Candid shots of a migrant wiping down her employer's car or washing the family dog are occasionally taken by close friends as a joke. But if these stolen shots are shown teasingly by the photographer to a group of intimates, the subject of the prying camera is more likely to threaten to tear up her workaday image than to treat it as a keepsake. Noticeably omitted, too, from the carefully posed photos the women favor is the sight of the domestic worker in the widely disliked black or pastel maid's uniform with white apron that some households insist upon, particularly for formal dinners and parties. The informal uniform, of pressed t-shirt, jeans, and rubber thong sandals or tennis shoes, is also erased from diasporic memorabilia. The life of drudgery is bracketed in what the Filipinas capture of themselves on film. Seen instead are views of the Filipina migrant in her day-off finery of high heels, lipstick and eye make-up, pearl earrings, and brightly colored feminine dresses or cotton suits. It is these images, set against the backdrop of Hong Kong's tourist attractions and upscale shopping malls, that are selected to document the women's lives overseas. They assert the migrant's knowledge of the world, altering and enlarging what she is entitled to appropriate as hers and preserve for posterity. Standing alone or with her arms intertwined with her smiling friends, she comments obliquely on Hong Kong's desire to render the maid unseen by locating herself firmly in the doorway of the glittering Tiffany's or the starkly elegant Jil Sander boutique. To viewers of the anthology of images she creates, she will permanently inhabit the global city's most luxuriously appointed public spaces.

These acts of reclamation are made more evident in videotapes of a favorite leisure-time activity for Filipinas overseas—the beauty contests that are sponsored by church groups and hometown associations and are a culminating annual event for many groups. In one of many pageants that I attended (the 1996 Search for Miss Star of the Orient), the formulaic introductory sequence was soon followed by a vision of the hometown association dancers exploding across the stage in matching bright pink miniskirts. Shimmying in unison, their arms and legs flashing upward and outward, they alternately hid and called attention to a backdrop in which "Search for Miss Star of the Orient" was painted in huge letters across Hong Kong's unmistakable skyline. What was paraded was not the silently enduring figure of the servant, but young women in buoyant possession of the city and, indeed, of the entire "Orient."

Throughout the Miss Star pageant, there was a continuous reconfiguring of the social geography of the domestic worker's world. During the "candidate in their sports wear" segment, the squash rackets, golf clubs and baseball bats of employers were borrowed to enter those public domains that barred the foreign migrant. What was accentuated was the ease with which the women contestants could command these spheres. Toying with the audience, primarily made up of their peers, they playfully mimed pitching baseballs out into the audience or pausing in their simulated hikes uphill to drink extravagantly from bottled water.

During subsequent standardized sequences, such as "candidates in their international costumes," dresses shot through with sequins and richly embroidered Indian saris or Chinese *cheong sam* drew gasps of admiration from the audience. They knew that borrowing such a garment required dozens of phone calls, the ingenious planning of quick exchanges in the markets near the women's workplaces, the calling in of favors, and the piling up of new social debts. Without an extensive network of contacts, it was impossible to prepare the array of costumes needed for a pageant, find a place to practice for the talent segment of the contest, or sell enough tickets to guarantee winning (which was less a matter of who was loveliest or could best belt out a song than who could persuade the largest group of supporters to buy tickets to the event). The beauty pageants were thus not just rituals of inversion or status reversal (Stoeltje 1996; Dirks 1994) but rituals of expansion in which a new self was celebrated in all its inventiveness and social connection. What would be memorialized—not only in photos and videotapes, but in multiple artifacts—was the migrant's starring place in a conceptual order devised by her own community in its alterity. To the formulaic question, how does it feel to be Miss Star of the Orient (or Miss Republic of the Philippines Teen Popularity Queen or Miss Manila-East), she would answer without tears, embarrassment, or feigned modesty: "it feels wonderful."

But the memorabilia generated by this event went not only to the winner but to all participants. Heavy brass trophies and plaques, tiaras, scepters, capes, sashes, ribbons, banners, programs, certificates, spike heels, theatrical makeup, pressed flowers, costumes and dresses, dozens of photographs by friends and often by a professional photographer, videotapes, cassettes, and other items ensured that everyone who had contributed to the event would have "souvenirs," in the words of the migrants. These photos would be handed around to Filipina friends, and, where the migrant had her own room in Hong Kong, might be displayed on bureaus or kept easily accessible in drawers. Once at home in the Philippines, there would be more photographs, of the migrants with a contented town mayor or church official, since the stated aim of the contests was the securing of charitable contributions for a hometown church or civic project.

In detailing these material, sensory memoirs of the diasporic experience, I want to accentuate their performative nature. Performance, Serematakis (1996) suggests, can be understood in three senses. It is first, a manipulative theatrical display, in which viewers may be persuaded to look and feel differently about the social relations depicted than they had prior to the enactment. It is second, an instantiation of codes: in the case of the beauty pageants, mention of such culturally honored themes as "uplifting the family," "praying to God," "doing one's best," or "progressing in life" struck responsive chords in an audience of peers. Such phrases induced the Filipinas present to cheer and applaud. But performance has a third set of dynamics as a sequence of acts that demand perceptual completion by a viewer. Photos, videotapes, and other material objects that memorialize performances are inherently transitive. An audience is imagined and expected to respond. The performer engages in a dialogue with her observers. The images she creates transfix the audience and invite their interpretation.

In the Filipina migrants' photos and video cassettes, it is significant that the everyday world of domestic work is largely unseen and inaudible. The dull daily routine is thus subject to an act of social forgetting or ignoring that allows the viewer's delighted imaginings to come to the fore. The photos of women in their finery, poised confidently against a global city's touristic backdrops, at once limit and refuse the unpleasant experiences of their daily work and evoke a expanded world that welcomes the audience at home into a new terrain of possibility. The photos, documenting a sequence of consumption not easily available in the Philippines to anyone but the rich, become a class assertion for future generations, erasing the daily trials and insults of their subject's life as a domestic worker. It is not that the women migrants consciously intend to deceive the present and future family. The hazards and hardships of migrant work overseas are well known even in remote rural areas, through the constant flow of newspaper accounts, films and plays that have chronicled Filipinos' work abroad since the mid-1980s and earlier. Rather, through their omissions, what the photos sustain is a solidarity that helps the migrant and her kin endure the dislocations of their separation. The photos reaffirm the migrant's inclusion in a cultural community in which it is a sign of cohesion and closeness to avoid speaking of what is painful and humiliating. At the same time, the photos and other migrant memorabilia communicate powerfully, expressly because they bypass language, opening up rich realms of visual, tactile, and audible (in the case of videotapes and cassettes) meaning. Sensory reperception by the viewer fills in what these objects suggest, supplying positive notions of the migrant's experience overseas and reducing worry and discomfort. The Filipinas, visually linking themselves with the pleasure and adventure of the fast-paced city, play with the power relations of the disapproving Hong Kong society. Consciously and unconsciously, they manage to intervene in a discredited identity. Fashioning an autobiography that edits out the negatives of their work abroad, they create instead a chronicle of achievement which can be read with pride by future generations.

Home as Audience

Diaspora studies have broadened in recent years to encompass people who were formerly known as economic migrants because they chose to cross borders in pursuit of work. From this perspective, what distinguishes a diasporic community is not necessarily its traumatic dispersal from an original homeland. Rather, it is an enduring ethnic consciousness, a troubled relationship with the host society and the dream of returning to an idealized ancestral home (G. Smith 1999; Cohen 1997). By these criteria, the Filipinas who work in Hong Kong are clearly a diasporic group.

Scholars of diaspora have argued, moreover, that a key aim of studying such displaced peoples is to gain insight into the impact of deterritorialization on their imaginative resources (M. Smith 1994: 18; Breckenridge and Appadurai 1989). Yet, to date, migrants' cultural production has been analyzed primarily in the context of the contributions that a play, piece of mural art or other aesthetic offering makes to its own particular genre (Gomez-Pena 1998; Herrera-Sobek 1998) or as a form of protest against the status injuries to which migrants are often subject. Efforts to examine diasporic experience have tended to overlook the probability that a diasporic community creates its self-representations in dialogue with multiple audiences, actual and spectral, both here (in the new society) and there (in the homeland).

As this chapter has argued with respect to Filipina domestic workers in Hong Kong, one such audience is indeed the host society, which enjoys the women's household labor but would otherwise consign them to the city's back corridors. In response partially to this unwelcoming reception, the Filipinas' self-portrayals reclaim their public presence, although not as "maids"[12] or "Philippine girls" (*banmui*), but as Ms Personality, Ms Vintar-Hong Kong, or well-groomed urbanites consuming the city's tourist attractions. A very few photos, displayed in magazines for Filipino migrants, capture the women in more casual clothing with their *alagas* (Tagalog for the employers' children they care for). It is notable, however, that in these shots the women are never wearing a maid's uniform, but appear relaxed and smiling, as if having a good time with their young charges. What is erased, as I have earlier emphasized, are the buckets and mops and dust rags that form the stuff of everyday life for domestic workers.

Asked why these mundane images are left out of the photos sent home, women answered: "we want to put our best foot forward," "I don't want my family to know how hard life is here," or "it's better to send photos of the happy times." Home, serving as an emotional anchor, becomes a place whose serenity must itself be protected. Upbeat self-portrayals serve as reassurances to kin that "everything is fine," that "we're happy, don't worry," in the words of several Filipinas. These selective self-representations, usually shown to friends before being mailed off, may also operate as self-assurances that a transformed self will meet with home approval. For as Nicole Constable demonstrates elsewhere in this volume, extended discussion with the women migrants indicates that beneath the idealized depictions, memories of home are often fraught with ambivalence. Some wonder whether they can reinsert themselves into their former lives and relationships, after experiencing what Tadiar (1997) calls "the partial liberation" of an overseas existence in which new social pleasures and opportunities are interspersed with dull routine.

Thoughts of return are also structured by the cultural meanings that have long been attached to travel and migration. In the ancient Philippines (and, indeed, throughout maritime Southeast Asia), the greatest male prestige was acquired through surmounting the dangers of travel to foreign lands. As an aspiring migrant wrote illustratively in the 1940s, he, too, fancied returning a hero from work in the United States "in the style of our old legends (in which) a . . . man had gone forth to slay the winged giants and devils in the days before history" (Margold 1995: 281).

While migration as a "journey of achievement" was once linked only to men, women overseas workers have been included as "the new heroes" of the Filipino national economy since the beginning of Corazon Aquino's administration. Thus, when Cardinal Jaime Sin, archbishop of Manila, visited Taiwan not long ago, he told an audience composed mainly of Filipinas: "in our country you are called bayani—new heroes. You are here for us even as soldiers go forth in a war" (*South China Morning Post* 1996).

Contributing, too, to the women's hopes and expectations of economic success are the remembered visions of returnees who were "nobody, before they left" (in the words of one Filipina domestic worker) but whose steady stream of remittances gained them new treatment at home as "celebrities" or "honored guests" at local events. News stories and photos published in local migrant magazines offer similar promises of prestigious status for returnees from abroad. Former domestic workers are seen visiting a newly refurbished village plaza or freshly painted fence donated by their association of Filipinas overseas. A grateful mayor or school principal often stands in attendance, confirming that it is not only the migrant's family but the entire community who benefits from the dollars she brings home. Underscoring these expectations is the long-standing habit among migrant Filipinos of postponing their return home if they feel they cannot meet the material demands of their extended families. A sizeable number of the Filipino farmworkers who migrated to the United States in the first two decades of the twentieth century never went home. Pride prevented their return as impoverished old men. Their letters and photos, too, avoided mention of the harsh life they encountered as agricultural and cannery workers, dishwashers, houseboys and hotel clerks. As one former farm worker admitted, he, like many others, had been "too proud to write home the truth about our existence here" (Scharlin and Villaneuva 1992: 23).

Such omissions in cultural expression are made more understandable by Serematakis's theorization of cultural performance as not only coming from within, but responding to the particularities of its own time and context. From this perspective, cultural performance represents a dialogue with history and audience (1996: 7) That does not mean, however, that photographic self-portraits have historical authenticity as their goal. The imagination of multiple audiences from homeland to host societies contributes to the rearrangement of past and present by the subject/object of a posed photograph.

The comment of Bing, a young male migrant to the United States, reveals this most powerfully. Speaking of photos he had received in the Philippines from his father, then a maintenance worker in Saudi Arabia, Bing recalled:

When I saw the smiling photos he sent home, I would think that he's trying to keep his sanity, trying to convince himself and us that he was fine. His letters, too, said everything was okay. But I'm the only son and on his trips home, he and I would go out drinking. Then he would tell me the real stories. Once when he was home, one of his roommates overseas went crazy. He picked up a big hammer and bashed every man's head in while they were sleeping. If my father had been there then, he would have been killed. From the photos, you would never know how difficult his life there was.

Bing's father continued to send home smiling self-portraits throughout his time overseas, despite his moments of candor with his son. Bing himself admitted, with a defensive grin, that even though he was a political activist with an understanding of the structural forces that allotted Filipinos low-level jobs overseas, he never sent home photos of himself in the uniform he wore daily as a parking-lot attendant. "Only pictures of me in a business suit, looking successful and competent," he said. "It's what's expected."

Like Filipino migrants of other eras, the Filipina domestic workers in Hong Kong see themselves presenting their visual autobiographies through frames and filters of their own making. Yet, their "journeys of achievement" are coerced by states, marginalized by the global economy and largely unappreciated by their host societies. As indicated above, the expectations of home and family exert a further persuasive pull on the migrant's subjectivity, shaping the notion of self they wish to claim publicly.

In writing of the highly migratory villages of island Southeast Asia, Carsten (1995) suggests that social memory is constructed as much from what is untold as from what is narrated and recorded. By editing out aspects of life overseas and accentuating others, the Filipinas' visual records of their diasporic experiences operate as comforting reassurances to self, kin, and community of the migrant's well-being. They are promises, too, of her investments in home, the place where her present family resides and her future family will be created. Expanding on Carsten's argument that an onward-looking kinship system is useful to mobile populations in allowing them to embrace newcomers, we can see here that future-oriented notions of kinship also serve the returning migrant. Through the mediation of posed photographs and videos, the Filipina domestic workers forges an autobiography for future generations. In this highly selective visual account of her journey abroad, she erases the indignities of household work and sustains a reassuring vision of herself as appreciated and welcomed by her kin and her homeland. The only question that remains is whether or not the generations to come will read between the lines of the migrant's cultural performance and wonder what is missing.

Part II
Provisional Return

Chapter 4
Viet Kieu on a Fast Track Back?

Lynellyn D. Long

At the Hong Kong airport, a small crowd of people pushed and jostled one another for a place in the line while two smartly dressed Chinese flight attendants looked on disapprovingly but made no effort to organize the chaos. It was shortly before Tet, the Lunar New Year, in late January 1998, and the Vietnamese were worried about returning home in time to prepare for the festivities. The plane was reportedly overbooked.

Two distinct groups of passengers boarded the plane: Hanoians returning from official visits to Eastern Europe and Viet Kieu (overseas Vietnamese) returning from Western countries for Tet. The Hanoians were dressed in austere gray, brown, or black suits while the young Viet Kieu wore the latest designs from Hong Kong, New York or Paris, including platform soled sneakers. Most of the Vietnamese passengers were middle-aged or elderly men, Communist party elite, while the Viet Kieu were diversified by gender and generation. I sat across the aisle from three Canadian Vietnamese: the oldest, in her early seventies, wore an *ao dai* (Vietnamese dress from French colonial times), her middle aged daughter, a conservative blue Western suit, and her daughter tight jeans and black leather jacket. The oldest, who did not speak English, was indifferent to our conversation, the middle carefully recounted in schoolbook English her excitement of returning home to an ancestral village in the North for the first time since early childhood, and the youngest stated in fluent Canadian English that she was "cutting school."

The mountains bordering the Red River Delta were shrouded in fog when we landed in the plain of wet rice paddies. As the plane set down, the mood within the cabin was subdued. Outside the day was cold and overcast. On the damp tarmac, stern-faced, khaki uniformed guards escorted us in a 1950's Russian bus to a dark, dimly lit shed where we queued up again, but this time in long, dutiful lines. The elderly Viet Kieu woman kept opening her passport and rechecking her visa. After a seemingly interminable wait, the customs officials waved us on. Outside again, I saw the three women embracing their relatives, who had arrived with roses and umbrellas. Witnessing the excited conversations of a warm family reunion, I reflected that such returns were first and foremost about reestablishing family and kinship ties.

Over the next four and half years in Vietnam, I would have many opportunities to observe Viet Kieu and Vietnamese interactions, interview Viet Kieu, read and hear various interpretations of different press accounts, and develop some long term relationships with a few families who returned to Vietnam or who hosted overseas relatives. The study that follows combines analyses of interviews, press accounts, and observations of Vietnamese-Viet Kieu interactions, from January 1996 to June 2000, a very interesting and exciting period in Vietnam.

This particular period encompassed an economic boom, a deep recession brought about by the Asian Currency Crisis, and a return to moderate but steady economic growth. The government also faced demographic pressures from a growing young population (over 50 percent were under twenty-five years of age) who were born after the war. Despite the economic fluctuations, the society continued to open its doors to a broader world, and the Viet Kieu played a vital role in that process.

I begin with an overview of the political and social entrée of the Viet Kieu into Vietnam, which is based on press accounts from the period. I then examine the specific experiences of Viet Kieu—why they returned, their refugee and resettlement experiences, and the relationships they formed with Vietnamese on return. This section, based on in-depth interviews with Viet Kieu in Hanoi and Saigon, shows how specific sets of experiences and relationships underlie people's eventual decisions to return and then to remain or leave. Finally, I analyze the larger role that Viet Kieu returns play in facilitating Vietnam's social and economic transition (Doi Moi) during this period.

Categorizing Viet Kieu

In early 1997, the *New York Times Magazine* in "Saigon: The Sequel" reported that "Americans—ambitious, romantic and too young to remember the war—are making Ho Chi Minh City the new expat capital" (Paterniti 1997: 22ff). The story offended many expatriates and Vietnamese alike because it focused on the experiences of one young, disaffected Anglo-American. The story profiled several young Americans involved in fast money, motorbikes, and win or lose all business operations. The Viet Kieu in particular were portrayed as naïve colonialists involved in some vast dating game centering on Saigon's well-known Q Bar. In Hanoi and Saigon, many wondered why the Americans were center stage as the last expatriates to re-appear and a distinct minority in the small international communities of both cities.

This story in the American press presaged a series of articles about returns of Americans to Vietnam, the most notable being that of Robert MacNamara, who returned in the summer of 1987 and met with General Giap and other former military leaders (Shipler 1997). MacNamara came expecting reconciliation and apologies on both sides, whereas the Vietnamese politely accepted his apologies

but did not offer their own. For the Americans, the visit was a failed attempt to re-
vise the historical record, whereas the Vietnamese Government expected new investments and was highly supportive of visits of returning members of Congress
(including Congressman Pete Peterson of Florida, Senator John Kerry of Massa-
chusetts, and Senator McCain of Arizona), who had served in Vietnam, and were
attempting to lift U.S. trade and aid sanctions on the country. Congressman Peterson eventually became the first American Ambassador to Vietnam; and during
his tenure (during the last months of the Clinton Administration), Congress lifted
the economic sanctions (Mydans 2000).

The *New York Times* story evoked a Graham Greene quality in depicting the
irony of malnourished children on Hang Gai or Hai Ba Trung selling the *Quiet
American* to returning GIs. In that sense it avoided the revisionist history that typ-
ified much of the information around Congressional visits (in part to gain acceptance for changes in policy toward Vietnam in the U.S.).[1] Nevertheless, one of
the most penetrating analyses of the period was Doonesbury's ironic return—a
GI who capitalized on his past to develop a new market. Trudeau's lampoons
probably best captured what was really at stake and not surprisingly, provoked a
spate of angry commentaries in both the American and Vietnamese press.[2]

Several Viet Kieu living in Hanoi feared that the *New York Times* story further
jeopardized their already tenuous and somewhat ambivalent status with the Vietnamese authorities. Many had found it difficult to obtain work permits, and if not
sponsored by a company or international organization on arrival, their requests
to remain beyond a tourist visa were usually flatly denied. For example, one
young, highly educated and talented Viet Kieu, who wanted to volunteer her time
and spoke barely a word of Vietnamese, was nevertheless treated as a potential
security threat and instructed to leave immediately as soon as her three month
tourist visa expired.

In the officially sanctioned English press, the Vietnamese Communist Party
provided their own interpretations of the returns. The February 1996 *Vietnam Economic Times* cover story extolled Nguyen Binh's success in bringing Federal Express
to the Vietnamese market (Korsmoe 1996). Based on "official" Government data,
the *Times* reported that more than 800,000 Viet Kieu returned between 1990–95
(with the number rising annually) and that $600–$700 million was being remitted
each year through official channels (Korsmoe 1996: 16). The reporter reminded
the public that the overseas Chinese had played an important role in that country's rising economic growth and foreign investment in the 1980's. However, the
Times reporter also noted that there were only 50 Viet Kieu licensed joint ventures
in contrast to 236 Japanese firms (17). The article failed to mention that the Viet
Kieu were primarily concentrated in the south (and therefore less visible to the
Government in Hanoi) and at the forefront of investors there. In the Ho Chi
Minh City American Chamber of Commerce, they comprised at least 20 percent
of the recorded 296 members (American Chamber of Commerce, personal
communication 1997). They were also concentrated in the banking and finance
sectors.

While underscoring some of the advantages of being an overseas Vietnamese doing business in Vietnam, the *Times* warned that the Viet Kieu should keep "a tight watch on their attitudes and beware of coming across as too arrogant" and that "Know-it-alls waving western degrees rarely last long" (Dung 1996:21). The story praised Viet Kieu who made a humanitarian contribution, gave up selfish ways, and searched for an emotional connection to their birthplace. "Those who fail to make the transition remain foreigners in their own homeland," the writer warned (Dung 1996:21). The article provided the Government's own moral and political regime for returning Viet Kieu. The Viet Kieu would be welcome provided they made no demands on local resources, did not make local people (especially Party officials) feel inferior, did not flaunt their western privileges and brought in capital.

The *Vietnam Economic Times* explicity categorized different groups of Viet Kieu returnees (Korsmoe 1996). The *Times* cited: (1) pre-75ers and earlier emigrants; (2) the '75ers, the "Old Regime" (also known as the "Saigon Regime"); (3) late '70s/early '80s—"the boat people, wave I"—those with experience under the Communist government but not under the Doi Moi ("Renovation") reforms; (4) 1980s: "the boat people, wave II" with a high percentage of northerners as well as southerners; (5) Orderly Departure Program (ODP): family reunification, 1985–96; and (6) those from Eastern Europe, "quasi-Viet Kieu" (Korsmoe 1996: 19). While asserting that the post 1975 groups (primarily Wave II and ODP) comprised the highest share of returnees, the article provided no empirical evidence. The limited understanding of children of employees of the former government (usually referred to derisively as the "Saigon regime") was also contrasted with the less Westernized and strong language skills of the later immigrants (19).

Interestingly, this official typology reflected the visa regimes and varying statuses of different overseas groups as much by who was omitted. For example, the article made no mention of Viet Kieu from China, Laos, Cambodia, and Thailand who along with the Eastern European returnees the Government routinely afforded a higher status in terms of access to local Vietnamese prices in a dual economy, visa requirements, working privileges, and freedom of movement. For example, Viet Kieu from former Eastern bloc countries and Vietnamese citizens paid half the plane fares of foreigners and Viet Kieu from Western countries (*Viet Nam News* 1997: 1).

The article also did not distinguish those who sided with the Communists but nevertheless immigrated to the West prior to 1954 (such as Ho Chi Minh himself). The pre-1975ers included many French Viet Kieu (e.g., former Mandarins and nationalist forces in the north) who left in 1954 following the French defeat at Dien Bien Phu, but also Viet Kieu who were members of the French or Vietnamese International Communist Party (ICP) who migrated for economic, educational, or political reasons. Thus, merely spending time in Western countries, regardless of one's political allegiances, made one a Viet Kieu as well.

Finally, the typology did not distinguish short versus long-term returnees. Many

Viet Kieu at the time were returning only during Tet to visit relatives, whereas others returned to live and work in Vietnam. The former sometimes used the occasion to see whether they would eventually want to immigrate—and later, these provisional returns sometimes turned into long-term commitments. Those who eventually came to live and work in Vietnam had usually established themselves well in another country and left several years earlier (interviews and conversations in Hanoi and HCMC 1997). As a group, they had enough resources and/or financial backing to return, were well educated, and had solid ties in their resettlement countries.

Ambivalent Expectations

The *Vietnam Economic Times* article allowed the government to begin to define a specific role for the Viet Kieu in Vietnam's transition to a market economy. Unofficially, the Government recognized the adverse effects of an earlier outflow of needed skills and issued invitations for Viet Kieu attending the top graduate programs in the U.S., France, and elsewhere to return to provide technical assistance (government official, personal communication 1997). For example, a fifty-year-old Viet Kieu banker, educated at the Sorbonne, was invited to return from Paris to advise the Prime Minister's office on trade and investment. Ironically, this particular individual was the son of a former cabinet minister in the "Saigon regime" and his parents were right wing conservatives who were part of an Orange County, California movement to retake the country. While initially suspicious of the offer, as a banker he recognized a good investment opportunity and took his chances. Over a series of subsequent visits, he increasingly realized that his return to Vietnam had less to do with the success of his technical assistance or economic ventures than with an increasing desire to retain a Vietnamese identity for his French children. The Prime Minister's office initially appreciated his advice and supported several return visits, but became increasingly less supportive of his reestablishing a local identity. When the banker brought his French wife to stay with other Westerners, the Government authorities quickly moved them into an authorized guesthouse, where they could keep a close watch on his activities.

Some Viet Kieu, particularly in the first days of Doi Moi, returned to Vietnam to demonstrate their adoption of Western ideological values and assumptions. In turn, the Government authorities closely monitored such visits to ensure that a positive account would ensue. In her autobiographical account, for example, Le Ly Hayslip (1989) observed tensions with local authorities in an earlier homecoming to Danang in 1986. Returning just after Doi Moi, she was closely followed and monitored throughout her stay. However, her account focused less on contemporary Vietnam and the actual changes or relationships she encountered and more on the memories that the return evoked of her own life during the war and as a refugee. While a personally moving account, it made little attempt to engage with contemporary Vietnam except as a place requiring humanitarian assistance.[3]

In contrast, the Government recognized that some professionals provided needed capital and skills (versus humanitarian contributions) and increasingly, began to see this group of Viet Kieu returnees as a potential resource. In 1997, the Government made the unprecedented decision to hire Ho Trieu Tri, a Viet Kieu architect, to restore the Hanoi Opera House, a French colonial landmark, modeled after the Paris Opera and one of the most visible landmarks of the city. The story made the front page of the *Viet Nam News*, the major English daily (Binh 1997). Putting the article in the English daily was also a way for the Government to signal to the expatriate community that their capital and investments were increasingly welcomed. The Ministry of Culture and Information reported choosing Tri, who had settled in Paris shortly before April 1975, from a field of six bidders. The *News* noted approvingly that in restoring the Opera House, Tri struck a balance between the old French designs and utilizing local craftsmen and materials (Binh 1997:4). Such syncretism allowed the Government to remain politically and socially correct towards the Vietnamese worker while demonstrating support for the upcoming Francophone Summit (held in Vietnam later that year). Ironically, very few Vietnamese spoke French, but the Government welcomed the Summit, which brought needed capital and investment and spurred an immediate growth in building construction. While the Vietnamese would never have allowed a French Viet Kieu to restore a statue of Ho Chi Minh (whose mummy was sent routinely to Moscow), they were willing to allow a French Viet Kieu restore a colonial landmark that for the most part, would be only used by Senior officials and foreigners. Once restored, the Opera rarely published an advance schedule of events, and any that could be obtained came from the Ministry of Culture and Information. Thus, the Opera House represented a separate designated space within which to develop Viet Kieu and French-Vietnamese relations without contaminating socialist ideals.

In many ways the Viet Kieu played a pivotal role in Vietnamese society during this transitional period. Since *Doi Moi* was initiated in 1986, the Government alternately embraced and rejected relations with Western capitalism. Likewise, relationships with the Viet Kieu waxed and waned on both sides during this period. However, the overall trend was an increasing integration of the Vietnamese economy into regional and world markets (Ljunggren 1997:30) and growing acceptance of the Viet Kieu, as a critical kinship link to those larger markets. To explore the changing relationships in detail, I interviewed professional Viet Kieu, living and working in Hanoi and Saigon.

Interviewing Viet Kieu in Hanoi and Saigon

Over the summer and fall, 1997, I conducted extensive, semi-structured interviews with four men and seven women. Three lived in Ho Chi Minh City and eight in Hanoi. They came from the United States, France, and Germany[4] and ranged in age from the mid-twenties to forties. Professionally, they worked as a doctor, banker, engineer, teacher, pharmacist, businessman, directors of nongovernmental organizations (2), and lawyers (3). Five were married and six single. Of those married, four women had foreign, non-Vietnamese husbands (a fifth was engaged to a British citizen) and one Viet Kieu man had a Vietnamese wife. Only one person in the group already had a child; another was pregnant. All had parents born in Vietnam except one whose father was French. All but two were born in Vietnam; one was born in Canada but grew up in Vietnam, and the other (whose parents emigrated in the '50s) was born in France but her family retained their Vietnamese citizenship and returned during her childhood. The age of departure ranged from four to nineteen years of age.

Among the group, one had parents who left during the 1950s, seven left just before April 1975, and three after 1975: two in what the Government deemed the First Wave and one in the Second. Unlike overseas Japanese, however, who distinguish between different generations, the appellation of Viet Kieu includes up to at least two generations (and perhaps, any person with ethnic Kinh ancestors). Despite their patrilineal system, the Vietnamese considered the interviewee with a French father to be Viet Kieu (and not French) since his mother was Vietnamese. However, if this person had instead grown up in Vietnam, then he would have been labeled an Amerasian and considered of mixed Vietnamese ethnicity. As a whole, the interviewees exemplified the various boundaries of official definitions of Viet Kieu-ness—living abroad in a capitalist, Western country, being exposed to Western values and practices, having at least one Vietnamese parent (even if they lived abroad), and emigrating with one or more generations.

At the time of interview, all but one person had lived in Vietnam over a year; that one was making plans to live and work in Vietnam. That particular situation allowed us to discuss some of the immediate impressions and considerations for returning. Most had been in Vietnam for about two years at the time of interview and had a professional position and employer, who had arranged for their visa. Two women married to non-Vietnamese returned because of their husbands' work.

Several interviewees observed that they played a pivotal role in their families between the two cultures. Their older siblings and parents maintained their primary social ties and networks with the ethnic Vietnamese communities while their younger siblings had primarily non-Vietnamese, Western friends in the resettlement countries. These returnees saw themselves as a bridge between two worlds by maintaining dual sets of social networks. All reported having Vietnamese and non-Vietnamese friends in both their resettlement countries and in Vietnam. In addition, those who reported leaving Vietnam during mid-adolescence reported difficulties adjusting to life elsewhere and saw the return to Vietnam as a way to address some of those earlier tensions.[5]

As a group they were often by position or training, leaders in their immediate professional groups, the broader expatriate community, or an emerging Viet Kieu social network.

Common Experiences of Return

Three common themes emerged across the interviews. First, all Viet Kieu recounted a journey—entailing a series of significant experiences—that led them back to Vietnam. Although some initially claimed that professional opportunities led to their decision, they later described specific actions taken to create such opportunities. Second, all discussed significant relationships and social networks that led to their decision to return. In every case, interviewees cited relationships with parents. Several people observed that their parents' unwillingness to discuss past lives in Vietnam provoked their own curiosity and determination to return. Because of their return experiences, some interviewees also challenged the stories told by parents and their parents' memories of Vietnam. Implicit in these challenges was a need to construct a new social and generational account of the refugee experience.[6] During the interviews, people also discussed other significant relationships and most described having ambivalent relationships with Europeans, Americans and Vietnamese. Directly and indirectly, they challenged both the assimilationist Western and an essentialized, Kinh (Viet) ethnic identity models. Third, all interviewees addressed how the experience of return reframed their own identities and kinship ties, which in turn affected their plans for the future. The analysis that follows addresses all three.

The Journey

Most Viet Kieu described a sense of inevitability about their return—as fate or destiny. As Ha (female, 1975) observed, "It just feels like this is what is supposed to happen, it doesn't feel as if I have a choice." However, when leaving Vietnam, they presumed they were leaving for good and would never be able to return. Only after Doi Moi could they imagine returning and realized they might be welcomed back. Once the return became possible, several echoed Mai's (female, 1975) observation that, "I always knew I was going to come back some day." Thus, this sense of inevitability or fate was recast to reflect changing social and economic relationships that justified return on both the part of the returnee and the receiving society. Returning became morally right once Vietnam underwent a renovation. Tuyet (female, parents, pre-1975) observed, "I always planned to return. I needed to resolve a lack of rootedness." Likewise, Yen (female, 1975) said, "I needed a change. I always wanted to come back to live and work in the back of my mind. It was a dream come true for me."

Difficulties in adjusting to his citizenship country, however, made Hieu (male, Wave II) want to return:

If you leave after 14 or 15, you never adjust to the language. I always have to watch my grammar all the time. I feel that no matter how hard I struggled to improve my English, I know that I can never express myself as I would have been able to in Vietnamese had I never left Vietnam. Furthermore, while I was living in the U.S., my Vietnamese did not get any better. In coming back to Vietnam, I also hope to be able to catch up with the Vietnamese that I have lost, or have never learned, while I was in the U.S.

In contrast, Phuong (female, 1975) portrayed her return within the context of other life decisions and as part of how she related to the world in general. She reported, "I was supposed to go into the Peace Corps and took a year off first to travel in the U.S. and Mexico." For Nguyen (male, First Wave) and Loan (male, First Wave), returning to Vietnam fit with larger professional plans and career intentions. Some wanted to contribute some public service in developing countries, and given family histories, chose Vietnam in particular. Upon further reflection, Yen remembered, "I always wanted to come back to Vietnam since college, although prior to that I had no desire to come back, but then I knew I wanted to work in a developing country. I came for humanitarian reasons. I wrote a letter to my boss' boss." While there were differences in the extent to which people said that they had some control over their returns and/or responded to certain inevitable processes, most echoed Mai's observation that, "I felt like I have a destiny with Vietnam but it is a destiny that I create as well." This blend or duality of inevitability and destiny, which resonated within Vietnamese culture, with individual will and volition, which resonate in Western ones (Fitzgerald 1972), reflects the particular Viet Kieu perspective on the event.

Situating the Past

The interviewees described early memories of Vietnam in visual images. Tui (female, 1975) recounted, "I have memories of Dalat—of green fields and of beaches. I remember my house being bigger." "I remember all the big trees and lakes, the tea fields, Binh Thanh market, holding on to my father's hand tight, wearing red pants," recalled Ha. Several cited well-known tourist or vacation places (e.g., Dalat highlands and Nha Trang beaches) and/or the countryside. Loan recalled spending summers in his mother's family farm outside Saigon. Several observed that they were surprised at the smallness of a former home when they located it again.

The images were often fragmented. Diep (female, 1975) observed, "they are broken pieces of memory; nice memories of a summer house." In Proustian fashion, she noticed that certain sights and smells back in Vietnam evoked or triggered these memories, "When I came back three years ago to visit sometimes I would eat a piece of fruit that I had never seen in North America but that I would know, I've eaten this before, been on this beach before."

Because most people left at a young age, they lacked coherence in their accounts but instead recalled a series of random events and images. However, Ha developed an explicit narrative, "most of it centered around the house, I didn't remember the rooms and upstairs, but escaping from bed in the middle of night and shadow puppet shows. I remember being driven to meetings, getting home late because of a school teacher."

Time in these memories was generally organized around school and school schedules; long hours spent in classes each day punctuated by summer holidays and breaks. Several people described the departure or changes in 1975 as an extended vacation. Those who left in 1975 rarely mentioned the war except to observe that a father or other relative was away for periods of time.

Those who remained in Vietnam after 1975 described a distinctly different set of memories even if they departed only a few months later. They recalled the terrors of warfare, assumption of communist control, political insecurity, and scarcity of food and other essential goods and supplies. For example, Loan described a rocket exploding in his back yard. He reflected how chaotic the last few days of the American withdrawal were in contrast to a controlled and organized Communist assumption of power in Saigon. His family waited another five months to be evacuated by the French Government and during that time, he recalled his parents' fears of the new regime as soldiers came door-to-door, "even though my parents had no association with the former regime and had done nothing wrong."

Nguyen remembered food shortages, leaving the French school in Saigon to learn Vietnamese in the local school, and his parents' economic difficulties during this period. Both parents were teachers and his father, a German instructor, lost his job. His father then tutored at home and his mother supported the family while they waited for his brother to clear the draft so they could obtain permission to leave for Germany. It took another five years before his family was allowed to immigrate.

Hieu remembered being "thrown into an atmosphere where everyone is Communist Party or Communist youth; it was very tense for me to be in the university." He recounted:

the negative politics of how people were trained and individuals interacted with one another. The School wanted to mold me in a certain way. In school everyone was watching one another to ensure that no one is doing anything that is not in the right direction of the Party's line and policy which were very hard and rigid at the time.

Yet, Hieu later reflected:

I felt my decision to leave in 1979 was very much an impulsive one without much careful consideration—a decision was made under the pressure of having to live under a very oppressive environment and the general fear of most people from the South for the unknown future having to first live under Communism.

Hieu's, Nguyen's and Loan's memories suggested why the later refugees and immigrants may have encountered more difficulties returning to live and work as compared to those who left in 1975 (or earlier). Already having direct experience with the new Government, this group left largely because they did not support the values and expectations of the new regime. However, they were also more impressed with the changes that the Government had undertaken and sympathetic to the reform process. In Hieu's case, he later regretted his rash decision and wondered if he should have remained.

Departure Experiences

Viet Kieu who left in 1975 at a young age described the actual departure as an extended summer vacation bounded by leaving school in Saigon and entering school in the United States or Europe. Tui and Phuong at the time thought that they were going on another summer holiday trip and compared moving from place to place to a camping trip. Ha recalled ironically, "Great, very exciting. As a little kid, I was too dumb to know what was going on. I was going on a holiday. The camps in Guam had nice beaches, blue water." Such descriptions also allowed Viet Kieu to portray refugee experiences in familiar Western terms to which non-Vietnamese Westerners could relate.[7]

Departures by sea entailed more difficult voyages than those by air. In April 1975, Yen's father, a navy captain, led a group of Vietnamese refugees out of the country. They drifted at sea for several days picking up other refugees on rafts. As they ran out of food and provisions, the refugees threatened mutiny and plotted to kill her father. Her mother tried to maintain peace by providing clothes and distributing provisions. Despite the horrors of that time, Yen reported it to her American classmates as "how I spent my summer vacation when I started school on September 5. I told about the stars in the open sky, going away quickly, drifting at sea."

Diep did not return from Canada at the end of that summer. She and her brother just stopped coming to Vietnam after the Communists assumed power until their family returned to Hanoi in the early 1990's. Her parents recognized that they would have to leave and planned for their eventual departure by buying property near an aunt in Canada.

Those who left after April 1975 portrayed specific emotions related to the departures. Loan remembered his parents' and other adults crying on the plane. These memories shaped his later decision to become a lawyer as a means to address injustice. Loan also remembered his father's bitterness against the new Government. Nguyen remembered his family's relief at leaving. Both believed they would never return.

Hieu escaped on a boat from the central coast of Vietnam. He wrote:

The following eight days were surreal! At night, the boat only had one dim light above the compass for the captain to continue the journey through the nights. I was not sick and therefore was asked to assist the captain watching with a small flashlight for waves, which might come from the sides of the boat and tip it over. We saw many huge ships, some did not stop, others stopped to provide us what we need like compasses, maps, food, and water, but not accepted to take us up on their ships. We went through a small storm and the boat made scary loud cracking noises while everyone prayed so loudly. Other nights, the water was so calm, and it was as scary as being in the storm with our little boat in the vast ocean. One day we almost got to land but then we saw military boats come and pull us away back to sea. We were lucky for not encountering any pirates, and finally arrived on a scarcely populated island in Indonesia.

Arrivals in Resettlement Countries

Those who left in April 1975 for the United States passed through one or more refugee camps; first in the Philippines or Guam and then in Camp Pendleton in California or Indiana Town Gap camp in Pennsylvania. Some described the camp experiences as part of the extended vacation, whereas others felt hardship for the first time. Ha described Camp Pendleton as "long snaking lines of adults waiting to get exit visas." "I liked the powdered eggs," she joked. Yen recalled,

We made it to Camp Pendleton. We spent three months living in tents at the base of the mountain. It was really cold out at night. We slept in a hall room on balloon—you know those blown up mattresses. That was a scary time. We didn't play. It was really hard be-cause we were always cold. I remember the communal bathrooms and showers, little lights always dark, walking miles to get to the tents for dinner. A group of people would go ahead first to see if they were serving chicken. If not, we would not make the long walk. We were very well fed, though, never went hungry.

In contrast, Loan's family relocated directly to a relative's house in France. He remembered waiting a long time at the airport, however, for his paternal grand-parents to arrive. Nguyen's family was taken to a Red Cross villa on Kurfursten-damm (K'udamm) Street in Berlin. "You know what that's like," he observed ironically, "not exactly a refugee camp." Refugees in Germany stayed at the villa until they acquired enough German to make their own way. "Since we all spoke German well," Nguyen reported, "My father quickly found us an apartment and got us out of there so others could come."

Pham spent several months at a camp in Indonesia until United Charities and a priest in New York sponsored him. At the same camp, Hieu recalled,

We slept on long bunks with mosquito nets side by side. The food ration for each week was limited to a head of cabbage, some eggs, rice, sugar and salt; and once in awhile, there was a truck carrying fish for the camp and I saw people run out to catch them like savages.

In both cases, they described deprivations, having little to no social support, and not being in control of their lives. They also recalled receiving English language training in the camps and processing centers. Their descriptions of camp life par-allel those of relief workers' and researchers' of the Southeast Asian camps and processing centers in the same period (Tollefson 1989; Long 1993).

Across many refugee situations, international relief assistance at the time ware-housed refugees for long periods and treated them as welfare recipients rather than as actors who made conscious decisions about their own economic and po-litical circumstances (Tollefson 1989; Long 1993; Harrell-Bond 1986). Neverthe-less, the Viet Kieu described a markedly different resettlement system for those who went to Europe versus those who went to the United States or Canada. Those in Europe had some initial language training in centers and then through friends, relatives, and other social networks found their own places to live and work. In contrast, many of the refugees who went to the United States or Canada lived in camps and processing centers until sponsored by a church group, American friend, or family member.

Relationships

Most Viet Kieu described feeling out of place and being treated as alien in their new homes. Tui recalled, "When I went to school, I realized this is it. All the kids in the class were staring at me. I was the only Asian in the class. The American students in Fall River didn't give you the time of day. They were rich children of farmers. I lived for the weekends and being with other Vietnamese." "We were very visible in the neighborhood, the only Asian family in Larkspur," Diep said.

Family often mediated this initial sense of rejection and alienation. Initially on her arrival in Canada, Diep observed, "I have no impressions. I remember the snow. But, we were both so young that it didn't really matter, because we were surrounded by a large family. It was the same group just in another place." Yen said, "Going to school was tough, I didn't speak English at all. Everyone wanted to help though because we came at the right time. We had a lot of support and American friends. It was different for those who came later. It didn't matter. I was so young and we had all our relatives, friends, and family around. It was just the same group in another place."

Likewise, church ties and social networks sometimes mediated the initial sense of alienation. As noted earlier, churches or humanitarian organizations sponsored many refugees who resettled in the United States or Canada. While waiting in the refugee camps, refugees often had to shop for sponsors. In Tui's case, her father was a Lutheran pastor and the Lutheran Church immediately sponsored her family. The Church continued to provide a social network and support system as the family relocated several times looking for better educational and employment opportunities. Eventually, Tui's father founded a Vietnamese American Lutheran Church, which had a large, active congregation in a major city. Tui's own faith and her family's religious affiliations and ties formed her primary relationships in the new society.

Sponsorship and the development of new religious social ties led to some religious conversions. Phuong and Mai's families were also sponsored by Lutheran congregations and after being assisted by a Pastor's wife, Mai's family converted from Buddhism to the Lutheran Church. Mai suggested that the decision, in part, reflected the need to create a new social network because several Vietnamese families converted and joined the Vietnamese Lutheran Church in her town (which served much the same function as Tui's father's church in a major city). After a few years, however, Phuong's family moved west to join her aunt and uncle, thereby reaffirming kinship as their primary social support system.

Anglo-American families, who knew the interviewees' families from the military, university, or trips to the United States or Vietnam, initially sponsored Ha, Phuong, and Yen's families. In each case, the Anglo-American family initially housed them and assisted the Vietnamese family in finding a place of their own.

Yen appreciated that initial support: "My whole life I've been very lucky starting with childhood—not going to bed hungry."

Ha, however, resented being so dependent. "The Wilsons had two young sons," she recalled. Upon arrival to their sponsor's place, she celebrated her brother's birthday with the sponsor's youngest son but her sixth birthday was forgotten a month later. "We spent the summer locked up on their sun porch learning English," she added. Ha also felt very competitive with the American students. "I knew I should be in the purple reading group," she said with some irony. She described life as a series of obstacles that she overcame to succeed in university and eventually, graduate from medical school.

Several people noted being particularly lonely during high school and not having close American or European friends until university or graduate/professional school. Tui never felt she belonged and was lonely in each place she went. Mai and Ha, however, eventually developed both American and Vietnamese friends. During high school, Ha befriended some twin sisters. "I became obsessed competing with them," she recalled. Mai, Lan, and Ha initially had non-Vietnamese, American friends and only developed Vietnamese social networks later in life. Likewise, Loan's first friends were non-Vietnamese French and in Nguyen's case, non-Vietnamese German. Only in university did they befriend other Vietnamese. In contrast, Tuyet's friends remained non-Vietnamese French.

A math teacher became a surrogate parent for Ha during a particularly lonely period of her life. "Arthur was the first person to knock really hard," she explained. They remained in contact over many years even though they had a major falling out over his liberal academic interpretations of the Vietnamese-American War.

During university, Loan, Nguyen, Mai, Lan, and Ha joined Vietnamese student groups. Ha, however, found them too conservative and competitive. In contrast, Mai and Yen benefited from a group of young professional Vietnamese interested in humanitarian and social development projects both with Vietnamese youth in their communities and abroad.

In Germany Nguyen was the first Vietnamese in his school to graduate from *Real Schule* (secondary school). Working his way through school, he had little leisure time to spend with other German students. On his graduation day, he completed a double shift and arrived late to the ceremony. One of his most significant memories was entering the graduation hall to hear the Director announce to the crowd, "Well we got our first foreign student but it looks as if he doesn't want to take his *arbitur* (academic diploma)."

Hieu, who arrived in the U.S. as an adult, was extremely lonely and at first found it difficult to make friends. Although he contrasted the U.S. to Communist Vietnam as a "very safe place, at the same time, I didn't realize that there were other dangerous elements. But at the time, I remember thinking that no one who knows me would hurt me." However, Hieu found it difficult to form close relationships at work. "I felt very alone at work." He also observed, "It was very difficult for me to recuperate from the humiliation of the whole ordeal of having to put my life out at the mercy of others." He eventually formed friendships—both

Vietnamese and others—in law school. Likewise, Diep described forming friend-ships with other Vietnamese Americans during pharmacy school. Phuong, how-ever, had no attachment to other Vietnamese Americans during law school but made other good American friends during this period.

The interviewees reported a variety of emotions and relationships in the reset-tlement countries. Ha observed, "I hated Boston, Harvard. Boston is creepy, the most racist place. What was really creepy was that none of my white friends knew what I was talking about." In contrast, Nguyen felt at home:

I grew up German. I had a very good time. I remember on 9th November 1989, it was dis-orienting again. For the second time, the country I knew no longer existed. It was the sec-ond time I had faced all that. First, in Vietnam and second, in Germany. My parents kept saying though, "why can't Vietnamese approach each other like that?"

Like Nguyen, Tuyet reported feeling most at home in France and in Europe in general. Similarly, Phuong preferred to be in the U.S. because of its wide-open spaces and mentioned her specific affinity to the land there.

However, several Viet Kieu objected that many Americans continued to relate to the Vietnamese through the lens of the war. Hieu observed, "their memories are frozen with respect to Vietnam and the war. I wish that I could bring them here [referring to Vietnam] to show them what it is about Vietnam." Ha observed that many Vietnamese Americans also lived too much in the past:

There are a lot of things to mourn but it didn't feel very constructive. They organized around public service but it soured because of fighting and class conflicts, not just how yel-low and white but the kids of soldiers were sitting in the class next to Judge's children. It was venomous, really, really bad. Those are the types of people I can see going to their graves angry—so much self-righteousness.

Relations with Parents

Several interviewees observed that their parents rarely talked about their refugee experiences with their children. "Our parents just never talk about these things. We don't talk much about them either," explained Diep, and her brother Pham concurred. Mai and Ha, however, objected to this silence. "Most of the Viet-namese families who settled in the U.S. are dysfunctional in one way or another. The teenagers rebelled," Mai observed. Ha said her parents fabricated the truth, giving socially acceptable interpretations, and most of all keeping silent.

Faced with silence, some sought out elders or other relatives to tell them what really happened. Tui took her son to Saigon to record her grandmother's story. Ha met an aunt who was willing to talk openly about Ha's parent's past lives. Diep and Pham reconnected with their grandfather. Before coming to Vietnam, Ha re-alized that "All my relatives made me feel like I was crazy, came from nowhere."

Several people recognized the separation and loss the parents must have suf-fered. "My mother regretted not taking her relatives—our grandparents. My mother's mother died while we were in the U.S. and she wanted to get my grandfather to the U.S. but he died first. My parents had difficulty adapting to the U.S.—there were lots of fights, it was a difficult time," Tui recalled. Phuong remembered that it was harder for her father than her mother to adjust—"She was more outgoing." Phuong's father died when she was still a child and Phuong and her siblings never developed a close relationship with their stepfather. Mai's mother also died in the U.S. of cancer at an early age, which the family attributed to the chemical exposure she received while working in a very difficult job in a nursing home. Loan's father never completely adjusted to life in France and died while Loan was still a student at university. Pham and Diep's parents lived apart—their father in Canada and their mother in Boca Ratan. The children separated as well—Pham stayed with his father in the north while Diep went south with her mother.

Tui described her parents' guilt and shame. "Every time my father went out, he was ashamed that it was not his country, while my mother was living with guilt that she did not take her parents over." In contrast, Tuyet realized that her father felt guilty for leaving in 1945 and not participating in the war. Loan observed that his father refused to talk about Vietnam and died a very bitter man. "When I first landed in Saigon again, I cried for my father who would never see all this again. I remembered his last voyage."

Several people described their parents' difficulty accepting their children's new cultural values and norms. "There was a lot of pressure to achieve," Mai reported. "My generation is a bridge." "My parents try to re-create a Vietnamese life and culture," Tuyet observed. Having grown up abroad, she had primarily European friends and had long ago left behind her parent's social network.

The children's desire for social relationships also caused tensions with parents. "We just didn't tell our parents where we went when we would go out dancing on the weekends," Tui observed, recalling how her sister and she met a group of Vietnamese American friends each weekend. Ha reported that her parents tried to deny what was happening. Describing a confrontation with her mother, Ha said, "That day I chose to tell her I was sleeping with my boyfriend, she was shocked and in denial. But, she stopped a moment and asked if I was using birth control. Then, she just acted if it all never happened."[8] In face of their children's opposition and determination, however, Diep and Pham reported, "They really can't push us, they learned to quit, they've given up long ago; they are never happy with who we choose."

Parents had varying reactions to their children's decision to return to Vietnam. "My parents supported me. They said, 'it is your decision, go there and do your best.' They were concerned because they knew the cultural differences between the two worlds," However, Ha said, "My mother and grandmother were super duper paranoid about the Communist regime." Several others used the word "paranoid" in describing parents' or relatives' reactions to the government. For example, Pham said, "My brother in the U.S. is very paranoid; he says to us, don't write your name on the fax—use your initials." Yen reported that when she tried to return earlier, "I was going to go but my parents flipped and said 'you would be arrested, it is dangerous. I forbid you to go. So, I went later." Although they agreed two years later for her to be relocated to Vietnam with her work, Yen observed:

my father didn't want me to become attached to people here. 'You could learn to trust them and you know that you don't trust them.' My coming back for Dad was particularly hard, he doesn't trust the Communist party; Mum has always wanted to come back.

In assessing his own parent's responses to the changes in their lives, Pham observed, "culturally a lot of time, they don't think it is right to say it. They are very careful in what they say and do. It must be difficult for them."

Relations with Vietnamese

The Viet Kieu described dynamic and changing relationships with the Vietnamese. According to Yen, "We were walking money bags in '93. They would charge and over-charge us. Relatives would come up and ask us for money. Their first impression was that Vietnamese are very wealthy." Tui, who had lived in Vietnam for several years, described numerous visits from the local police in the early 1990s. "My landlord didn't know what to do with me in those days," she observed. Tuyet recounted, "They were curious about my physical appearance. My cousins asked a lot of questions. We were the rich family from France—funny for us because in France, we were normal."

Several people observed that the Vietnamese perceptions of them were changing and the north/south distinction was becoming more marked than Viet Kieu/Vietnamese. "People that I have met, born after the war, after the 1975 draft, don't have any memory or problems by South Vietnamese or Americans so they are able to look at us like other foreigners," Hieu explained. In Hanoi, Tui observed, "It is better to be an overseas Vietnamese than a local southern person, they respect you more." Mai reported, "I am treated more differently because I'm a southerner than as an overseas Vietnamese."

With the rapid economic changes and access to larger markets in Vietnam, Viet Kieu were becoming less visible and differentiated from other expatriates in the society. "People here don't think I'm Vietnamese. They are more likely to think I'm Singaporean, Thai or Chinese. Sometimes they even say to me 'you speak really good Vietnamese for an Indian,'" Yen laughed. Tuyet observed that people did note her nationality and "were curious about my physical appearance. They sometimes guess Thai or Indian."

With the recent reforms, Phuong argued that the Viet Kieu should change their approach to relating to the Vietnamese. She was appalled at seeing four or five Viet Kieu at the airport try to bribe the customs officials by slipping five or ten dollars in their passports. "They were physically shaken up, that's the mentality of the overseas community. Just slip a few in the passport." When asked to provide a bribe (money or her expensive wedding ring), Phuong cancelled the trip and returned to the airport a few days later leaving the ring at home. However, she reported that even her Anglo American husband was surprised at her unwillingness to pay a small bribe to take the trip as scheduled.

Several interviewees observed that the Vietnamese usually presume that Viet Kieu know how "things are done here" and will make the necessary under the table payments. " 'You can understand how it is' they say to me in a negotiation," Tui reported. Pham depended on relatives, however, to know the right approach. "Money under the table is a new concept for me. Our father's family helped us a lot with this," he said. Others were less accepting of the Vietnamese system. "I get disappointed because of the greed because people here don't trust the system or government yet. You see a lot of 'get what we want, what we can get' here," Yen said.

Some Viet Kieu complained about cross-cultural differences in communicating. "Vietnamese are full of questions. I used to be honest in answering, tired to help with jobs but inevitably, it didn't work out." Diep said, "Maybe the lower class is more nosy. They ask everything. How much do you charge, how much do you pay but not everyone is like that"; she added that her mother warned her that the concept of "thank you" was not known in the north. "They never say thank you," she stated.

Phuong observed that her relationships with the Vietnamese worsened when she married a Western man and lived in an expatriate compound. "They expect me to get them all jobs," she complained. Diep and Pham observed that the Vietnamese "don't like Vietnamese women hanging out with Westerners. They don't like to see a Vietnamese woman with a Western man." On the other hand, Pham stated that he would not want his sister to marry a Vietnamese man because the "males are too chauvinistic, macho. The wife has to have a good job but still come home to cook, clean, and look after the house. Her husband expects her to have both qualities." Their parents who lived in Hanoi were also "hesitant of us going out, they don't think we understand as much—think it is dangerous. If I hang out with the girls here, it is not the same as hanging out with girls in the U.S., my mother says."

Most interviewees developed relationships with Vietnamese through their work or kinship networks. They rarely met friends from the past and when they tried to do so, Tuy found that the contacts were casual and superficial. According to Nguyen, "It is not easy to make friends, on a business level, we get along well but there is no intersection in interests, languages, and hobbies." Diep discovered that she was not sufficiently proficient in Vietnamese but that even if she were fluent, she would only meet her coworkers. Phuong said that when she was not working, she had very few Vietnamese friends and the only friendships she made had been through work.

Everyone addressed the issue of Vietnam's transition.[9] "It is becoming a modern society, becoming Westernized—promoting democracy and capitalism," Yen observed. However, Loan argued, "the transition is going to take a long time, the expectations were so high." "It's a great place for workaholics—you just work all the time, there is nothing to do so you go to work," Diep observed. For others, however, the pace was too slow. "I'm a city person. I'm bored here, too," said Nguyen.

In contrast to the focus on capital in relationships with Vietnamese, Yen (a banker) reported that the Vietnamese taught her, "you don't need a lot to be happy. You don't need to have 60 pairs of shoes. People here are fairly inventive. At 32, I feel stupid saying okay, materialism is not everything but unless you live here, you don't know that. I hope Vietnam doesn't lose a lot of its culture." Diep admired a local woman motorcycle driver because "she is the only person I've met who realizes that here is much better than the outside."

Changing Citizenship and Kinship Ties

Reestablishing trust in Vietnamese terms was renewing kinship and ancestral ties again. These ties are affirmed annually in specific rituals at family altars and ancestral graves, which was why many Viet Kieu initially returned for Tet. While the interviewees themselves (who remained) did not necessarily attach the same importance to performing these rituals in Vietnam, the Vietnamese invariably saw the reintegration of their Viet Kieu kin in these terms. Vietnamese who entertained overseas kin during Tet often remarked how important it was for the Viet Kieu to worship at the ancestral altars again. At the same time, they expected the returnees to bring back resources, gifts, and money for the family. In our local community in Hanoi, for example, our Vietnamese neighbors often remarked when a new house went up (or an old one was refurbished), that "their Viet Kieu relatives helped them" or "that place was paid for by their Viet Kieu cousins." Both gained new economic and social resources—access to capital, an emerging market, and enriched family and kinship ties (creating more complex, transnational networks at home and abroad).

Reversing its earlier hostility to western Viet Kieu, government policies increasingly reaffirmed these news ties by providing favored status and treatment. In 2000, the Government instituted a new policy to afford western Viet Kieu the same terms of treatment for visas, residence status, property rights, and local airline fares, etc., as other overseas Vietnamese and the local population. Faced with the Asian currency crisis and a dramatic downturn in its earlier phenomenally high rates of economic growth (decreasing from 7–8 percent to 2–3 percent per annum), the Ministries of Foreign Trade and Investment and of Foreign Affairs decided to encourage Western Viet Kieu investment because they feared to lose the economic momentum gained earlier. Thus, notions of citizenship were flexible and adapted to the changing social and economic circumstances (Ong 1999).

Although the Vietnamese and the Government increasingly granted a place for the Viet Kieu both within families and as part of citizenship regimes because of their links to capital and investment, the Viet Kieu themselves responded in different ways. Those who had made a long-term commitment to live and work in Vietnam often developed complex, temporal notions of kinship and citizenship that permitted flexibility of movement and social and economic capital.

At the end of our meetings, the interviewees invariably discussed where they claimed citizenship and whether their kinship ties were primarily in Vietnam, the country of resettlement, or both places. Despite the common interest in citizenship and kinship allegiances, their answers varied.

Diep and Pham's family were determined to remain in Vietnam. In coming to Vietnam, they again expanded their kinship networks to include grandparents, cousins, aunts, and uncles of both parent's families. Following a family developmental cycle or trajectory, they re-established ties with the mother's relatives (Oxfeld 1993). Within their father's residence, they also re-established a fraternal stem household (as both sons eventually returned to live and work in Vietnam).

"My parents are going to stay here so I don't really ever want to be too far from them," observed Diep. Her observations suggested the increasing importance in this family of maintaining transnational kinship ties across different locales (similar to those Ong describes of overseas Chinese). Diep planned to marry a Vietnamese American but recognized that her husband would not give up his medical practice to live in Vietnam. They would eventually establish a conjugal family in the U.S. However, her own compromise was to develop a small business in Vietnam with her mother and brothers, and thus, her work would bring her back to Vietnam "two weeks out of two months." Maintaining ties in both places, she celebrated wedding rituals in both the U.S. and Vietnam, which reflected the traditions of each place, established a profession and license in the U.S., and opened a small business in Vietnam.[10]

In the initial interview, Diep's brother, Pham, reported that he had no definite plans to leave but asserted that he was certain that he would not stay in Vietnam forever. "Probably not, not too compatible, the mentality is too different here," and he added that he planned to return either to the U.S. or Canada depending on business opportunities. Diep chided him for this remark: "Our nationality is Vietnamese. We like both. Our base will be the U.S. but we don't want to be far from our parents." Pham retorted, "here we are Vietnamese, in the U.S. we are Americans. But we are more visible here." However, once his brother joined the household, together they expanded the family business in Vietnam. Later, Pham spoke of remaining in Hanoi for many years if not forever and just visiting Canada now and again. His decisions reflected an evolving family trajectory that included a fraternal stem family in Vietnam with transnational ties to conjugal families in the U.S. and Canada. For both Pham and Diep, it was important to maintain various options so as to hedge one's risks. Given assurances of such flexibility, Pham was willing to make a commitment to remain in Hanoi. Over time, both individual and family strategies reflected the changing social and economic opportunity structure. The increasing ease of economic relations for this family allowed them to reestablish a more flexible but also a more layered and dense set of kinship relations in Canada, the U.S. and Vietnam.

Mai planned to return to the United States to marry a British boyfriend. Both she and her future husband were involved in international issues but she did not discuss any direct kinship ties with Vietnam, nor did she consider herself Vietnamese. Coming to Vietnam, she explained, helped her to see the importance of organizing the Vietnamese American community and working with Vietnamese youth in the U.S. She was interested in politics and organizing other Asian groups as part of a larger Asian American voting bloc and interest group. Reestablishing ties to Vietnam empowered her sense of being an actor in the U.S. political arena and re-enforced her own citizenship status there. "We need Vietnam more than it needs us," she observed.

Nguyen and Phuong planned to move to another country in Asia, where business opportunities were better. As Nguyen explained, "Somehow I see my future not in Vietnam. Vietnam is one of the stops to move forward, it is too small to stay here. I will miss it by the time I leave but I know it is not my future here. The future is in Asia. I'd like to go to Singapore or Malaysia." Phuong also encouraged her husband to move to Singapore or Jakarta to expand his professional opportunities. Nguyen and Yen observed that they were afraid of losing their technical skills if they stayed in Vietnam too long and they wanted to return eventually to the headquarters of their organizations. Yen explained, "Eventually I have to go back, work wise I have to be in the head office where it is happening." All three—Nguyen, Phuong, and Yen—had developed strong professional identities which governed their decisions about place. Their notions of being Asians rather than Vietnamese or nationals of a western country reinforced that professional sense of a global citizenship, responsive to the increasing flexibility of both labor and capital.

Ironically, Nguyen sympathized with the East Germans who had lost their rootedness. As a German, he observed that they were *Fass ohne Boden*, a pot without its bottom. In contrast, through his professional experiences, Nguyen had achieved a certain status as a German, which many easterners who are unemployed and dislocated lacked. In effect, he suggested that in global markets citizenship status not only confers but also follows economic opportunities.

Even though Yen planned to return to her organization's headquarters, she had assumed her Vietnamese name and changed her passport accordingly. She argued, "There will always be a part of me that is Vietnamese in behaviors and habits. If you ask whether I am Vietnamese or American, I would say that I have an American heritage, but my roots are here." Of all the Viet Kieu, she perhaps best accorded with Vietnamese perceptions of the Viet Kieu's place in their society. Yen took advantage of the economic opportunities in the West but her kinship and ancestral ties (and sense of place) remained in Vietnam.

In returning to Vietnam, Ha rejected the Vietnamese American community even though she increasingly saw herself as an American. Yet, she also continued to question what it meant to be American. "I didn't get along with other Vietnamese Americans. They liked to go to Vegas, it's a very Vietnamese thing. They liked Vietnamese pop music. Maybe they are more American, very materialistic, backstabbing and sniping. But, there are things about me that wouldn't last here." She eventually returned with her husband to the U.S., where she gave birth to a son. The return to Vietnam was a way to address the silences in her own life and overcome her sense of being denied a past which in turn allowed her to establish a family in the United States. While she no longer expected to settle or raise her family in Vietnam, she reestablished strong ties with her paternal uncle and his family and planned to ensure that her son maintained these relationships. By returning to Vietnam, she developed what she considered an authentic Vietnamese American identity grounded historically and ancestrally.

Tui was very ambivalent about where she belonged, although she planned to return to the United States. Given her personal life history, it seemed that she would be lonely wherever she went. "America is not my country. Here I feel like a foreigner, Vietnam is not my country either. The U.S. is more comfortable because of family there. We will go back because of family ties." However, she resolved her ambivalence in how she raised her son, whose father was Anglo-American. "I let him wear diapers [as the Americans] but I also let him pee on the streets." Unlike Ha, Tui's loneliness brought her to seek stronger ties with her family's church and its social networks (which overlapped with those of her husband).

Hieu wanted to stay in Vietnam and ensure that his children would know Vietnamese. However, his status was already too tenuous, and he was uncertain how long he would be allowed to remain. Later, he wrote, "The U.S. has welcomed me, but I think my pride has kept me from feeling it is my home." He also realized that, "All my family are now in the U.S. and are doing well financially. I have many nieces and nephews who are living in the U.S. and I think are facing with a rather different set of racial issues similar to those of other Americans. I don't think that they understand how to feel being a refugee." He worried that his fiancée, a Vietnamese American, would not want to live in Vietnam, and did not know how to resolve this dilemma. "If you leave after adolescence, your identity is more contested. You never completely understand the grammar of the new language." By returning, he determined that his primary attachments were in Vietnam, but, given his earlier political history, he could not be certain of being welcomed there.

Loan planned to stay as long as it made sense. He observed that "you can never be sure here. The work can always change and you have to leave." He was equally uncertain whether his French Viet Kieu wife would be happy as well. Both suggested that their kinship ties were stronger with the Viet Kieu community in France. In part because of his marriage, Loan said that ultimately they were French and would return there.

Tuyet, too, observed that she would return to France, in contrast to Loan, but more for reasons of citizenship than kinship. "The paradox is that in coming here, I've learned how French I am. Vietnam is a very beautiful country but more of a myth, a myth which is disappearing, the country of one's grandparents," she reflected. Even as she tried to distance herself from that past, she realized that "when someone says something against Vietnam, I feel it. I don't want to be disinherited, rejected as a stranger."

Recapturing Trust and One's Sense of Place in Vietnam

Although many young Viet Kieu wanted to develop ties to Vietnam that transcend their parent's (or their own) previous refugee experiences, most describe
ambivalent relationships and challenge both Western assimilation and Vietnamese essentialist models of ethnic identity. Returning to Vietnam allows many
Viet Kieu to establish a sense of place based on their own memories and experiences and to expand family relationships and kinship ties. For the Vietnamese
government, the Viet Kieu were increasingly important to the process of Doi Moi
(renovation), in developing trade with western markets and encouraging an infu-
sion of capital. However, the Viet Kieu also embodied the problems of relating to
the West and official government discourse mandated appropriate Viet Kieu
practices within an existing socialist moral and political regime.

Returnees' accounts—whether of Robert McNamara or Le Hay Slip—in the
Western popular press—often serve as evidence for revisionist histories of the war.
For Western countries, especially the United States, the return of Viet Kieu (along
with other Westerners) represents a final victory against communism in which
young capitalists or old warriors win on the new battlefield, the market. Such portrayals underscore the continued failures of communication and more often than
not, foreign investments and joint ventures fail. Revisionist histories also typically
make Vietnam the subject, America the object, and seek to understand what
America did wrong (Vlastos 1990). As Clark (1991: 199) observes, revisionist histories "transform individual experience into an icon of communal redemption."
However, trying to reinvent the past or achieve communal redemption has no relationship to contemporary Vietnam. As these accounts demonstrate there are
many different reasons for returning and many varied experiences of return.

Trinh (1991: 163), a Vietnamese American critic, argues for redefining the nature and boundaries of politics in relation to personal meanings, yet maintaining
the tension between the two. In so doing, return decisions along with issues of
place, kinship, and citizenship are critical entry points for understanding contemporary Vietnam's transition and what Vietnam is today.

Allowing the Viet Kieu to return was for the Government part of a larger
process of opening its economy and society to the West. In the Vietnamese press,
the return of Viet Kieu was initially a chance to atone for past wrongs and to give
up selfish ways. In so doing, one was welcomed home again and one's ancestral
ties were reaffirmed. The official Vietnamese version of the homecoming often
affirmed an essentialized "Vietnamese" identity, based on proper, moral social
practices and behavior and respect for common ancestral ties. Thus, one returned
not only spatially but also, morally home. In so doing, both sides gained social and
economic resources through enriched family and kinship ties.

Yet, the interviewees and Vietnamese people themselves contested the official
narratives and conditions of return in their own daily experiences. Reasons for returning as well as receptions varied and there were many evolving return histories. Vietnam itself was undergoing a rapid social and economic transformation

in ways that had little to do with the war or the earlier communist regime. The various return trajectories and particular life histories captured some of the complexities of the transition process.

In encouraging the Viet Kieu to return, many Vietnamese themselves again affirmed that family and kinship ties matter most (personal observation; Jamieson 1995). Yet, Vietnamese and Viet Kieu alike were often ambivalent about the homecoming. The ambivalence reflected differing expectations of proper moral relations, kinship and ancestral ties, and ultimately, of place and citizenship.

The Viet Kieu defined some of the shifting boundaries of who is Vietnamese in this period of historical transition. For most, coming back to Vietnam was a process of establishing trust through the creation of shared experiences, place, and kinship ties. The refugee experience involves a breakdown of trust or habitus (Daniel and Knudsen 1995). Unlike their parents, siblings, and friends who mistrusted the communist regime, the Viet Kieu tested the relationships, tried to understand the former ties, and often developed stronger and denser kinship ties and social networks. As a group, they were increasingly confident in their ability to negotiate with Vietnamese society.

Some people returned to understand the silences and to know the stories behind their parents' reticence so as to build better relationships in the future. While their parents had a discourse rooted in shared experiences and memories, Vietnam, for many of their children, was theoretical (Knudsen 1995). Coming back to Vietnam grounded one's images and memories and established a new set of experiences. Often, the return represented liberation from a restrictive, secretive, or painful past. As Trinh (1991: 14) observed, "the return to a denied heritage allows one to start again with different re-departures, different pauses, different arrivals."

An important aspect of the return experience was establishing a sense of place. As Giddens (1990) observes, a dynamic of modernity is the separation of space from place. In describing the returns, many Viet Kieu seemed to be trying to relocate space with place in their lives. Memories of former houses, streets, fields, and trees became specific experiences with normal dimensions again. Certain smells were associated with a specific fruit. Space being relocated in place was not just a set of distant images, stories, or disembodied voices but encompassed specific sensory experiences, histories and relationships.

Yet, those who returned also acknowledged the continuing ambiguities of space, time, and relationships in their lives. Citizenship and social and kinship ties were multi-layered. To the Government one's status implied varying degrees of trustworthiness from trusted, "socialist bloc" insiders to completely untrustworthy agents of foreign imperialist forces (the Rambo raiders and CIA agents of an earlier era). Viet Kieu also implied degrees of citizenship to be regulated and taxed according to one's degree of spatial and moral distance. On the part of the Vietnamese people, the Viet Kieu had financial and social obligations to assist one's kin as part of reaffirming ancestral ties. Yet, they often regarded their Viet Kieu relatives as Vietnamese first no matter from whence they came or went.[11] To be

Vietnamese was both an ethnic identity, which implied shared roots and histories, and an attachment to a particular place.

The Viet Kieu on the other hand established their sense of place in several parts of the world and extended their notions of kinship to fit with various geographic locale. In the popular press, being Viet Kieu often implied a relatively small group of savvy, young expatriates in Hanoi and Saigon who often spoke excellent Vietnamese and had loose social connections to one another. As bricoleurs in other societies, some were Vietnamese in personal relationships and Western in work and professional relationships (White 1997). Others ultimately rejected both Vietnamese and Western models but affirmed a larger Asian transnational citizenship (to enlarge their professional opportunities). Many asserted creolized definitions of citizenship, drawing on different referents at various points in time and space. For some, being back in Vietnam made them more French or American, while for others, re-returning to the United States or France again allowed them to feel more Vietnamese again.

What one is not, as Barth (1969) observes in his classic discussion of ethnic boundaries, often affirms what one is. As this study shows, such oppositions are permeable, historically situated, and subject to social and economic negotiation. By returning to Vietnam, the Viet Kieu and their Vietnamese kin, who receive them, have extended these boundaries far and wide. By encouraging these returns, Vietnam enlarged its own space in the global economy.

Chapter 5
Chinese Villagers and the Moral Dilemmas of Return Visits

Ellen Oxfeld

A Bad Class Marriage. When Qiufang decided to marry the Chen's son, her parents were so upset that they made her kneel in front of a portrait of Chairman Mao for an entire day! The Chen's son came from a bad class category, because he had overseas relatives, and Qiufang's parents were afraid that with this kind of connection, the rest of their family would be discriminated against. Finally, Qiufang ran away to the neighboring village where the Chen's son lived and married him anyway, but she did not see her natal family for seven years. As time went on, however, her family began to see that it really wasn't a bad match after all. Her husband's family began to receive a lot of money from their overseas relations in Indonesia. Now Qiufang's parents really like their son-in-law.

An Unfilial Visitor. Xiuling Ji's elder brother came to visit from Taiwan last year. But instead of first returning to his mother's grave to worship her, he decided to take a trip around China, and visited lots of scenic places such as Kunming. Later he returned to Mei Xian [his native place], and he was immediately struck down by a severe illness for over one week!

The "reopening" of China in the late 1970s made it possible to revitalize a host of dormant links between Chinese villagers and their overseas Chinese relatives. This chapter examines the return visits of these overseas relations from the point of view of the residents of Moonshadow Pond, a Hakka village of 800 in Mei County, Guangdong Province, in southeast China. The visitors are all natives of Moonshadow Pond who emigrated either before the Liberation or during the early years of Communist rule. These visits are provisional returns ranging from a few days to a few months of each year, and the visitors are usually welcomed warmly by village residents. But the visits have also had a profound impact on Moonshadow Pond life, introducing contending notions of status and obligation and sometimes producing tensions between residents with and without overseas kin.

I lived and conducted fieldwork in Moonshadow Pond from 1995–96, and again in the summer of 1997. The village's residents are Hakka, a distinct ethnic and linguistic group who are dispersed throughout a number of provinces in southeast China.[1] They are nonetheless considered to be members of the majority Han Chinese rather than to be members of an ethnic minority.

Since the reform of China's economy in the early 1980s, and the decollectivization of agriculture, the economic life of Moonshadow Pond like that of many rural areas in China has changed dramatically. From the early 1950s until the late 1970s, agriculture was the mainstay of the economy, and families lived primarily off the collectively worked land. Now, most families in Moonshadow Pond utilize the land allocated to them in order to provide themselves with rice and vegetables, but they also rely on the wage labor or small business activities of some family members to augment their livelihoods. Many of the young people in the village migrate to large cities, such as Shenzhen and Guangzhou, which are hundreds of miles away, in order to earn money as factory workers, cooks, or drivers and to remit funds home. Other villagers work nearby in road and home construction, or they cultivate fruit trees or fish ponds in the village or operate small stores. A few villagers have also prospered in the ranks of the bureaucracy in the nearby county capital, or in private businesses within the village itself, including the local doctor, a family that runs a car shuttle service, and a family that makes items for use in religious ritual. School tuitions, medical bills, and new homes can simply not be paid for with the proceeds of subsistence agriculture.

In addition, since the early 1980s, the renewed relationships with and return visits of overseas kin have also played an important role in the economic and social life of Moonshadow Pond. However, as the stories at the start of this chapter illustrate, these reestablished contacts with overseas Chinese kin are accompanied by a number of new ironies surrounding the status of those with overseas connections as well as new anxieties about what is to be expected from these visitors. With the death of Mao Zedong, and the onset of the reform era in the late 1970s, China's political leaders changed their attitudes and policies toward links with the outside world, including connections with overseas Chinese. The class label system was abolished, and those descended from landlords, rich peasants, and other "bad classes," including those with overseas Chinese connections were no longer pariahs. But as overseas Chinese return to visit their village relations, new sets of questions arise. What is to be expected from these returning kin? What are the ground rules for relationships between those who emigrated and those who were left behind? How are the actions and decisions of those who return to be judged?

In the anthropological literature on China, particularly on southeast China, a number of ethnographies have already investigated the connections between emigrants and their native villages. Many of these works focus not only upon the economic impact of emigration, remittances or investment, but also on the impact of return upon local communities. They ask how emigration, remittances and return affect class structure and infrastructure (J. Watson 1975; Woon 1984, 1989; Hsu 1996; Hsing 1997; Lever-Tracy 1996a, b), as well as whether they unravel or help to strengthen traditional cultural forms, such as the lineage (Watson 1975; Chen 1940; Woon 1984, 1989). A number of recent works also examine the allure of transnational Chinese culture for those who remain on the mainland (Liu 1997; Yang 1997).

Although these issues will be considered in this chapter as well, the focus and point of departure differ from previous works. I concentrate on the ideas and expectations villagers hold about return and on the moral and social dilemmas that return engenders. This examination also adds a new dimension to the treatment of return in the Chinese context because previous works either focus on pre-liberation China or on Hong Kong or deal with the role of remittances but not with actual return (Lozada 2001; Woon 1989).[2] Finally, unlike a number of other contributions to this volume, I focus here on return from the point of view of those who remained behind rather than on the experience of the returnees. After all, it is not only the returnees who wrestle with contradictions between imagined and actual homelands. Those who remain behind must sort out multiple and often contradictory images of homecomings.

In what follows, I show how villagers construe their visiting foreign kin in several ways. Villagers expect them to remember their family and commemorate their ancestors. But, as shown in the second of the opening stories, they may also view returnees as foreigners whose priorities are not congruent with those of the villagers. Further, while overseas kin are viewed as potential benefactors, as the first story suggests, both their public and private contributions are subject to a variety of interpretations, and these contributions also generate new social frictions. As such, when villagers discuss their expectations about the obligations of visiting overseas kin, they articulate a number of competing moral visions. When this occurs, they make judgements about the overseas returnees *and* about other villagers who interact with them. Thus, the return "home" creates a complex and contested moral space.

Before going further, an explanation of terms is necessary. There is some debate about whether persons of Chinese descent who live outside China should be called "overseas Chinese" or some other term such as "diaspora Chinese" (Nonini and Ong 1997b), "persons of Chinese descent" (*huayi*), or simply "Chinese people" (*huaren*) (Skeldon 1995). I use the term "overseas Chinese" for the purposes of this essay. This English term comes close to the written terms of reference, *huaqiao* or "overseas Chinese, and address, *haiwai qiaobao* or "overseas compatriots," used in local documents and letters to refer to Chinese residing abroad.[3] A term sometimes used in colloquial speech to refer to Chinese visitors from abroad is *fan ke*, or "foreign guests." (I will have more to say about the derivation and implications of these terms in sections below.)

Although people in Hong Kong are not technically "overseas," and Hong Kong is now part of China, I include Hong Kong relatives as "overseas Chinese" in this essay. Until 1997, Hong Kong was not only part of a separate political entity, but also part of a vastly different cultural, economic, and social world. Relatives who returned from Hong Kong to the village were treated in much the same way and were the objects of similar sets of expectations as those coming from more distant areas, and letters from lineage, village, or township leaders addressed to "overseas compatriots" were also sent to Hong Kong relatives.

Historical Antecedents

To understand the significance of return migration to China, one needs first to understand the fluctuating role that diaspora has played in Chinese life for the last several centuries. Although Chinese migration and return migration in the 1990s and beyond are influenced by present day structures of the world economy, it would be wrong to view these movements as new phenomena (Appadurai 1990; Clifford 1994; Basch et al. 1994; and Ong and Nonini 1997 for discussions of diaspora and transnationalism in terms of the contemporary global economy).

During the early decades of the Qing dynasty (1644–1911), the Chinese state banned emigration. Indeed, the Qianlong emperor stated that emigrants had "'deserted their ancestors graves to seek profits abroad'" (Duara 1997: 43), and emigrants who returned were often executed in order to deter others from leaving (42). However, in the waning years of the Qing dynasty, the imperial court, much like the reform minded Communist leaders of the post-Mao era in China, realized that emigrants might provide an important source of wealth that could be used profitably to enhance Chinese development. By the 1880s, imperial policy toward emigrants had reversed itself, and by 1902 the Qing government was actually sending envoys to Southeast Asia to encourage the Chinese merchants there to invest in China.

The use of the word *huaqiao*, or "overseas Chinese" also begins in this period. Hua simply refers to China or Chinese, and, as Wang Gungwu points out, "the word *qiao* is "an ancient word whose main meaning is 'to sojourn, or reside temporarily away from home.' The first clear use of the word . . . occurred in an official document in 1858. . . . Up to this time, a whole range of other terms, some most uncomplimentary, were employed to describe Chinese who resided overseas" (Wang 1985: 72).

Between the downfall of the Qing dynasty in 1911 and the establishment of Communist rule in 1949, China experienced breakdown in civil order, invasion by the Japanese, economic disaster, and civil war. During this period, many areas of southeast China witnessed large rates of emigration. Indeed, as Woon reminds us, overseas Chinese remittances "helped balance the trade deficit of China in the 1920s" (Woon 1984: 276).

In Moonshadow Pond, emigration during the turbulent first half of the twentieth century was often viewed as the only alternative to destitution. Emigration from Moonshadow Pond, as from most parts of Guangdong Province, was heavily gendered (Woon 1984). Most of the emigrants were male, and most went to India, mainland Southeast Asia, or Indonesia. Often they never returned, leaving wives behind as virtual widows. Later, at the time of Liberation in 1949, a few men emigrated because they had been soldiers in the Nationalist army and feared retribution. Finally, in the early 1950s, in the wake of land reform instituted by the new Communist government, a few more villagers emigrated. In this case, the émigrés were individuals who were in "bad class" categories, mostly those who feared that as former landlords they might be beaten or even executed.

As in earlier historical eras, the Communist government went through several changes of policy toward emigrants and their families. During the 1950s and early 1960s, relatives of overseas Chinese were able to receive some remittances, but return visits from emigrants were not encouraged and rarely took place. Then, during the Cultural Revolution era (officially 1966–68, but with an influence continuing well into the 1970s), almost all contact between overseas Chinese and mainland kin was cut off. Overseas Chinese who returned, such as refugees from Indonesian political violence, were "attacked for their bourgeois values and wasteful practices" (Godley 1989: 333).

"If you had an overseas Chinese relative," one villager told me, "they might even accuse you of being a spy. So most people, if they had any connections, just kept it a secret." Many villagers used a popular slogan of the period, "self-reliance and arduous struggle" (*zi li geng sheng, jian ku fen dou*) as an example of wrong-headed ideals. "Imagine if overseas Chinese could have invested in China all along," one resident told me, "we would certainly have been more well off by now!"

After 1978, the policy was reversed again and contacts with overseas Chinese were actively encouraged (Godley 1989). Confiscated property and bank accounts were returned to overseas Chinese (Godley 1989; Woon 1989). On the national and provincial levels, investment by overseas Chinese capitalists now plays an important role in the expansion of China's economy, especially in the southeast, the area from which the bulk of the émigré population originated. Even at the township and village level, donations and investment of overseas Chinese have played an increasingly important economic role in villages that were once home to emigres or their ancestors.

While it is true that an overseas compatriot need not return in order to make a contribution, such donations are often realized during the course of a visit, and may even be the occasion of a banquet or ceremony in honor of the donor. When villagers speak of overseas returnees, they often refer to acts of beneficence. I therefore begin my examination with an analysis of the way villagers discuss overseas visitors in their role as benefactors beyond their immediate families, and of the contradictions within these images and the social relationships they attempt to describe. Following this, I examine villagers' understandings of their visiting kin in terms of two other models—they view them as family and lineage members with unbreakable ties to ancestors and living relatives, but they also view them as foreigners who may no longer honor these ties. Throughout my analysis, I emphasize the competing and contradictory desires and moral judgements that return visits engender among villagers.

Returnees as Benefactors

Although immediate family members may receive help from a returnee, villagers also view returnees as benefactors who extend a helping hand beyond the needs of their closest kin. All villagers are aware of the significant role overseas Chinese play in economic revitalization. They often compare different regions of Guangdong as well as different villages in their own area in terms of the frequency and strength of their connections with overseas Chinese. In Moonshadow Pond, 23 out of 165 families (14%) say they have an overseas Chinese connection. But while only 14 percent of families have a direct connection to an overseas Chinese, several recent village projects could never have been completed without their help. The first project was the renovation of the local primary school, including the donation of desks and benches in the early 1980s, followed by the construction of two new bridges in 1983 and 1986, renovation of the ancestral temple in 1989 and an old residence hall belonging to one of the larger lineage branches in 1996, and, finally, paving of some dirt or old brick roads in the village in 1992 and 1996.

Donations from overseas donors to public institutions and projects are now deemed so important that cadres and even ordinary village residents are involved in trying to solicit them. Villagers often organize themselves into committees which recruit funds from overseas Chinese in order to garner support for local projects such as road paving or renovation of the primary school or lineage branch temple. A former head of the production brigade, an administrative area that includes Moonshadow Pond and one other village, often touted his success at soliciting help from overseas Chinese as his finest achievement in office. And, at the next higher level of administration, that of the township, some cadres are actually delegated the official responsibility of soliciting overseas Chinese donations. If an overseas Chinese returns and is residing in the district during the Chinese New Year, township cadres will always make a courtesy call on New Year's Day.

When I asked villagers why they thought overseas Chinese would contribute to village projects, they often mentioned what may be called a "primordial" connection between overseas Chinese and their ancestral villages. People are expected to have emotional connections (*ganqing*) toward their native villages that will automatically generate an interest in contributing. "Your native village," explained my landlord, "is your root (*gen*), and it is only natural that you would want to help." In Chinese popular religion, one's native village is the home of one's ancestors, to whom one's obligations never cease, an issue that I explain in more detail in the following section. Traditional Buddhist notions are also attached to these explanations as well. For instance, the notion of *gongde* ("beneficient works") is often cited in discussions of overseas Chinese donations. Charitable giving is supposed to have good repercussions not only for oneself and one's family, but also for one's descendants.

However, villagers see other aspects of giving beyond primordial connections or the building up of religious merit. In general, giving increases one's status or "face" (*mianzi*), and this possibility of raising status through giving certainly applies to returnees as well as to permanent residents of the area. Villagers nonetheless view this phenomenon somewhat ambivalently. They welcome donations, but on occasion they may deride the pride that can motivate them.

For instance, just a few miles up the road from Moonshadow Pond was the home of a former smuggler who had grown up in the Indian Chinese community. In India he had run afoul of the law, and he had therefore returned to his native village in China to build a house for his elderly mother. Despite his former occupation, as well as conflicting relationships with his own sons and three former wives, none of whom returned with him, he endeavored to attain a solid reputation in his ancestral home by making generous public and private donations. After several years of giving, however, he experienced financial troubles. Both his family members and unrelated villagers explained his predicament as stemming from the fact that he "loved 'face' too much" (*tai ai mianzi*), in other words, that he was too concerned with raising his status by public giving, and therefore went bankrupt.

"When a *huaqiao* returns to the area," my landlady told me one day, "he almost always takes the local level officials out for a big meal, and also gives them *hongbao*" (little red envelopes in which money is placed). While gift-giving is an important part of social interaction throughout Chinese society (Yang 1994; Yan 1996; Kipnis 1997; Hsing 1997), villagers in Moonshadow Pond view this kind of behavior as an especially prominent feature of overseas Chinese, primarily because so many returning *huaqiao* have more financial resources than their rural cousins.

This ability of overseas Chinese to dispense money and other gifts also has implications for villagers' moral evaluations of each other. There is much to be gained from cultivating relationships with wealthy visitors, but villagers will harshly judge a person who is seen as playing up to an overseas Chinese visitor, with whom he or she does not have a close family connection, purely for the purposes of monetary gain. Many like to quote an old proverb that says, "last night you were just a three pound dog, but today, you are my third great uncle" as a way of expressing the rapidity with which relationships change when a person suddenly becomes rich. My neighbor in the village described for me one day, in very disapproving tones, how one man in Moonshadow Pond had recently toadied up to a returnee in order to get funds to buy a special motorcycle for his son, who was disabled. This returnee was a former Nationalist soldier who had fled to Taiwan forty years earlier, but now spent a few months each year in Moonshadow Pond, since it was his native village. Stories also traveled throughout the village of individuals who impugned others' motives in front of this same retired soldier, ostensibly for the purpose of gaining his favors for their own benefit.

Nevertheless, those who receive help are supposed to appreciate it. A woman in the village who had a job cooking for the returned Nationalist soldier decided to quit her job because she was tired of his infamous bad temper. Since he had supported her beyond her salary, including paying her daughter's high school tuition, many people said she should have stayed longer and swallowed the insults.

The most extreme example of taking advantage of overseas Chinese deep pockets was that of a professional gambler. One of his most frequent tricks was to go to the county capital, not far from the village, and lure overseas Chinese into a variety of gambling games and card tricks. Because of his skill at both gambling and deception, he often won big in these games, effectively emptying the pockets of the visitors whom he engaged in play. But the hapless victims of his gambling talents were strangers. He would not have been able to take such advantage of returnees to his own village.

Returnees as Kin

In one sense, the return of overseas relations to Moonshadow Pond is only a continuum of returns that all Chinese experience. As Charles Stafford points out in his fascinating study of separation and reunion in China, "narratives and rituals of separation and reunion" are highly elaborated in Chinese society (2000: 177). Many of these reunion rituals revolve around the New Year's celebrations when family members from all over China and even further away return to their natal homes (46).[4] At this time, not only the living, but also the ancestors, and certain gods such as the God of Wealth (Caishen), are invited to return—both ancestors and gods enticed back with offerings.

Returning *huaqiao* are different from other family members who return because they return less frequently than family members who live within China, and because they return from societies with different political or cultural compositions. As shown earlier, expectations surround their return that would not surround that of a son returning to visit his home village from a Chinese city, or a married daughter arriving with her husband to share a New Year's feast with her natal family.

It is important to define what is meant by kin in the rural Chinese context. Moonshadow Pond is a single lineage village, and all village residents (except for women who have married in) see themselves as connected by descent. They use the term *ziji ren* ("persons within the same circle") to refer to one another, and most returnees share this identity with other residents of Moonshadow Pond. Individuals related through marriage are referred to differently as *qinqi*, a word that is often translated into English as "relatives," but which has a more specific connotation in the Chinese case. After arrival in one's ancestral village, a returnee may also choose to visit friends or *qinqi* in other villages. But these villages are by definition not their home. "Home" is where one's descent group resides.

In Moonshadow Pond, as in many other villages in southeastern China, an ancestral temple stands at the center of the original area of settlement. It honors the lineage ancestors as far back as the village founders (said to have arrived in Moonshadow Pond in the seventeenth century). To the side of this temple is a second structure honoring the descendants of one lineage branch. Arriving at the village for the first time, or returning after a long absence, an overseas returnee is expected to proceed to the entrance of the village and make offerings to the village gods who protect it. Visiting kin should then go to the ancestral temple, and after that ascend the mountains surrounding the village to worship at their more immediate ancestors' graves.

Moonshadow Pond residents expect returning *huaqiao* to make offerings to village gods and ancestors before going anywhere else. This applies to both men and women. For while men's names are recorded for posterity in the lineage history, the daughters and daughters-in-law of the lineage are also expected to honor the remote ancestors of their fathers or husbands, as well as to visit the gravesites of their own parents and grandparents. Family members from the village also expect returnees to host at least a small banquet for their closest relations.

However, villagers feel that long years abroad may diminish returnees' sense of connection with their ancestors. And, they like to tell moral vignettes about the eventual fate of people who ignore the specified rites of reunion and commemoration of ancestors and consequently, are struck with misfortune or ill health, much like the hapless individual in the second of the stories that begins this chapter.

"*Huaqiao* who are not born here don't have a concept about their ancestors," my landlord said to me one day. He was equally perplexed by his elder brother, a former Nationalist soldier who had fled to Taiwan in 1949, and now returned every few years to visit. Why had his brother bought a flat in the city when everyone knew that when you grow old you would want to return to your native village? This proved, my landlord asserted, that his brother had a very strange way of calculating things (*da gui suanpan*, literally "use the abacus in a strange way"). My landlord contrasted his brother unfavorably with a sister-in-law. Although this sister-in-law resided in Taiwan and never visited the mainland, she sent money every Chinese New Year to my landlord and his wife, so that they could buy offerings to give to the ancestors on her behalf.

The ideal of remembering the ancestors connects easily to the notion that *huaqiao* have a responsibility for their living relatives as well. Villagers often write letters to relatives with whom they have not been in contact for years, and whom they have never met. Indeed, while living in the village I translated into English several letters written to second-generation relatives who no longer could read Chinese. Some letters were attempts to reestablish ties, while others were more direct pleas for help. The latter may occur when a family member has been struck with a serious illness and overwhelming medical expenses, or in the context of wanting to build a new house.

This expectation of help from returning kin also contains the roots of discord among those who remained behind. My notes are filled with examples of disputes that center upon money remitted from abroad. Usually the problems begin when one family member claims that other family members are hoarding remittances that were supposed to be dispersed. At other times, a family member will complain that an overseas relative is helping one branch of the family more than others.

"The closer someone is to you the more they act like a stranger" (*yue qin yue jian gui*) said a friend of mine. In her estimation, her paternal uncle had not been particularly helpful to their family when he returned for a visit. Yet, these expectations and reactions are just a more extreme example of general tendencies at work in contemporary rural China. As Anagnost (1989) points out, there is still a strong egalitarian current running through the Chinese countryside. This current is influenced by ideas of reciprocity operative in the countryside before the Communist era (which encouraged banqueting and contributions to ritual functions on the part of the elite), as well as by the continued influence of the Maoist period with its emphasis on destratification and radical egalitarianism. Anagnost points out that while the official press is skeptical about customary means of satisfying reciprocity norms such as banqueting, it encourages contributions to village infrastructure. As such, expectations regarding visiting kin remain high from all quarters. In her study of social relationships in urban China, Mayfair Yang relates a story about a woman who never returned to her native place, precisely because she dreaded the number of gifts she would have to bring (Yang 1994: 113).[5]

One must keep in mind that post-reform changes in the Chinese economy exacerbate the disparities that can be created by overseas remittances. During the Maoist era, when relations with overseas kin were almost completely severed, there were few ways one family could become vastly richer than another. Flaunting wealth would in any case make one politically suspect and even be dangerous, especially during the Cultural Revolution era. In addition, there was simply little way to differentiate oneself economically from fellow villagers. Everyone worked for the collective. One's labor contribution was measured in work points recorded by the accountant of each production team, and a large part of the payment was in staples rather than in cash. One could earn more by working longer hours, or perhaps collect more work points by taking on more taxing and more highly valued jobs within the production team. A family might also bring in more work points if most family members were able bodied workers rather than young or elderly dependents. Beyond this, there was little a family could do to differentiate themselves economically from others.

After the early 1980s, many families built new homes, television became ubiquitous, and clothing and diet became much more varied. Meat and fruit became much more common features of the diet and were no longer saved for a few holidays a year. To make a long and complicated story of economic transformation short, money makes a difference now that there are things to buy. Competition for the attention of overseas visitors must be viewed in this context as well.

Not surprisingly, while Moonshadow Pond residents expect and desire assistance from their own relations, visits by these returning kin help nurture an undercurrent of grudging resentment among families. And, this is not purely about finances, but also about more symbolic kinds of status. In ways that remind one of the famous Trobriand *kula* trade, many people told me that the same item given as a gift was much more desirable than if one had purchased it oneself. When a friend of mine from Hong Kong visited her relatives in Moonshadow Pond, she gave gold bracelets to three older women with whom she was friendly. A fourth woman felt snubbed and mentioned these gifts to several others. Likewise, my landlady's daughter told me how her mother-in-law wanted to say that I had given her a gold bracelet, and she would gladly give me the money to purchase it—as long as she could say it was a gift from me.

Of course, in addition to the status achieved from displaying relatively small gifts, there is also the question of much larger amounts of financial assistance. Some gifts can help a family build a house, buy an expensive consumer item, or start a business, and thereby have a significant impact upon their economic circumstances. While almost all residents of Moonshadow Pond have experienced increasing prosperity in the post-Mao order, they have also witnessed the emergence of much greater economic differentiation between families. Overseas connections are not the sole explanation for this, but they do play a role. Villagers know which families have overseas connections, and they know which of these connections have added to the economic well-being of the family. Pointing to the success of Jinsheng Ge, the village doctor, my neighbor said to me, "Of course they are well off. Not only is their business successful, but also Jinsheng Ge's mother has connections with her uncle's family in Thailand and her brother's family in Hong Kong. *We* had to make it without any help from *huaqiao*."

Despite the jealousy it may engender in those without overseas connections, willingness to help family and kin is still the most prominent value by which villagers assess the moral caliber of returnees. This emphasis is evidenced in the case of one particular category of kin—the men who fled China in the wake of the Communist victory because they were Nationalist soldiers. All but one of the former soldiers who fled Moonshadow Pond had abandoned wives and families in their retreat, married again, and started new families in Taiwan. Although they had virtually no contact with their families throughout the Maoist period, they were able to reestablish connections during the reform era initiated by Deng Xiaoping. Indeed, the subject of former Nationalist soldiers who return to the mainland to visit children and first wives was recently a popular subject of television dramas and movies in both the PRC and Taiwan.

In Moonshadow Pond, four emigrants fit this description in whole or in part. In one case, the former wife also fled the village, remarried, and started a family elsewhere. She left her son with her husband's brother, who raised him while she remained in contact. In another case, the entire family was able to flee. In other families, the wives who remained behind did not remarry, but remained in their in-laws' homes to raise their children. All these men have returned to the village at least once, some living in the village with their adult children for several months at a time. All who left children and spouses behind have sent back considerable remittances, enough to distinguish their families economically from those of many other villagers. When I asked villagers about whether these men should have remained faithful to their first wives, no one said they believed they should.

What was important, they said, was that they should remember from where they came and help their abandoned families.

One former soldier has actually returned and built a house in the village where he stays for several months each year. But unlike the others, he returns primarily to avoid his familial relationships in Taiwan rather than to reconnect with abandoned family members in China. This retired soldier was unmarried when he left China, and he is unable to get along with any of his sons or his wife back in Taiwan. Although he has a sister in China who lives in the county capital not far from the village, she also has little to do with him. Villagers noted that he had no close kin to care for him, and that he had to pay people from a different sublineage to tend to him when he became seriously ill. His presence in the village, therefore, is viewed ambivalently, since it is the direct result of his failure in familial relationships. While treated respectfully, he is also the focus of negative gossip, much of it relating to his bad temper and familial relations. "Guosheng Ge has money," people say, "but he does not always *zuo ren*," a Chinese expression which means to act humanely. The respect he may have garnered as a result of his wealth, as well as the implicit status he grants to the village by returning to it (an issue I discuss in the next section), is diminished considerably because of his bad family relationships.

In certain ways, the standards used to evaluate returnees as kin, the expectations and the disappointments, are not all that different from the standards which would be expected from any economically successful kin. But unlike kin who return to visit from cities within China, *huaqiao* are different *because* they are foreign. This creates a number of conundrums for the villagers. Can one expect perfect filiality and familial devotion from those who have lived and acculturated to foreign customs and culture abroad? Are there limits to familial loyalty?

Returnees as Foreigners

The villagers' doubts about whether returnees understand ancestral ideology is a good example of how returnees come to be seen as embodying at least some foreign attributes (since villagers also doubt that foreigners honor their own ancestors). Indeed, as mentioned earlier, visiting relatives from abroad are sometimes referred to as *fanke* ("foreign guests"). Both words convey the category outsider, since family and lineage members visiting from within China are not usually referred to as either "guests" or "foreign."

Although some returnees may reside in the village for several months at a time, and may gradually acclimate themselves to the pace of village life, other visits may be brief, lasting only a few days, and the visitors may stay at a hotel in the nearby county capital rather than with relatives in the village. This choice is explained as resulting from the returnees' inability to "adjust" (*xiguan*) to life in the countryside after years of a much easier life abroad. Indeed, residence abroad is viewed as having a profound and irreversible impact upon returnees. For instance, villagers were surprised that I traveled by bicycle since returnees rarely do so.

They assumed that the *huaqiao* reluctance to use a bicycle was an attitude picked up from living abroad. Similarly, as noted earlier, the failure of a few returnees to give priority to ancestral ritual was also explained as a result of long years abroad.

Huaqiao foreignness is also embodied by their legal status and by their ideological orientation toward state and party. Legally, *huaqiao* have a somewhat liminal status. When they first visit they must register with a special *huaqiao* office in the local public security bureau. However, unlike the situation during the Cultural Revolution period, their access to their relatives is unrestricted, and they can stay in China for longer periods of uninterrupted time than ordinary foreign visitors. Spending time with these foreign kin exposes villagers to heterodox opinions that may implicitly or explicitly critique Party hegemony. I have heard visiting relatives criticize local newscasts, newspapers, and other media as both narrow and slanted. One villager told me that he had never thought about how limited the daily newscasts were until his uncle visited from abroad and complained about them.

Since it is much harder for villagers to leave China than for *huaqiao* to return, returnees often create a window on the rest of the world. It was not uncommon for villagers to ply a visitor with hours of questions about Taiwan, Hong Kong, or another far-flung country from which he or she was visiting. One might view this give and take as an element of larger processes of cultural globalization or transnationalism (Appadurai 1991, 1996; Basch et al. 1994). But, if it is part of a transnational process, then it is the localization of the global (Watson 1997) that is most notable here. Whatever stories are told, and however returnees decide to comport themselves, they are quickly pulled into the local world of gossip, moral judgments, and status evaluations. In this case, it is important not to overestimate the global or transnational side of this process.

Likewise, returnees may also be viewed as a potential political threat because they occasionally articulate views that are critical of state power or of its media. However, in Moonshadow Pond, at least over the short term, there is insufficient evidence to view returnees as having any kind of unsettling effect on state power at the local level. In fact, returnees often legitimize this power by treating officials to banquets and plying them with gifts and money in attempts to either gain favors or at least ensure an uneventful visit. And when returnees donate to a visible public project such as a school, local cadres are always present at the ceremonies acknowledging these gifts and thanking the donors. Obviously, the marginal legal status of returnees is also significant here. Despite any ideological heterodoxy returnees may inject into the local scene, their actual behavior does little to challenge local or national political structures and even supports them.[6]

Conclusion

The opportunity to reunite with overseas kin is welcomed enthusiastically by the residents of Moonshadow Pond, but it also creates an unsettled space of discourse. In this space, desire for status and material wealth is both expressed and satirized, expectations of family loyalty are both fulfilled and sometimes shattered, returnees are both family and foreigners.

The idea that overseas visitors are guests as well as family, is yet another contradiction in the discourse about them. Not only are returnees family, lineage mates, and potential benefactors, but in addition, they are "guests." Moonshadow Pond residents take great pride in their hospitality, and they say that hospitality is a specialty of Hakka culture. Guests are greeted by acknowledging the time and trouble they have taken to visit, and a common polite expression uttered upon the arrival of a guest is to exclaim "so much heart" (*hen you xin*), tipping one's hat so to speak to the long or difficult journey that the guest may have just endured.

Villagers told me that being a good host was a matter of "face" (*mianzi*). Any guest, no matter how rich or poor, must be treated with hospitality, merely because of the guest's thoughtfulness in visiting. In this sense, there is an egalitarian aspect to the notion of hospitality. But in reality not all guests produce the same amount of status for their hosts. As we have seen, the higher the status of the visitor, the more "face" is gained by the host.[7] Gifts from overseas visitors not only add to a family's status by increasing its wealth, but they also add to the recipient's relative status in the village merely by association with the overseas donor.

Admittedly, there is a strong relationship between gift giving and social status in Chinese society, regardless of the connection with overseas return. Those with many connections (*guanxi*) have high status and more "face" (*mianzi*), and one way these are rendered visible is by the number of gifts one receives (Yan 1996). Similarly, return is a common occurrence for many rural Chinese families (Stafford 2000), even if only from the nearest county capital. Nevertheless, in both return and gift giving, the involvement of overseas returnees accentuates the process of status enhancement. As such, those with fewer overseas connections lose out in two ways; they lose out on material help, and they also lose in an arena of status competition.

Yet, as shown in this chapter, even in the case of those without overseas relations there is a complex play of moral and status evaluations. Those who have no overseas connections may always take solace (and the moral high ground!) by demonstrating that they did not manipulate relationships merely for material benefit. Further, while returnees are welcomed as kin and benefactors, their foreignness can lead to transgressions of local moral expectations, especially in the familial realm—troubles and potential embarrassments that are avoided by those without close overseas relations.

Thus, returnees become enmeshed in a web of local judgements about both themselves and their hosts. Glorious as any visit may be in itself, it also becomes the template for a host of competing imperatives and expectations.

Chapter 6
Changing Filipina Identities and Ambivalent Returns

Nicole Constable

> For all of us, in good times and bad, the image of home is multilayered, and the notion of return is unsettling
>
> —Carol Stack (1996)

> Diaspora women are caught between patriarchies, ambiguous pasts, and futures. They connect and disconnect, forget and remember, in complex, strategic ways.
>
> —James Clifford (1994)

Hong Kong is one of the wealthiest cities in Asia, a center of world trade, a place of many comings and goings. It is an international hub, whose social and cultural landscape is heterogeneous, hybrid, and transnational. Hong Kong's population of 6.4 million includes over 130,000 Filipino domestic workers, representing the territory's largest non-Chinese minority. In the 1970s only a few hundred Filipinas worked as "domestic helpers" for expatriate employers in the colonial city. These workers' popularity quickly grew among the burgeoning middle-class Chinese population, which found it increasingly difficult to attract local Chinese women to do paid household work. By the 1990s well over 10 percent of Hong Kong's population employed domestic workers. Women of numerous other nationalities (among them Thai, Indonesian, Sri Lankan, Indian, and Malaysian), are included among foreign domestic workers, but by far the largest group is women from the Philippines. The majority of Filipinas are between the ages of twenty and forty, most are Roman Catholic, and approximately a quarter are married. Contrary to many locals' expectations, Filipina domestic workers do not come from the poorest or least educated sector of the Philippine population. The vast majority have graduated from high school, and some come from middle-class families. They come to Hong Kong on two-year contracts, with temporary work permits administered by the Philippine Overseas Employment Association and the Hong Kong labor and immigration departments. Employment contracts stipulate that domestic workers should be provided with room and board and a minimum salary. In 1995 minimum monthly wages were HK$3,750 (U.S.$480), one of the best domestic worker salaries in Asia. By far the largest group of employers today are local Chinese who have recently joined the ranks of Hong Kong's growing middle class and belong to double-income households (Constable 1996a, 1997a, b).

The reunification of Hong Kong with the mainland in 1997, serves as an important backdrop to this chapter. A topic of concern, the reunification created a context in which discussions of home, or perhaps more accurately homelessness or dislocation, were common. The practical issue of where one would be after July 1, 1997 had to be addressed by both Chinese and non-Chinese. Filipina domestic workers—some of whom had begun to "feel at home" in the course of completing several two-year contracts in someone else's home—commented to one another, sometimes regretfully, about the inevitable impermanence of their stay, and they spoke of returning to the Philippines for good, or entertained fantasies of working in other new and exciting places. Despite Chinese and Philippine official assurances that they would be permitted to stay, workers expressed concern (Manila Chronicle 1997a, b, c). One Filipina domestic worker wrote in *Tinig Filipino*, a magazine published in Hong Kong for Filipino overseas workers,

By the year 1997, Hong Kong will be returned by the British Government to China. This is really a big issue, not only for the Chinese people but for us Filipinos too. The year 1997 is killing people's minds. For us migrant workers, we really are affected with this issue. . . . We do not know what will happen in the later years. So while we still have the chance, try to save as much as you can and bring a bag of money home. (Manguera 1996: 22)

Notably, the reunification had different implications for Filipino Overseas Contract Workers (OCWs) versus for Chinese locals. To some Hong Kong Chinese, reunification represented a desired end to foreign rule; a return to the homeland or the motherland. Yet not all Hong Kong Chinese openly expressed such unambiguous optimism. Many viewed the changeover with apprehension, nostalgia, or considered it simply a shift from one colonizer to another (Chow 1992). A Chinese school teacher, explaining her ambivalence toward reunification, said to me "how would you feel, if your adoptive parents (the only parents you've ever known) returned you to the natural mother who wanted you back and had given you up long ago?" Hong Kong, as Chow writes, "knows itself as a bastard and orphan" (1992: 157). Hong Kong Chinese might see themselves as returning home or, in a sense in exile at home. One Chinese employer, commenting on the difference between her own situation and that of foreign domestic workers, noted bitterly that "at least *they* have a home to go back to."

Filipino OCWs would unanimously agree that they do have "a home to go back to," yet home is not as simple and unambiguous as the Chinese employer's comment implies. Reunification raised many issues for overseas workers, the most obvious being financial. A *Tinig Filipino* article entitled "Are You Preparing for Your Future?" captured a common feeling:

Everyone of us dreams someday of going home to the Philippines to be with our loved ones—far from the daily toil of cleaning toilets, washing other people's clothes, living with strangers who look down on us. But what will happen to us when we go home? . . . Many of us are trapped by the realization that, once we go home we would have no source of income. (*Tinig Filipino* 1995: 36)

Accompanying the economic concern is the more subtle question of "how will I *fit in* when I go home?" This question is a more private, personalized, or idiosyncratic concern than the collective economic one that is easily articulated and much more openly discussed. The anticipation of what it might be like to go back for good are based on experiences of brief ten- or twelve-day visits spent in the Philippines once a year, or every other year. A short story by a Filipina domestic worker, published in Hong Kong primarily for an audience of OCWs and entitled "The Great Divide," speaks directly of the possible feeling of alienation in its opening lines: "After being away from home for eight years now, Diane felt like a stranger in her parents' home. The whole house was no longer the same haven from which she used to derive so much comfort" (Torrefranca 1992: 31). Domestic workers express regret at the thought of leaving Hong Kong. Anonas writes "Surely we will miss Hong Kong" when "the time comes for us to go back home for good" (1995: 28). "Ahhh—Hong Kong" writes Mendoza, "we have managed to mingle with your flow of life," and she expresses her "secret protest" against leaving what has become "like a home away from home" to many foreign workers (1996: 26; see also Arellano 1992).

In this chapter I address questions about the meaning of home—in its various and contradictory forms—for Filipina domestic workers in Hong Kong. Drawing on interviews and literature collected in Hong Kong between 1993 and 1997, I argue that even though most women stress their economic motivations for working in Hong Kong, these comprise but a small part of the many complex reasons why they come, why they remain, and why they return. Five brief sketches of domestic workers frame this study and raise broader issues. These five women, like most I met, stayed in Hong Kong much longer than they had originally planned, and like the other women they all considered economic motivations critical to their decision to emigrate. I focus on these women not only because they are among those whom I knew best, but also because they expressed various degrees of ambivalence toward return, and various degrees of success in reconciling parts of their diasporic lives. Collectively they illustrate a spectrum of attitudes toward home based not solely on their identity as migrant workers, but also on their identities as wives, widows, daughters, and/or mothers.

These particular cases raise broader questions about the nature of home and exile: In what sense, under what circumstances, and in what ways, has Hong Kong become home for Filipina domestic workers? To what extent are their images of the Philippines as home transformed by the process of migration to Hong

Kong and return? How are migrant imaginings of home—in relation to family and gender—reconfigured by migrant experiences? Finally, what are the implications of these imaginings given the social realities of return?

Home, Diaspora, and Exile

English words such as "home," "homesick," "holiday," and "DH contract" are commonly interjected into Tagalog, Visayan, and other Philippine languages in Hong Kong, creating, for example, in the case of Tagalog and English, what is popularly referred to as "Taglish." A domestic worker might use the English phrase "going home" to mean returning to either the Philippines or to her place of residence in Hong Kong. Although a worker might say "It's late and I'm going home," another might comment "it's not *my* home, it's my employer's home." Some workers will say that they "feel at home" with their employer or in Hong Kong. Referring to Central District on Sundays, one domestic worker stated "This is a piece of home . . . I come here each week and it doesn't feel so bad to be away from home" (*Manila Chronicle* 1997a: 8). A Filipino journalist advises Filipinos who "feel homesick" in Hong Kong to go to Statue Square in Central District where they can "feel . . . right in Luneta, Quiapo, or Divisadora" (Madamba 1993: 56). Similarly, Arellano (1992) notes that because of the clusters of Filipinos and Filipino food, games, magazines, and languages spoken, some regions of Hong Kong have become like a "home away from home." More often "home"— with its powerful emotional implications—refers to a worker's place of residence in the Philippines, as in the poem entitled "My Beloved Home" by a domestic worker in Hong Kong. Of her house in the Philippines, Ragus writes, in somewhat anthropomorphised terms:

> You are a gift of God; Meant for me
> Long before the first beat of my life.
> You are my House; Which hands had built
> Which minds had formed; With love,
> You became my Home. . . .
>
> May my Home be steadfast and unchanged
> With open doors awaiting my return;
> For whether a success or failure I become;
> Where else can I go, but back to my Beloved
> Where I can be myself—Home is where my heart is. (1992: 57–58)

Scholarship and folk wisdom shared by Filipinos and English speakers provide contradictory notions of home. Is home, as the English proverb indicates, "where you hang your hat" (the physical location where you work or happen to be, such as an employer's flat in Hong Kong)? Or is it, as Ragus concludes "where your heart is" (a place of emotional attachment, a social space where family and lovers reside)? While the first proverb stresses more explicitly, it seems, the geographic location where you happen to be, the second suggests that "home" is identified more with affective ties or social relationships. Ragus's poem, evokes a sense of home as both the house in her native country and the affective ties that are connected to it. Like Rushdie's remembered childhood residence in Bombay, a focal point in his *Imaginary Homelands* (1991), it is useful to conceive of home as involving some degree of both location (at least an imaginary one) and relations—thus constituting a social and physical "space" as opposed to simply a "place" (Abbas 1994: 442). Ragus's home, in other words, is a place—rendered unchanging and two-dimensional by her absence—or alternatively as a space that cannot be separated from the social, political and cultural dimensions of her life as a migrant worker in Hong Kong.

Some important contributions to the study and conceptualization of home come from literary and cultural studies. Edward Said, for example, has explained how home and exile are integrally connected, he outlines key distinctions between types of emigres, and he describes "true exile" as a "condition of terminal loss" and insurmountable sadness (1984: 159, 166–67), yet also views it, more positively, as the basis for an important "plurality of vision" (172). Writing about post-independence African writers in exile, Parker further problematizes Said's notion of home—suggesting that one can, paradoxically, be more at home in exile (1993: 67). Rushdie's nostalgic remembrances of home in Bombay are written from outside India. England may be a place that lacks certain sentimental attachments for Rushdie, but it has provided him with safety and the practical comforts of a home in which he can presumably "find satisfaction with the task of writing." Similarly, domestic workers may sometimes feel more at home in Hong Kong even while they continue to imagine the Philippines—in particular ways—as home.

Filipina domestic workers are of course not, strictly speaking, exiles, since they express some degree of choice in going to Hong Kong, but they are in some ways *like* exiles (Said 1984: 159–67). They often feel forced by economic and personal circumstances to go abroad. Overseas contract labor is undoubtedly, inextricably connected with global economic and historical processes (particularly the labor export policy of the Philippines, and the demand for cheap household labor in Hong Kong) (Constable 1996, 1997a, b). At times for some, life abroad is overwhelmingly experienced with sorrow as loss and deprivation. For others, however, like the exiled emigre writers Parker describes (1993), their native Philippines may be the space where their affections center, yet they may also experience Hong Kong as a source of satisfaction, as a place where they participate in meaningful activities, and it can serve as a refuge of sorts. Despite the hardships entailed in the work they do there, Hong Kong is a place in which foreign workers can sometimes feel "at home," the space from which they develop a "plural vision" (Said 1984: 172).

Said (1984: 159–62) urges us to think beyond the literature of exile and the literary figures who have produced it, to the experiences of the masses who have lived through it. Yet there exist relatively few explicitly ethnographic (as opposed to literary or fictional) explorations of the emotions and experiences of returning home (notable exceptions include Stack 1996; Lavie and Swedenburg 1996; Feld and Basso 1996; Schiller et al. 1992). Yet the burgeoning literature on transnationalism in anthropology and cultural studies illustrates the way in which migration does not necessitate an emotional or material severing of ties with home, but can form the basis for a multi-sited community, an important point also borne out by studies of Filipino migrant workers (Constable 1996a; Margold 1995, this volume). Clifford calls for greater awareness of distinctions between diasporic situations and experiences (1994). He argues that the ideal type model of diaspora proposed by Safran overlooks "the principled ambivalence about physical return and attachment to land" (1994: 305, emphasis in original). Although a minor point in Clifford's article, the theme of ambivalence toward physical return is one I seek to develop here, because it appears in many Filipina narratives of return.

The engendering of diasporic situations is also of central importance (Clifford 1994; Buijs 1993; Georges 1992; Wiltshire 1992). The vast majority of Filipino domestic workers in Hong Kong are women, and most are unmarried and in their twenties and thirties—an age when "normally" they would be at home, married, and having children of their own, rather than cleaning the homes and caring for the children of their employers (Constable 1996, 1997a). As Clifford notes, women may gain greater "relative independence and control," or alternatively, "life for women in diasporic situations can be doubly painful" as women struggle "with the material and spiritual insecurities of exile, with the demands of family and work, and with the claims of old and new patriarchies" (1994: 314). Yet "despite these hardships," women "may refuse the option of return when it presents itself, especially when the terms are dictated by men" (314). This is not to say that men always or necessarily control the conditions of return. Women also attempt to negotiate return on their own terms.

Migration has transposed women's household work onto a grand transnational scale wherein Filipinas perform the household chores of middle-class Chinese and expatriate women. Home for most Filipina domestic workers is no longer congruent with the household in which they reside. Instead, home is tied to ideas of family back in the Philippines, even as that family is reconfigured by their own absence and remittances. As the examples that follow suggest, life in Hong Kong poses new challenges to their identities as wives, daughters, and/or mothers. And some women seem better able than others to successfully link the two facets of their lives, and to imagine and enact ways to challenge or reconfigure gender and family roles from afar (Georges 1992; Wiltshire 1992). Rather than point to the commonalities of experiences that are linked to the same broad historical, global, and political processes of migration, the following examples demonstrate the diverse experiences of displaced persons.

Acosta

Acosta, like the other women described below, stayed in Hong Kong far longer than she originally planned, but like them she was willing to discuss her prolonged stay in more than superficial terms. I came to know Acosta in 1993, her fifteenth year of work in Hong Kong, and briefly caught up with her again in 1997. She was married, in her forties, the mother of a teenage son and daughter. In an interview, Acosta told me of her excitement at returning to the Philippines, about the all too brief "honeymoon period" she experienced when she reunited with her family, the pleasure she felt at unpacking the multitude of gifts that she had carefully selected and accumulated over the past two years, and then the subtle shift that took place sometime within the two-week visit, which left her with an impatient, urgent desire to return to Hong Kong. As she explained, "This is how it always is. When I go back home for a week or ten days we [my husband and I] get along very well. He is attracted to me and we are very happy. But any longer than that and I am thinking . . . I just want to come back here again." After a week Acosta began to worry that she could not maintain the level of excitement in general, that she did not fit in, and that she would not satisfy her husband sexually. Her friends told her that she "should not worry about exciting sex" at her age. After spending most of her married life away from her husband, she seemed frustrated that they could not maintain the relationship of their youth. On trips home, she becomes "just a nagging wife and we fight a lot. He always wants to know where I am going and I get angry." Unlike in Hong Kong, "I have to tell him where I am going all the time."

Acosta only hinted that her dissatisfaction was a result of having spent time in Hong Kong. Home no longer satisfies her and she soon becomes unhappy and restless. She likes to work in Hong Kong, and life is "not so exciting back home." The relief she expressed on her return to Hong Kong seemed almost palpable. She quickly resumed her busy work routine and in her spare time still scanned the street markets for bargains—gifts she would accumulate to send back with neighbors or townmates, perhaps a new blouse for herself. She had become—for many reasons—more comfortable in Hong Kong than in the Philippines.

Yet despite the concerns Acosta expressed to me in deep confidence about her desire to settle there, the Philippines remained her "home" and she fully intended to return there one day for good. She fondly stroked photographs of her children, and beamed as she showed me pictures of the material improvements afforded by her remittances. She insisted that life was good in the Philippines; she was convinced that her husband was faithful (with one brief exceptional interlude) and that her children loved and appreciated her despite their repeated pleas that she "come home for good."

The last time we spoke in 1993, Acosta assured me that she was on her last contract. Pointing to her ambivalence about Hong Kong and home, she explained that her daughter—in her late teens by then—was "threatening to come to work as a helper" in Hong Kong, too. While sufficient for her, it was not the future she had envisioned for her daughter. "I came here so she wouldn't have to!" she said in an exasperated tone, and she was planning to go back to convince her daughter—once and for all—not to come. The key, she thought, was to tell her daughter that she herself was finally finished with Hong Kong. Acosta expressed frustration at this ironic (yet not so uncommon) twist of fate, repeating "I came here so she wouldn't have to."

In the summer of 1997, it was difficult to recapture the intimacy of our earlier conversations. When I expressed surprise that she was still in Hong Kong, she stressed the standard explanation. The "main reason" she kept coming back, she said, was "to earn more money for my family because it will be more difficult to live there with little money. I don't know how long we will be allowed to stay in Hong Kong [after 1997], but I will stay just a little bit longer." A friend of Acosta's said more bluntly, "Acosta has been away so long, she is just afraid to go back." Another domestic worker offered the following explanation. "It could be because she has been here so many years. She has got used to the way of life, every-thing. . . . If you're here for a long time and you go back to the Philippines, you see how poor it is, the traffic in Manila is so bad, the transportation so bad. I think Hong Kong is so much more organized; the technology is newer. I think there are some people who come from the provinces, it changes the way they dress, how they eat. They become like their employers."

The feeling that "it is sometimes difficult to go back"—described to me in more or less poignant terms by several women—was not uncommon, yet many women were extremely reluctant to talk about it. It is much easier and far more acceptable for workers to explain the return to Hong Kong as simply and overwhelmingly eco-nomically motivated. I was told on countless occasions, "We come back because we need to earn money!" "I came back because I have many debts to pay back." "We come back because we have our families to support." With the approach of 1997 the question was no longer only "Why do you come?" but "Will you stay?" or "How long will you stay?" An online newspaper recorded typical responses:

Enticed by the money, Virginia Bernardo, 40, left her job as a saleswoman in the Philip-pines and headed for Hong Kong seven years ago. Her four sisters also came to fill their billfolds. "I'll wait to see what the situation is like after the handover," Bernardo said. "But I plan to work one more two-year contract, save more money and try to start a business at home. . . ."

Cresencia Dalpasen, 26, said that she had also come to Hong Kong for the money. Dal-pasen has been with the same employer since arriving in October 1994 and said she plans to "stay in Hong Kong after July 1 to keep earning money, but if there are any problems, I'll go home." (*Daily Yomiuri* On-Line 1997)

Economic motivations are without a doubt an important and primary factor in women's decisions to work overseas. Yet, money is also the easy answer, the gen-erally most acceptable answer, and to some extent an automatic and incomplete response that tends to cover up the richness and idiosyncrasy that ethnography can sometimes uncover. If taken as the *only* answer, economic motivations obscure other more painful, less comfortable, less socially acceptable, but equally impor-tant—and sometimes contradictory—answers that linger below the surface as suggested by Acosta's ambivalence.

Women who forget that they are in Hong Kong for economic reasons, however, are quickly corrected or criticized. Domestic worker Cayog begins her *Tinig Filipino* article by conveying a sense of the seductive attraction of Hong Kong: "Hong Kong is a beautiful place where people of different nationalities spend their holidays. We see lots of beautiful and fantastic work of expert hands here that tend to conquer our minds and our hearts. Sometimes because of this, we develop the desire of not leaving this beautiful place" (Cayog 1996: 22). The main point of the article, however, is to remind women of the "human suffering" behind Hong Kong's deceptive "gleaming lights," and, like Gamboa, she urges Filipinas to "remember that we are here to work and not for pleasure" (Gamboa 1996: 22).

Another pat answer to the question why women return to Hong Kong—often paired with the economic one and equally acceptable—has to do with family obligations, filial piety, and family relations. That is, many women go to work overseas out of a desire to help their families, a motivation that is highly valued in Philippine culture. It is considered honorable and admirable for a daughter to delay or sacrifice marriage in order to work abroad for the sake of her parents and siblings. The sacrifice of a married woman who misses the day-to-day experiences of family life in order to provide for her family is also appreciated. But what this answer—like the economic one—neglects, is that some women also go abroad to get away from parents, in-laws, siblings, husbands, and children.

Attempting to probe beyond the realm of filial piety and finances, I talked to women I knew about others who had admitted to me that they were not so eager to go back to the Philippines. The response reflected another clear pattern. I was told that in cases like Acosta's there must be "something wrong at home." Marites, a volunteer at a nonprofit organization for overseas workers, after hearing about Acosta, offered the following account of her friend Delores who "had little choice" but to return to Hong Kong because of the "trouble at home."

Delores learned that her husband was going with another woman. But he looks after the children, and of course she appreciates the fact that he is looking after the children well. But it is breaking her heart, so there are times that she will drink with some friends and shout it all out—all the things that she feels, all the heartache and the pain. She went home for a holiday. And then she had mixed feelings about whether she would treat her husband nicely or show him the bitterness she has learning that this is going on. . . .

She said, "I think I was very, very strong at one time and then would be very nice and soft to him another time and because sometimes it just flashes in my mind and I feel stiff. Another time again I will be nice and ask him if he wants some coffee. And this confuses him. But I don't understand why it confuses him because he knows what he's doing. And I say 'why would you be so angry at me? You know what you are doing.'"

And she decided that maybe she needs some space and she goes to visit her parents and she stayed there for a week. And her husband didn't like that. "You've only been here for two days and then you go to your parents for a week!"

"They are my parents, don't forget. They are my parents!"

"But you have a family."

"Yes I have and that is why I'm spending my holiday with my family. But I have something to hash out with you."

But he didn't want to talk about it. He started punching her. She said, "I was like a punching bag. I was blue and black all over my face. I was bloating because of hits—And how would I take this? And he would say I am so proud to have so much money. And I said 'no I am not—If I had a lot of money I would not go back and clean other people's toilets. If I have lots of money I would not go back.'"

"Now that you are rich you act like this."

"I said 'No. I just want to make sure I still have my pride here; I still have my person, my being here with all my spirit intact, because of what you are doing to me. I thought I am doing something good for my family. Now you are doing this to me. You are only giving me heartbreaks.'"

Really she was devastated. She came back here. Why would she stay? He almost killed her.

Workers recounted such stories of women who were physically abused at home, had unfaithful husbands, faced separation, or had children who were angry or hostile toward them for having left. Since it was considered abnormal not to want to return home, those who did not go back were assumed to have problems there.

Very few women openly acknowledged at first or in initial interviews that they actually enjoyed life in Hong Kong or even preferred it in some ways to being back in the Philippines. Speaking of returns to Hong Kong simply in terms of the money earned or filial piety, was a way to avoid the possible existence of an underlying contradiction between the self-sacrifice and duty of working abroad to support family, and the fact that for many women Hong Kong is not necessarily experienced as a total selfless sacrifice. Despite the hardships, there are also many pleasurable aspects to life in Hong Kong.

For some, life in Hong Kong is a source of independence, new pleasures, and new senses of personhood. Despite the implications of lowliness from the perspective of many Hong Kong employers, being an overseas domestic worker carries a certain prestige, and a much higher social status than being a "helper" in the Philippines (Dumont, 2000). Workers might dress in elegant, stylish clothes for outings on their day off, for posed photographs they send home, or while attending popular Filipino charity functions that belie their lowly status as maids (Margold this volume, Constable 1997a, b). Laura, a forty-five year old domestic worker, revealed her sense of the "kind of woman" who has difficulties going home. As she described to me in 1996:

When I go home I wear simple work clothes. The same shirt I wore when I came! No makeup. No jewelry. No earrings. Some people go back all sexy, all dangling! So big, skirts very short. . . . ahhh, high heels! So embarrassing. They have trouble. It's easy to adjust if you go back to your country. You go back with shirts and jeans—and lots of money in your pockets! But some Filipinas—waaahh! I buy this one, I buy that one, I buy three necklaces, the earrings, the fingernails, the lipstick. Then they go back as a "one-day millionaire." . . . A few days later you have no money already. They call them one-day millionaire. The rest of the days they are bankrupt and unhappy.

Laura advised domestic workers to resist temptation and "remain the same" in Hong Kong. She interpreted superficial changes in clothing and appearance as a sign of deeper changes, and future discontent. Although blue jeans and T-shirts are not necessarily a reliable indicator that no deeper changes have occurred, Laura had a point. Women like Acosta who dress up and say they feel "like their own boss" in Hong Kong, may experience a sense of diminished class identity when they return to the Philippines as so-called "one-day millionaires." Acosta was initially motivated to work in Hong Kong out of a sense of familial duty, and a concern for the future, but her sense of duty was also accompanied by more personal, individual desires and a competing sense of personhood that grew with her prolonged stay overseas.

Although Acosta agonized about whether it was better for her to be with her children or to send them money from abroad, for her Hong Kong was the home away from home described by Parker. She was empowered by the independence and freedom she negotiated for herself there. She described Hong Kong as a place where—despite the rules and regulations—she felt "free." In Hong Kong she had become "her own boss," in a sense unknown to most other overseas workers. Unlike most domestic workers who work full time for one employer, and live in the employer's home under his or her watchful eye, Acosta had made her own arrangements to live with several Filipinas. Her contract was, she explained, a "scam" agreed on by her and her "main employer." He paid her only a fraction of the amount stated in her contract, and in exchange required her to work for him only a few hours a day. Although part-time work—or "aerobics" as it is euphemistically called—is illegal for foreign workers, it is not uncommon, and Acosta's employer knew she worked for several employers. Acosta skillfully negotiated her numerous part-time jobs, earning substantially more money than she would have with a single employer. She arranged her own hours and refused to work for employers she did not like. Although vulnerable because of the illegality of her work, she seemed both confident and proud of her ability to work the system. She did not relish giving up her autonomy to her husband's various demands at home. With her in Hong Kong, they could still both feel like the boss. Acosta did not give up her family or her home when she left; she sent them money, photos (of herself dressed up and well posed in Statue Square), and letters, and telephoned them regularly—attempting to link the two places, despite the difficulties, into one life, or one "transnational migrant circuit" (Rouse 1991: 14, Margold this volume). She insisted that the Philippines was still "home" even though she clearly felt more "at home" in Hong Kong.

When Acosta returned for infrequent visits to the Philippines, she experienced what Dorinne Kondo has aptly described as a fragmentation of self (1990). As a Japanese American in Japan, Kondo describes her sense of awareness of the apparent fragmentation of her identity into American and Japanese pieces. Filipinas like Acosta can experience a fragmenting of their Hong Kong and Philippine identities such that when they return home, "the different elements, instead of fitting together to form at least the illusion of a seamless and coherent whole . . . strained against one another" (1990: 14). Like Kondo, I would argue that selves that appear "coherent, bounded, and whole" are in fact an illusion. Nor is international travel or movement between vastly different social contexts necessary for fracture to become evident. But the degree of fragmentation and the illusion of coherence are crucial issues. Although not limited to situations of migration, displacement, and exile, fragmentation of self can be heightened and an illusion of unity more difficult to maintain in such situations. Going back to the Philippines heightened Acosta's awareness of the incompatibility of her two selves, resulting in a sense of panic and an urgency to return to Hong Kong, where she had spent four-fifths of her married life, almost half her life, and where she could continue to view herself as a worker and a wife and mother, though one who fulfilled her duties from afar. She discouraged visits from her family and minimized her own trips to the Philippines. Home in the Philippines was most comfortable from her position in Hong Kong as an imagined faraway place; from there it remained insulated from the reality of everyday life, conflict, and interaction.

Molly

One day in early July 1997, I had lunch with Molly and her employer. I first met Molly in 1993 when she was expecting a baby, and I have known her employer, an eighty-year-old scholar, for about ten years. As I described to Molly my recent interest in how some foreign domestic workers prefer Hong Kong to the Philippines, I expected the usual dismissal or resistance to my topic. To my surprise, she interrupted me, grinning, and said "That's me! That's me! Yes, I'm one of them!" She explained—more openly, explicitly, and confidently than Acosta ever did—that she preferred to be in Hong Kong and was quite "at home" there. She said that she did not miss her three-year-old son when she was away from him. "I don't miss him" she said cheerfully, "because I have never lived with him!" Her son has stayed with his maternal grandmother and his father since the week after he was born. "You don't enjoy seeing him?" I asked, my question betraying my own bias. "Of course I enjoy seeing him! I go home often. Several times a year." "Doesn't that make it harder to come back?" "No, I'm *always* happy to be back. I am one of the very lucky ones. With a good employer . . . and I owe him a lot of money!" She smiled warmly toward her employer.

Molly showed me photos of her son (whom she had named after her employer), her husband, and their beautiful house in the Philippines. Despite her unpretentious style, some people in her town were jealous and gossipped about her. As she explained, they said she must be either a prostitute or her employer's mistress in order to earn such good money. The gossip doesn't bother her—"I know it isn't true," she said and, pointing upward, continued, "and He knows it too." She showed me photos of a barbecue, a picnic under bauhinia blossoms, and other outings with Filipina friends in Hong Kong. She explained that she has much more "fun and freedom" in Hong Kong than she would have in the Philippines. There she would have to "learn to plant rice." I could not tell if she meant this literally or figuratively. Her husband was a college teacher, a high-status but low-paying occupation in the Philippines, but his family owned a plantation. Yes, she insisted, "life would be much harder," and she would have to learn to plant rice if she went back! Several years earlier she had told me she would stay in Hong Kong as long as her current employer wanted her to. This time she said she was "very, very happy" because her family had finally agreed that she could stay in Hong Kong as long as she wanted, and they had agreed that when to come back was entirely her decision.

Molly, in other words, considered Hong Kong a home away from home in which she had successfully negotiated a new role for herself, one that her family (husband, parents, and in-laws) could live with, at least for the time being. As she explained, it was not simply that her family had resigned themselves to her decision, or that they had accepted it because they appreciated the material benefits they would enjoy. They thought she had already earned enough. Rather, what pleased her most was that they had allowed her to make the decision and seemed to respect her choice. Molly visits home at least twice a year. Her husband and son have visited her in Hong Kong, and her employer has become well acquainted with her family in the Philippines. As an older bachelor, he considers Molly like family. Unlike Acosta, who expressed more ambivalence about her return to Hong Kong and her visits to the Philippines, Molly, it seems, managed to weave both sides of her life together into an apparently less conflicted, fragmented, or partitioned sense of self. She was, as she explained, a mother and wife, but on her own terms, not the way she would have to be had she remained in the Philippines.

Fely

Fely contrasts with both Molly and Acosta in important ways. I have known her for over three years, and have had the opportunity to observe and talk with her in the course of many visits and overnight stays at the flat where she worked in a largely expatriate and affluent region of Hong Kong. Visiting her and her employers allowed me to observe both sides of an employer-domestic worker relationship. In her early twenties when she first came to Hong Kong, Fely only intended to stay for one contract (two years), yet she had recently signed her sixth contract and completed her eighth year in Hong Kong. Her extended stay cannot be attributed to the fact that she felt "at home" in her employers' flat, for all concerned—even the toddler she cared for—seemed acutely aware of her lower status as "helper" and how this distinguished her from other members of the household. Yet she remained in Hong Kong in 1997 and signed a second contract with her current employers, despite a difficult and demanding job that was far more stressful, and allowed far less freedom and flexibility than Molly's or Acosta's allowed them.

About halfway through her fifth contract, Fely married Danny, who was introduced to her by an uncle during a visit to Manila. Shortly after her marriage, Fely returned to Hong Kong, uncertain how long she would remain and under pressure from Danny to come home soon. Hoping to finish her contract, feeling some responsibility to her current employers, not having saved a lot of money, and unsure what she would do in the Philippines, she convinced Danny to let her stay a little longer, and urged him to try to join her in Hong Kong. Sympathetic toward Fely's position as a newlywed who was separated from her spouse, her employers seriously considered signing Danny's contract in order to allow him to come to Hong Kong. But they found it difficult to provide the justification to hire two full-time workers required by the labor and immigration departments. They did not in fact need him to work for them, but, as for many other overseas workers there was the possibility that he could do "aerobics" while allegedly working for one full-time employer.

Despite the fact that she liked Hong Kong far less than Acosta and Molly, and that she unambiguously considered the Philippines home, Fely preferred not to re-turn very often. She had not gone back for over a year—despite having four weeks off in December 1996 when her employers went abroad. "The more I go home" she said, "the harder it is for me here." She described how, during her first con-tract, she was fairly happy until she returned to Hong Kong after her first visit home. "Returning to Hong Kong was awful" and she experienced her first and most severe bout of homesickness, so she decided to go home as little as possible, "and since then life has been easier." Fely found her current work extremely de-manding, the hours long, and the relations with her employers sometimes strained, but she enjoyed spending her time off with church friends and shopping for bargains. She had a knack for style and she and a friend earned extra money on Sundays selling clothes.

Fely only vaguely anticipated changes in her life when she returned to the Philippines. She did not think the changes would be because of her experiences in Hong Kong but, rather, because she would be returning as a newlywed. She was not sure where she would live or what occupations she or her husband would have, but she thought that if she could save money, her return would go more smoothly. Fely's sense of self, in contrast to Molly's, was more closely linked to an imagined future life in the Philippines than to her present life in Hong Kong. Her marriage linked her sense of self more securely to the Philippines. Remaining in Hong Kong and avoiding trips back home has, paradoxically, enabled Fely to maintain her sense of a more coherent and unified self situated in the Philippines.

Virginia

Virginia, in her early thirties when I met her in 1994, was politically active and worked hard to establish a labor union for domestic workers in Hong Kong. From a conservative family in the Philippines, she first arrived in Hong Kong in 1988, leaving behind a husband, and a two-year-old son in her mother's care. She stayed with her first employer for only three months. They did not get along and agreed it would be best for her to find a new employer. Her second employer's household included a married couple, three teenage children, and a *popo* (grandmother). After she had worked for them for eight months, she received a telephone call in-forming her that her husband had died:

It's really terrible. This is one of the things I can't forget. He was sick. Yes, and actually they [relatives] know and they don't want me to know that he's getting sick—even my husband he don't want me to know about his illness and don't want me to know the problem,—so after I get this message on the telephone, I'm crying a lot; I drop the phone and then cry, cry. I'm not ashamed to cry. I cry. So my popo says in Chinese to me "Don't cry." So I feel, oh, I feel so sad.

Her employers were very understanding, attempted to comfort her, provided money for funeral expenses, and allowed her to return home.

So I went to the Philippines. And when I arrived I was scared because I see the coffin. I don't want to go in the house. Of course when you go home you want your husband to greet you—and he's already lying there inside the coffin. It's really terrible I don't like to come inside. I move backward and I'm so upset I cry and cry again and again. Even on the airplane, I cannot take it. My parents, the people there say "calm yourself," and "it's okay," but, when I arrive home, from the gate I see the coffin and I move backward. Before I would always hallucinate [fantasize] that he is in Hong Kong, staying with me, before he died. And that is why when I visit home, I feel that there's already something wrong.

When I asked if she wanted to go back home, she answered, "Of course I always wanted to go home. But I have to support my child." Her son does well in school and her goal is to send him to university. After her husband's death she returned to work for the same employers until they migrated to Canada a year later. She located a new employer who allowed her to participate in labor activism and agreed to accept a lower salary in exchange for greater flexibility in her work hours. Usually she was satisfied with this arrangement, except when she received a message from home saying they needed money. "Ahh. . . . This is my problem," she sighed. "I don't have my own house. My earnings are for the schooling of only one child. How much worse for those who have many children."

Virginia said that her work and union activities kept her so busy that it was difficult to return to the Philippines, but her son has visited her in Hong Kong: "If I don't have time, he comes. Because I cannot leave the work. I have very big responsibility here." Her son, aged nine, wanted her to come home:

He doesn't want me to work. "Why do you need to go to Hong Kong?" "Why do you need to be a DH [domestic helper] when in Philippines you can also be a DH?" . . . And then he told me that "my friends told me that money is not important. More important is that you should stay with me. I don't have a father anymore." Anyway, I just answer him that "I can buy a computer, I can buy nice clothes for you," just to compensate when he's asking me; "And you see, you can go to a very nice school because I'm in Hong Kong."

Her son preferred her presence to that of her presents. Despite Virginia's goals for him, like Acosta's daughter, her son's ambition was to come and work in Hong Kong:

He says to me, "Oh. Maybe when I'm grown up I can come to Hong Kong also and do domestic work. To earn money for you. You can stop working and I can do domestic work." He's a boy! He's thinking like that also! To earn money, to help is to be a DH also!

Actually there are domestic helpers who used to stay in Hong Kong for almost ten or 15 years. After they send their children to school and then to university they will bring them here to become domestic helpers. It is like a trend, a cycle. You just earn money to send you children to school. After they come to school they come here as DH. Because the economy is so bad—even if you graduated from university.

Virginia considered being married as an OCW better than being single. She described what she considered the unfortunate fate of some single women as follows:

If they stay in Hong Kong, they cannot marry any more because they have this feeling of being responsible. Like my sister. She came to Hong Kong just to give financial support to the family, then after that she's not just giving financial support. She lets my niece to go to school, and after that she has many, many more burdens, and so she prefers to stay here. So she's still here, and, like Sara, she's still single.

Though I did not know Virginia as well as I knew Acosta, she seemed to express far less ambivalence about remaining in Hong Kong. Although her son pressured her to come home, she balanced this pressure with the sense that she was also badly needed by the workers who depended on her in Hong Kong. It was clear to me and to other women who knew Virginia that she was deeply dedicated to her union activities and received a sense of reward from her involvement and leadership role. Through her activist work, she discovered skills she did not know she had. She hinted at the disapproval of her relatives "in the military" if they knew of her labor activism. Her husband's death also clearly colored her reluctance to go back to the Philippines. She could still imagine him in Hong Kong, as she had before he died, but the stark reality of his absence confronted her whenever she went back.

Elsa

Though active in different circles from Virginia, Elsa and her sister Belle were also politically active, and their political conviction and activism contrasted with Acosta's more independent and entrepreneurial approach to life in Hong Kong (Constable 1997a). In the summer of 1996—anticipating changes that might accompany Hong Kong's reunification with the mainland—both Elsa and Belle told me we might not meet the following summer because they planned to leave Hong Kong within the year. By late 1996, after more than ten years in Hong Kong, Belle, in her early forties, returned to the Philippines to head a non-profit migrant organization in Manila, where her younger sister also worked. Elsa, almost 40, had remained in Hong Kong since the late 1970s, and she laughed when I reminded her that a year earlier she had predicted her departure: "I decided I will stay in Hong Kong as long as I'm allowed to do it because it has to do with financial concerns. I told myself that if I still have the opportunity to work in Hong Kong to earn money, then I have to keep at it. Nowadays I'm still saving money for my future. Because I don't know if I will get married or I will remain single, but I have to be prepared, financially."

Elsa was very much at home in Hong Kong. She spoke some Cantonese, had learned to cook Chinese food, and had her favorite street markets and dim sum restaurants. Like Acosta, she negotiated an uncommon living situation where she was not required to live with her employer but, rather, shared a flat with several Filipinas. She enjoyed her work and had much opportunity to interact with other Filipinas when she volunteered at the Mission for Filipino Migrant Workers.

Since Elsa and Belle left their low-paying assembly line jobs in Manila to come to Hong Kong years ago, the family's economic situation has improved. Besides her sisters in Manila, Elsa had a younger sister who was a domestic worker in Italy, a brother in the Philippines who helped his parents look after their small farm, and another sister who worked for duty-free shops in the Philippines. Elsa and her sister in Italy helped support the rest of the family. Although Elsa had no children or husband in the Philippines, she gave the impression of being extremely well integrated into events there. "I don't go home often," she said, "but I know exactly what is going on there!" Like the Mexican migrants in California described by Rouse, Elsa has managed to "participate in familial events from a considerable distance" (1991: 13). She kept in close contact with her parents by phone and mail, and was intimately involved in decisions about their house, finances, and investments in material goods. She felt very close to her siblings, and enjoyed her visits home at least once a year. Like Molly, she moved back and forth between the two places with relative ease, keeping in touch with friends and family in both places. During her 1996 Christmas holiday, she arranged a reunion of Filipino friends from Hong Kong in Manila, including some who had permanently returned to the Philippines, with others who were visiting for the holidays.

Elsa thought it noteworthy that neither she nor any of her siblings were married. "My brother is likely to marry, but so far none of the girls, and the youngest is already in her early thirties." Although she said that she would "like to have a husband and children," she was wary of pursuing romantic involvements in Hong Kong, and, like her younger sister in Italy, she tried to deter "interested men." As Elsa explained, "there are few Filipino men in Hong Kong and many women, so the men have their choice and can move from one to another." She also considered non-Filipinos dangerous prospects. Over the years she has told me many cautionary tales of abandoned, sometimes pregnant, broken-hearted Filipinas—including a close cousin—who returned home under very different circumstances than they had envisioned:

I was exposed to a problem here of Filipinas. Some have taken into a deep relationship. They become pregnant. After that it becomes a big problem because the man will run away from them and . . . will not take the responsibility. I don't like to have the risk. And my family have very, very—have trusted me. . . . One of my cousins was impregnated by a foreigner who did not marry her. He married a Chinese woman. So she went back home and she doesn't care [about] the gossip, the heartache that was inflicted on her by some of our relatives. Only her parents, her close relatives are very supportive of her. She did not plan to go home like that.

Elsa entertained the possibility of adopting a child when she returned to the Philippines. Having been away for so long, however, she might encounter difficulties since assuming the care of a child in the rural Philippines is based on informal channels and normally takes place over a prolonged period of time, as the parents, child, and prospective parent gradually come to a suitable arrangement. However, at the time it seemed that Elsa would remain in Hong Kong as long as she could. Her family greatly appreciated her contributions; she had a good and very flexible employer, and her work at the Mission gave her satisfaction and allowed her an escape from the tedium of household work.

Comparisons

Acosta, Virginia, Molly, Fely, and Elsa have all remained in Hong Kong longer than they originally intended, yet they justified their continued returns in different ways. Fely's explanation appeared the least complicated: she remained in Hong Kong to save money to facilitate a more comfortable future married life in the Philippines. She explained her short-term reluctance to go home as simply a way to avoid homesickness. Fely's sense of self seemed squarely located in her imaginings of the Philippines. Hong Kong offered her—in her own words—simply "a place to earn money," a practical solution to an economic problem. She enjoyed aspects of her life there but did not expect to miss Hong Kong when she eventually leaves. The longer she remains, however, the more difficult it will likely become for her to experience her return in simple and unambiguous terms.

The other four women expressed more complicated reasons for staying in Hong Kong. Her husband's death in her absence transformed home for Virginia, creating new obligations but also new opportunities. Although Molly was most articulate about her preference for Hong Kong because of the personal freedom and independence it afforded her, Elsa and Virginia also unambiguously considered life in Hong Kong personally rewarding and enjoyable. As Elsa said in 1994, "Hong Kong is an exciting, clean, and beautiful place. I have many friends here, and I do good work. Most of the time I am very satisfied here."

Acosta expressed a higher degree of ambivalence than the other four women about her returns to Hong Kong and the Philippines. Unlike Molly and Elsa, whose families expressed some approval or acceptance of the changes they have experienced while away, Acosta thought her family would want everything "like it was" when she returns, and unlike Virginia, she seemed reluctant to admit how much she had changed. Acosta's was perhaps the most "partitioned"—harshly disjointed or dualistic—sense of self (Nandy 1995), which explains her greater ambivalence toward return. While Molly and Elsa said they wanted to stay in Hong Kong as long as they could, Acosta was more ambivalent. She preferred to be in Hong Kong, but thought she *should* return to the Philippines. Once there, she could not settle down. When she learned she was pregnant after a brief visit to the Philippines in 1980, there were already hints of her ambivalence. As she described it, her employer's children "were crying, oh they were crying when I said I need to go back to stay together with my family." They said, "You do not want to come back any more?" and she answered, "I don't think so. I have to have also my own baby." But her behavior lacked conviction and she repeatedly de-layed her departure until the end of her pregnancy. Then she returned to Hong Kong, despite her husband's objection, when her daughter was just a few weeks old. For her, Hong Kong was a source of both pleasure and guilt. Hong Kong, moreover, was good for her but not for her daughter, and although she thought she ought to return permanently, she clearly preferred to be in Hong Kong.

Despite their different situations and attitudes toward Hong Kong, Molly, Fely, and Acosta are likely to return to the Philippines as married women, and, like them, Fely also expected to become a mother. In 1997, Fely seemed to express the least ambivalence about returning to the Philippines, and anticipated the need to rework relations back home solely on account of her new role as a wife. Molly and Acosta are likely to miss the freedom and independence of life in Hong Kong. Elsa, who, like Molly, has negotiated between the two places quite skillfully and comfortably, has no clear traditional role to which she will return. If she returns in her forties, childless and unmarried, she will necessarily—to an even greater degree than the others—have to create a new space in the one she left behind. Paradoxically, this may be easier for Elsa to accomplish than for Acosta or Vir-ginia. Although Acosta has a family and a marriage to return to, her children grew up in her absence, and her short visits home suggest that she bristled under pressure from her husband to perform wifely duties. Virginia will return as a widow, perhaps alienated from her son because of her long absence and from some of her kin because of her political activities. Unattached, Elsa may be in the best position to utilize the new networks that she has created, activated, and main-tained between Hong Kong and the Philippines. Like her sister Belle, Elsa may settle in Manila, away from her parents, and make a fairly smooth transition from her activist work in Hong Kong to another activist organization in Manila. The changes Molly and Acosta have made to their family roles may be harder to main-tain when they leave Hong Kong. As a single and childless woman, Elsa's position has been structurally altered by her time abroad. That is not to say that women who are married or have no children will have an easier time. They too will have to rework relationships.

Unpacking Home

Most Filipinas go to work abroad "in desperation, under strong economic and so-cial compulsion" (Clifford 1994: 314), as other migrant workers, but once the process of transnational labor is in place, new reasons to continue coming to Hong Kong and new rationales for staying are set into motion. Migrant workers reshape gender and family roles and relations as well as economic ones. Relations in the Philippines are altered in minor and major ways. Hong Kong clearly affords many Filipinas a degree of personal and economic independence that many are reluctant to give up when they return to the Philippines. New friendships are established in Hong Kong, and life there, despite difficulties, can take on a sense of normality. In this context, some women begin to question basic assumptions about what it means to be a worker, wife and mother, as they carve out new identities and political spaces in Hong Kong, and thus resist or delay returning home.

Carol Stack ends her afterword to *Call to Home* with the following excerpt from a conversation: "*You can definitely go home again,* Eula Grant told me one afternoon on her porch in Burdy's Bend. *You can go home. But you can't start from where you left. To fit in, you have to create another place in that place you left behind*" (1996: 199, emphasis in original). As Stack points out in her preface, "going home requires reworking traditional relationships between men and women, husbands and wives, parents and children" (1996: xv). Unlike African American migrants to the northern United States, Filipina domestic workers rarely have the intention of settling permanently in Hong Kong. Yet both groups share with other return migrants the necessity of "reworking" and "creating another place [space]" upon their return. Filipinas discover, like other return migrants, that it is not always easy to fit back into their old lives and relationships because they have changed and home has been altered by their absence.

The diasporic experiences of domestic workers are—as illustrated above—gendered in a number of ways. Overseas work fundamentally alters the experiences of young women: mothers spend long periods of time away from their children, husbands or lovers. Others do not marry or have children, avoid relationships with men, or embrace (homosocial or homosexual) relationships with other women. Men who remain at home may lose the traditional role of breadwinner and find themselves performing duties once performed by women. Women migrants, moreover, may find themselves in the unfamiliar (traditionally male) role of breadwinner or political leader, and they are applauded as the nation's new economic heroes for performing other women's household duties abroad. Men of 30 or 40 who work overseas are less likely to sacrifice having a family—or to fundamentally alter their familial roles as provider—by going abroad in their youth. They are still likely to marry and to have children. But women OCWs who have children often sacrifice the experience of motherhood, and, like Elsa and Belle, are likely to remain unmarried and childless. Elsa might adopt a child and yet remain unmarried. Virginia might—like Belle—carve a new role for herself in the Philippines, drawing on her experiences as a migrant worker and labor organizer. Molly continues to negotiate her position in her extended household so that the empowerment and independence she gained in Hong Kong could become more permanent.

Hong Kong has also exposed women to new material desires and different class identities. The cases described above raise many questions about the complex class dimensions of the experiences of domestic workers. Foreign domestic workers are lower class from the perspective of their employers, but they come from a variety of backgrounds in the Philippines. Some come from poor, landless families in the provinces; others from professional, middle-class, or landowning families. Their remittances, moreover, can have either a short- or a long-term impact on the family's economic and social status. Accustomed to identifying herself as a professional working woman of sorts in Hong Kong, Acosta is likely to experience a sense of downward mobility when she returns as a "one-day millionaire" to the rural poverty of her family in the Philippines. Her remittances have had no significant long-term impact on her family's financial situation so far, and she will miss being "her own boss." For women such as Molly, the change may not seem as great. She anticipated having to work hard, but she will return to a beautiful new house, and to her status as the wife of a college professor in a landowning family. Elsa and Belle's work in Hong Kong has allowed their family to buy a small parcel of land, build a house, and secure their sister a coveted position as a domestic worker in Italy. Though they will still be poor by local standards, working as activists for returned OCWs in Manila will afford them greater prestige than their first jobs as local helpers and assembly line workers.

Unlike those they left behind in the Philippines who "are principally aware of one culture, one setting, one home," Filipino overseas workers are—like the exiles Said describes—"aware of at least two, and this plurality of vision gives rise to an awareness . . . that—to borrow a phrase from music—is *contrapuntal*" (Said 1984: 172, emphasis in original). While not, strictly speaking, exiles, Filipina migrant workers develop a plural vision that allows—perhaps requires—them to create a new place in both in Hong Kong and in the Philippines. As we have seen, a plural vision can be both alienating and inspiring, a source of awareness and dissatisfaction, and a source of pleasure and apprehension (172). In circumstances of change and mobility, a plural vision no longer permits the self the illusion of a unified, bounded, or coherent whole.

Precisely how these women will fit in when they ultimately return to the Philippines (which they most likely will) remains to be seen. Migration has provided them with new experiences, desires, options, and visions, but with no ready formulas for successfully transplanting them. What is clear, however, is that many women express some ambivalence about return, and so for now they continue to make themselves at home, away from home, in Hong Kong. And when they return to the place where they were born, they will be, more than likely, in a different space and therefore remain, in a sense, in exile.

Part III
Repatriated Return

Chapter 7
Returning German Jews and Questions of Identity

John Borneman

This chapter examines German Jews who were forced to flee the Nazi regime, sought exile in one of the Allied countries (United States, USSR, France, England), and repatriated to East and West Germany within a decade of the end of World War II. The motivations for return to either East or West Germany are explored, as is the influence of locations—in exile and return—on the way German-Jewish identification is articulated. The study takes place toward the end of the Cold War and in its immediate aftermath. With German unification in 1991, Germans in the East, in particular, experienced a dissolution of their motive for return (to build an anti-Fascist state), and they, along with the entire East German population, were integrated into an enlarged Federal Republic. The German-Jewish experience of repatriation is particularly instructive in that it demonstrates how this small group of survivors experienced the discontinuities between culture, religion, nationality and citizenship. At a time when ethnonationalism in discrete, sovereign states is posited as the only viable form of group identity, German-Jewish struggles to move beyond this form are indeed an alternative that deserves attention.

Who Is a German Jew?

A major contention in contemporary debates about identity politics is that theories of modernity have led to an overemphasis on the aspects of coherence, unity, and continuity in identities. Significance, or even health, is attributed only to those identities that display coherence around single characteristics (such as, for example, ethnicity, sexuality, or nationality), appear unified between domains of experience (such as work and family), and can be narrated in a continuous history (usually around tropes of suffering or production). This overemphasis results in neglect, if not pathologizing identities that are disjunctive and not easily narrated as part of a continuous history. In this chapter, I examine the autobiographies of a small number of German Jews who left Germany before 1939 and returned to one of the Berlins after 1945. German-Jewish identity in this century has been marked by a series of disjunctures in categories of belonging, in particular by discontinuities between culture, nationality, and citizenship. I shall address the question of the meaning and significance of these disjunctures for German-Jewish selfhood among the small group of German Jews still living in Berlin.

This chapter is part of a larger project, which I completed with Jeffrey Peck (Borneman and Peck: 1995). In June 1989, we began ethnographic interviews— some of which we later filmed—with formerly exiled German Jews in order to address three questions. We asked: "Why did some German Jews voluntarily return after 1945 from exile in one of the Allied occupation countries to East and West Germany, more specifically to East and West Berlin? Did postwar experiences change the way in which people imagined themselves to be German Jews? Who in fact is a German Jew? History intervened in this project: the Wall opened on November 9, 1989; the East German state dissolved and its territories and people formally united with the Federal Republic on October 3, 1990. The extreme flux of this period, now called *die Wendezeit*, during which we both regularly visited or intermittently lived in Berlin, continually dissolved many of the divisions and tensions that we were studying, only to replace them with newer and emergent ones not immediately identifiable. It forced us to continue our research for several more years.

We began by trying to identify all German Jews living in Berlin who had experienced exile in one of the Allied occupied countries and returned to Berlin. No one, of course, keeps such lists. Moreover, the very category "Jew" or "German Jew" has been a politically contested one, by the Germans in the East and West, by the various members and organizations of the international Jewish community, and by the different Allied occupation forces. For obvious reasons many Jews did not want to identify themselves as such, least of all for the purposes of citizenship or statistical quantification. Subject positions are always also political stances, placing an actor in an historical tradition and a present-oriented field of power and interest. Thus, the number of "Jews" one cites will always be partially determined by polemical, political, and factual considerations. With these caveats in mind how might one identify a German Jew?

A census published in June 1933 registered 500,000 Jews living in the German Reich (around one percent of the total population), of whom approximately one quarter were foreign (non-German) Jews. Approximately another 100,000 people who were not registered had at least one Jewish grandparent. Of those registered by the government, around 72,000 lived in Berlin. Between 1933 and 1945, approximately 270,000 were able to leave Germany; more than 165,000 were murdered; about 15,000 survived the camps, and another 2,000 survived underground (Benz 1991: 10). In the spring of 1945, "as many as 100,000 Jewish survivors [the majority not being German Jews] found themselves among the eleven million uprooted and homeless people wandering throughout Germany and Central Europe" (Peck 1991: 5). Between 1945 and 1950, the number of Jewish "displaced persons"—the official category used by the Allies—rose to nearly 200,000 (Jacobmeyer 1983: 421–52). International Jewish agencies then engaged in a massive and relatively successful effort to remove the Jewish population from Germany, so that by 1950 the number of Jews in Germany had dwindled to around 15,000. Of this small group, 6,000 were displaced Jews from Eastern Europe who settled in Germany, another 2,000 were Jews from other countries, and only the remaining 6,000 were German-Jewish emigrants or returnees (Yahil 1971: 496–500). Those who remained in or moved to Germany after the war became a pariah people in the eyes of groups such as the World Zionist Organization, the World Jewish Congress, and the Jewish Agency, all of which issued ultimatums to the effect that all Jews must leave Germany (Peck 1991: 9).

The relation of Jews to the Allied occupiers and to German authorities was entirely different. Within weeks of the defeat of the Third Reich, exiled Jewish Germans began returning to Berlin to serve—initially the Soviet Union, shortly thereafter the other three occupation forces—in rebuilding Germany. The great majority of these returnees were highly skilled, politically motivated, Jewish anti-Fascists who had worked in the opposition during the war. Some had begun this oppositional activity on the side of the Republicans during the Spanish Civil War; they saw the fight against Nazi Germany as a continuation of these earlier battles and the return to Germany as part of an international anti-Fascist struggle. Many identified themselves more strongly as Communists and members of the German Left than as Jews, and many were prominent personalities whose return to Germany was expected and hoped for by a small group of non-Jewish German friends and anti-Fascists who had also survived the war. On the whole, however, Jews who returned within the decade after the war report that most people living in or occupying Germany at that time treated their return—and their Jewishness, to the extent they revealed it at all—with total indifference.

In this chapter, I illustrate my arguments by citing five of the 23 autobiographical interviews we completed, which is approximately half of the people we identified as German Jews who also fit the categories of this project. We selected people based on categories that revealed a particular range of experiences and differences in age, gender, nationality, and county of exile; we did not select them randomly. We also maintained a nearly equal balance between those living in the East and West, between women and men, and between two generations. I will limit myself here to a discussion of members of Generation I, those born between 1904 and 1926, raised in Germany, who left between 1932 and 1939, and were in exile during the war in one of the Allied occupation countries (USSR, United States, Great Britain, or France). They returned between 1945 and 1956 (except for one, who returned in 1979) to either East or West Germany, and eventually to one of the Berlins.

For the purposes of our study, we identified people as Jewish either because they subjectively identified themselves that way or because they were so identified by ancestry, from the outside through shared blood on the male side (a category employed by the Nuremberg race laws) or through shared blood on the female side (according to Jewish religion). Thus, several of the participants in this study who had been labeled Jew at various times in their lives insisted that they were not Jews. Obviously, we are aware of the danger in hypostasizing an identity for someone who insists that they do not belong to the group in question. We recognize and respect the right of people to represent themselves as they wish. On the other hand, our goal is not to prove people's belonging against their wishes but merely to indicate the relation of subjective identifications to the two definitions of belonging listed above.

Our open-ended, autobiographical discussions extended anywhere from one to six hours at a time. In eighteen cases we returned for a second interview, in eight cases for a third. The discussions were taped and carried on in the language chosen by our partners, either German or English. About one month into the interviews, we decided to make a video documentary about these people, in addition to our book project, and thus selected nine people for filmed interviews. Since August 1989, we have met again either singly or together all of the people now included in our book. After transcribing, translating, and editing the initial interviews, we made the resulting protocols available to the interviewees for further corrections and comments.

The Decision to Leave

Specific reasons given for leaving Germany ran along two axes of comparison: those who returned from *exile* in the United States or the USSR and *to citizenship* in the Federal Republic of Germany (FRD) or the German Democratic Republic (GDR). My purpose here in citing these interviews is not to demonstrate a typical experience but to illustrate the range of responses to any particular issue. Half the individuals of this generation whom we interviewed belonged to the Jewish *Gemeinde* (community) in East or West Berlin, all of those in the East except two were members of the Socialist Unity Party (SED), while only one of all those in the West whom we interviewed belonged to a political party. Among the reasons for leaving Germany, approximately half singled out fear of discrimination, persecution, and/or murder because of their Jewish identity; one left to join a boyfriend in the USSR the year before the Nazis came to power; one left both because he suffered from an occupational blacklist (for political and ethnic reasons) and in order to fight in the Spanish Civil War; many said that they left out of political opposition *and* because they were Jewish. Concerning the country of exile/ emigration, no one went to the United States out of political conviction; two went to the USSR to work for the revolution. The others ended up going to countries that agreed to take them in, with no prior preference for refuge there.

Case 1. Ruth Benario was born in Berlin in 1910, left for the USSR in 1932, and returned to East Berlin in 1954.

I had a friend who was world-renowned in physics. He was in Genf and Lucern, was general-director there for five years. [Today he's] a very famous man, also with respect to East-West relations, and he's made a name for himself in the peace movement. I've recently found him again, after thirty-three years. I can tell you about that later. That's always funny and really accidental, how everything plays itself out in life, especially with our generation. He was supposed to go to take someone with him, and said, "Good, you come along." I said, "No. I'm not going along." I'd just begun working in a photography studio. That was 1932. And we cabled back and forth to each other, daily, until one day I suddenly said to him, because something funny had happened in the meantime, "Okay, that's enough of this story. I'll come along."

Like many women we interviewed, Frau Benario offers an explanation for leaving that, despite her independent spirit, makes her decision contingent on the life of a male friend. Although she designs her entire life story as one motivated by accidents and by unintended consequences of intentional actions, she also attached particular significance to events in which she ends up going along with men, particularly boyfriends and lovers. It may well be that freedom of movement for women at that time, even for relatively wealthy and independent women like Frau Benario, was limited by the extent to which they could attach themselves to men who had mobility. Earlier in her story, Frau Benario had described to us the circumstances of her childhood: raised in a private villa in the wealthy Dahlem section of Berlin, painted by Kokoschka; she drove a car and took private flying lessons. Yet perhaps the most fateful decisions of her early life, the move to the USSR, was a result of following a boyfriend there. The year after she arrived in Moscow, with Hitler firmly in power in Germany, she decided not to return. Though her boyfriend (the famous physicist Viktor Weiskopf) moved on to Denmark (and later to the United States), she made a life for herself in Moscow.

Case 2. Ernst Cramer was born in 1913 in Bavaria, emigrated to the United States in 1939, and returned to West Germany (as an American citizen) with the Allies in 1945: "Hm, you know that as so often in life, very much, very much is naturally accident, isn't that so?" After explaining that he had rejected his first offer to leave Germany in the fall of 1934 because it was to go to Israel, he continues,

After I rejected this first offer to emigrate, I had approximately three other offers to emigrate to South Africa. Finally, I decided, after, after the ordinance, after they passed the Nuremberg Laws, that a young person simply couldn't live here any more. I then began working in agriculture—through the youth movement in which I had worked. In 1937, I formally joined one group. We didn't want to join the Zionist group because we said there were too few positions there and too few licenses to go to Palestine back then. . . . We then tried to find places elsewhere in the world. We wanted to find a place where we could remain together as a group and then settle together in South America. That also proved impossible to realize, and then came 1938. . . . After that the motto here was: just save yourself if you can. And I had a possibility to emigrate to Kenya, as well as to America. I went to America. . . . I was in Buchenwald in '38, and then in the summer of '39 I emigrated directly to America.

The specific circumstances that finally led to Herr Cramer's exile are idiosyncratic. He told us that a Gestapo man finally convinced him to leave but in the most unexpected way. The man offered him the position of heading the *Reichsvertretung der Juden in Deutschland* (the official body said to represent all Jews living in the Third Reich). But the man offering him the position also assured him that even if he accepted it the Gestapo would soon arrest him. It was only a matter of time before they got to him and the other Jews. Therefore, Herr Cramer said, he was ironically thankful to the man for so clearly outlining his options, and he immediately left for the United States.

Case 3. Goetz Berger was born in 1905, became a lawyer and a Communist during Weimar, left Germany in 1934, went to fight in the Spanish Civil War in 1936, and was imprisoned in a concentration camp in France before escaping to the USSR in 1943. He returned to East Berlin in 1949. "In 1933, I was kicked out of the lawyer's profession, naturally. There was a law that forbade anti-racists as well as Jews from practicing this occupation, called the *Berufsbeamtengesetz*. [Though this law was aimed at civil servants,] it was also applied to private occupations such as law. I had to leave the republic, illegally." Herr Berger explains that his association with Jews at that time was a symbolic one, that he did not identify himself subjectively as a Jew.

Now, you have to look at it as follows: Before Hitler, we had many Jews, relatively many Jews were in the so-called free occupations, lawyers and doctors, for example, above all this was true for Berlin. In other places, it wasn't so concentrated. That connection had much to do with German history. The Jews were not allowed to enter the military in old Prussia, nor in the Weimar Republic. They weren't allowed to enter higher levels of administration, nor diplomatic service, and they were practically not represented at all among the farmers. . . . And now it came to a very negative decision, in my opinion, that in commerce the Jewish element was very strong. In the '30s, even already in the '20s, the large commercial centers, shopping houses, were well developed. These stores were nearly exclusively in Jewish hands. . . . Now the Nazis had an easy time playing with this, especially among the petty bourgeois, among the commercial interests and the small dealers. They felt, and objectively they were correct, threatened by the large concerns. And through this, Nazi propaganda, the racist Nazi propaganda using these categories, fell on fruitful soil.

Herr Berger then makes a similar argument for the intelligentsia, which also had a high proportion of Jews. During his narration, he always refers to the Jews in third person, though much of this history is one in which he is personally situated, given his own family history, political orientation, and occupation.

As to why so many Jews did not leave Germany, Herr Berger explains,

Well, I see the primary, the most basic reason why Hitler came to power is that the German people, especially the intellectuals who were not politically sophisticated and did not want to be politically informed, that they always said, "Politics is something ugly. Politics spoils the character. We don't want anything to do with politics. We are suspended in spiritual/intellectual spheres [schweben in geistigen Sphären]." Therefore, they didn't bother. This became the fate of many Jews. . . . I knew several myself, who had remained in the Hitler period, long after they could have left, when they had the means to leave, but they said, "Good God, what we see in the newspapers, that can not be reality. In the end, after all, Germany has produced Goethe and Herder. Germany is a civilized country. And besides, there are laws and we have rights, and we haven't really done anything to anybody." What they failed to see were the political relationships behind it all. This unpolitical thinking, this rejection of all that is politics, this was very widespread among the Jewish middle class.

Several aspects of Herr Berger's explanation are striking. First, in substantiating his own cosmopolitan identity, one that in the Enlightenment tradition transcends religion, race, and nationality, he works with the same dichotomy as the apolitical Jews he criticizes: he posits politics as a domain divorced from culture, rather than culture as the very site of politics; he differs from those he criticizes only in that he emphasizes politics over culture, whereas they prioritize culture over politics. Second, he differs from the other two individuals cited above in deemphasizing coincidence and contingency as motivating his history and instead resorts to objectively identifiable structures in his arguments to explain history, of which his own history is only a specification. Third, his insistence on referring to Jews in the third person and refusal to position his own history as one determined by Jewish history can be explained again partly by reference to his cosmopolitanism which transcends race and religion. Also he firmly believes the personal is the opposite of the political, with the former being less significant. Fourth, the "political" for him is antifacism.

Case 4. Hilde Eisler was born in 1912 in East Galicia, at that time part of Austria, later Poland, currently part of Ukraine. When she was six months old, her family moved to Antwerp, Belgium. Two years later the First World War broke out. Her father was drafted into the Austrian army, and her mother, labeled an enemy foreigner by Belgium, resettled in Frankfurt, Germany, where her mother's parents had been living for many years. Frau Eisler grew up, then, in Frankfurt, in a fairly integrated wealthy family—her father was a banker in Poland and her Belgian relatives were in the diamond business—though as an Ostjudin (Jew from the East), she was never fully accepted by the Westjuden (Jews from the West) in Germany. After spending a year in prison for underground activities against the Nazis, she began her exile from Germany in 1937, landing in New York in 1941. She was deported from the United States during the anti-Communist hysteria of the McCarthy purges in 1949 and resettled in East Berlin.

I was placed on a visa as the quasi-engaged woman of my husband [Gerhart Eisler]. It was like this: I didn't get a Mexican visa from the people there, those who organized it all from Paris. Why? To this day I still don't know. Something didn't work out, and then he [Gerhart] offered to put me on his visa. I had worked in the resistance in Germany; I was imprisoned. I worked illegally, giving out illegal literature against the Nazis. I was arrested, spent a year in prison, was then deported to Poland. . . . From there I went to Czechoslovakia, and from there I was able to go to France. I worked with Gerhart Eisler in Paris. I first met him there working with anti-Fascist radio programs. And he passed me off as his fiancee, so that I could get on his visa. But I wasn't engaged to him. We were only friends. We later married in America, in Connecticut.

Much like Frau Benario, Frau Eisler ties her fate to that of a man, one with whom she was initially quasi-engaged and later married. She insists that her reasons for going into exile are both because she is Jewish and because she was in the political opposition.

In accounts of the circumstances of leaving or escaping Germany, the two German Jews cited here who took refuge in the Soviet Union were, so they maintain, driven by circumstance and political convictions. Hence they offer political explanations, including a political explanation for German racism, for Hitler coming to power, and for their forced exile. For those German Jews who took refuge in the United States, explanations for leaving tend more frequently to emphasize Jewishness and German racism without placing this in a political context—unless, that is, they would end up returning to East Germany instead of the Federal Republic after the war. Those who returned to East Germany from exile in the United States also offered accounts for leaving Germany similar to those of their peers who were in exile in the Soviet Union. I suspect that there exists a strong positive correlation between the degree of politicization and exile in the USSR, and between this politicization and the decision to return to the GDR from exile. These accounts also seem to indicate that the politicization occurred most frequently before leaving Germany, not during life in exile. Why some returned to the East Zone/GDR instead of the West was most dependent on a disposition to see the Party and world ideology as movers of history. Compared to their counterparts who went to the West, those who went to the East were less convinced of personal fate as determinative of their own lives.

The Decision to Return

Decisions to return, when, and to what country were equally varied, as shown from five examples below.

Case 1. Frau Benario returned in 1954 to East Berlin after twenty years in the USSR and two in China.

We asked the Red Cross to repatriate us. I had been in the Soviet Union long enough. I wanted to go back to Germany and help with the rebuilding of Germany. I took that step, and I asked that the man Hart, Dr. Hart, Dr. Camillo Hart—he was my third husband, so to speak, all without papers—and I asked them if I could take him along with me. However, he was either supposed to go back to Romania (where he'd been imprisoned in a concentration camp before the Russians freed him) or to Vienna (where he was born). He wanted to come with me to Germany, but the Russians didn't want to release us from our duties [for me that was because I worked] as translator for the radio.

Why return to the GDR, we asked.

For me it was clear. My husband said, "We're not unpacking. We're going immediately on to West Germany, to West Berlin." I said, "Without me." The people there [in West Germany], I really don't like them. But especially important is that I'm in agreement with what they want here, by and large, not in the narrow sense but with socialist democracy. I'm for that. And still more specifically the people [in the East] protected me from the concentration camp, so that I couldn't just simply turn my back on them. I cannot do that. . . . The thing is, this [going to the West] was taken for granted when one comes out of the Soviet Union. But I couldn't do it. I couldn't immediately go on over to the Federal Republic. That's exactly the opposite [of where I was at]. And back then there was the Cold War, and everything was much worse than now, still more antagonistic and less friendly for the people who came back from the East. That all fit tightly together. For me it wasn't an option. I didn't have to do what all the others were doing—go West.

We asked whether as a Jew she had second thoughts about returning to Germany. "I've never had inhibitions [because I am a Jew], for at the time I went [to the Soviet Union] such a thing didn't really exist. There were Germans, you know? But there weren't Jews, and Christians, and Catholics, and all of that. And when I came back, I went about exactly the same way that I did before I left." Frau Benario remembers pre-1932 Germany as one where German identity was not exclusively inhabited by non-Jews, where Jewishness was not an icon for difference. "Jews, and Christians, and Catholics, and all that," meaning other particularistic forms of identity, were neither seen as coterminous nor in opposition to Germanness. Although she herself does not use the word *cosmopolitan,* she is remembering a time, at least in the circles she frequented, when a nonparticularistic, nonethnic, nonreligious identity was preferred. She hoped that she could resume this kind of identity after her return to Germany. Her reason for returning to East rather than West Germany she explains variously throughout our interviews with her: because she didn't want to shock her daughter, because she owed something to the Russians since they saved her from the Nazis, because she sympathized with socialism. Ultimately, she often concluded that she felt more comfortable with those in the East because her own history in the intervening twenty-two years was more closely tied to theirs, and she did not want to be alienated from this history.

Case 2. Herr Cramer returned to West Germany with the Allied occupation army in 1944 after six years of residence in the United States. "We wanted to stay in America, but the positions they offered me there interested me so very little. And there was so much to do here, things that were very close to my, no, not my heart, that sounds so. . . . I had the feeling I could do more here than [in America]. I got a job [that enabled me] to remain in Germany." In contrast to Frau Benario, whose reasons for return often focus on concerns of loyalty, belonging, and Cold War ideological fights, Herr Cramer offers an explanation that stresses contingency, accident, a dependence on circumstance. We never encountered any Jews who returned to West Germany out of conviction, though some, like Herr Cramer, developed a positive sense of belonging in their work and interactions in the intervening years.

Case 3. Albert Klein, the oldest of our discussion partners, born in 1904, returned to West Berlin in 1979. He initially went into exile in 1935, because of fear of persecution as a Jew. His exile took him to Vienna and Riga, ultimately landing him in Lithuania, which was shortly afterward annexed by the USSR. He remained in Lithuania working in the theater until 1979, when he emigrated to Israel. "For me, to return was always a task (*Aufgabe*). I always thought that I would come back to Berlin. Berlin is where I grew up and I have certain obligations here." He explained how he had promised his first wife, who was murdered in a concentration camp, that he would return to Berlin. ["In all these years] I've been in no political party, have wanted no privileges, because I knew that somehow I'd come back to Berlin." Klein remembers the decision to return as made before he left. He remembers having made a pact with his first wife about an obligation to return. He never portrays his Jewishness as being in opposition to other identities or even to different citizenships—German, Lithuanian, Soviet, or Israeli. Perhaps more than the other people we interviewed, Herr Klein embodies the idea of a cosmopolitan identity that did not seek to transcend any particularities but rather combined them in different, idiosyncratic ways.

Case 4. Herr Berger returned in 1949 after fighting in the Spanish Civil War, four years internment in a concentration camp in France, and six years exile in the USSR. After mentioning that he came from a politically engaged family, that his father was a pacifist, he explains his decision to return.

We said, it concerns eliminating the roots of fascism in Germany for all time. We fought against fascism before the war, during the war, and we wanted to [do that] also after the war after we returned to Germany. And we all shared the perspective to return to Germany. For we wanted to help build a democratic, anti-Fascist, and, from this perspective, a socialist Germany. Now, it was our task, since we were all old Socialists, old anti-Fascists, with experience, with knowledge of an international nature, now it was our task. . . . We looked at our task as a political one, an ideological, humanistic one. . . . First, we had to drive this antihumanism out of the German people, yes, and we wanted to help do that. And because of that, it was clear to us that we would return to Germany.

This particular explanation is a distinctly East German one, especially in the way in which democracy, antifascism, and socialism are linked as part of an *Aufgabe*: task, mission, obligation. This *Aufgabe* is not the same as that of Herr Klein. Herr Klein's mission was a personal one, to honor the memory of his murdered wife, to reclaim home, to deny the Nazi victory of a *Judenfrei* Germany. In contrast, Herr Berger sees himself as part of a historical mission (political, ideological, humanistic)—thus, his use of "we" instead of "I"—a Communist intent on eliminating fascism.

Case 5. Frau Eisler left Germany in 1936 and returned in 1949 to East Berlin. She had been deported from Ellis Island in New York after three months imprisonment for refusing to inform on her husband, Gerhart Eisler, who, in addition to his anti-Fascist work, had also been a leader in Communist party organizing in the United States during the war.

[I did not want to return] but I didn't have any other option. There were no options for me because, first, I was married, and my husband definitely wanted to return—he was politically engaged. And second, I would have found no sympathy with my American friends if I would have, so to speak, deserted. There would have been a big scandal had I remained. The Americans would have exploited that. They would have made a big deal out of it.

So it was clear to me that I would return. . . . I didn't have a permanent visa. . . . The Americans offered me one so I could stay—if I would have betrayed him, betrayed how he managed to leave the U.S. [He had escaped as a stowaway on a Polish ship.] But I didn't do that.

Much like her counterparts who went to West Germany, Frau Eisler's decision to return was not one made out of loyalty to a cause or ideology but was contingent on circumstances. In her case, the decision was to follow her husband to the East. To this day, Frau Eisler, whose American citizenship was revoked when she left, cannot visit the United States without being arrested. Although she claims to always have had Communist sympathies, her return was perhaps more attributable to gender (we found only one example, that of Frau Benario's "husband," in which a man followed a woman back) than to political convictions.

In sum, we could not isolate a primary reason for return that holds across all or even a majority of the cases. It may be that Jewish Communists were more eager and enthused about returning to the East because they and East Germany were more anti-Fascist than those who returned to the capitalist West where a consistent ideological explanation was unavailable. Yet this conviction may often have been an ad hoc, ideological justification for material circumstances that made the return to the East the best of the relatively few choices available to German Jews at that time. In most cases, practical considerations—offers of work, McCarthyism in the United States, Stalinism in the USSR, deep ties to German language and culture, ties to place—were determinative of who returned and to where.

Division and Identity

Initially, Jews who had returned to Berlin were not radically affected by the Allied division of Germany. In fact, many wanted this division—as just punishment of Germany for the war, as a necessary lien on European security, and, especially for those in the East, as an opportunity to eliminate fascism and construct socialism. The Jewish *Gemeinde* (Community) in Berlin remained united until 1953. A majority of the early returnees to the Soviet Zone/GDR settled in the Pankow area of East Berlin. Officially acknowledged as "victims of fascism," and treated the same as other categories of Nazi victims, they received priority in apartments (only eight percent in Berlin of which survived the war undamaged; see Luize and Hopfner 1965: 574), and many were immediately incorporated into high-status political, cultural, and administrative work. For most of these people, political identity was more important than religious and ethnic aspects of Jewishness. In any case, political authorities in the East encouraged the development of nonreligious and nonethnic identities, and most residents, Jews and non-Jews alike, accommodated themselves to this norm. At the same time, the state did recognize the principle of "freedom of religion." The community organized itself accordingly, along religious lines, and some people did practice a Jewish identity—much as others practiced Catholic or Protestant identities—within the state approved and controlled confines of the confessional community. Given no alternative but a Jewishness reduced to religious practice, many East German Jews suppressed parts of their own histories, in the extreme case even hiding aspects of a Jewish heritage and history. Hence their children were often left on their own to rediscover or nurture relations to Jewishness or the Jewish community if they were so inclined. In 1986, a group called *Wir für Uns* (colloquially, "for ourselves"), comprised of approximately two hundred members, began meeting regularly in East Berlin to cultivate a broad range of primarily nonreligious-based Jewish traditions (Kirchner 1991: 35; Ostow 1990: 47–59).

As the Cold War heated up in the early 1950s, people in the East and the West, including Jews, were increasingly asked to take sides against the other half. In 1952–53, a wave of persecution of "cosmopolitans" and "Western immigrants" in Prague and Moscow had repercussions in East Germany. Jewish communities were searched. The Parliamentary representative and chairman of the Jewish Communities in East Germany, Julius Meyer, was arrested. Five of the eight leaders of the East Berlin Jewish Community fled overnight to West Berlin in January 1953. The result of the exodus was a call from the rabbi for greater Berlin, Nathan Levinson, for all Jews in the GDR to move to the West. Many responded to this call and on January 19, 1953, the Communities were officially divided (Beigel 1953; Ostow 1989: 1–9).

Despite this turbulent political history, approximately 1,500 Jews were registered as living in greater Berlin in 1956. But the number of Jews in the GDR continued to decline dramatically, even after the building of the Berlin Wall in 1961, whereas the community in the West, somewhat larger to begin with, stabilized. By 1986, the number of Jews registered by the community in the GDR had declined to 350, with 200 registered in the East Berlin community (Richarz 1988: 20). Approximately half of those with whom we became acquainted, either personally or through hearsay, were not registered by the community and thus not part of the official statistics. Most came from professional classes and worked in the same, or related, occupations from which they had been banned during the Nazi period. By the 1980s, the East German regime, in search of the international recognition already accorded the Federal Republic, began to curry the favor of international Jewish organizations and thus granted most Jews in the GDR a relatively privileged status, with more travel and business opportunities and better access to political authorities.

For West Berlin Jews, 1952 was also a decisive year, for at that time the Federal

Republic began actively encouraging some prominent Jews to return. In its striving for international recognition and its desire to isolate the GDR, it formulated a reparations policy, not primarily oriented to the Jews who had suffered under the Nazis or to relatives of those who had been killed but focused on the state of Israel and the Jewish people as a group. Through policies earmarked as antifascist in the East and *Widergutmachung* in the West, both German states, but especially the Federal Republic, gained prestige and legitimation in the international community. In light of this effect, Y. Michal Bodemann (1983) has argued that the major "function" of Jews in postwar Germany became one of doing "ideological labor" for the two new states. Because the Federal Republic was more successful at this game of international politics—until 1973, only thirteen states refused to go along with West Germany's Hallstein Doctrine and recognized the GDR—it experienced a net gain in Jews during the Cold War. From 1955 to 1959 alone, six thousand Jews migrated to West Berlin/West Germany; more than 60 percent came from Israel, with most of the rest from Latin America. It should be stressed that most of these immigrants were either of Sephardic ancestry or Ostjuden, not German Jews; they were not returnees but new to Germany and German culture. The Jews in the GDR, on the other hand, though smaller in number than in West Germany, were primarily German Jews, either the products of so-called mixed marriages, concentration camp survivors, or returnees from exile (Kirchner 1991: 30). Following the logic of the Cold War from the other side, the GDR developed a different, often contradictory, policy regarding Jews. Initially it supported Jewish claims for indemnity but after the summer of 1952 suspended all outstanding restitution claims. Likewise, its policy toward Israel, initially extremely supportive, also became increasingly hostile over the years. Additionally, as pointed out above, official anti-Semitic persecutions in the Eastern bloc, especially but not exclusively under Stalin, caused a steady flight west. The West German Jewish community, under the leadership of Heinz Galinski from 1949 to 1990, worked closely with the FRG in welcoming those from the East.

By 1989, the time of our study, Jews (with minimally two Jewish grandparents) living in the two Germanies were estimated at 70,000, although only about half of them were registered as members of the Jewish community. If one includes converts to and others closely identified with Judaism, this number might approach 100,000. Of those registered by the communities, approximately 5,000 lived in the East, 25,000 in the West. Of this total, about 2,000 lived in East Berlin, 6,000 in West Berlin. Included among those in West Germany were approximately 10,000 to 12,000 Soviet Jews who had immigrated since the 1970s (Bodemann 1993; Bodemann 1983: 28; Ostow 1989; and Richarz 1988: 25). Today more than 50 percent of all Jews registered with the community in West Berlin come from the former USSR (Hammer and Schoeps 1988). Of these numbers, only a small fraction are "German Jews." Of this fraction of German Jews, we were concerned with only those who had lived in exile in one of the Allied countries and returned to Berlin.

Living in East or West Berlin altered the way in which Jewishness and Germanness were articulated, and unification has again forced a rearticulation of this relationship. New German-Jewish identities were formed in dynamic interaction with East and West German state and social patterns of integration and postwar identity formation. To oversimplify the major differences, Jews who returned to the East were assimilated into a nationality based on a universalistic ideology of antifascism and socialism. Theoretically, anyone could become East German if they believed in this ideology. Jews who returned to the West were assimilated into a nationality based on a particularist ideology of membership in a blood-based German Volk. Theoretically, only those who were German by blood—and this included German Jews—could become West German. In practice, these state administrators never adhered strictly to these national ideologies. West German citizenship was also guaranteed to anyone who had been a legal resident in the former Reich, as well as to all *Volksdeutsche*, Germans by blood, living in the East bloc. Moreover, it was West German practice to offer citizenship to all European Jews, many of whom were stateless after the war, regardless of their nationality or cultural background. Thus, German Jews who returned to the West fit into a larger category of European Jews in which the German part of this hyphenated status became a sign of citizenship alone, and the Jewish part became a sign of cultural distinctiveness, if not radical otherness. As mentioned above, German Jews who returned to the East tended either to omit the reference to Jewishness altogether, to downplay its relation to otherness by emphasizing its secular qualities, or to reduce it to a religious practice and membership in the *Gemeinde* (the Jewish community). The following five cases illustrate these differences.

Case 1. In August 1989, Ruth Benario, who returned to East Berlin in 1954 after twenty-two years in the USSR, responded to our request to explain how she relates Germanness to Jewishness: "I am a German Jew." To the question "Do you find that burdensome," she responded, "No. God, you sense things, sometimes there's a trace of something or other. But where don't you find that in life? That doesn't matter. . . . But I will say it, for I am it, and I'll remain what I am. I'll always be a Jew."

In the summer of 1989, we asked her about her relationship to the Federal Republic.

It's really seldom that I meet people over there whom I like. The size of the people over there, I feel, isn't right. And their attitude, the way they behave, the way they speak, the things about which they're interested. I am not like that! I'm not that and I don't like that kind of person. . . . It's frightfully difficult for me to get used to these people. . . . It's precisely that way with a woman, a friend of mine whom I've known since our childhood. I just recently began to think about why that is so, just the beginning of this year. I say, "Well, how's it going? What have you gone through?"

"Nothing at all," she says. "I'm always fine."

We were in Zurich back then. She went from exile in London to Zurich. I was so perplexed that she didn't go through anything at all during this period when we had to deal with Herr Hitler and Comrade Stalin, and where so many have gone through so much, such hard times. And that people are first really formed through this experience—that's something they don't at all understand. You see, it's the same for Frau X and her husband in West Berlin. They were in America. They also didn't live through anything that happened, who we were back then, and what we had, and how it all began. And that was for me really remarkable, how I came to this understanding, that they naturally lead a totally different life than we are able to, because we see it from a totally different standpoint. . . . And they are very nice and all, but they don't understand anything, what happened to us because of what we've lived through, how that penetrates us. Or it appeared to me that way. They're very loving and nice, kind, but that's not the point.

Frau Benario expresses the relation of Jewishness to Germanness as something experiential, as part of her personal history. Her history, she reminds us, was made possible only because Stalin saved her from Hitler. Later, of course, she explains how she was also terrorized by Stalin while in Moscow, even exiled in Siberia during the war. Throughout our interviews with her, she stressed her desire to help others, to feel for and live with and for others, as the major motivating force in her life. She feels closest to those people with whom she shares the same experiential history. Her strongest criticism is reserved for her German-Jewish friends who were unable to comprehend her history, an inability she attributes to not having "gone through anything," to exile in America and postwar life in West Berlin.

In an interview two years later, in 1991, she reformulated her relationship to the newly unified Germany. "The Jews aren't well-liked in Germany. And the idea of a Jewish state is even more unpleasant. It's difficult to explain to them that other people want to live just like the people here." Her unstated reference was to German xenophobia and the growing violence against foreigners, in particular asylum seekers and Turks, that accompanied unification. With respect to her own identity, she states, "I don't feel German. I feel Jewish. I am not a German. I don't have anything in common with the whole German people. I was in fact rubbed the wrong way when I came back from the Soviet Union. At that time a friend asked me if I wasn't happy to be back in my home country again. And I said, I am sorry I came back. I find nothing homey here. I'm here to help. That's all."

Between 1989 and 1991, something had indeed changed for Frau Benario. In our first interview, she cried several times in reciting the events of her return, of how, after years of cramped living quarters in Moscow, she was given a large apartment with a kitchen, living room, dining room, and separate bedrooms. In 1991, she began to remember this return as something she regrets—and regretted as early as the 1950s. In the enlarged Federal Republic, she is already beginning to reformulate Jewishness and Germanness as oppositional identities.

Case 2. Herr Cramer returned in 1944–45 with the American army after six years in the United States. About his identity, he said, "I am a German Jew." When we asked about his decision to stay, he replied,

It wasn't a decision, no, it didn't work out that way. I didn't say one day, like Hitler said, that I'd decided to become a politician. I never decided to live here in Germany. Rather, it just presented itself that way. You accumulate so many things like that, like how I entered the American army. I feared that it wouldn't again be possible to build some kind of Jewish life [in Berlin] because I couldn't imagine that during the Hitler period there were still people who thought otherwise here in Germany. Then I came back and suddenly I noticed that, like so much in life, it's not always black and white. Nothing is black-white. It's all various shades of grey, everything is a little faded.

Herr Cramer's initial return to Germany was with the press division of the army. After several years, he returned to the United States, where he had obtained citizenship during his exile. Realizing that there were few career opportunities for him there, he returned to West Germany a second time, this time as a civilian working to establish the West German press (for Springer Verlag). He did not expect full integration and now attributes early problems to his own aloofness and distance from most people. Eventually he joined the Christian Democratic party and worked his way to the top in Springer Verlag. Today he is very proud of the way West German political institutions have developed, and he sees himself as having made a significant contribution to this through the development of an independent press. His personal aloofness never hindered his career, for neither the Federal Republic nor West German society required the kind of ideological integration or agreement demanded by the GDR. In fact, both of his children have left Germany, one for Norway, the other for the United States. He sees their decisions as exercises in freedom of choice, not as rejection of what West Germany offered them. For Herr Cramer, Germanness and Jewishness were never and are not now oppositional identities. Although one might suspect that Herr Cramer served an alibi function for the right-wing German press for whom he worked and for postwar West Germany—a single Jew serving prominently—Herr Cramer never experienced his work for Springer and his life in West Berlin, or so he told us, as a Jewish outsider treated as a token by the insiders. Indeed, as we interviewed him in the executive suite of the gold-capped, glistening Springer building in Berlin, he appeared to us very much an insider.

Case 4. Herr Berger, who returned in 1949 to East Berlin from an internment camp in France (via the USSR), denied altogether any links between his subjective self and either Jewishness or his life in exile.

I am not Jewish. Isn't that clear? I was a Lutheran until I left the church. That was self-evident for me. . . . I'll be quite honest with you. In the old socialist community, where I saw myself as a Social Democrat and a Communist, sometimes as a Socialist, we shared a word, just once a word from Marx: "Religion is the opium of the people." On the other hand, the International, in which it says "No higher being will save us, no God, no Kaiser, no tribunal." And then we have to look at the entire history of Prussian Germany, where the church has always stood on the side of reaction.

For Herr Berger, there was no alternative to socialism, and, as he explained to us elsewhere, to anti-Fascism. Judaism was religion—here he agreed with the official definition of the East German state—and religion cannot save people. In German history, religion, as he sees it, had always served the forces of reaction.

But Herr Berger has another criticism of German Jews, to which he points in explaining why so few returned to Germany. "I beg of us to judge them with care. But many Jews didn't come back for economic reasons. After 1945, Germany was a field of ruins, and it was difficult to make a career here. On the other hand, I believe that the politics of Stalin, in which one can certainly see definite anti-Semitic tendencies, worked to scare away many. It was worse in the Soviet Union, but that is Stalin, please. That's not socialism [we are talking about]; with Lenin it was the opposite." Herr Berger then explained how Lenin had many well-known Jews in his close circle of friends and advisers.

The line of Herr Berger's argument goes as follows: Jewishness means above all religion as ideology—and he distances himself from all religion. Moreover, neither Jews nor any other group can be delineated by blood or race. The fact that he and members of his family were identified by the Nazis in this way seems to have strengthened his resolve not to identify subjectively with the categorization Jew. (In a discussion with a close mutual friend, he once confided how his aunt was forced to give up her house pets once laws were passed making it illegal for Jews to keep domestic animals. Yet he refused to give us even this memory of Jewishness.) Much like Marx in "On the Jewish Question," he appeals for a nonreligious, nonethnic, nonracial identity based on international solidarity. Marx went further, of course, and also argued that Jews would never achieve selfhood and equality within Europe unless they were freed of the stereotypes attached to Jewish culture: greed, money, haggling, and commerce.[1] This criticism is also implicit in Herr Berger's explanation of reasons why German Jews did not return.

Case 5. Frau Eisler returned to East Berlin from the United States in 1949. In our interview in August 1989, she explained, "The GDR gave to me for the first time in my life the feeling that I was a citizen with equal rights. I could vote in the GDR for the first time in my life. I feel like an absolutely equal member of the society here. I feel cared for and secure, ever more now. . . . And, as I said, my journalistic work was a great source of satisfaction. I also sit on the board of the Committee of Anti-Fascist Resistance Fighters, and I am thankful for the carefulness and way and manner in which they treat the anti-Fascist resistance fighters here." About the Germans and German identity, she described her sentiments, "Actually, disrespect, abhorrence, loathing about what they tolerated, if they weren't all criminals themselves."

When we asked her to describe her own complex relation to politics and Jewish selfhood, she said, "I've always said that I am a Jew. I've never been silenced about that, but this conscious Jewishness, that's something the Holocaust made me." Asked to explicate this "something," she replied, "First, I am a Jew. I feel myself a citizen of the German Democratic Republic. I am a GDR Jew." Much like Herr Berger, she has taken on a GDR identity, a state identity that emphasizes Staatsburger, formal citizenship, over membership in any ethnonational identity. But, unlike Herr Berger, she has resisted any integration into the German Kulturnation, instead emphasizing her own cultural identity as a Jew. Her own relations to America and the United States from her period of exile are omitted entirely. Though she remembers these experiences fondly, and stated that she would love to visit her relatives and friends in the United States once again, she did not indicate any personal bitterness or animosity for being denied an opportunity to reconnect with this part of her past. For Frau Eisler, identity is necessarily discontinuous. Her identification with culture, Jewishness, is set alongside her citizenship, GDR—but she is a national nowhere. Moreover, though Jewish by birth and fate, she insists on keeping this cultural identity separate from categories of race and religion. Her citizenship, by contrast, is the one thing she has chosen, based on a shared ideology.

We had several more interviews and letter exchanges with Frau Eisler following the opening of the Wall. During this tumultuous period, she was alternately withdrawn or active in representing her life and that of her husband in the public sphere. In a letter dated April 7, 1991, she referred us to an interview she had given in March 1990 to Manfred Engelhardt, which he edited and published (Engelhardt 1991). In this interview, she lays the blame for the collapse of the GDR on the scandalous leadership of the *Nomenklatura*, "What I am so appalled by is that the leaders in the Party isolate themselves. [They] have no idea what is happening among the people. They have forgotten everything, although they themselves suffered under fascism." She laments the fact "that our chance was wasted and that we now must live through such a decline, that the people don't want to hear from us anymore."

On April 30, 1991, Jeff Peck went back to Frau Eisler with our film director, Martin Patek, for a filmed interview. The following excerpts are from an interview that took place, then, a full seven months after formal unification of the two Germanies. This translation, edited and shortened, is mine.

Jeff: How do you feel about all these events [since 1989]?

Frau Eisler: Very divided. Naturally, I am happy that the Wall has fallen, for I have always had my reservations about how long one can imprison a people. That is very positive. But there are also many negatives. [Among these negatives, she lists a "general insecurity" about the future, unemployment, and rising criminality. She also mentions the singular and virulent anti-Semitism that had "broken out" in Germany, which she also finds threatening.]

Jeff: After the war you came back to the GDR. Now you are sitting in the Federal Republic, a country that you never really wanted [to be a citizen of]. How do you feel about that?

Frau Eisler: I must be honest [with you], it doesn't really matter whether I am now a citizen of the Federal Republic, or was a citizen of the GDR. It's simply . . . it doesn't concern me.

Jeff: Do you have a stronger feeling about being Jewish now than you did before?

Frau Eisler: I don't feel any more Jewish now than before. I understood myself to be Jewish before; that is my identity in the first instance. It was always important to me and it will remain important.

Since our first interview, Frau Eisler has changed significantly the way she portrays her identity. The unification of Germany has not resulted in a more unified identity for Frau Eisler, but in more discontinuities in her life course. No longer able to reference the GDR as part of her identity, she now has only her Jewishness, for she is living in a state with which she has shared an oppositional history. She mourns the loss of parts of her identity tied to the GDR: resistance fighter, anti-Fascist, Socialist. After commenting on her disappointment about the "perversions" of East German socialism and her disappointment with this "great fiasco," the failure to realize socialism in the GDR, Jeff asks her if she is sad. She replies, "Of course I am sad that it has come to this. We had once imagined [we would] build a democratic, better, actually more just, humanistic Germany. That was the reason the people returned, that was the great hope of the people who came out of the KZ [concentration camps], who were persecuted as anti-Fascists. Naturally, it's a great defeat, a defeat we have suffered. We have to live with that."

Conclusion

This chapter has examined how the identities of German Jews who returned from exile following World War II to live in a divided Germany have been marked by discontinuities between categories of culture, nationality, and citizenship. Rather than begin with the necessarily reductionist categories of the state, the census taker, the doctor, the rabbi, or the psychologist, I went directly to German-Jewish returnees and to their personal histories. These histories reveal emergent and changing subject positions, variously willed by individuals, determined by outside authorities, or negotiated between the two, with regard to states, nations, religions, ethnicities, and, most strikingly, with regard to the Cold War. These positions should not be confused with "opinions" or "values," idealist artifacts with which the cultural is often confused; rather, subject positions directly index the material conditions in which people actually live.

Formerly exiled German Jews offer privileged insights into the relations between identity, exile, and politics because they are an extreme and exceptional case. As Carl Schmitt has argued, politics is made by who decides on the exception, and the Jews have often served as the exception in German, if not in European, history.[2] This "decision" has not been just a German or Jewish one, but one of world-historical dimensions, part of a "global ecumene" (Hannerz 1992) in which a transnational flow of images and interactions has contested the meaning of "German Jew." The German Jew today is a living presence in a space where they were consigned to death and memory. The fact that non-Jewish Germans tend to project onto them qualities and meanings that they had no part in generating should not lead us to privilege these projections in our studies (R. Gay 1992: 467–84). Today these often philosemitic meanings, not restricted to the German Jew but often extended to the European Jew, include guardians of memory, the conscience (and origin) of the West, and a litmus test for German democracy. In this highly emotional and political field, the specificity of the German-Jewish subject, particularly those who returned to Germany, has been blurred and confused, if not effaced.

It is commonplace in the popular media to assume that Germanness and Jewishness are radical alterities that entail mutually exclusive identities, to stress the cultural autonomy and timelessness of Jewish culture as distinct from the same aspects of German culture, and to think of the "Jewish community" as a homogeneous, distinct group that never changes. We have inherited this conceptualization of culture from German romanticism and nineteenth-century debates on cultural nationalism, and anthropologists have been perhaps the major carriers of this basically Herderian tradition. It is, however, extremely misleading to assume that culture is thing-like, a set of essences distinct from other essences that endure over time, passed on by generational transmission (Moore 1994; and Clifford 1988). The German Jew has a historical and syncretic identity, fundamentally shaped in interaction with the experience of diaspora and with the political division of the Cold War.

With this in mind, one does no justice to German-Jewish identity by considering the Jews as always external to the Germans, by assuming that the Jews have always had to choose between cultural autonomy or assimilation into an unchanging Germanness, or, conversely, that the Germans have to fear being Jewified, recalling the Nazi notion of a *zersetzende Geist* (a decomposing, perverting spirit). Indeed, the very idea that the Jews could so easily pervert the Germans indicates a basic Nazi insecurity, even admission of an inferiority complex, that German spirit was itself incomplete and thus open to influence by a projected "outside" that was already "in."

This kind of thinking was reinforced by the idea of a homogeneous nation, written into the West German Basic Law of 1949, that Germanness is inherited by blood, that because a German is necessarily limited to a single citizenship, she or he must choose to which culture s/he belongs. As is well known, this ethnocultural ideal of German nationality has never been historically realized. At least since the Middle Ages, Germans have been divided into many competing principalities, each with distinct tribal identities. In the last several centuries, millions of ethnic Germans have been living outside any German state along with millions of non-Germans (primarily Slavs and Jews) living within the different German states. The ideal of homogeneity was further reinforced by an assimilationist model of the "Volk" that has traditionally assumed the Jews, alone with the Gypsies of all the peoples in Europe, to be nonassimilable to the major "nationalities" on the continent. The inspiration for this idea is the nineteenth-century Mazzini formula, that a culture, nation, and state are isomorphically related, a program on which the Zionist movement also modeled itself (Brubaker 1992; Hobsbawm 1990). This model of an ethnocultural nation-state continues to inspire the leaders of the vast majority of the 190 states in existence as of this writing, despite the fact that only a handful have anything approaching a homogeneous nation. But in Germany, a territorial component was ultimately added to the ethnic/descent qualification—in 1999, eight years after unification.

German Jews never fit neatly into this either/or question, for clearly they could be either, neither, or both German and/or Jew. In their lives, culture, nation, and state are more often than not disjunctively instead of continuously related. In this sense they are a "third" with respect to the binary German/Jew or native/foreigner in that they resist easy categorization and thus pass back and forth between them, between German and Jew, between native and foreigner. During their periods of exile, many Jews had obtained another citizenship (Soviet, American, British) and become fluent in other languages, further complicating the program of a continuous national history and bounded cultural identity expressed in a single language that realizes itself in a state.

By repatriating to Germany, these German Jews challenged and destabilized the assertion of the binary opposition German and Jew, and in that sense were harbingers of a reconciliation between the countries Germany and Israel. Germany is today not only Israel's most important trading partner but also a consistent voice for Israeli interests within European politics. In passing between cultures, nationalities, and citizenships, German Jews have hovered in-between belongings, resisting to some extent the radical choices between East and West, Jew and German, Israel and one of the German states.

The Jews in this study returned from three different experiences of exile—the Soviet Union, the United States, and England, the nations of the "morally correct"—following World War II. They returned from this position within the morally correct to the land where the genocide took place. For those in the East, as I have already mentioned, the return was justified above all in antifascist terms. They claim they returned to eliminate fascism; they remained on the side of morality. For those in the West, the reasons for return vary tremendously. Few have anything to do with morality; most returnees claim that they just got caught in Germany and then made the best of it. But, to the extent that some justified the return to Germany in moral terms, it was to build a democratic Germany. This difference between the condensed symbols of antifascism and democracy was a major theme of debate in the unification process. Since the unified Germany was redone according to the West German model of democracy, and since the "morally correct" Soviet Union has dissolved, the antifascist subject position of people in the East, Jews included, was harshly criticized and severely undermined. For none of the Jews with whom we spoke was the unification of Germany a major goal or reason for return. Some, indeed, returned only because Germany was divided, and because they thought that this division was right. Suddenly they found themselves to be displaced peoples again in a country not of their choosing.

The point I want to make is that both exile and place of return, East or West, provided different locations for articulations of German-Jewish relations to the Holocaust, the division of Germany, and now unification. First, the Holocaust affected this group directly, but, unlike those who survived the war in one of the camps or in hiding in Germany, they survived in exile, and exile is remembered as life not death. Second, memory of the Holocaust has been shaped by return, by being positioned as German citizens living in German culture. Memory is shaped by direct confrontation with the site of Holocaust culture—place, sounds, sights—that other Jews remember from afar. Thus, return has entailed a different living out of the Holocaust trauma, a kind of reconciliation condemned by many Jews in America and Israel. But this working-through further differs for those who returned to the East instead of the West. Devoting one's life to eliminating Fascism, even if considered a failed project by some of the participants themselves, is not the same kind of working-through as dedication to building a free press or fostering democratization.

What a successful anti-Fascist working-through entails remains highly disputed. However, it would be oversimplistic to claim that the East German anti-Fascist policy was totally ineffectual, or even, as some claim, counterproductive. An opinion survey done between October 1 and October 15, 1990, indicated that West Germans were much more anti-Semitic than were East Germans. In response to the question of whether Israel was a state like any other, to which Germany had no special obligation, 57 percent of the West Germans responded positively, only 40 percent of the East Germans. In response to the question of whether the Jews instrumentalize the Holocaust, 45 percent of the West Germans said yes, compared to 20 percent of the East Germans. In response to the question of whether Jews have too much influence over world politics, 44 percent of the West Germans said yes, while only 20 percent of the East Germans agreed (cited in Benz 1991: 21). To be sure, the opinions indicated in surveys are hardly reliable reflections of what people actually do, since they usually reflect back the opinions of the questioner. In this case, the questioner was the American Jewish Committee, which I presume had no interest in showing West Germans to be more anti-Semitic than East Germans. The only conclusion I want to draw is that the anti-Fascist policies of the GDR, and reeducation more generally, should not be dismissed lightly since such efforts had some influence on opinion and behavior (Borneman 1996). How enduring and significant these changes are is a matter for further research.

Lastly, given the end of the Cold War, is the Jewish returnee to Germany again repositioned? Certainly the dissolution of the Soviet Union coupled with the unification of Germany has dramatically changed the configuration of power as to who can determine morality. And with the elimination of the GDR Jews in the East have been directly challenged to reexamine their postwar lives. Although the United States claims for itself moral leadership on a world scale, it appears as if the issue of right is increasingly being decided at a national level. Even if this trend does not continue, Jews in Germany no longer occupy the contested space they did during the Cold War. Nor are they likely to reoccupy the phantasmic space of "the exception" they did in the nineteenth century (P. Gay 1978; Gilman 1991; and Gilman 1986). The increase in xenophobia and antiforeign actions in Germany has often been directed at Muslims and Arabs, it has not been paralleled by a similar increase in Jewish anti-Semitism. German Jews appear to have lost their iconic status, though they are not yet merely a sign in the forest of symbols. What do we have to learn from the experiences of German Jews? "If their success was largely illusory in immediate terms," writes the German-Jewish,

American historian George Mosse, "in the long run they presented an attractive definition of Jewishness beyond religion and nationalism" (1985: 20). At a time when ethnonationalism in discrete, sovereign states is being posited as the only viable form of group identity, German-Jewish struggles to move beyond this form are indeed an alternative that deserves our attention.

Chapter 8
Repatriation and Social Class in Nicaragua

James Phillips

> Sorrow has been a challenge
> the future a hope.
> We build, as though a poem,
> creating, erasing, rewriting.
> —Nicaraguan poet, Vida Luz Meneses

Since 1934, Nicaragua has experienced forty-five years of repressive dictatorship, a bloody revolution that killed 50,000 people, eleven years of revolutionary change during which civil war killed another 50,000 people, and a decade of peace that many say is simply war by a different name. Adding to these man-made disasters, like the horsemen of the apocalypse, have come tidal waves, hurricanes, volcanic explosions, and other natural disasters. This is the immediate context in which thousands of Nicaraguans have left their homelands for temporary or permanent exile. It is also the context in which thousands have repatriated.[1]

This chapter concentrates on those who left Nicaragua during the civil conflict of the 1980s, and analyzes the experience, especially the repatriation, of these exiles within a context of socioeconomic class differences and emerging class awareness in a society penetrated by transnational economic interests. The cultural components of social classes in such situations shape different experiences of exile. The large majority of the refugees from Nicaragua in the 1980s were peasants. The conditions that shaped their displacement to Honduras and repatriation to Nicaragua were part of a social class transformation—the proletarianization of peasant populations—that threatened the continued existence of the peasants as a viable socioeconomic group (Mintz 1974).

In Nicaragua, this process of class transformation through refugee status and repatriation took place in a context of conflicting national agendas about how

Nicaragua was to be integrated into global economic systems. It may be understood not only as a coincidence of war or natural disaster, but also within a context of, and perhaps as an integral response to the developing demands of a global economy. For many peasant refugees, repatriation meant the end, not of displacement, but of being a peasant.

Defining Refugee, Repatriation, and Return

Article 14.1 of the 1948 Universal Declaration of Human Rights states that, "Everyone has the right to seek and to enjoy in other countries asylum from persecution." In a now-classic formulation, the 1951 Geneva Convention Relating to the Status of Refugees included reference to "a well-founded fear of being persecuted for reasons of race, religion, nationality, membership of a particular social group or political opinion." It also stipulated that, for these reasons, the refugee is unable to gain protection in her country of nationality and therefore crosses national boundaries in search of protection from such threats. Finally, the Geneva definition included an inability or unwillingness to return to one's country of nationality due to such threats. As Malkki points out, these attempts to define refugee were primarily a response to conditions in Europe during and after World War II (1995b: 497ff).

In the thirty years between these classic formulations of the status of refugee and the events discussed in this chapter, situations in Africa and Asia, forced a rethinking and reformulation of the meaning of refugee, both as a legal status and as a sociological and ethnographic concept. The concept of refugee began to reflect a more diverse causality and population. The Organization of African Unity admitted civil war and disorder due to disasters as situations in which people flee across national boundaries in search of safety and security. In many areas, extreme poverty, natural disasters, civil conflict, and governmental repression often seemed to co-occur as a complex of conditions from which people might flee as refugees. The nexus of poverty and political repression as a contributing factor in validating claims for refugee asylum in the United States was upheld in immigration hearings involving people fleeing Haiti in the early 1980s (e.g., *Haitian Refugee Center v Civilletti* 1980). In Latin America, and especially in Central America, civil conflict relating to social and political change emerged as a major context for the creation of refugee populations (Phillips 1994a). Nicaragua during the 1980s was an example.

Three further refinements in the understanding and use of the refugee concept have developed. The earlier concept of the refugee as an individual and refugee status as an individual's experience seemed inadequate in situations where large groups and even whole populations moved across national boundaries. Investigation has turned increasingly to attempts to understand group experiences (Malkki 1995b). Second, the diversity of refugee populations has begun to gain attention, replacing assumptions of uniformity and interchangeability. Recognition of the particular and differing refugee experiences of women, children, the elderly, indigenous and tribal peoples, and different socioeconomic classes has become increasingly important. The present study concentrates on class differences as relevant in shaping the meaning of the refugee experience.

Third, attention has turned increasingly to analysis of the refugee experience as a dynamic process, not simply a static category or status. Within this process, attention has focused on (1) the forces that move people to leave their homeland; (2) their adjustment (or lack thereof) to life in a host country, whether in camps or in host communities; (3) the resolution of refugee as a legal status and a social identity, that is, how one stops being a refugee. International organizations have commonly recognized three durable resolutions of refugee situations: permanent settlement in a host country; resettlement in a third country; and repatriation to the country of origin. Increasingly, these three imagined outcomes have become inadequate in accounting for the creative, diverse, and complex ways in which refugees and refugee populations stop being refugees. The current study focuses on repatriation as a complex, problematic process. In sum, these expansions in our understanding of refugees reflect a conceptual and theoretical critique of the essentialism of earlier attempts to define "a single, essential, transhistorical refugee condition" (Malkki 1995b: 511).

In the context of Central America during the 1980s, at least two additional complications to the concept of refugee deserve attention. Refugee situations in this region during this period occurred largely in the context of struggles over societal and political change. The civil wars in Guatemala, El Salvador, and Nicaragua, which generated thousands of refugees, were struggles over social, economic, and political change in those countries. In most cases, these movements were rooted in a history of poverty and political repression, but the dynamics of pervasive armed civil conflict introduced further complexity to the refugee experience and further complications to the concept of refugee. People fled the dangers of war (Nicaragua, El Salvador), the imagined dangers of impending changes (Nicaragua), or the brutal reaction to attempts at change (El Salvador, Guatemala, Honduras). This situation affected the way refugees began to identify themselves and to transform their refugee identity. For example, many Salvadorans gradually began to envision their repatriation as agents of change in their own country, while many Nicaraguans did not, (Phillips 1994c). The present chapter is an attempt to understand one refugee situation in a larger context of struggles over changes that are shaped by larger national, international, and global agendas. As such, it represents a critique of much of the literature that sees refugee situations as a "problem for development" devoid of larger political implications (Malkki 1995:506).

The second complication of the refugee situation in Central America concerns the process of crossing international boundaries, an integral part of most definitions of refugee. Here one encounters the difference between legal and ethnographic uses of the term refugee. The idea of an international boundary may be a legal and political reality, but it is not necessarily a sociocultural reality for those who are termed refugees (Hansen 1991: 102–3). In a study of Salvadoran refugees in southwestern Honduras during the 1980s, Montes (1989) provides a descriptive analysis of the social and cultural continuity along the border between El Salvador and Honduras. Similarly, peasant farmers who crossed from northern Nicaragua into southern Honduras in the 1980s were moving into a social and cultural context not significantly different from that which they had left. Although sometimes potentially deadly to cross (Dilling 1989), the international boundary was porous, with constant flows of population back and forth in both directions. This sociocultural continuity, ease of access and adjustment, and repeated transience also shaped the complexity of movement, and of the meaning of terms such as repatriation and return.

Repatriation and return are sometimes used interchangeably. More often, repatriation has a formal and restricted meaning, while return is used informally and refers to any situation in which people go back to a country of origin. Repatriation often refers to a situation in which people consider themselves and are considered by others to be in a host country temporarily, with the intention of eventually returning permanently to a country of origin. As used in this chapter, repatriation can be either the decision of refugees themselves, or the policy and program of a host government or international agency assumed to have protective responsibility for the refugees (usually the office of the United Nations High Commissioner for Refugees, UNHCR or, in Spanish, ACNUR). Repatriation usually implies relatively little attempt or intent by either refugees themselves or host populations and governments to adjust or assimilate refugees into the host country. The dynamic of repatriation is toward the country of origin.

By contrast, return can be usefully applied to situations in which refugees or immigrants have already settled more-or-less permanently in a host country, and return to a country of origin for a temporary visit. Return can also refer to the adoption of a transnational lifestyle in which people move back and forth between two countries. Finally, return can be used in circular movements in which refugees actually return home and then back to a host country several times before permanent repatriation or resettlement. In such cases, refugee populations and individuals are often connected in complicated ways to other border populations—such as guerrilla forces—and to their movements and agendas. This situation may require a more nuanced understanding of what is forced and what is voluntary. It can complicate both the identity of being a refugee and the repatriation process. Such is the case discussed in this chapter.

When Peasants Become Refugees

Wolf defines peasants as "populations that are existentially involved in cultivation and make autonomous decisions regarding the process of cultivation" (1969: xiv). Unlike the farmer, the peasant, "cleaves to traditional arrangements which guarantee his access to land and to the labor of kin and neighbors. Moreover, he favors production for sale only within the context of an assured production for subsistence" (Wolf 1969: xiv). The traditional arrangements upon which peasants depend include local community relationships of kinship and ritual obligation, as well as relationships to local authorities, large landowners, or others who may exercise control or ownership over the land and resources that the peasant needs for subsistence. Some of these important others are brokers or gatekeepers between the peasant and the larger society beyond the local peasant community. This way of life is supported by values and perspectives that may differ markedly from those of other social classes. In general, the peasants of Nicaragua have historically conformed to this description.

In traditional peasant communities the exploitation of the peasantry by the larger society and its local agents and brokers is normally masked, or embedded within the network of social relations and values unless or until the traditional arrangements are ripped away by events and processes dictated by development of the larger society. This leaves peasants consciously vulnerable and forces them to face directly the larger society—a process Mintz calls proletarianization (Mintz 1974). It may certainly be argued that such disruptions of peasant life have increased in recent decades. Discussion of the displacement of peasant populations is sometimes oriented within the context of an emerging global economic order rooted in the colonialism of previous centuries and heading toward the increased integration or globalization of local and national economic systems and communities (Phillips 1994b, 1998; Mintz 1974; Wolf 1969).

A growing literature of case studies contributes to this line of analysis. For example, Grosfoguel uses the term "depeasantization" to describe the penetration and demands of the global economy in the Caribbean and the region's integration therein (Grosfoguel 1995). In his study of the forcible displacement and permanent transformation of three Mexican peasant communities by a hydroelectric dam project as part of Mexico's integration into the North American Free Trade Agreement (NAFTA), Quesada Aldana argues that this result, and similar results in other parts of Mexico, are not accidental but are deliberately planned by government and international lending agencies. "The purpose may have been to depeasantize (*descampesinizar*) the Mexican countryside, in order to remove any obstacles in the way of development of big business, both national and international" (Quesada Aldana 1998: 8).

While the displacement of peasant communities and the decline in the proportion of peasants within societies are often described within a global economic dynamic, peasant displacement is rarely explicitly discussed as a major contributor to the formation of refugee populations. Many cases of peasant displacement are internally contained within the boundaries of a single country and not defined as refugee situations.[1] Many of the refugee populations that have been studied are not primarily composed of peasants. Studies of refugee populations that are composed primarily or entirely of peasants may not adopt a descriptive or analytic framework that emphasizes social class as a crucial characteristic. Studies of refugee populations are often concerned with the local and internal dynamics of the situation, and may not include discussion of national or global economic forces.

Most of the refugee flows within Central America in the past three decades have been overwhelmingly composed of forcibly displaced peasants (Ferris 1987). The approach adopted here analyzes refugee situations involving many Nicaraguans during the 1980s from the perspective of social class differences, and specifically of peasant displacement and class transformation within a global economic framework.

Peasant Displacement in Recent Nicaraguan History

Nicaragua has a history of both peasant displacement and refugee situations which during the past half-century have been symptomatic of the movement from a semi-feudal agrarian structure to the threshold of integration into neoliberal global economic systems. When the Somoza family seized power in 1934, the agrarian landscape consisted largely of a *minifundia* of many small, peasant-owned plots, a *latifundia* of large family and corporate-owned plantations (especially cotton-growing enterprises on the country's Pacific slope), and a ganaderia system of middle-sized family-owned cattle ranches. Peasant displacement during this period was mostly internal, as peasants in some areas were forced from their plots by expansion of family and corporate plantations. They then went to the cities, or squatted on marginal lands. In a few cases, the Somoza dictatorship resettled displaced peasants in *colonias*, parcels of land in more remote areas. Meanwhile, Nicaragua's economic elite became increasingly divided between those who wanted to modernize the economy by intregrating it into larger, global systems; and those who feared any departure from the older, semi-feudal regime.

The Sandinista uprising that ended the Somoza dictatorship in 1979 was initiated by upper- and middle-class urban, educated professionals and students. Peasants, however, provided many of the fighters and the material and moral support for the insurrection (Bedana 1991; Phillips 1994b: 11–12). At the time, the brutality of Somoza's attempts to suppress the uprising shocked international observers as news media reported these events. (For example, the Cuban newspaper *Granma* carried daily stories with photos of the killing of civilians and the bombing of the city of Esteli.) Resistance to Somoza crossed class lines, and included wealthy businesspeople and professionals as well as poor peasants. Thousands of peasants fled the violence for the relative safety of neighboring Honduras.

With the Sandinista victory and the departure of Somoza in 1979, many Nicaraguans in Honduras returned home, while former members of the Somoza elite and some officers in his National Guard fled to Honduras, Costa Rica, the United States, and elsewhere. Some of those who fled the Sandinista victory eventually formed the core of a resistance movement that later called itself the Nicaraguan Resistance. Others called it simply *la contra*, the counterrevolution. By the early 1980s, Resistance forces were making armed incursions into Nicaragua from bases in southern Honduras and northern Costa Rica. They became a vehicle for those who wanted to end Sandinista rule and integrate the country more closely into global economic systems (Eich and Rincon 1984). The armed struggle created violent, insecure situations in which thousands of peasants and whole communities were uprooted from the land and the social networks in which they had traditionally lived.

Conflicting Projects of the 1980s

During the 1980s, two different and conflicting projects formed the context for the armed struggle. Each project envisioned a different fate for Nicaragua's peasants. The revolutionary development project of the Sandinista government proposed a mixed economy in which rural peasant farmers would play a more prominent and privileged role than under Somoza. The agrarian reform concentrated on replacing the traditional agrarian class relations with a situation in which peasant farmers and strengthened peasant communities worked together in cooperative forms under the guidance and with the support of the state. Some progress was made toward achieving this goal, especially in the early years of Sandinista rule. This project was oriented inward insofar as it concentrated on increasing internal production and meeting the basic needs of the poorer sectors of the country's population (Central American Historical Institute 1984; Kaimowitz 1984).[2]

An alternative project to transform Nicaragua's rural agrarian society was furthered by those in Nicaragua and the United States who were interested in expanding a neo-liberal global economic system. The role envisioned for Nicaragua's peasants was that of a mobile and relatively inexpensive labor force, while large areas of land were transferred from peasant control to the control of those more integrated into the developing global economy. The advancement of this project required the proletarianization of the country's peasants, their transformation into a mobile work force, and the rupture of traditional ties to land, place, and community. In effect, this meant the elimination of peasants as a viable socioeconomic class.

Pervasive Conflict

Outside observers often called the war in Nicaragua in the 1980s a civil war. Divisions occurred in families of all social classes, but peasant families were particularly stressed inasmuch as they depended heavily on all family members for survival and support. Peasant families with members fighting on one side of the conflict were often worried about reprisals from the other side. Wealthy families usually had more economic and political resources to deal with such threats. Yet this conflict was more complex, for the war not only divided families, but also provided an excuse for the reemergence of long-standing local conflicts between neighbors, large landowners, and local peasants. Beyond this, the war was international, involving both Honduras and the United States as well as Nicaragua.

This multi-level conflict fueled by old social tensions and new ideas about low-intensity warfare eradicated a clear and relevant distinction between combatant and civilian and eventually, between combatant and refugee.[3] Government agrarian reform workers and Ministry of Housing workers who worked in peasant communities, and nonmilitary installations such as grain storage facilities and rural health clinics, were major targets of resistance forces. This situation posed enormous problems for local peasants. In a typical case, a father and daughter were severely injured when the truck in which they were riding struck a land mine. When asked why he was riding on a road he knew could be mined, the father replied that he lived there. To protect themselves, isolated rural peasant communities formed local self-defense militias and patrolled the perimeters of their communities constantly. U.S. officials routinely referred to peasant farming communities as military targets.

The lack of any secure civilian space in Nicaragua's northern countryside shaped the refugee situation in several ways. It raised levels of fear and insecurity in peasant communities and encouraged many to leave for Honduras. It also led to the blurring of differences between refugee and combatant, and posed problems for the international community in deciding who was a refugee. For example, a U.S. Government report discussing the Nicaraguan refugee camps in southern Honduras admitted that the identity of camp residents as refugees was problematic. Refugee camps were important recruiting grounds for nearby Resistance forces who had easy access to the refugees, while humanitarian aid intended for the refugees was allegedly diverted to Resistance forces (Ferris 1987: 34).

Class Differences, Resource Bases, and Concepts of Self and Place

Between 1982 and 1990, thousands of Nicaraguan peasants were internally displaced, and thousands more of all social classes fled the country as refugees. Among the social classes there were significant differences in the pattern and subjective experiences of being a refugee. Differential access to economic, social, and cultural resources shaped these variant experiences.

For many wealthier Nicaraguans, having enough money to travel quickly to the United States and to establish oneself successfully usually correlated with access to a transnational social (business or professional) network and cultural resources such as higher education and a cosmopolitan lifestyle, values, and experiences. More profoundly, many of Nicaragua's elite were already at ease with the idea of participating in and taking advantage of international and global systems, and with defining their primary community in transnational and non-local terms. Most wealthy and middle-class Nicaraguan refugees went to the United States or to major Latin American cities.

Lacking significant economic resources and international networks, and with a locally rooted sense of self and place, most peasant refugees went the few kilometers across the border to rural southern Honduras (or northern Costa Rica). Once there, they lived in refugee camps, while some survived among the local peasant and small-town populations. Although legally an international passage, this border crossing provided familiar cultural and social continuity for northern Nicaraguan peasant refugees. This very continuity posed problems for Honduran authorities, who had reasons for wanting to control and confine the Nicaraguan refugee population, but were often unable to identify them.

Class Differences in Reasons for Leaving Nicaragua

Decisions to leave one's homeland and seek refuge elsewhere are usually complex. During the 1980s, outsiders often assumed or claimed that Nicaraguans were fleeing their country for ideological reasons, specifically opposition to or fear of the communist tendencies of the Sandinista-led government. A closer analysis reveals that most refugees of all social classes had other, more practical and immediate reasons which were related to ideological differences only in complicated ways, if at all (Bedana 1991: 17)

The problems of running a business during the conflict of the 1980s were important considerations for many wealthy business people. These problems included sabotage and damage to infrastructure, a war economy that left little money for repairing or expanding old or damaged infrastructure, shortages of fuel and materials, travel restrictions within the country due to dangers in the war zones, disruption of trade with the United States, and more. The real or anticipated negative consequences of Sandinista government policies toward business were also a concern, related practically and implicitly, to ideology. These considerations pushed some Nicaraguans to leave. Some also were pulled by the opportunity to become established abroad in countries such as the United States whose economies offered more opportunities and played a more important role in global systems.

The war was most immediately and intensely felt by peasant communities. As Alejandro Bedana writes, "The peasants were both the subject and the object of the civil war, but they did not start it" (1991: 13). As a class, the peasants were the primary intended beneficiaries of the agrarian, economic, and social policies of the Sandinista government, and the primary object of the military and psychological warfare of the Resistance forces. The war took place where peasant farmers chiefly lived and where their identity was rooted. Most casualties were peasants.

The overwhelming concern of peasants, especially in the northern zones of conflict, was immediate safety and security. Dona Josefa, who had already lost two sons in the war, repeated a refrain often heard among both refugees in Honduras and displaced peasants in Nicaragua:

We were afraid, afraid for our children. We're afraid because they [the Nicaraguan Resistance] strike [our communities]. What we want most is peace. The *contra* destroyed everything, crops, homes. They killed our sons. It's a very bad situation.

Not only was the situation frightening, but the refugee's resources were often destroyed as well. Dona Josefa, for example, came from a peasant community that was attacked and burned by Resistance forces, along with four other nearby communities. She lost her land, her house, and most of her possessions. Resistance fighters destroyed many peasant communities or attacked them repeatedly, making it impossible for peasants to remain. Many were internally displaced and others went to Honduras.

Young people and their families worried about the military draft. They were concerned (with good reason) about death or a permanently disabling injury, and about removal from the family economic unit which depended on their work. The ordeal of Dona Casimira, a peasant refugee from a small community in northern Nicaragua, was typical. "My son went into the military [Sandinista Army] to defend us. He was killed in an ambush a year ago. My other children would have to serve. But having lost one, I don't want to lose any more," she said early in 1986. Sometimes, young people slipped away to Honduras to avoid conscription, then returned quietly to their families.

In some areas where Resistance forces operated most freely, they disseminated propaganda about Sandinista government intentions, promised better living conditions and even cash for those who went to Honduras, and threatened community members who wanted to remain in Nicaragua. Resistance forces kidnapped individuals, often in roadside ambushes or raids on communities. Sometimes, Resistance forces simply marched whole communities to Honduras at gunpoint, including in one case a village of 152 people. The author personally documented several of such cases. The particular case of the village of 152 was corroborated by a villager who was able to return to Nicaragua, as well as by foreign aid workers and Catholic nuns who lived in the area and worked with the villagers. Some of these situations blurred the line between creating refugees and forcibly conscripting young people into the Resistance forces. They also gave new meaning to the term "forcibly displaced."

Conscious ideological preferences usually played a minor role, if any, in peasant refugees' decisions to flee or to repatriate. Dona Marta, was a peasant refugee woman whose son joined the war at the age of thirteen and was killed. Later she said he had not died for anything as petty as political ideology. "All this talk about communism, we don't know anything about it."

Class Differences in Refugee Camps

Wealthy and middle-class Nicaraguans lost land, businesses, clientele, and professional positions when they left Nicaragua, but in many cases they were able to transfer some assets to their host country, and to establish themselves in new ways. For most peasant refugees, the situation was radically different. While some lived among the Honduran population in small towns and rural areas, the majority was placed in camps in southern Honduras.

In 1988, ACNUR estimated that there were 25,000 Nicaraguan refugees in Honduras. About half of these were English-speaking Miskito Indians living mostly in the eastern department of Gracias a Dios (La Mosquitia). The rest, about 12,000, were Spanish-speaking Ladino or mestizo Nicaraguans concentrated in three camps in the southern department of El Paraiso, not far from the Nicaraguan border. These numbers fluctuated during the early 1980s, but gradually climbed until 1988. In that year the numbers began to decline as people repatriated.

Life in the Nicaraguan refugee camps in El Paraiso was structured and controlled by formal and informal power structures. By the mid-1980s, ACNUR had primary responsibility, but major policy decisions were set by the Honduran military and the Honduran National Refugee Commission (CONARE) headed by an army colonel. During this period, members of the Nicaraguan Resistance moved relatively freely within the refugee camps and recruited among the refugees. The Resistance had several training camps and safe havens in southern Honduras, not very far from the refugee camps. By manipulating treats, threats, and truth, Resistance fighters exercised control in the camps. They provided cigarettes, other small luxuries, and sometimes food rations; threatened reprisals against the family members in Nicaragua of refugees who talked of returning home: and spread rumors as another means of control. A particularly potent rumor was that Sandinista authorities would kill or jail refugees who returned to Nicaragua.

The resistance blocked news and information about amnesties proclaimed by the Nicaraguan government, and specifically targeted Nicaraguans who were charged with providing information about such amnesties (Phillips 1994c: 110). There were also allegations of U.S. government involvement in efforts to control or distort the flow of information from Nicaragua to the refugees in Honduras. In 1988, Miskito leader Brooklyn Rivera, often a skeptical critic of Sandinista government policy, claimed that the United States Embassy in Honduras had exercised its influence to prevent him from entering Honduras to provide Nicaraguan refugees with information about repatriation (reported in the Honduran daily, *El Tiempo*, March 29).

When others were present, refugees were very reluctant to talk about this informal power structure controlled by the Resistance. Some made oblique reference to the pervasiveness of *orejas* (spies, literally "ears"). In private, refugees spoke to members of international agencies of their desire to return to Nicaragua and their fear of what Resistance forces might do to them, to family members in Nicaragua, or to those they would leave behind in Honduras. As ACNUR's representative in Honduras publicly admitted that the refugee camps were used by resistance forces, and that this was a difficult problem to resolve (*El Tiempo*, March 7, 1988). He had told the author the same in a private interview sometime earlier. The informal control structure in the camps, while far from complete, helped Resistance forces to obtain new recruits and discouraged large-scale repatriation to Nicaragua.

Attitudes Toward Repatriation

Class-related differences shaped differences in attitudes toward, and patterns of, repatriation. Wealthier refugees often had the resources, the transnational networks, and a vision of their own identity that encouraged them to understand their time abroad in terms of opportunities not available in Nicaragua, even in peacetime. They were more likely to shift attention from repatriation to permanent resettlement in a host country, especially the United States. Even the arrival of a formal peace and a change of government in 1990 were not incentives compelling enough for many to repatriate. Many returned to Nicaragua for occasional visits, often to reclaim land occupied by peasant cooperatives or other occupiers, or to recoup assets held by others or by the government during the Sandinista period (Phillips 1994c: 16). These resources were integrated into a personal economic base centered outside Nicaragua. Opportunity lay in resettlement rather than repatriation.

Peasant refugees in camps in Honduras focused on home as a particular locale within Nicaragua where all of their assets—material and social—were located. Identity and long-term survival were rooted in place. Far from being an interruption to economic and social security, repatriation was as a step toward normalizing and securing one's economic and social life. Opportunity lay in repatriation rather than resettlement.

This attitude toward repatriation as opportunity was reinforced by the conditions of refugee camp life in Honduras. For most refugees, the material conditions of camp life were not a significant improvement over life back home, and were often worse. The flow of aid from international and governmental relief agencies did not significantly change this situation. Aid was a constant reminder of the peasant refugee's dependency and the insecurity of her condition. Aid depended on the charity or good will of outsiders, and could be an instrument of control as much as of support. Honduran authorities, international aid agents, and the Nicaraguan Resistance could manipulate the flow of aid for their own purposes. Public accusations of such manipulation were frequent (e.g., *El Tiempo*, June 23, 1988).

Life in the refugee camps was hardly more secure than life in Nicaragua. The forced conditions under which some refugees had been brought to Honduras further contributed to the sense of insecurity and powerlessness associated with life in the camps.

Under such conditions, repatriation became more attractive, and news of changes in family or local conditions back home influenced attitudes about repatriation. Upon hearing that a son dodging conscription in the Nicaraguan Army had (or could receive) amnesty from the Nicaraguan government, some refugee families tried to repatriate. In other cases, news that the local situation back home had been *tranquilo* (peaceful, with no combat, raids, or military attacks) for a while was enough to move some refugees to attempt repatriation.

Along the Honduran border, a pattern of frequent and multiple returns became common among the refugees. Throughout the war there was a constant, but variable, flow of refugees between Nicaragua and Honduras. The same individual or family group sometimes appeared in Honduras several times, only to return (often at night) to Nicaragua. For many refugees, these multiple returns were a testing of the waters. Sometimes refugees did not stay home, but returned to Honduras if the situation they had fled was not resolved or if they were forced back to Honduras by Resistance forces. One ACNUR representative attributed this pattern to the power of Resistance forces and, more generally, to the refugees' ongoing vulnerability. ACNUR representatives in Honduras expressed concern about individual repatriations in a situation where Resistance forces and others had free reign to threaten, manipulate, and exercise physical and psychological force over refugees.

These situations of return would probably not be considered formal repatriations by international agencies and governments. Still, they may be considered more than temporary returns, for the intent was always to return permanently, if possible.

Government Attitudes Toward Repatriation

Although the Nicaraguan government favored repatriation of its citizens, it was also concerned about the capacity of the shattered economy to reintegrate thousands of refugees into productive lives. The government's other concern was the difficulty of reintegrating demobilized combatants—both Resistance fighters and the government's own army—into daily life, and healing the wounds of internecine conflict. Security was an added problem. Could the returning refugees and Resistance fighters be trusted to abandon their attempts to overthrow government authority, once back in Nicaragua?

Honduras—which hosted thousands of Nicaraguan refugees and resistance fighters, as well as thousands of refugees from El Salvador and Guatemala—was also divided by conflicting fears and concerns about repatriating Nicaraguans. Hondurans had a history of accepting Nicaraguan refugees, most recently during the bloody insurrection against Somoza in the late 1970s. Before the refugee camps were constructed in the early 1980s, peasant refugees from Nicaragua regularly found shelter in small towns and peasant communities in southern Honduras. The historical, social, cultural, and geographic affinity of the two peoples ensured a degree of acceptance and hospitality.

But Honduras is a poor country. Authorities worried about the popular perception that the Nicaraguan refugees were better off than their Honduran hosts. In efforts to demonstrate fair treatment of the refugees, ACNUR inadvertently added to the invidious comparison by claiming, for example, that the infant mortality rate in the Nicaraguan refugee camps was five percent, while in the surrounding Honduran countryside the rate was over eight percent (reported in the Honduran daily, *La Tribuna*, June 24, 1988). Honduran authorities worried about the radicalizing political effect of such perceptions of relative deprivation among their own poor peasants and were eager to see the Nicaraguans repatriate.

Hondurans had other reasons for wanting to repatriate the Nicaraguan refugees. Most Hondurans, including the country's military leaders, were opposed to becoming involved in Nicaragua's internal war. As always in Honduras, national sovereignty was a sensitive issue. The Nicaraguan refugees were a reminder that the war which foreign powers were waging was spilling over into Honduras, and the country was a staging ground. Vastly increased levels of U.S. economic and military aid, both desired and resented, as well as a large diplomatic presence in the country during the 1980s were additional reminders. Both civilian and military leaders were concerned about the presence of Nicaraguan Resistance forces and their recruitment among the refugees. As a member of the Honduran Congress stated: "We are an occupied country. We have four armies on our soil—the U.S., the Nicaraguan Resistance, the Salvadorans [being trained by U.S. military in Honduras], and our own army." On the other hand, repatriation was a sign of return to normalcy, which was likely to decrease United States aid to Honduras. This last concern proved to be accurate.

The Reagan administration was slow to support repatriation of Nicaraguan refugees. The refugees' presence in Honduras was both an embarrassment to the Sandinista government in Nicaragua and an excuse for sending humanitarian assistance, at least some of which was likely to go to Resistance forces. For its part, ACNUR wanted to repatriate the refugees as soon as possible, given the unstable and complicated conditions in the refugee camps. But ACNUR was also sensitive to its mandate and its public image as protector of the refugees' safety and rights.

This was the complex political landscape in which repatriation was contemplated and attempted. The litany of differing fears, concerns, and agendas was instructive of the usefulness of refugees as a political factor for other interests. The corollary is that such refugee situations continue to exist without the implementation of durable solutions because it is in the interests of various parties and stakeholders that there be refugees.

Here it is worth recalling that the refugees in question, like the overwhelming majority of refugees everywhere, were rural poor, mostly peasants. There is a certain ironic historical continuity in the realization that, even when they flee as refugees, peasants continue to be used to serve the interests of other sectors of society. Nicaraguan peasants and refugees were often well aware of this irony and of their role in the plans of others.

Formal Repatriation, Peace, and Change of Government

A formal, organized repatriation process for the Nicaraguan refugees in Honduras was initiated in May 1987, when the governments of Nicaragua and Honduras signed a joint agreement with ACNUR for the systematic voluntary repatriation of the Nicaraguans. Under this program, ACNUR reported more than 6,000 Nicaraguans repatriated in the year from May 1987, to May 1988. The Honduran state refugee agency, CONARE, reported that almost half of these repatriations occurred within the first two months after the repatriation agreement was signed. The repatriates included Miskito peoples in eastern Nicaragua as well as Ladino

Nicaraguans in the western part of the country. Thereafter, the number of Nicaraguan repatriations slowed until the Central American governments (except Belize) signed the Esquipulas Two peace accord in 1988.

Esquipulas Two included a variety of points. In countries with ongoing civil wars, governments were to begin peace negotiations with their armed opposition, and to strengthen democratic political participation. The governments also agreed to promote and expand the ongoing voluntary repatriation of refugees. Every Central American state (including Belize) hosted thousands or hundreds of refugees from its neighbors. For Nicaragua, Esquipulas Two meant facilitating the repatriation of hundreds of Salvadorans and Guatemalans to their homelands, while accepting back thousands of Nicaraguan refugees from Honduras and Costa Rica.[4]

After Esquipulas Two was ratified, Nicaraguan repatriations increased again to about 1600 in the first two months. ACNUR's chief representative in Honduras attributed this to the refugees' perception that peace might be at hand, as well as the implication that the agreement to promote democracy would restrict the powers of the Sandinista government, and assuage the concerns of both refugees and Resistance fighters. "The commitment of the governments to fight to democratize the nations with the goal of establishing peace in those countries where there is war, has inspired the confidence of the refugees to return to their countries" (Waldo Villalpando, quoted in the Honduran daily, *La Prensa*, March 2, 1988).

Shortly after signing the Esquipulas Two accord, Nicaragua's Sandinista government instituted a process that led it to a peace agreement with the Nicaraguan Resistance in 1989 (the so-called Sapoa Accord). The government also held its second round of national elections in February, 1990, which resulted in a change of government in Nicaragua.

Repatriation: The Nicaraguan Resistance as Refugees

During the Nicaraguan conflict of the 1980s, the lives, identities, and fortunes of refugees and resistance fighters were often difficult to separate. They shared common peasant origins. The nature of the war and the power structures that directed life in refugee camps ensured, at the least, a confusing or fusing of refugee and combatant as terms of common discourse. This close and problematic relationship continued during and after repatriation, and helped shaped events in Nicaragua in the years after formal repatriation. Peace and a change of government after the February 1990 Nicaraguan elections posed a problem for many Resistance fighters. Now that peace had come, would they no longer be considered combatants? Were they now refugees?

Complicating this question was the presence of another group—families and dependents of Resistance fighters. Even as repatriation of the formal refugee camps was proceeding in late 1989, ACNUR registered about 7,000 Resistance fighters in training camps and safe zones in southern Honduras, and about

30,000 family members and dependents of these fighters—more than the total number of formal refugees. Most dependents were concentrated in camps and small settlements apart from the formal refugee camps (General Accounting Office 1991: 12ff).

The Sapoa Peace Accord of 1989 brought a formal ceasefire and stipulated the reintegration of Resistance fighters into Nicaraguan society. Many Resistance fighters and their commanders in Honduras remained wary, and did not disarm or return until the government set the date for national elections. At that time, some returned to participate in the election campaign against the Sandinistas. Uncertain of the outcome, they left their families and dependents in Honduras, along with the remaining fighters. With the Sandinista electoral defeat, repatriation of the remaining combatants and 30,000 dependents became a primary task.

In May 1990, ACNUR assumed responsibility for arranging the voluntary repatriation of all Nicaraguan Resistance fighters and their dependents still in Honduras. By then, many Resistance fighters realized that a very different government was in place in Nicaragua. Resistance leaders also realized that, after the 1988 presidential election in the United States, U.S. government support for the war had waned. Now that a primary objective of U.S. policy had been achieved with the Sandinista electoral defeat, U.S. interest would turn elsewhere.

While still concluding the repatriation of Nicaraguans from the formal refugee camps, ACNUR faced two new major tasks. The first was to provide for the material needs of the former Resistance fighters and their dependents still in Honduras until their repatriation to Nicaragua could be completed. Throughout much of 1990, ACNUR conducted food and health programs for this population. The food program embroiled ACNUR and Resistance commanders in an ongoing dispute over the adequacy and equitable distribution of the daily per capita rations. Resistance commanders continued to exercise control over their own camps and the large population of dependents. Working through this command structure, ACNUR distributed food supplies to Resistance commanders who, in turn, were responsible for ensuring that meals were adequately provided in communal kitchens.

Accustomed to receiving larger rations during the war through U.S. government agencies (such as USAID), Resistance leaders complained that ACNUR's rations were too small. There was evidence, however, that, "Resistance commanders used some of the food provided by UNHCR [ACNUR] to bribe local [Honduran] government officials and sold some for personal gain" (General Accounting Office 1991: 16). Meanwhile, some former Resistance combatants and dependents complained that they were not receiving food rations, even though the U.S. Embassy in Honduras and the Red Cross verified that ACNUR was providing adequate supplies. Similar accusations were heard throughout the latter years of the war. Thus, despite their changing status from combatants to something else, some Resistance commanders acted as they had in the past. At times, they seemed intent on distinguishing themselves from the refugees, and resisting the circumstances and pressures, especially from ACNUR, to classify and treat them as refugees. For example:

According to the former combatants and others with whom we spoke, the Resistance viewed itself as the victor in a civil war and responsible for the election victory of Chamorro as president [and the defeat of the Sandinista Front]. Consequently, the former combatants believed that they were entitled to be treated better than refugees ... ACNUR, on the other hand, viewed the former combatants and their dependents as being very similar in needs and composition to the Nicaraguan refugees in UNHCR-assisted camps and, therefore, it provided them basically the same food ration as it provided to refugees. (General Accounting Office 1991: 14)

This ongoing negotiation of status illustrates how the year-long transition process of repatriating the Resistance forces and their dependents, which was not completed until early 1991, marked not only a geographic and material transition but also one of identity and identification. The repatriation of Resistance fighters gave them a status similar to that of the Nicaraguans who were repatriated from refugee camps, but many of them continued to regard themselves as combatants. This process, in which they tried to maintain a combatant's identity while being increasingly identified as refugees, contributed to a class-oriented militancy which characterized the response of many repatriates to the conditions and problems of their re-assimilation into Nicaraguan society.

Land, Credit, and Class Interests: Repatriation and Its Discontents

In the early 1990s, Nicaragua faced the daunting tasks of reintegrating thousands of refugees and former combatants, establishing a lasting peace, rebuilding a war-torn economy, and resolving the still unfinished struggle between contrasting projects of national development. Although a formal peace prevailed, the struggle continued through the formation and implementation of economic and social policies within Nicaragua.

Economist and university president Xabier Gorostiaga articulated one contending vision of the role of the peasants and small farmers in rebuilding the country.

The [peasants and small] farmers have the energy and potential to become the critical subject for the reactivation of economic development, the consolidation of social and democratic stability in Nicaragua, and the arrest of the extremely serious environmental degradation. (Gorostiaga 1993: 2)

Gorostiaga advocated credit preferences for peasant and small farming production cooperatives as a means of helping to resettle and stabilize these groups. This vision of the role of peasants in rebuilding Nicaragua may be seen as an extension of the Sandinista project which placed the peasants at or near the center of national development. Throughout the civil war, the Sandinista government had worked with peasant farming communities to ensure internal food and export crop production, mostly in peasant production cooperatives, and it had developed with peasant farmers simple, low-cost means to curb soil erosion and promote re-forestation—two central environmental concerns.

Gorostiaga also observed that Nicaragua's peasants and small farmers were key to healing the social wounds of the civil war and to promoting social stability. This largest sector of the population had suffered the most in the war, and it had access to traditional cultural resources rooted in the daily life of small rural peasant communities in Nicaragua and values, beliefs, and practices geared to the resolution of local and interpersonal conflict.

These cultural resources included an understanding of what is needed to live in communities with close-knit, local, and interdependent social networks where conflict needs to be kept within acceptable limits. They also included a sense of the peasant's dependent and passive position in society, given that the ultimate authors of events, including the civil war, were not other peasants but rather powerful, often distant, elites. A common refrain of Nicaraguan peasants, both refugees and the internally displaced, was echoed by Dona Josefa during the most intense period of the war. Although she blamed other Nicaraguan peasants for doing the actual killing and destruction, she saw a more distant (if still personal) source. "I wish someone would put their hand on President Reagan's chest and tell him to stop killing us."

These values and perspectives were accompanied by a religious faith which included rituals of traditional Catholic piety such as the Way of the Cross, the Rosary, veneration of the Virgin Mary, and special Holy Week and Easter observances, as well as the popular interpretation of events and problems in the light of Biblical parallels. Such beliefs and practices helped people interpret war, violence, and conflict in a way that promoted forgiveness and tolerance along with prophetic social and political criticism.

Gorostiaga's vision of the role of the peasants and small farmers in reconstructing Nicaragua coincided well with the major objectives of the returning peasant refugees—peace, land, and credit. Because other visions of Nicaragua's future and the peasants' role in it prevailed, all three of these objectives remained elusive.

The first years of the new peace in the early 1990s were characterized by the struggle of displaced Nicaraguan peasants for land and credit. Returning refugees and peasant communities internally displaced by the war joined recently demobilized soldiers from both the Sandinista Army and the Nicaraguan Resistance to form mixed bands (*los revueltos*, the "scrambled"). They demanded that the new government honor what they regarded as a promise to provide land and access to credit. The government argued that it could not possibly provide enough land to fulfill the demands of returning refugees, demobilized combatants, and internally displaced communities. Moreover, land titles and ownership were complicated. During the 1980s, the former (Sandinista) government had settled displaced peasant communities on lands abandoned by large landowners who had fled the country. The new government's ensuing development philosophy seemed to favor larger landowners and attempts to "rationalize" agricultural production.

Even when land was available to returning refugees, the government was unable to provide substantial credit to peasants and small farmers because the expected aid and loans from the United States were not forthcoming. International financial institutions demanded that Nicaragua follow policies that largely ignored the peasants and small farmers.

Unable to obtain land or credit, bands of *revueltos* threatened to take land by force, and to disrupt government agencies. When large landowners returned to Nicaragua to reclaim lands they had formerly occupied, peasants on the land often vowed forceful resistance. Dire threats were exchanged between returning large landowners and peasant communities. In one case, when a former landowner returned to Nicaragua to reclaim his land, he found a peasant community settled there. A community leader told the author, "If that landowner returns with his goon squad there will be bloodshed, because we will fight."

Conclusion

Patterns of polarization that characterized the armed conflict of the 1980s began to shift. Former enemies—Sandinistas, Resistance fighters, refugees—joined in pursuing common needs. What the repatriated refugees and the former combatants of both sides had in common were their peasant origins, their need for land and credit, and their sense of betrayal by the authorities. Repatriation brought the refugees face to face with a changing Nicaragua. For many of them, repatriation revealed the extent to which their lives had already been transformed by revolution, war, and displacement. The traditional arrangements of economy, community, and society had been ripped away or severely strained. It is possible that the destabilizing effects of war and displacement made peasant refugees more vulnerable to the conditions they encountered upon return—conditions that seemed to encourage the emergence of class-oriented awareness even as these same conditions posed a threat to the continued existence of the peasants as a viable social class. For many, repatriation did not mean the end of displacement, but rather the end of being a peasant.

In Nicaragua, the forces that promoted rapid and violent "depeasantization" turned peasants into refugees. This process upset the traditional arrangements and removed peasants from the land, communities, and resources that seemed to define and support peasant existence. Underlying this dialectical transformation, the restructuring of Nicaraguan economy and society for integration into a new global order was a contested but powerful process.

Meanwhile the economy and living conditions of most of the country's peasants continued to deteriorate. Three years after the majority of Nicaraguan refugees had returned from Honduras, Gorostiaga voiced the desperation of many people:

If we do not overcome the growing impoverishment, there can be neither peace, nor democracy, nor development, nor natural resources because the growing misery is devouring the future. (Gorostiaga 1993: 1)

For Nicaragua's peasants, the words of poet Vida Luz Meneses—"creating, erasing, rewriting"—is not a hope fulfilled but a bitter irony.

Chapter 9
Refugee Returns to Sarajevo and Their Challenge to Contemporary Narratives of Mobility

Anders H. Stefansson

> Migrancy, on the contrary, involves a movement in which neither the points of a departure nor those of arrival are immutable or certain. (. . .) Always in transit, the promise of a homecoming—completing the story, domesticating the detour—becomes an impossibility.
> —Iain Chambers (1994:5)

> What I missed most (while I was in Germany) was my family and friends, the language and the whole environment, sociality and most of all the easy-going way of life. I missed to live where I'm born. I missed to be "under my own sky" (*podneblje*).
> —Bosnian repatriated refugee, August 2001

Refugees and the scholars who study refugees often hold radically different perceptions of mobility, home, and return, as indicated by the two quotations above. The aim of this chapter is to explore the discrepancies between the level of theory and the lived experiences of refugees. The experience of forcible displacement sets in motion powerful processes of identity formation by which the construction of idealized images of homelands and hopes of one day returning to the places left behind emerge as turning points of exile life (e.g., Bisharat 1997; Eastmond 1997; Malkki 1995a; Safran 1991; Zetter 1994). Based on a study of refugees who have repatriated to Bosnia-Herzegovina from a variety of host countries, this chapter examines what happens when the so-called "myth of return" (Al-Rasheed 1994; Anwar 1979; Zetter 1999) becomes reality and the visions of home and return, nourished during exile, engage with the profoundly transformed and difficult circumstances of everyday life in the places to which the refugees have returned. Refugees returning to Bosnia-Herzegovina enter a society troubled by grave political and economic problems, preventing a large part of the returnees from going back to their original homes. Coupled with discrimination and resentment from those who stayed behind many returnees nurture feelings of marginalization and alienation. Others, however, emphasize the joy of linking up with their prewar, "normal" lives.

Repatriation Discourse: The Glorious Homecoming

During the 1990s the scale of refugee repatriation has increased dramatically, both in the developing countries and within Europe, in particular in relation to refugees from the former Yugoslavia. Already in 1980 UNHCR described repatriation as the best durable solution: "Voluntary repatriation, whenever feasible, is of course the most desirable solution to refugee problems" (1980: 1, in Warner 1994: 160). In 1992 the same organization proclaimed the 1990s to be "the decade of voluntary repatriation" (Allen and Morsink 1994a: 1). Indeed, it is estimated that around 12 million refugees have returned to their countries of origin during the preceding decade (Koser and Black 1999: 3). The new political emphasis on repatriation stands in marked contrast to priority given to resettlement and integration (or assimilation) of refugees into Western host countries which dominated the international agenda during most of the Cold War period. Among the manifold reasons behind this policy shift are the fall of the Berlin Wall, which has rendered refugees ideologically superfluous, the growing number of asylum seekers in Europe (especially from developing countries), the rise of what has been termed "the new racism" (Barker 1981) or "cultural fundamentalism" (Stolcke 1995) in the West, the image of increasing numbers of refugees fleeing *en masse* from situations of civil war in which people are considered to be persecuted collectively, and a general reorientation of refugee policy away from an "exilic bias" and towards a "source control bias" (Aleinikoff 1995: 258), emphasizing tight visa regulations, temporary protection, voluntary repatriation or even "imposed return" (Chimni 1999). Thus, whereas the UNHCR principles of "return in safety and dignity" (UNHCR 1996) are still in place, recently the organization has begun to loosen the ideal of *voluntary* repatriation.

Repatriation-oriented policies are legitimized by what scholars in this field have labelled a "repatriation discourse" (Koser and Black 1999b: 4), characterized by problematic assumptions like "all refugees want to go home" and "the best place for refugees is home" (Sepulveda 1995: 83). In stark contrast to the currently dominating constructionist anthropological theories of place and belonging, the institutions dealing with refugees tend to depict repatriation as a homecoming to a former way of life and a familiar cultural environment, as a fairly straightforward re-establishment of the conditions from before the displacement, not only for the host country and the home country but also for the refugees themselves, the "end of the refugee cycle" (Black and Koser 1999). This is a line of thinking resting on cultural fundamentalist suppositions about the relationship between people, place and identity (Warner 1994).[1]

The Impossible Homecoming in Repatriation Research

Several scholars have mourned the lack of research on the issue of refugee repatriation (Allen and Morsink 1994a: 1; Coles 1985; Sepulveda 1995: 83; Warner 1994: 161). However, the increasing scale of refugee repatriation within recent years in turn has led to a plethora of studies on both the imagination of home and return in refugee diasporas (e.g. Al-Rasheed 1994; Anwar 1979; Graham and Khosravi 1997; Kibreab 1996b; Malkki 1995a; Ray 2000; Stefansson 1997; Zetter 1994; Zetter 1999) as well as on actual repatriation and reintegration processes (e.g. Allen 1996; Allen and Morsink 1994b; Black and Koser 1999; Cornish et al. 1999; Cuny et al. 1992; Habib 1996; Stefansson 2000; Stepputat 1994; Van Hear 1994; Zarzosa 1998). Armed with newer theories on globalization, deterritorialization and transnationalism, much of this literature dismisses the static assumptions about belonging and cultural identity guiding public repatriation policy discourse. Instead, repatriation researchers emphasize the dynamic nature of notions of home and return among forcibly displaced people caused by change over time in the country of origin and in the identities of the refugees themselves. The repatriation discourse does not pay attention . . . to questions of time and changes that can take place for the refugee, in the country of origin, and the relationships between the two (Warner 1994: 169).

For many refugee groups exile turns into a long-term condition (e.g. the Palestinians, the Tibetans, the Iranians), with the likely consequence of a development of multiple attachments, for those refugees who have the luxury of a choice implying a decision to stay in the host country, as a sort of practical home, while continuing to be culturally and spiritually connected to the home country, as merely "the place of nostalgia" (Graham and Khosravi 1997: 131). Evidently, for descendants of refugees and migrants, either living away from the originary homeland or embarking upon "ancestral return" (King 1986: 6), the meaning of home becomes even more contested (Hirschon 1989; Tsuda 2000; Voutira 1991). The refugees who *do* repatriate, whether voluntarily or involuntarily, often face significant difficulties in re-integrating into the socio-economic and cultural environment of the countries of origin, for example with regard to housing, jobs, securing sustainable livelihoods and attitudes from authorities and those people who stayed behind in the home countries (Koser and Black 1999b: 10–11). Besides, for various reasons, be it matters of security or livelihood, a great deal of returnees do not settle in their original areas or homes (Eastmond and Öjendal 1999; Hammond 1999).

Obviously, this means that the experience of repatriation is no simple or glorious homecoming. Rather, in the terminology of some repatriation researchers, "return may be more traumatic than the experience of flight and exile itself" (Sepulveda 1995: 84), return may be felt like "a reverse culture shock" (Graham and Khosravi 1997: 126), a travel to "an unknown wilderness" (Pilkington and Flynn 1999: 190) or, more optimistically, a "new beginning" (Hammond 1999: 229), "a new and challenging environment" (Koser and Black 1999b: 11). Accordingly, returnees often feel like "outsiders" (Cornish et al. 1999) or "strangers at home" (Stefansson 2000).[2] Therefore, it has been suggested that central concepts within repatriation discourse, like "return", "re-integration" and "reconstruction", somehow implying a return to the past, need to be replaced by "a more proactive theory of return migration" which instead emphasizes construction, creativity, innovation and cultural change (Hammond 1999).

Although these critical theories offer important correctives to the fundamentalist assumptions of repatriation discourse, much repatriation research, in its justified revolt, has come to embrace the equally untenable assumption of "an impossible homecoming" (Jansen 1998: 85): "Refugees involved in voluntary repatriation are not returning home. They are, in fact, returning to their country of origin, but no more" (Warner 1994: 170). The advocates of repatriation (like many refugees themselves) close their eyes to the sad fact "that we have no homes and will continue to be homeless, and therefore that that we can never return home in the way that the nostalgic idealism of a politics of place would lead us to believe" (169). In fact, the displacement of the refugee is no more than "the incarnation of the homelessness that is part of all our experience" and essentially "we are all refugees" (168). From this perspective the impossible homecoming is the unavoidable outcome of various sorts of change (in the homelands, in the identities of the refugees and on a global scale).

However, does it logically follow that transformation is incompatible with a sense of being at home? On closer inspection theories evoking the idea of the impossibility of homecoming are very abstract in their nature and not strongly grounded in empirical realities. During the last year or so I have gradually realized that my own fieldwork material, on the repatriation of Bosnian refugees, would need quite a bit of twisting to correlate with the notion of the impossible homecoming. Also, a recent attack on the anti-repatriation discourse (Kibreab 1999) calls for a more balanced, less theoretical approach to repatriation. Here it is rightly argued that it is misleading, and indeed inappropriate, for academics who celebrate the deterritorialization of identities in a world of increasing globalization and interconnectedness to put the displacement of refugees on a par with the generalized condition of homelessness (Said 1979: 18, Kibreab 1999: 385). For most refugees in the world there exists no alternative to voluntary repatriation, as they live in deplorable conditions in third world countries where "the alternative (to repatriation) is to languish in camps and to live indefinitely off handouts, or to suffer from harassment, round-ups, arbitrary detention, extortion or even deportation" (Kibreab 1999: 390).

Repatriation remains the best solution to many refugees because, notwithstanding the assumptions of a deterritorialization of identity, the importance of links with specific places and homelands has not diminished:

in a world in which many rights such as equal treatment, access to sources of livelihoods, access to land, rights of freedom of movement and residence, are determined on the basis of territorially anchored identities, the identity people gain from their association with a particular country is an indispensable instrument to a socially and economically fulfilling end (407).

This shift in orientation away from the postmodern focus on matters of identity, and the imagination of home, towards political structures and livelihood conditions points to a reconceptualization of home. In the remaining part of this chapter I explore how the "pragmatic" perception of home among Bosnian returned refugees paves the way for the development of more complex theorizing on refugee repatriation, highlighting both socio-cultural transformations *and* continuities. For the Bosnian returnees, home refers to the possibilities of reestablishing a sense of normal life, which in its turn is defined by three key issues: creating sustainable livelihoods, finding a place of relational identification, developing a site of cultural attachment. (cf. Olwig 1998).

The Political Context of Repatriation to Bosnia-Herzegovina

During the war in Bosnia-Herzegovina (BiH) an estimated 2.3 million people were displaced from their homes. Of these, around 1.3 million found refuge outside BiH, primarily in other countries in the former Yugoslavia, Western Europe, and North America (CRPC/UNHCR 1997: 3). The return of refugees and internally displaced persons (IDPs) was inscribed as a cornerstone in the Dayton Peace Agreement (DPA) which put an end to the war in December 1995. Until the end of January 2003 approximately 425,000 refugees have repatriated to BiH and 510,000 IDPs have returned to their pre-war homes (UNHCR 2003). In the light of the mass exodus of refugees from BiH, and due to a political demand not to reward the strategy of ethnic cleansing, most Western European governments, in close consultation with the UNHCR, granted temporary protection to the refugees.[3] Their acceptance of relatively large numbers of refugees was based on the expectation of mass repatriation when the situation in BiH stabilized. As the war dragged on, some host countries decided to grant the Bosnian refugees permanent rights of residence; thereby, the decision to repatriate was left in the hands of the refugees, while the authorities continued to encourage and support voluntary repatriation to BiH. A notable exception from this pattern was Germany, which has carried through its policy of temporary protection and returned the majority of its 330,000 Bosnian refugees, especially during 1997 and 1998. From other Western countries, only relatively small numbers of refugees have chosen to repatriate. The emphasis on repatriation has been much less explicit in host countries in the region itself (in particular the Federal Republic of Yugoslavia and Croatia) but the often appalling economic conditions of Bosnian refugees in these places have indirectly forced a number of refugees to return.

To argue that the BiH to which refugees return is a radically different country than the one they knew before the war is an understatement. BiH gained its independence from the Socialist Federal Republic of Yugoslavia in 1992 and immediately became engulfed by war over this issue. During the war large parts of the infrastructure, housing stock and cultural and religious monuments were destroyed. Apart from the large number of displaced people, the majority of whom have not returned to their former areas, about 200,000 people lost their lives due to the conflict. The DPA aims at keeping BiH unified but at the same time divides the country into two entities, the Federation of BiH and the Republika Srpska (RS), with a weak central government in Sarajevo. While the international community has managed to bring largely peaceful conditions to the country and has brought about a large-scale material reconstruction, BiH remains a fragile political construction, tormented by serious socioeconomic problems. Although nationalist parties were ousted in some parts of the country in 2000 from the end of the war they have dominated, and continue to influence the political scene whereby they have succeeded in minimizing minority return through a combination of violent incidents, bureaucratic obstructionism and discrimination. In practice, BiH operates as three mono-ethnic entities, with three separate political systems of power, armies, and police forces as well as education, healthcare and pension systems (ICG 1999).

"Volunteers" Versus "Expellees"

Given the troubled situation in BiH, many returnees nurture strong feelings of frustration, marginalization and alienation, which on the surface of would seem to support the idea of the impossible homecoming. Perhaps the strongest indication of the accuracy of this line of thinking is the obvious fact that several hundred thousands refugees have not (yet) decided to return. However, these negative attitudes are opposed by statements of positive identification with and belonging in Sarajevo and/or BiH and the joy of being home once again.[4] The clearest pattern to this complexity of the experience of return is that returnees who repatriated voluntarily (volunteers) express feelings of belonging, whereas returnees who repatriated involuntarily (expellees) typically give voice to feelings of disenchantment and estrangement. In general, the experience of return very much depends upon the conditions of life in exile and the circumstances of return.

However, the distinction between volunteers and expellees obviously is not absolute: in practice it is often difficult to distinguish between voluntary and forced return, as all refugees are exposed to different kinds of social pressure with which they then develop strategies to address. Further, the same person often expresses both feelings of belonging and alienation, according to different contexts (time, setting, mood, theme of conversation etc.). Moreover, sometimes volunteers experience that the conditions found upon repatriation cannot match their, to some extent idealized, imaginations of home and return, while, in contrast, some of the expellees acknowledge that their fears of return have turned out to be somewhat exaggerated.

Creating Sustainable Livelihoods

While migration movements are often explained in terms of economic consider-ations, in the general understanding refugees flee from political persecution, not economic hardship. However, the fact that traditionally most refugees have tended to stay abroad has sometimes been seen as a result of concerns about livelihood; from this perspective, repatriation entails a lowering in the living stan-dards of the refugees. Indeed, for most refugees who return to BiH the issue of livelihood[5] is of central importance; the decision to return or stay in the host country very much rests upon considerations about the economic and material conditions in BiH, and the everyday lives of most informants are dominated by efforts to establish sustainable livelihoods. The question of being home and con-siderations about identity (personal, national, ethnic, religious) are more or less sidelined by concerns about livelihood; at least they are seen as luxury issues which are only deemed relevant to reflect on for those returnees who have solved its livelihood situation in a satisfactory manner. Feelings of belonging and alien-ation thus largely follow livelihood patterns. With some exceptions, refugees who have returned voluntarily usually enjoy much better living conditions than do those who have returned against their will. This is hardly surprising, as an im-portant reason for not wanting to return, in the first place, is the unsolved mate-rial situation expected to be found in BiH. Faced with the possibility to stay in the host countries, few refugees return voluntarily to insecure material conditions in BiH. Most volunteers have had the opportunity to visit BiH a number of times before eventually repatriating, thereby returning well-considered, well-organized and well-motivated, generally to secure accommodation and jobs, in marked con-trast to the situation of the expellees.

The war in BiH had devastating material and economic consequences. Despite over five billion dollars that international donors have poured into BiH over the last five years, economic development has been slow, with unemployment rates in some areas of up to 50 percent. Most of the state-owned companies that domi-nated the Socialist Republic of BiH have been shut down. The economy is characterized by a crippling combination of pre-war socialism and a raw form of early capitalism in which every transaction with the authorities depends upon *veze*, that is, connections and contacts, knowing the right people, or alternatively upon corruption (ICG 1999: 35; Macek 2000: 103). The situation in Sarajevo is slightly better due to the city being the capital and economic center of the coun-try, with most international institutions and organizations having set up head-quarters there.

In general, these economic difficulties are exacerbated for returnees because of a degree of structural discrimination from the Bosnian authorities and the possi-bilities of those who stayed behind during the conflict (the stayees) to take over va-cant jobs and housing in the meantime. The discrimination of returnees takes more or less direct forms, ranging from a denial of their right to repossess their homes and some types of jobs, to payment of higher fees for having their telephone reconnected, to converting their foreign diplomas into Bosnian ones, to having job applications turned down because of "better qualified candidates" (meaning stayees). Due to the continued ethnic division of the country, many refugees are unable (or unwilling) to return to their original homes in ethnic minority areas. Many Bosnjak (Bosnian Muslim) refugees from Republika Srpska have settled down in majority areas in other parts of the country, a large number in Sarajevo. In the new places they have to live with relatives or rent or buy new accommodations, which is often quite expensive. Even returnees who lived in Sarajevo before the war may experience that the process of evicting the temporary residents (IDPs and others) can be extremely time-consuming, and in some cases impossible. Thus, many refugees return to a situation where they have lost either their pre-war accommodation or their prior job, and in quite a few cases both. The living conditions of returnees who are caught up by a combination of unemployment and lack of access to their own housing are often desperate. With low pensions and virtually non-existant social welfare, they are left to their potential savings from the stay abroad and the hospitality of relatives, in addition to their abilities to create new sources of sustainable livelihoods.

However, the livelihood conditions of returnees are not always as dire as indicated above. At this point there still exists a radical division between the living conditions of those refugees who return from Western countries and those from countries in the region. During their stay in the Western host countries, some of the refugees were able to work, or live on social welfare, which made it possible for them to save up occasionally significant amounts of money which then could be used to rebuild war-damaged housing, provide the foundation for income-generating opportunities and secure themselves a job in the public sector (rumors suggest that some employers take bribes). Many Western European countries facilitate and economically support the return of refugees to BiH through various kinds of repatriation programs.[6] All these opportunities are rarely available to returnees from non-Western host countries. Also, in some cases besides, in the Western states, refugees have obtained language skills and professional qualifications that put them in an advantageous position compared to stayees in relation to the job market, particularly for attractive jobs in international organizations and foreign companies.

It must be underlined, though, that the level of (dis)satisfaction with livelihood conditions in BiH among returnees is not based on absolute, but relative demands, as the possibilities of creating sustainable livelihoods in BiH are compared with the livelihood conditions in exile as well as with the material conditions refugees were used to before the disintegration of Yugoslavia. Therefore, for refugees who live in poor conditions in host countries, repatriation may be considered a comparatively attractive solution, particularly if repatriation entails the repossession of homes. But even for refugees in Western countries, the standard of living in BiH can be perceived to be better than in the host country. In this way, livelihood conditions in BiH can be both a source of satisfaction and frustration among returnees as well as an incentive to repatriate and a reason for staying away. Obviously, this does not imply that livelihood conditions and feelings of being home are locked in a one-to-one relationship, that home is merely "where you make it" (Graham and Khosravi 1997), but in the Bosnian context the feeling of having a "decent standard of living," in relative terms, forms a kind of minimum basis for positive identification with a particular place. However, other issues also affect such feelings of attachment; such as social relations in Sarajevo.

Social Relations in Postwar Sarajevo

Besides the obvious fact that the access to social networks is a key element affecting the possibility of securing sustainable livelihoods, not least in the post-war Bosnian society where the state is largely incapable of fulfilling the obligations towards its citizens and plagued by widespread corruption and nepotism, there is also a more emotional side to the structure of social relations. As a result of war, the demographic composition of BiH has changed to such an extent that even those refugees who return to their own areas do not return to the same social environment. Around 200,000 people were killed or perished during the war; approximately 900,000 persons continue to live as refugees outside BiH; 600,000 are displaced within the country itself; and an unknown number of Bosnians have emigrated. It is estimated that the overall population of Sarajevo has decreased from 510,000 in 1991 to approximately 360,000 in 1999, despite the arrival of at least 90,000 displaced persons during the war (ICG 1998). These demographic transformations have caused the development of three significant social cleavages: returnees (and refugees) versus stayees, ethnic (or religious) divisions, and locals versus newcomers (or town people versus people from the countryside).

Returnees, Stayees, and the Monopoly of Suffering

Would they (the stayees) have us back at all? I wondered if those who had stayed at home were considering us as traitors. In spite of all the packages we had sent down to them, I sensed that there was a gulf between those who had stayed and us who had fled. My father realized that well-educated, experienced people were in demand in the bank. But they also let it be understood that it would not be popular if they employed a *deserter and refugee* as a boss who should give orders to *the patriots* who had defended their country. A *patriot* will not take orders from a *deserter.* (Bosnian teenage girl, Edita Dugalic, returning from Germany (Kusterer and Dugalic 1998: 12, 33, 58; my translation from Danish)

The return of refugees evokes a variety of attitudes from their compatriots who stayed behind in the homeland:

The reception of returnees by those who stayed behind can vary as much as reception in a new society, particularly when the period abroad has been long. It is an obvious fact, but it bears noting that both the returnees and the home community will have changed during the absence of the migrants. . . . For those who stayed behind, among the reactions to returnees may be welcome, toleration, grudging acceptance, rejection, antagonism or conflict. (Van Hear 1998: 56)

The experience of return to BiH rarely belongs to the glorious kind. Whereas the official attitude of the Bosnian government is that all refugees are welcome to repatriate and help rebuild the country, in practice authorities privilege IDPs, demobilized soldiers, and relatives of people who were killed during the war in the labor and housing markets. Besides this structural discrimination, many returnees feel that they are being accused by the stayees of betraying Sarajevo and BiH by fleeing abroad.[7] For example, some people wear a T-shirt with the words: "I was here from 1992–95—where were you?" One popular war song includes the lyrics:

Sarajevan *raja* (people) / While Bosnian cities burned / You were far away / When it was difficult / You left Sarajevo. . . . When you come back one day I shall greet you / But nothing will ever be the same / Don't be sad then, it is nobody's fault / You saved your head, you stayed alive. (Macek 2000: 145)

According to the returnees themselves, though, the accusations of betrayal and cowardice in reality mask a feeling of envy on the part of the stayees who nurture distorted images of luxurious life these refugees lived in Germany and other Western host countries from where they apparently return with "suitcases full of Deutchmarks and three Mercedes each." The situation and problems of the returned refugees as well as the large Bosnian diaspora abroad are almost absent themes in the media and the public debate, bordering on being a cultural taboo.

The returnees find it annoying that the stayees take no interest in hearing about the experience of being refugees in other countries but merely want to "preach" about the suffering of war. A returnee from Germany says that the stayees believe they have a "monopoly on suffering" that makes them morally superior, "small Gods." In many cases this mental division makes it difficult for returnees to develop normal relations with stayees, sometimes even with their own relatives and former friends. As another returnee from Germany explained:

We have all changed. People who stayed behind used to say that they have become a little bit crazy, and we who went away have had other experiences. I believe we have become developed, in all ways, with respect to education, behavior and culture. We have seen that it's possible to live better and more beautiful. In this way, we have become like minus and plus. There are not many common themes between us anymore. Many in our neighborhood think that our children are too free, they take on too little cloth, listen to too loud music, we're crazy because we have a dog in the house, that's typically German they say. To be honest I'm also tired of all their war stories. It was their own choice to stay here. I went away and thank god for that! All this make us very different and when there are no common themes to talk about then it's better not to have contact, to stay in your own world.

But as this statement indicates, the social cleavage also works the other way around as some returnees feel superior toward those who stayed behind because of their experiences in Western countries, which are often perceived in positive terms such as "democratic," "civilized," "developed," and "just," while the stayees are seen as negatively affected by their experiences of war, brutality and social degradation. Sometimes it is the returnees who accuse the stayees of cowardice and egoism as they opted to stay in BiH in order to keep their houses and jobs. From the point of view of many refugees, to leave BiH was a moral act, showing their anti-nationalist stance, refusing to take part in the primitiveness of war. A returnee from Norway talks about the hypocrisy and stupidity of those who claim to have stayed in order to defend the country:

I get really mad at those people who say that they stayed here in order to defend the country. Everybody says that they wanted to defend the country but I think that the only thing they defended was their own existence. Nobody had an idea that they were defending anything, you were lost. Your own friends were shooting at you, how is it possible to understand that? Where is the idea about the defense of the country? It is simply stupidity (*glupost*).

A returnee schoolgirl told me that as "poor" people (in this case meaning those who have stayed behind in troubled BiH) like to stick with "rich" people (referring to the returnees from Western countries); it can even turn out to be a social advantage to be a returnee.

The Ideal of Multiculturalism

Historically situated at the crossroads of different civilizations, BiH, and Sarajevo in particular, harbored a unique cultural, religious and ethnic diversity. As is well-known, through the practice of "ethnic cleansing" this pluralistic society has turned into a country which now consists of "three ethnic reservations" or "ghettos," in the words of several informants. In Sarajevo the Bosnjak part of the population jumped from about 50 percent prior to the war to approximately 87 percent, whereas most Bosnian Serbs, people of mixed nationality, and those who self-identified as Yugoslavs have left town (ICG 1998). Although the Sarajevo-based government of BiH during the war continued to be officially committed to the ideal of multiculturalism, and the city is one of the few remaining places in BiH with a significant proportion of ethnic minorities, as the war progressed Sarajevo became still more influenced by radical Muslim nationalism. After the war, a certain degree of mostly bureaucratic discrimination of ethnic minorities has continued to take place. The returnees who belong to the ethnic minorities in Sarajevo are targets of a certain level of resentment from at least a part of the Bosnjak inhabitants, not the least from the group of IDPs who fear that they will be evicted from their apartments when the local minorities return.

However, as opposed to other parts of BiH in Sarajevo, the ethnic polarization seems less problematic than other social divisions. Many local Sarajevans claim that they would prefer to live with their pre-war neighbors of different nationalities instead of the despised newcomers from other, less "developed" parts of the country. It is a common point of reference among original inhabitants of Sarajevo (returnees and stayees alike and across ethnic groups) to mourn the construction of new, huge, Middle Eastern-looking mosques, the increasing numbers of bearded men and "wrapped up" women in the streets of the city (signs of being believers), as well as the stupidity and absurdity of "ethnic politics." Few informants fail to point out the number of relatives and friends who belong to different national groups and the continuing existence of both Muslim, Catholic, Orthodox and Jewish religious institutions in the city. Thus, while the ethnic composition of Sarajevo surely has changed dramatically (and irreversibly), the memories and ideal of the multicultural society have not lost their appeals completely.

"Cultured" and "Uncultured" People

This points to the third major sociocultural barrier in Sarajevo, the one between local, original Sarajevans and newcomers (*dosljaci*). During the war, as large numbers of Sarajevans fled the city and displaced persons from other parts of the country took their place, the balance between the two groups has been significantly altered. The categorization of people into the local-newcomer dichotomy is simultaneously a native, moral distinction between people with a "town mentality" and those with a "countryside mentality," which again is linked up with other mental divisions between "cultured" versus "uncultured," educated versus uneducated, and modern and Western versus backward and Balkan (Bringa 1995: 58–60; van de Port 1998). Many original Sarajevans describe Sarajevo as "one big village," due to the invasion of "peasants" or "mountaineers" from rural areas who have brought with them their "village manners" and transformed the former sophisticated cosmopolitanism of Sarajevo into a place plagued by garbage, mafia-style criminality, corruption, nepotism, Muslim nationalism, cultural primitivism, improper language and so on. One returnee informant describes the behavior of the displaced population in this way:

Everything they do they do in a way that has no place in a city. They behave uncultured (*nekulturno*) they are uneducated, illiterates, have some customs that are strange to us, wash carpets outside, shake them out of the window, dump garbage out of the window. All this don't belong to the city. The way they talk. When they call on the telephone they ask "Hamo, is that you?" instead of telling their name. All this bothers me. The only thing that can change this is the return of the original Sarajevan population.

Naturally, returnees are differently positioned in respect to this division. Those returnees who lived in Sarajevo before the war are not targets of, but often participants in, this cultural discourse. On the contrary, the large number of returnees who come from other parts of the country are exposed to this sort of cultural ridicule. To some it is deeply annoying but to others it is only perceived to be a minor problem. Many returnee newcomers actually employ this repertoire of stereotyping by placing themselves in the "civilized" category in relation to other groups with even lower social status (notably the stigmatized Gypsy population, the Albanians, and people from Sandzak).[8] Indeed, the distinction between cultured and uncultured people has such a long history and imaginatory power, both in BiH and in the whole of former Yugoslavia, that even though it has taken on a new importance due to the massive scale of relocation during the recent war, few returnees seem to have difficulties in readapting to it.

In conclusion, despite the fact that postwar Sarajevo is characterized by significant changes in the landscape of social relations, it is also marked by a level of continuity. The issue of social relations has shown to be extremely complex: what is in one context a stigmatizing social category can turn out to be a factor of social prestige in other circumstances. For example, whereas in some contexts returnees are discriminated and resented by the stayees, in others they are welcomed.

The Search for "Normal Life"

For both returnees and stayees the nostalgia and search for "normal life" are powerful urges.[9] Whereas most often the emphasis is on the frustrations of not living a "normal life," and not living in a "normal society" or a "normal country," some returnees describe their repatriation to BiH as an effort to regain these things. For many returnees the experience of economic hardship and social stigmatization gives rise to feelings of cultural alienation, whereby they, in their own terminology, have become "strangers at home" or "refugees in my own country". The feeling of social alienation implies a prior identification with and attachment to a place (Tsuda 2000: 19), and many returnees stress that the war has transformed the once familiar city of Sarajevo into an alien place. Of course, this feeling of being strangers in a well-known place is not merely an effect of physical destruction and economic decline. A female returnee points to one aspect of this cultural deterioration:

Everything has changed here (in Sarajevo). I was born here, and Sarajevo is not at all like what it once was. Everything is primitivism, the way of life, the people in this building, the bus. Before the war we had achieved a European level. Our cities have become villages but not like villages before the war because they were clean. Now everything is dirty.

One obvious result of this sense of disenchantment with the present conditions in Sarajevo is a recalling and idealizing of the material and cultural situation of the past, both in terms of their own lives and of Sarajevo, BiH and Yugoslavia in general. In relation to the poverty and nationalism which dominate BiH today, Tito's communist Yugoslavia emerges as an economic and multicultural paradise. A second consequence is that many returnees nurture very positive, and sometimes clearly idealized, images of the life in their host countries (or in the West in general). Upon repatriation, returnees (re)interpret the qualities of their former home of Sarajevo and BiH in light of their experiences of living abroad. Most significantly, however, the frustrations with the home country are channeled into searching for better places, where the possibilities of leading a normal life are deemed to be more realistic. The dream of getting away, once again, is shared with many people who stayed behind during the war. According to a recent survey, more than 60 percent of the youth in BiH would leave the country if they were given the opportunity to do so (UNDP 2000). From some Western European host countries returnees have a right to regret their decision to repatriate and within a certain period re-enter the host country, and a number of returnees use this possibility or consider to do so. To a number of returnees, repatriation was predicated on their ability to acquire citizenship in their Western host countries, as this provides them with the ultimate freedom of transnational mobility and return to their host countries if repatriation turns out to be disappointing. In general, the strategy of the returnees is to retain as many economic channels, social networks and future opportunities for physical mobility as possible, hereby creating "mobile livelihoods" (Olwig and Sørensen 2002). In these cases, return clearly takes on a slippery meaning.

While certainly feelings of disenchantment and estrangement are abundant among Bosnian returnees, most simultaneously appreciate aspects of the Bosnian geography, culture and way of life. Despite the war-caused transformation of BiH, some aspects of culture die hard and a certain level of cultural continuity manages to survive. Among the most stated reasons for returning are that in exile refugees missed the landscape, the climate, the rivers, the smells, the language and in particular the Bosnian version of "the good life," with an emphasis on sociality (*druzenje*), hospitality, local food and drinking, strong family relations, etc. A young Bosnian female refugee who was visiting BiH explained to me that although she absolutely detested the political and social structures of the Bosnian society, and for those reasons did not want to return permanently to the country, she had discovered, much to her surprise, that the mentality of people was pretty much the same as before the war, and that still a feeling of relatedness across all the new ethnic and social cleavages had survived among ordinary people. This feeling of returning home to a familiar cultural atmosphere is exemplified by the statement of a returnee from Germany:

What I missed most (while I was in Germany) was my family and friends, the language and the whole environment, sociality (*druzenje*) and most of all the easy-going way of life. You probably won't understand it but it is something else to speak in your mother tongue. It was very demanding to speak in German, I'm much more relaxed when I speak my own language. Language is for me the basis of any identity. I missed to live where I'm born. I missed to be "under my own sky" (*podneblje*). What has brought me back is the Bosnia which is all too beautiful, the nature in particular. It's a different matter that everything else is destroyed, but the beauty of the country has brought me back and that's what I'm enjoying at the moment.

Many highly educated Bosnian refugees find it unsatisfactory to live on social welfare or earn a living through hard physical labor in the Western host countries and repatriate to reestablish a sense of a meaningful, normal everyday life by working in jobs which match their qualifications. Many elderly refugees feel socially excluded in the host countries due to language difficulties. The experience of being a foreigner is seldomly easy, as this returnee from Norway points out:

You're never a first class person in a foreign country. Stranger is stranger. A person is only a human being in his own place. Norway is a lovely country and the Norwegians offered us everything. I like the social system in Norway, the treatment of people. But the silence killed me [her family lived in a small town in the northern part of Norway]. It was terrible. After four p.m. when you see someone in the street you know that either it's a Bosnian or it's a cat! I can't imagine my life without Sarajevo. We live a good, normal life. We're satisfied, psychologically, that's the most important. I'm home in my own. We love our city and we love life here in Bosnia.

The Narrative of Mobility and the Aestheticization of Displacement

The notion of the "impossible homecoming," which has been queried in this chapter reflects more widespread recent developments within anthropology and related disciplines, as scholars within these fields of research are developing a new theoretical master narrative (Bruner 1986). This is generally known as a shift in orientation away from wholeness and toward a new focus on fragmentation, or from complex culture toward cultural complexity (Wicker 2000). But equally well this theoretical transformation can be characterized as leaving behind the narrative of (em)placement (or sedentariness), in which the theoretical gaze was pointed at immobility, stability, boundedness and cultural continuity, and adopting a new narrative of mobility, emphasizing aspects of physical movement, globalization, transnationalism, diaspora, cultural creolization and socio-cultural construction. In a revolt against the former anthropological portrayals of homogeneous and well-bounded "culture islands" (Fabian 1983), the metaphors of the hotel, the motel and the airport have been suggested as more suitable ones to depict the present state of cultural flux (Clifford 1988), with parallel calls for the development of an anthropology of "traveling cultures" (Clifford 1992) and even for a "nomadology" (Deleuze and Guattari 1988).

The obvious dangers in the anthropological narrative of mobility are twofold. First of all, it is dangerous to render commonplace movement and homelessness as conditions to which we are all, in the globalizing postmodern world, inevitably and equally exposed as the normal state of affairs. An apt illustration of this is the statement, quoted above, that "we are all refugees" (Warner 1994: 168). Regarding refugee studies, the numbers of which have vastly increased during the preceding two decades, one paradoxical consequence of the tendency towards a democratization of displacement could be that . . . the refugee once again disappears. This time they are the norm in a world that is uprooted and fluid. Just like everyone else, if more so, the refugee is mobile, uprooted, dislocated and lonely. If the world is a "nightmarish postmodern landscape of homelessness" then the refugee is simply one of many who travel this landscape, together with tourists, guestworkers, exiles, business consultants, expatriate experts, roving academics and the like (Shami 1996: 7).

The second major risk is to focus solely on the positive side of mobility, an "aestheticization of exile" (Malkki 1995b: 514) as a position providing an "originality of vision" (Said 1992: 366), a tendency especially marked within cultural studies and studies on transnationalism: "The idealization or romanticization of exile and diaspora can be just as problematic for anthropology (and literary studies) as is the idealization of homeland and rooted communities in works of refugee studies" (Malkki 1995b: 514).

Formerly dark visions of modern fragmentation, meaninglessness alienation, and the homeless mind (Berger et al. 1973), have given way to a conceptualization of mobility and uprooting as a liberating and empowering condition; mobility, for many people is becoming their true home. In this process, home has emerged as a kind of metaphysical, imagined space more than an actual physical, geographical place. Whereas some years ago scholars were being accused of depicting the refugee's territorial and cultural uprootedness as a pathological condition outside the normal sedentary and national order of things (Malkki 1992), recent studies on refugee and migrant diasporas tend to dig into the aesthetic image of mobility as a creative condition through which people on the move, apparently linked up with each other in transnational networks, construct new homes and identities by maximizing the economic and cultural potential of multiple locations. Today, at least within the academic world, it is rather sedentariness which is becoming pathologized, as the crisis of mobility is turning into a crisis of "involuntary immobility" (Carling 2002).

However, as the stories of my Bosnian informants and many other refugees around the world indicate, clearly there are qualitatively different kinds of displacements; and to equate, say, the situation of the refugee with that of the tourist, or the expatriate, or even with the "'postmodern' manifestation of existential homelessness" (Kaplan 1996: 140) would be tantamount to erasing the varying political and economic contexts within which different kinds of travellers move:

As travel, changing locations, and leaving home become central experiences for more and more people in modernity, the difference between the ways we travel, the reasons for our movements, and the terms of our participation in this dynamic must be historically and politically accounted for. (Kaplan 1996: 102)

For anthropologists and other intellectuals it might make sense to talk about "being at home in continuous movement" (Rapport and Dawson 1998a: 27) or "home . . . is where one best knows oneself" (Rapport and Dawson 1998b: 9), but it would be foolish to expect that refugees and other unprivileged people embrace such dissipated notions of belonging. In the case of refugees a multitude of constraints severely limit their freedom of movement and ability to feel at home in exile, not least pertaining to restrictive refugee policies, the increasing political prioritization of repatriation, the economic hardship of refugee life in many parts of the world and the social stigmatization of the refugee label. In such an environment it may be tempting to go home (if that is at all an option).

Pragmatic Transnationals

In this chapter I have shown the complex and contested nature of perceptions of home and return which are at play in repatriation and re-integration processes. Refugees repatriating to BiH voice both feelings of socio-economic marginalization and cultural alienation as well as feelings of belonging and the joy of being home. This fieldwork material then instantaneously rejects the repatriation discourse and its celebratory depictions of repatriation as an unproblematic homecoming. At the same time it seriously questions the idea about the impossible homecoming which informs much of the academic research on repatriation. Despite the apparent differences between public policy repatriation discourse and its critics in the academic world, these two lines of thinking on repatriation seem to be united in a fundamentalist conceptualization of belonging and home, as an identification with a place and community frozen in time; from the former perspective this constructs return as natural, from the latter point of view dreams of going home become an illusion.

The presently dominating anthropological narrative of mobility makes us prone to ridicule the simple-minded assumptions of identity of repatriation discourse, in addition to nationalism and other static approaches to belonging. But this narrative simultaneously provides a certain theoretical blindness, an uncritical stance, towards notions such as the impossible homecoming and the more general aestheticization of displacement, in this way glossing over aspects of cultural continuity and coherence—in other words, all that which does not change. If we instead reconceptualize home in more pragmatic terms, then we will come to acknowledge that there exists no a priori opposition between change, not even war-caused change, and feelings of going home to or being at home in original locale. After all, feelings of belonging do not rest on objective factors but are situated in the subjective realm.

The Bosnians have suddenly become a transnational people, dispersed over large parts of the world. Likewise, Bosnian refugees have developed transnational identities based upon multiple attachment to several places (Clifford 1994). Many Bosnian refugees continue to reside in Western host countries, with their economic and social security while staying in contact with relatives and friends and keeping informed about the political and cultural developments in BiH through mass media and vacations in the homeland. Similarly, those refugees who have returned to their country of origin rarely cut themselves off from the outside world (physically, economically or emotionally). In this sense, they have become pragmatic transnationals, not cultural fundamentalists. The majority of the repatriated Bosnian refugees take home to be a synthesis of a site of livelihood construction and an environment of relational and cultural attachment. Some have found it, others keep searching.

Chapter 10
The Making of a Good Citizen in an Ethiopian Returnee Settlement

Laura Hammond

> We see our life as two lives. The life before 1977 (Julian Calendar, or 1984 Gregorian Calendar, when we fled to the Sudan) and the life after. The life before was better because we were in our homes. But this is a new life and we must try to make it as complete as possible.
>
> —Ada Bai returnee, April 1995

There is a popular conception that when refugees repatriate to their country of origin, they return to their homes. Studies of post-repatriation experiences portray people picking up the pieces of their lives, mending the social, economic, and cultural fabric that has been torn and reinserting themselves into the societies from which they have been exiled. As Liisa Malkki points out, botanical metaphors of displacement as uprootedness and return as transplantation are based on the expectation that the returnee will thrive in his or her original environment, and that a refugee's proper place is his or her area of origin (Malkki 1995a: 15–16). Contrary to the impressions given by these perspectives, repatriation is more often an opportunity for proactive change than a return to the status quo.[1] Refugees who return after a prolonged absence from their countries of origin are not always able to return to their previous houses or villages but must establish new homes. They must define their relationship to their new physical environment, as well as to the altered social and political order (particularly following a regime change), in an entirely new way. Identity, group membership, and physical survival come to be negotiated in new ways as people call into question the basic tenets of their existence.

In this chapter, I examine the post-return experiences of people living in the Ada Bai returnee settlement in northwestern Ethiopia. I argue that return may vary both qualitatively and in terms of its duration, and should be understood as a process by which the returnee establishes the social, political, and economic ties that define him/her in a meaningful way as a member of a community whose primary ties are to the country or region (but not necessarily the village or city) of origin, rather than to the location of exile. I describe this process of integration as involving the creation of a new code of citizenship, where power and legitimacy are redefined both by pressure from above (by political leaders) as well as negotiation from below (within the community).

My observations are based on an eight-year engagement with the returnees living in Ada Bai, the largest of three settlements established in June 1993 near the commercial farming town of Humera in the Tigray region. From November 1993 to July 1995, I lived and conducted ethnographic research in this settlement, to which 7,500 ethnic Tigrayans had repatriated after living for nearly a decade (1984–93) in refugee camps in eastern Sudan. My objective was to examine the process of integration that they were involved in, to determine whether self-sufficiency was in fact a realistic objective, and to understand the challenges of return from the perspective of the migrants themselves. I have returned to the settlement periodically since then (most recently in April 2001), and have tracked the transformation of community identity, or put in other terms, the creation of a homeland.

The lens through which I describe the enactment of this process of homeland creation is the returnees' approach to natural resource management and conservation practices following their repatriation to Ethiopia from eastern Sudan. Returnees effectively fashioned their behavior, and manipulated their use of natural resources, to define a particular relationship to the social and political order, an order which they were both faced with and actively involved in (re)creating. Distant from the center of political power not only geographically, but economically and socially, returnees developed their own rules for accumulation of power and participation within the wider discourses of regional and national reconstruction. Their relationship to the hegemonic order (which itself was in a state of flux and recreation) was largely voluntary; however the *form* of their allegiance was of their own making.

Construction of a new system of social practice did not need to (and in some cases clearly could not) entail the adoption of patterns of behavior common or familiar prior to flight into exile. Upon coming back to their country of origin, returnees were unable, and in many cases uninterested, in picking up where they left off before they became refugees. Rather, in the context of repatriation, resource use and conservation practices took on new forms that had to do with the opportunities and limitations presented by the environment of return and the new realities of life in a postwar context.

Peace and postwar contexts are typically short-lived in the Horn of Africa. In 1998–2000, war came to the people of Ada Bai again, as a bitter conflict between Ethiopia and Eritrea was fought over an ill-defined border. Many young men left the village to fight in the central and eastern parts of Tigray against what they perceived of as an invading army. Towns near Ada Bai were evacuated,

but except for a one-month period in which they sought refuge from bombard-
ments at a nearby water source, the people of Ada Bai did not leave their new
homes. When I returned after the war was over (the government denied foreigners access to the area due to its proximity to the border), I found the community
stronger and more secure than I had ever seen it before. The processes I observed
when the community had been newly formed continued and deepened such that
there was no longer any question that Ada Bai was their home, the place to which
they belonged.

Conditions of Flight and Arrival in Sudan

The people of Ada Bai were among an estimated 200,000 people from the central and eastern highlands of Tigray Region who fled to Sudan in 1984–85 to escape war and famine (Abbry: 132; Hendrie 1996: 35).[2] The war, which had been
raging since 1975, had intensified, and combined with severe drought to make it
impossible for people to remain on their farms. The journey took four to six
weeks: due to the insecurity caused by the war, particularly fear of air attacks,
people traveled mostly at night. The popular rebel movement—the Tigrayan
People's Liberation Front (TPLF) and its humanitarian arm, the Relief Society of
Tigray (REST)—assisted people to move, providing guides and transit centers
along the way to distribute food and medical care.

When they arrived, the refugees were exhausted, emaciated, sick, and weak. At
first, the humanitarian effort was focused on bringing morbidity and mortality
under control by providing emergency assistance: food, water, shelter, and medical care. Despite these attempts, death rates skyrocketed; the deaths in Wad
Kowli camp, where most of the people I lived with had stayed when they first arrived in Sudan, were among the highest that had ever been recorded in a refugee
camp (CDC 1992). One old man recalled to me, "Death was uncountable
there . . . The refugees became sick from . . . the climate and the food [in their
weakened condition, people were unable to digest the food they were given].
There was [deadly] diarrhea." A woman found the place difficult to describe, "At
Wad Kowli, so many people were dying I can't explain it. So many people died
every day that you didn't even want to go to the graveyard. You simply dumped
people in the grave and left."

So bad were conditions in the camps that many people chose to return to
Tigray in 1985 even though the war was continuing. REST organized the repatriation of 154,000 refugees from Sudan against the advice of international organizations who were afraid that conditions were not safe and that return would
render the former refugees inaccessible to aid workers who were unable to work
inside the war zones in Tigray (Hendrie 1996). Refugees who opted to stay in
Sudan said that they would not return for fear of continued war and hunger, conscription into the government army or forced resettlement (Clay and Holcomb:
1986 104; Clay, Steingraber, and Niggli 1988: 44–45). These refugees were determined not to return to their home areas until the war ended and the govern-

ment was replaced. Those who were able to return relatively quickly or regularly were most successful at preserving their claim to their houses and farms. Those who remained away longer lost their property and had to face restarting in a new place once they repatriated.

The Politics of Confinement in the Refugee Camp

The returnees with whom I lived in Ada Bai had been settled in the Saffawa camp after Wad Kowli was closed for health and security reasons.[3] Saffawa was originally intended to be a reception center, a place for refugees to stay for a short time before either being integrated into an agricultural production scheme in the Sudan or else voluntarily repatriated to Ethiopia.[4]

Although the refugees had their own elected leaders, who were in most cases representatives of REST,[5] ultimate legal authority in the camps was held by officials of the Sudanese Government's Commissioner for Refugees (COR). COR was responsible for distributing relief items made available through UNHCR and various NGOs, and, together with the Sudanese police, with maintaining law and order in the camps.

By all accounts, this authority was often abused. Women in Ada Bai told me that in the Sudan they had been particularly vulnerable to having their wares destroyed (particularly alcoholic beverages and cigarettes, which were both illegal to sell and to consume), or of being beaten or raped. Men, too, said that they regularly faced punishment by the Sudanese police if they were caught trading illegally or otherwise transgressed the laws, which were often unfamiliar to them since they differed from Ethiopian laws.

At Saffawa, no refugee was allowed to hold land, although some did so illegally by renting from local Sudanese landholders or squatting on a rare unused piece of land. Others supplemented their assistance allotments through petty trading or daily labor on the nearby plantations. If a refugee was discovered by COR or the police to be farming land for himself and his family, he was subject to arrest and confiscation of both the land and the harvest. Under these circumstances, most refugees said that they chose instead to work on the large commercial sesame, sorghum and cotton plantations for daily or piecework wages, or to support themselves through petty trade.

In the struggle for survival in a place where they were prevented from practicing many of the trades they had relied on in their country of origin, refugees had to weigh the risks and benefits of breaking rules and laws in order to eke out an income. Despite the prohibitions, collecting and selling fuelwood, brewing and selling alcoholic beverages (for women), squatting on or renting farmland, and petty trading (for men and, to a lesser extent, women) were essential economic practices for most refugees. The goods and services that Ethiopian refugees provided were in great demand to the Sudanese themselves, even if many were illegal. Those who emerged as powerful members of the community included traders who brought clothing, vegetables, and other goods from the cities for sale in the refugee camps, women who ran bars, pharmacy owners, and those who worked for international organizations.

The politics of confinement that characterized the organization of power relations in the refugee camps bred a sense of individualistic opportunism, and power came to be vested more in personal wealth and access to material resources (not only cash, but also multiple ration cards, food, jobs with international organizations, farmland, etc.) than in traditional prestige factors such as family name or history.

A Politically Important Repatriation

In May 1991, the TPLF led a coalition of rebel forces, calling itself the Ethiopian People's Revolutionary Democratic Front (EPRDF), into the capital and overthrew the Marxist government known as the Derg. The President, Colonel Mengistu Haile Mariam, had fled the city a few days before, and was ultimately granted asylum in Zimbabwe.

One of the top priorities of the new government was to bring the refugees home from Sudan. At the end of the war it was estimated that 160,000 refugees remained in camps in Sudan (ARRA: 1992). Many of the TPLF's leaders had lived as refugees themselves during various stages of the struggle, and were committed to bringing their compatriots home. Mass repatriation would demonstrate that the new government had removed obstacles for people to return with confidence and in dignity to their home country.

Most refugees did not need to be persuaded to return to Ethiopia: the opportunity to return to a Tigray where peace prevailed was enough incentive. However, the role of individual choice was minimal: the refugees had been politically mobilized for years to be ready to return as soon as they were directed to do so by their leaders. This does not mean that repatriation was not voluntary, but rather that the notion of choice was influenced very much by group dynamics. The group sought stability and a sustainable way of life. Thus, return represented an opportunity to claim the rights and privileges guaranteed to Ethiopian citizens that would bring about this kind of security.

Despite their eagerness to repatriate, the reality of return was vastly different from what most people had imagined for themselves. Prior to their return, they had been told that it would not be possible to reclaim the farmland they had left behind in the highlands of Tigray region, where they still had relatives. Since population pressure on the land was great (the average holding being less than one hectare, or four acres, and in many cases as little as one-fourth that amount), local government administrations had redistributed the land of the refugees to those who had remained in the highland communities. Further partitioning of holdings to make room for returnees would render individual farms too small to be able to produce sustainable livelihoods.

To accommodate the returnees without placing too much pressure on local highland community resources, the new government of Ethiopia designated three settlement areas in the far northwestern corner of Ethiopia, close to the Sudan and Eritrea borders, near the town of Humera. This area had previously been administered as part of Gondar region but, following the redrawing of regional boundary lines by the new government, now came under Tigray's jurisdiction, and had a local population that was a diverse mix of ethnic Amhara, Tigray, Kunama, and other groups. Returnees were offered plots of farmland in this dry, hot, but fertile lowland area; most of the land allocated had previously been part of a failed state farm run by the former socialist government.

Home at Last?

The first two years following repatriation involved the forging of new relationships between farmer and farmland, homesteader and home, a process that demanded novel approaches to basic subsistence practices as well as a re-examination of notions of citizenship, communitarianism, and kinship. I joined the returnees in November, five months after their initial return. They were still living in temporary shelters and were finishing the last of the food rations that had been given to them when they repatriated. The processes that I describe in this chapter had hardly begun; people were literally trying to figure out how to situate themselves in this new environment, and did not seem at all certain that they were going to remain in the settlement.

Secure Access to Natural Resources?

Many returnees who repatriated from Sudan in 1993 told me that they had decided to come back to their home country in order to obtain secure access to farmland. This was one of the prerequisites to achieving a sustainable livelihood. A popular song sung by young girls in Ada Bai captured this sentiment:

> Those who were our brothers in Sudan
> Come back to your country,
> With our warm greeting of struggle.
>
> You, our brothers who are in a foreign country
> Come back to your country
> Because it is lighted with a big lamp of freedom
> We have been refugees long enough.
>
> I hope to come back to my homeland in order to farm
> In a place that is not your country
> You cannot own it like when you are home.
> I left my country eight years ago and now I am in a hurry.[6]

In Ada Bai, it was not possible to practice the kind of ox-plow based agriculture that prevails in the Tigrayan highlands. In fact, being only 40 kilometers (approximately 25 miles) from the Sudan border, the move kept them within the same agro-ecological zone that they had lived in as refugees, but not the same that most had known before leaving Ethiopia.[7] In addition, the returnee settlements were thickly settled, resembling large towns or refugee camps more than the scattered residential patterns of the highlands, where a house could be as far as one kilometer from its nearest neighbor.

The western lowlands of Tigray, in which Ada Bai is situated, has a reputation for being exceptionally fertile, and returnees were certainly aware of this when they moved to the area. The "black cotton" vertisol soil found throughout the area is rich, although its high clay content results in severe cracking during the dry season (Kibreab 1996a: 38). Much of the land around Humera, the administrative center of the area and located 20 kilometers from Ada Bai, had been used for commercial farming since the beginning of the twentieth century and mechanized farming began during the 1960s (McCann 1990: 121). During the reign of Emperor Haile Selassie, particularly from 1960–1974, private landowners cultivated large tracts of land with sesame, cotton, and sorghum. These commercial farmers were expelled following the nationalization of all land by the Derg in April 1974 (Clapham 1988: 157–94). The Derg set up its own state farm on this land, which was never very successful, owing to sporadic but heavy fighting (especially in 1978–79 when most of Humera town was destroyed in clashes between the Derg and the Ethiopian Democratic Union), inefficient management, and lack of popular support for collectivized farming.[8] After 1982, the farm was abandoned; tractors sat idle in large lots until they eventually disintegrated beyond repair.

The name Ada Bai is derived from the Tigrinya "Adi Abay" meaning "Big Land"; true to its name, it is a vast plain, bordered on one side by the Tekezze River (which also separates Ethiopia from Eritrea in this area) and by a smaller river known locally as the Rawayan, meaning "that which satisfies the thirst." Prior to the arrival of the returnees in 1993, it was home to a mere 100 agro-pastoralists who had migrated from Eritrea several years before. REST estimates that 2300 houses were built by returnees in Ada Bai during the first year, in 16x20 meter plots.[9] Wooden poles for construction of the traditional round huts with thatched roofs (known as *tukuls*) were brought from the forests at the edge of the plain. The *woreda* (district) chairman reported that 480,000 poles were cut to serve all three of the settlements during the first year following repatriation.[10] Upon reaching this calculation, local government officials began to become concerned that continued immigration to the area might deplete the available resources.

For farming purposes, households were to be allocated between one and three hectares of land, depending on the number of members.[11] In practice, very few people actually received the amount of land to which they were entitled. The Hiwot Mechanization Company (a parastatal agricultural production company) provided tractor disk plowing free of charge the first year and on a credit basis the second (at a rate of 100 birr per hour of plowing, repayable at harvest time). Much of the land that the returnees were allocated in the first year, however, was overgrown with thick bushes and trees and required clearing before it could be plowed by tractor. This was not possible for most farmers, as allocation took place in June and July, precisely the time that they should have started planting. Farmers estimated that it would take a single man one month to clear one hectare of land. Many farmers thus left their land idle during 1993 since it would have been too late for them to plant once they had cleared and plowed it. I arrived in Ada Bai in November, when the first crop cycle should have been harvested. There was little harvesting going on, and many people complained that they had not been able to grow crops and would need food aid to support their families until the next harvest. Together with a group of farmers, I visited the areas that they reported had been allocated (including the largest plot allocated to several hundred farmers that was located 50 km from the settlement!). Almost all of the land was standing fallow or with crops that would never fully mature.

The second year, more land was allocated earlier and closer to Ada Bai's residential area. Farmers tackled the problem of clearing individually, with each man (the vast majority of landholders were men) concerned only with his own plot of land. Those farmers who did succeed in clearing their land by themselves in time for plowing faced problems if their neighbors' land was not cleared, for it was impossible for the tractors to get through the uncleared land to plow. Immediately, disputes arose between farmers. Some argued that all who had been allotted land should be required to clear it right away, even if they did not plan to cultivate it that year, so that the tractors could get through to the cleared plots. Others complained that they were not able to clear the land, or that they could not afford the tractor plowing even on a credit basis, and so they saw no point in clearing land that they could not use. The story of one farmer illustrates the dilemma:

I started to clear [my] land but no one is clearing around me. I know that the tractor will not be able to get to it. The soil is like the place where we were before (in 1993). It is bad. I would [clear the land] anyway even if it was bad, but I can't if the others are not. There are about twenty people with land in that area. . . . It is hard for the donkey[12] to plow because there is strong grass in the area. . . . It is not possible to rent land because we have no money in hand. [The landholders] ask for the money first so we can't afford the price of rent.

To solve the problem of clearing the land, the *baito*[13] called on people to work together to clear several allotments at once. The *baito* chairman announced at one public meeting:

Some people still have not (been allocated) farmland and some have not cleared it. If the land is not cleared, the tractors may not be able to get to the land that is plowed. So until plowing takes place everyone should keep clearing. . . . Even if tractors arrive, if the area is not cleared they will not be able to plow it.[14]

Some agreed with this sentiment, and strove to organize people into *gudgeles*, groups of about 50 farmers each, to clear the land collectively. The proponents of the *gudgele* system rejected the benefits of individual labor and began to foster the notion of a collective work ethic to be undertaken for the common good. One militia member told me,

Our responsibility is to clear the land, and the government's is to give the seeds, so I will do my responsibility and if the government doesn't live up to its [side] I will leave the land. We are believing [hoping] that they will live up to their responsibility.

In this statement the image of a contract between the state and the peasantry can be clearly seen. A recurring theme emerged in my fieldwork: the idea that the government had a responsibility to provide at least some of the means by which peasants could attain self-sufficiency, and the farmers' acceptance, to varying degrees, that they too had responsibilities to fulfill in order to "deserve" these benefits from the government. Upon clearing his land, one man said to the *baito* leaders at a public meeting,

Even the places we have cleared have grown weeds. The [rented tractor] plows are late in coming and we cannot afford to rent animals to plow. Why don't you give us the money for seeds and hand tools now so we do not have to sit idle?

This farmer evidently felt that he had fulfilled his side of the contract by clearing the land, and that if the tractor plows were not going to come to fulfill theirs', then he should be entitled to take alternative steps to ensure that his crop was planted in time.

Some farmers received land that was already cleared, which had reportedly been under cultivation by Sudanese squatters for many years. These foreigners were expelled, and their land was given to the returnees. This might seem to have been an ideal arrangement for the returnees, except that the land was 50 kilometers from the residential settlement and situated in a swampy plain. Proper management of that land was virtually impossible, and the first harvest, on both near and far plots, was a near total failure. In subsequent years it was abandoned by Ada Bai farmers and alternative land located closer to the settlement was requested (and partially received) from the *woreda*.[15]

By the second year following return, most returnees had cleared their own land and found a means for plowing it, whether through a loan scheme offered by the Hiwot Mechanization Company or by renting, borrowing, or sharing draught animals (usually donkeys, but in some cases cattle or camels were used to plow). Most turned to their neighbors or farmers in Humera town to borrow or rent draught animals because, they said, the cost of tractor plowing was too high.[16] Very few people had any or enough of their own draught animals for plowing. Nearly everyone had to settle for only one pass through their fields with the disk plow, as both tractors and draught animals were in such high demand.

Those farmers who did eventually clear their land thereby increased their security over it. Elected officials agreed that someone who had cleared their land had invested in it sufficiently to guarantee him or her the right to retain it. Those who did not clear their land were more at risk of having it taken back from them and given to someone else who would be more likely to clear it. This put women at a particular disadvantage, as many who had no one to help them clear or plow were holding onto their plots in the hopes that someone would eventually wish to rent it from them. Single women were by far the most disadvantaged in terms of access to land.

These problems should perhaps be seen as pioneers' dilemmas. In taking over responsibility for virgin land, returnees also had to begin to bind together as a community to manage these resources. Individualism was in most cases not possible to pursue for long, and rules for management of the new resources had to be invented.

Exhausted or Inexhaustible Resources?

In addition to the challenges of having to work together to manage the new resources, an additional unforeseen problem of shortage of land, not only at the household level, but also at the *woreda* level, quickly emerged. Prior to 1993, little attention had been given to the notion that the natural resources in the Humera area might prove to be limited. As Bruce, Hoben, and Dessalegn point out, no one had ever explored whether "unutilized resources were indeed freely available."[17]

In January 1994, the *woreda* chairman told me, "We think there will be enough land for everyone. We are not worried about having enough now." This sentiment was echoed by a representative of the *woreda* Office of Agriculture, who said that the problem was not locating enough farmland but rather finding settlement sites for returnees with sufficient water, accessibility, and services. The *woreda* chairman admitted that allocation was made difficult by the fact that all landholding records had been destroyed during the war, and that it was not possible to determine exactly how much land was available. Nevertheless, in 1993 land was being offered to returnees, commercial investors, local residents (up to 10 hectares per household) and settlers from the highlands who were willing leave their home areas.

After the second movement of returnees from Sudan to Ethiopia in 1994, the local administration began to be concerned that there would not be enough land to allocate to all who wanted it if they continued to parcel it out as generously as they had the previous year. What had previously been thought to be an area of inexhaustible resources suddenly appeared insufficient to meet the farming demands of the local residents, returnees, commercial investors, and parastatal companies.

In early 1994, the results of a land use survey were completed. The Woreda Office of Agriculture estimated that roughly three quarters of the arable land was already allocated and that a large portion of that was being used for small-scale cultivation (10 hectares or less) caused a great deal of alarm among the local administration.

The tension between the needs of small-scale returnee farmers and the regional and national needs of cash-crop production increased as the benefits to be reaped from the revived commercial farms grew. Kibreab notes that

It is generally not concern for the well-being of such communities that prompts most governments to establish settlement schemes, but rather the desire to gain access to resources which were previously controlled by the subsistence producers concerned so that they [the governments] can allocate such resources, mainly land, to alternative economic activities such as commercial agriculture where returns are believed to be higher. Allocation of land formerly utilized by nomadic and small sedentary farming populations to cash-crop and/or commercialized livestock production is considered by many governments as an imperative, dictated by the need of optimal resource allocation. (1996a: 1–2)

Much of the sorghum being produced in the fields around Humera was being bought by private and humanitarian interests and brought to food-deficit areas of the country for sale or distribution as relief food. Furthermore, sesame exports provided an important source of foreign currency to the cash-strapped government. The farms, the largest of which are owned by private share companies whose shareholders are high-ranking TPLF members, were providing important funding for other public programs which promoted rural development and enterprise establishment. Promotion of commercial farming apparently came to take priority over individual allocations to small-scale subsistence farming by returnees. It was thought that returnees could support themselves adequately by working on the farms.

In 1995, regional repatriation priorities were altered when it was decided that the natural resources around Humera were being depleted. Returnees from Sudan were resettled in the Tigrayan highlands, with assistance from UNHCR and REST, without any guaranteed access to land at all. Before returning, people were warned that even though there was no assurance that they would get land in the highlands, no land would be made available for them in Humera either. They were advised that if they chose to move to the Humera lowlands after having been transported to their areas of origin in the highlands (there being no law preventing such relocation), they would not be given house or farm plots. A significant proportion of returnees in 1995 and 1996, however, took their chances and came to Humera to rent land from the commercial farmers and other landholders with the money they had received from what UNHCR deemed a rehabilitation grant. In fact, Ada Bai's population jumped from 7500 in 1993 to over 10,000 in 1996, largely as a result of the influx of returnees in 1995. Others returned to the highlands and attempted to establish themselves in off-farm trades. In December 1999, a *woreda* administrator in central Tigray told me that several hundred returnees to his area from the refugee camps in Sudan were still in constant need of food assistance four years after repatriating since they did not have any farmland and had not been able to find trade or employment to support themselves.

In addition to this measure, regulations against cutting green wood for building or firewood were handed down by the Humera *woreda* to the *baitos* and ultimately to the returnees. Wood was only to be taken from farm plots rather than from forests. Moreover, only those who were clearing their own land were allowed to manufacture charcoal for sale (from the wood they cleared). These restrictions were meant to slow the rate of environmental degradation and depletion of resources. However, when I visited Ada Bai in May 1997, I saw massive stacks of charcoal piled outside the *baito* office that had been confiscated from illegal charcoal producers.

The New Code of Good Citizenship

The land that was allocated to the first wave of returnees to Humera in 1993, was assigned by the *woreda* to the local *baitos* to distribute. There was, however, not enough land to allocate to everyone who was eligible. It was very difficult, well nigh impossible, to determine who should receive a piece of this limited land when so many who were in need were demanding it. The *baito* faced the choice of either allocating smaller plots to more people, or targeting those who were most in need of farmland, giving full allocations to fewer people. It chose to do both. Some households were allocated smaller plots than to which they were entitled. In addition, a series of selection criteria was devised to identify the people who were most in need of land. Others were denied land. The evolution of this set of criteria gave rise to what I call a "new code of good citizenship."

In the Tigrayan highlands, access to land, whether by residence (*diessa*) or inheritance (*risti*), defined farmers as members of a particular community. Writing on the relationship between land tenure and community identity in highland Eritrea, where *risti* was practiced, Kibreab says,

Land was perceived as serving as a lineage dating back many centuries which nurtured links with the past and the future. Persons without land were viewed as lacking roots, lineage or heritage. That was the rationale of prohibiting permanent alienation of land. (1996: 159–60)

Likewise, land under the *diessa* system tied people to a particular community not only through the individual plots allocated to all residents, but also through communal adjudication of common resources such as grazing land, water sources, and fuel lots (1996: 159). By removing these rights, the individual lost one of the principal features by which he or she was identified as a member of the community. Lacking this tie upon repatriation, the returnee was faced with the prospect of carving out a new identity in the community through obtaining access to land.

At the outset, it was difficult to define a notion of who was deserving of land because the community and its leaders had not yet evolved a well-defined code of proper behavior or of legitimate membership to the community. Many of the lines of social stratification, determined by internal community dynamics, had not yet been developed, and those that had applied prior to the experience of exile, no longer did so outside of the communities of origin. In the absence of an established definition of who was deserving of land, returnees started to think imaginatively of how they could distinguish themselves as members in good standing of the returnee community, such that they would not be overlooked when land was distributed.

The clearest way of doing this, in the eyes of the people, was to align oneself with the political leadership. Community members noticed right away who received land: members of the *baito* and militia,[18] priests, veterans, and families of soldiers who had fought for the TPLF during the war. This was partly the result of the fact that those who provided community service were otherwise unpaid, and allocation of land was seen as a way of rewarding them for having volunteered their labor. The suspicion of favoritism, even if such practices were defensible, led to some ill-feeling, but also encouraged people to evaluate how they could position themselves so that they too might be seen to be deserving of land as a reward for services rendered. They also saw that those who had received land as a result of their membership in a community group, had been more effective at lobbying for land than they might have been as individuals. They therefore began to form blocs through which they hoped to be able to lobby for access to farmland.

Among the first in the returnee settlement to try their hand at gaining power through organizing were the wives of traders. Traders and shop owners in Ada Bai had been told by the *baito* that as there was not enough land for everyone, and that as they had alternative sources of income, they were not entitled to farm land. The wives organized themselves and went to the community leaders demanding that land be given to them in their own names. One woman explained the process to me:

I told [the *baito*] that my husband had a trading permit, but I needed a plot of land for my children since trading is risky right now in Ada Bai. We have no certainty with trading because we are just starting. We want to have land as a security. If we have residence land (house plot), we feel we have a place here, but we need the [farming] land to feed our children's stomachs.

The *baito* considered her case, and the cases of others like her, to be legitimate and gave her an authorization paper to give to her neighborhood *gudgele* responsible for allocating land.

One of my neighbors, who was reluctant to "make waves" by joining the traders' wives protest movement, was urged on by her husband to petition the *baito* for an allotment of land. She reluctantly went to the *baito* to make a claim, and returned victorious with one hectare of land. She never let him forget that it was her land he was working, and it turned out to be the household's sole source of income since they did not have the money to purchase stock for their small shop and it remained closed for the duration of my stay in Ada Bai. One *baito* member justified the council's decision by explaining to me, "We haven't seen trade helping the family yet, so if [the traders' wives] asked for land we are giving them land. We hope that in the future they will not need it."

By July 1995, when I left Ada Bai, the third round of allocation was in progress. By then distinct rules had evolved by which people sought to obtain access to land.

While political loyalty was still the defining feature of those who were allocated land, the way that loyalty was expressed had taken on additional meaning. People would, for instance, participate in communal work projects such as laying the pipeline for the water distribution system, participating in community environmental sanitation campaigns (collecting and burning garbage) or conservation projects in the knowledge that if they did not, they would be fined and, they imagined, probably would not receive land. One lucky fellow was even given land in recognition of the service he had performed to the community for being the resident anthropologist's research assistant!

Voting for Land

One of the more disturbing relationships was the perceived connection between participating in local elections (voting) and obtaining or maintaining access to agricultural land. When elections were held in May 1995 to select representatives to the regional assembly and federal Council of Representatives, international observers were not allowed to monitor the elections. I dutifully stayed away from the polling station. At the end of the day, however, members of the Ada Bai Women's Association came to me to ask if I would drive some of the sick people who wanted to vote to the polling station. I agreed, delivering them to the election site without actually entering the station. The following is an extract from my notes of that day:

At around 6 p.m. I was asked to bring a woman to the polling station who had given birth two days ago. [With the help of two members of the Women's Association] we somehow managed to get a man sick with advanced tuberculosis into the car too. At the polling station two other sick people were coming out of the booths [supported by their relatives]. One woman could not walk. She had been brought by cart on her bed to vote.

Surprised that people would insist on going to the polls to vote even in such weakened conditions, I asked the woman who had just delivered the baby why she was voting. Did she really think that her vote was so important that she had to struggle so much to cast her ballot? "No," she said. "I am voting because if I do not I will not get any land this year." This was the first time I had heard of voting being associated with access to land.

That evening, I asked some of my neighbors what they thought of this woman's response. Without revealing what she had recounted to me earlier, I posed a hypothetical question to a female friend: "If you had just given birth to a baby, and you were bedridden, would you try to vote anyway?" Her husband, usually not one to speak for his strong-willed wife, broke in right away. "I would carry her on my back if I had to. If I didn't, we would lose our land." She nodded her agreement.

What is important in this case is not necessarily whether voting actually guaranteed access to land (or rather, whether not voting deprived one of access to land). More significant is the fact that such an action was *perceived* to have this effect, and that therefore the popular definition of being a good citizen, with access to resources, required this behavior. It should be noted that for most women, this was the first time they had voted and thus, this association was a new one for them.

Negotiation and Argumentation as Key Methods of Social Construction

This description of political posturing does not imply that there was a single structure of authority with which people felt they had to comply, or that all power was dictated from top down. People had agency and power, and in many contexts they were not afraid to use them. The myriad ways that people vied to win favor from the political leaders was a constant source of negotiation, discussion, disagreement and often amusement. Means of receiving recognition in order to get access to land were being invented all the time, and it was as much a victory for the individual farmer to find a new form of behavior that could be rewarded with access to resources as it was for the leaders to acknowledge compliant behavior, since the evolution of this code of conduct for new citizens helped them to govern the community.

Negotiations over the rules by which good citizenship should be defined were not always so unproblematic, however. Discussion of rules became something of a battlefield, as people found ways to complain when they felt that there was too much favoritism. Unsubstantiated rumors commonly spread that members of the *baito* were keeping the best land for themselves and their families, that they were stealing aid resources, particularly food, from the warehouse that were meant for distribution, and that if you crossed one member of the *baito* the wrong way, you would never get land. One priest was disliked by some people for disagreeing with several other priests[19] over the role of the church and the clergy within the community. He was accused of keeping for himself the contributions that people had given him towards construction of the new church. These rumors, even if unfounded, communicated to the leaders the strong message that they were being held accountable to the community. For the most part, forms of currying favor had to follow acceptable lines of conduct that the majority of the community tacitly or overtly agreed to, or else the person who had broken the code could be ostracized and criticized by the community. If the *baito*, the clergy, or any other source of institutional power abused their privileged positions egregiously, community members were not afraid to complain publicly.

Other forms of negotiation and argumentation took place in the sanctioned setting of the public meetings. Particularly during the first year of my stay in Ada Bai, these meetings were held with near annoying frequency, usually on a Saturday, Sunday, or feast day, and commonly lasted the entire day. Despite my discomfort at sitting in 120°F heat for six hours, I attended these meetings as often as I could because they gave me valuable insight into the means by which social rules were constructed. In these meetings, people publicly aired their concerns and doubts about the rule construction process, and forwarded recommendations for revisions.

In two instances, debates were held in public meetings concerning the use of land surrounding the houses. Some residents were concerned that the houses were too close together, and the danger of fire was so great that fences around residential compounds should be prohibited (a straw house could burn to the ground in fifteen minutes). They said that fences prevented access to those coming to help extinguish the fire and could even help to spread fires from one compound to another. Opponents of the motion said that the fences were needed to protect their animals at night and to maintain at least the semblance of privacy and security in such a crowded environment. This argument was presumably more important in the refugee/returnee contexts, where housing was crowded, than it would have been in their original highland homes, where houses are typically not built close together, spreading out instead across the mountain slopes, and walls surrounding compounds are usually made of stone. The debate was bitter, but in the end, the fences were allowed to stay.

The other debate concerned the planting of crops inside the residential compounds. In Sudan, it had been common for people to use what little land they had around their houses to grow vegetables, spices, and even cotton, to meet their household needs. This was necessary since pressure on the land around the camps was so heavy and resources so scarce. Having plants growing close to the houses, however, was acknowledged to encourage the breeding of mosquitoes, a major concern in an area where malaria is the leading cause of death. One group of residents thought that such planting in house compounds should be banned, whereas another said that the plants were necessary for providing food and cotton (a source of cash) for the household. Again, after a long discussion and a show of hands, the plants were allowed to remain. The principle of the need to debate publicly what might appear to be individualistic rights was strengthened through these instances.

Conclusions

Access to resources dictated the terms by which Ada Bai residents sought access to power, and ultimately through which they re-established their position as citizens of the post-war region and state. In most cases, behavior that defined the good citizen also helped to secure returnees' access to the very resources over which they negotiated, thereby creating stability and greater economic security. Returnees were successfully forming a code of what can be considered acceptable or proper behavior. They did this in response to directives issued from those in positions of authority as well as from below, through discussions, debates and arguments between neighbors and relatives—in houses, teashops, the marketplace, and at the water source—about the form that such behavior should take. While leaders may have required compliance in exchange for resources, their followers demanded accountability in exchange for support. The two relations existed symbiotically and were ultimately intended to lead to sustainable principles of re-source use.

When I finished my dissertation research and left Ada Bai at the start of the rainy season in 1995, households were much better off than they had been dur-ing the first year after return. Most had managed to become self-sufficient and to have enough access to cash and food to support their families. Rates of prevent-able illnesses such as diarrhea were down, as the water supply had been improved through communal labor, and nutrition was generally improved. Children were going to school, and families were investing in their homes and farmland. Still, I was not entirely confident that people would continue to stay in Ada Bai rather than return to their homes.

During return visits in 1996, 1997, and 2001, I saw the village that I had once considered to be fragile and unviable become more stable. Residents attributed this to the fact that life had become "more settled" and that they "knew the place" better than they had when they first arrived. Rules of good citizenship were bol-stered by regulations concerning environmental protection.

In May 1998, a bloody war between Ethiopia and Eritrea began. This was os-tensibly a dispute over the location of central and eastern parts of the border be-tween the two countries, although disputes concerning trade relations and treatment of each other's resident nationals fueled the enmity between them. Ironically, the location of the border in the area closest to Ada Bai was well-defined: the Tekezze River, which flows a few kilometers from the village, forms the undisputed western border between the two countries. Still, the conflict af-fected them in significant ways. With the border closed (including the bridge con-necting Humera with the Eritrea town of Om Hajer), local markets collapsed. In addition, the markets for Humera's main cash crops, sorghum and sesame, dried up. Sorghum previously had been sold in Eritrea; when this market was closed, it was not possible to divert all of the marketable stock to Ethiopian grain markets since transport costs were much higher. Sesame had been exported through the Eritrean port of Massawa. Transport to the far-off port of Djibouti (once Mas-sawa was closed to Ethiopian cargo) was so expensive that Ethiopian sesame could not compete on the global market. This resulted in a loss of wage-earning op-portunities for Ada Bai residents.

Although I was in Ethiopia working for the United Nations during the war, I had not been able to return to Ada Bai because, I was told by the Government of Ethiopia, it was inside the security zone and was not safe. I did manage to visit other parts of Tigray during that time, however. When the war finally ended, I went back, not knowing whether I would find the village still in existence, or whether my friends had been killed or lost their relatives in the war. I arrived to find that all of my neighbors were still living in the same place, and their lives had taken on an even greater sense of permanency in their new home.

Ada Bai residents told me that, despite the difficulties the war had dealt them, they had not wanted to leave their village. Former returnees from other settle-ments closer to Humera had evacuated to camps and been given relief food throughout the war, but the people of Ada Bai chose to remain where they were. Some took advantage of the fact that commercial farmers nearby were not planting during the war by squatting on the large plots to cultivate their own crops. People told me that when areas close to Ada Bai were shelled by the Eritrean military, they left their homes to seek shelter in a river bed approximately 10 km east of the village. "It was awful," they told me. "We were like refugees all over again." They came back three weeks later, as soon as the immediate danger had passed, and refused to leave again for the duration of the war.

I found my former neighbors, who had been among the poorest returnees and were childless when I first met them, with three children and a flock of more than 30 sheep. Despite the apparent improvement in their economic status, they were extremely distraught because, they said, Eritrean militia had raided five of their cattle. I observed a calf, no more than a few weeks old, being led to nurse from a neighbor's cow, as its own mother had been among the raided animals. The head of this household had spent the entire day with the *baito* lodging a complaint and trying to find a way of obtaining restitution. To my surprise, the same *baito* leaders that I had known during my first fieldwork period had retained their positions. They had become seasoned politicians, and had the trust and support of most of the residents. It was to these leaders that the people of Ada Bai turned when they felt victimized or attacked by their Eritrean neighbors.

Since the start of the civil war in 1975, rural Tigrayan society has been extremely politicized. The TPLF and REST continue to enjoy positions of authority and support throughout the region. People genuinely feel that these organizations helped them through a very difficult period, and many, probably correctly, feel that their lives have been saved by the actions of the movement. This feeling has been strengthened by the experience of the war. In addition to men enlisting in large numbers, households contributed their labor, wealth, and food resources to the military. Distrust of Eritreans has had a galvanizing effect on the community: it has enhanced the unity of Ada Bai identity and caused people to cooperate more in the face of a common perceived enemy.

The process I have described here by which a community code of good conduct is developed has continued and become more refined as a result of the perceived threat not only to national sovereignty but also to residents' own farms and homes. Eritrean territory is visible from Ada Bai, so the threat of invasion during the war, and even since the cessation of hostilities (as evidenced by the cattle raiding that had just taken place when I arrived in the village) was palpable.

The code of good community citizenship is, I suspect, not very different in form from codes of community membership in many societies. Community leadership is both a means and an end to legitimate access to resources in societies throughout the world. What is unique is that Ada Bai residents have had an opportunity to reexamine, sometimes but not always consciously, each of these tenets of community formation, to reinvent and redefine them in new ways. Relationships between power and resources are directly linked to the most basic level of subsistence.

In repatriating after nearly a decade (1984–1993) of living in refugee camps in Eastern Sudan, Ethiopian returnees in the northwest Tigray region were presented with new opportunities for proactive change. Rather than returning to a life or community that was familiar, these returnees settled together in a new area. The process of return was one not of homecoming but of creative change in which individuals and families established the social, political, and economic ties that defined them in meaningful ways as members of a new community. This process of integration involved the creation of a new code of citizenship, where power and legitimacy were redefined by both pressure from above (by political leaders) and negotiation from below (within the community). Through patterning of behavior and manipulation of rules concerning natural resource management, individuals generated new definitions of what it meant to be a good citizen.

Chapter 11
West Indian Migrants and Their Rediscovery of Barbados

George Gmelch

In 1987 Eric Hinds, twenty-two, single, and without prospects of a steady job, emigrated from his native Barbados to the United States, and settled with his brother's family in a West Indian neighborhood in Brooklyn. Over the next eleven years he held various jobs—deliveryman, baker, steel band player—while attending night classes at a local university. He married Esther Hollingsworth, another Barbadian emigrant, and they started a family.

On a visit to Barbados during Christmas 1997, the couple started to talk seriously about going home. Esther didn't want to raise her children in urban America, and Eric missed the Caribbean climate, sea, and more relaxed pace of life. So he began to apply for jobs advertised in the *Advocate*, a Bajan newspaper that circulated among his emigrant friends. Eventually he was offered a job with a small bakery owned by a relative. The salary was only half what he was making in the United States; Eric and Esther agonized over the decision. They would not enjoy the same standard of living they had in Brooklyn, but they would be home. After some months, they decided that what mattered most was the country in which they were to rear their children. And that was Barbados. Eric accepted the job and they returned home to the West Indies.

The Hinds are among tens of thousands of emigrants who have returned to their native lands in recent years. During the past decade there has been a stream of migrants returning from Britain and North America to many parts of the Caribbean, including Puerto Rico, Jamaica, and Trinidad, as well as to smaller islands such as Barbados. The actual number of emigrants returning home to countries like Barbados can only be estimated because as they pass through airport customs and immigration, they are indistinguishable from those returning solely to visit. But other indicators—the transfer of foreign bank deposits, construction of new housing in rural areas, and population increases beyond natural growth—provide ample evidence that return migration is rising sharply in much of the Caribbean (Gmelch 1992: 41–56).

This chapter examines the emigration and return of Barbadians from Britain and North America. While both ends of the migration cycle are described, the focus is on the experiences of Barbadians returning to the Caribbean and what it means to come home for both the individual and the society. In the early 1980s I conducted a survey of 135 Barbadian returnees.[1] The results of the survey, in which the varied lives and experiences of the migrants were reduced to statistical patterns, seemed too far removed from the reality of the migrants' lives that I knew. More interested in giving expression to what it meant to migrate and then years later return home, I began a second study involving in-depth tape recorded life history interviews with a smaller sample of twenty migrants.[2] The data in this paper are drawn heavily from the latter research, but it is also informed by the earlier survey work and from current fieldwork in a Barbadian village.

Emigration from Barbados

The Barbadians in this study left their island as part of a mass migration from the English speaking Caribbean to Britain and North America following World War II. Some went to attend university or vocational training courses, but most sought work. In the 1950s Britain began actively recruiting workers from its former colonies in the West Indies, India, and Pakistan. Labor was needed for the post-war reconstruction and for a booming economy. Tens of thousands of Barbadians along with other West Indians boarded ships for jobs in the United Kingdom. British companies and government agencies, including the London Transport Executive and the British Hotel and Restaurant Association, sent recruiters to Barbados. Villagers could take the bus into the capital city of Bridgetown for an interview. If they qualified, as most did, they were assigned a job, trained, and transported to England. Men, particularly, went to Britain to work in post offices, on the buses and trains, and construction sites. Women became nurses or worked in light industry. The Barbadian government, seeing emigration as a way to alleviate population pressure at home, loaned the emigrants money for their travel.

As Britain got back on its feet, however, competition for jobs between the Britons and the newcomers created hostility and resentment toward the colored immigrants (Davison 1962; Patterson 1969). The British parliament responded with the Commonwealth Immigration Act of 1962, restricting further immigration. By the late 1960s the flow of emigrants from the West Indies, India, and Pakistan had virtually ended.[3] However, the United States and Canada reopened their doors to immigrants, and a new stream of migrants began to head north.

The postwar era was not the first time Barbadians had emigrated from their island. Since the 1830s, when slavery was abolished throughout the English-speaking Caribbean, migration had been common. On Barbados and other islands with similarly dense populations and scarce resources, emigration was a necessary safety valve. In the nineteenth century, Barbadians went to larger islands within the Caribbean. In 1905 many signed up with American recruiters and emigrated to Panama to dig the canal. By the time the canal was completed in 1914, nearly one-quarter of all Barbadians had traveled to Panama (Richardson 1985). In the 1920s, Barbadians emigrated to Curacao, Trinidad, and Venezuela to work in the newly developing oil fields. Others went to Cuba to work in the sugar industry. And even before World War II, a small number had emigrated to North America and England, then affectionately known as the "mother country." But the flow to these "metropolitan" countries, as they are referred to in the Caribbean, was only a trickle compared with the torrent that followed after the war. In just two decades (1951–70), 14 percent of the Barbados population of 230,000 had left the island (Richardson 1985).

Barbados

Barbados lies in the eastern Caribbean, about 200 miles north of the South American continent, and east of the great arc of volcanic islands that sweep a thousand miles from the Virgin Islands in the north to Trinidad in the south. With a gentle terrain ideal for agriculture, Barbados was the archetypal "sugar island," producing sugar, molasses, and rum for its colonial master, Great Britain, for over 300 years. Most Barbadians are descendants of Africans who were transported to the island to work as slaves on the sugar plantations. Independent from Britain since 1966, today Barbados is better known to the outside world for its white sand beaches and sunny, tropical climate, which make it a popular tourist destination. Its reputation is far larger than its size, just 21 miles from north to south.

Why They Went

Nearly all the migrants in my survey left Barbados with the expectation that they would find better opportunities for themselves abroad, whether it be work, education, or joining a spouse. Many also desired to see what the "mother country" was really like, or "how the other half lives" (Chamberlain 1997). Especially in the 1950s and 1960s, some were also influenced by the fact that other Barbadians were emigrating and that it was the "thing to do." In the words of one Calypso artist, "The trek to England was the only craze" (Holmes 1988: 220).

The journey overseas was a momentous occasion, and the beginning of a new life. Most migrants had never traveled abroad before, much less been on a ship or airplane. To this day, the migrants can remember the day of the week they left home and the day they arrived abroad. The migrants were sojourners rather than settlers in that they all saw their stay overseas as being temporary. Most expected to be home within five years. Nearly all, however, stayed much longer.[4] The few who came back on schedule were mostly students who had no choice because their visas had expired.

Abroad, the migrants settled in cities and neighborhoods where they had relatives or friends, and where work was most available. Hence, most migrants found themselves in large cities—London, Birmingham, New York, and Montreal.[5] The migrants clustered in the inner city. The reason for this, as Peach (1968: 85) notes of British cities, is that the older, more dilapidated and therefore less costly housing is found near the center. Not surprisingly, as British towns evolve, the newer and more desirable housing is built further from the center.

Almost immediately upon arriving, they went to work. Norman Bovell, for example, arrived in London on a Tuesday, found a job on Wednesday, and began work on Thursday. Rose Thornhill disembarked from a ship, boarded a train, arrived at the mental hospital in York at 4:30 a.m. for a job she had been recruited for in Barbados, and was told to report to her nursing station for the 7 a.m. shift. The speed at which the migrants were employed indicates the high demand for laborers in England during much of the 1950s and early 1960s. That the migrants lost no time in finding work is not surprising given that a primary motivation for going abroad was the desire to make money. It is telling that most of the migrants can still recall their wages down to the shilling for each job they held.

The work they found was predominantly manual labor. They became van drivers, bus conductors, mailmen, painters, seamstresses, nurses' aides, and factory operatives. Typically the jobs available to them were the dirtiest, most boring, and worst paying. Most were jobs white workers did not want. For some migrants these jobs were of lower status than the positions they had left at home in the Caribbean, though the wages were generally higher.

Barbadians, like most immigrants to Britain and North America, did not wander far from the city in which they initially settled.[6] Remaining among other West Indians made it easier for the migrants to maintain relationships with fellow Barbadians who shared their interests and values, and who provided moral support, as well as information about jobs and economic opportunities. Even small groups of immigrants can have some economic and political weight if they are spatially concentrated.

If there is a dominant theme in the migrants' stories, it is how hard they worked. Some held two jobs. Most volunteered for all the overtime available to them. Rex and Tomlinson's study of immigrants in Birmingham, England, found that twice as many West Indians worked more than 48 hours a week as did white British workers. (1979: 113) Despite the extra hours, though, their weekly wages were not any greater.

Family

As a husband and a father, I am struck at how long many married migrants were separated from their spouses and children. In many cases, five years would pass without couples seeing one another.[7] During the interviews, I wondered how well the marriages of my middle-class American friends would have endured under such circumstances. But Valenza Griffith spoke for most Barbadian women whose husbands had gone abroad when she explained that, as long as one's husband was emigrating to better the family's position, you could not cry or complain. Rather, you passed the time until they came back or until you could join them by "keeping busy."

Separations between a migrant couple and their children were also common.

Like other West Indian immigrants, the children were left in the care of grand-parents or other relatives. Most parents believed that their children would be bet-ter off in the Caribbean, both because the village was a safer and healthier environment than the streets of Brooklyn or London, and also because more rel-atives would be there to look after their welfare. Abroad, with both parents work-ing, the children would be left with a child-minder. Good child care was difficult to find, and many immigrants had heard stories of children being neglected or abused by babysitters. When the migrants' stay overseas stretched into more years than they had originally planned, their children grew up during their absence. It was ten years before Norman Bovell saw his eldest child, and then she was not sure that he was her "daddy." Another elderly man painfully recalled his home-coming after more than twenty years abroad. His two sons, who were infants when he left Barbados, were in their twenties when they came to the airport to meet him. He had a photograph of them but was unable to recognize them in the crowd. When they finally located one another, his sons were not convinced that he was their father.

Racism

Many migrants encountered racial discrimination, especially in their search for employment and housing, such as the signs in windows and doors of flats telling blacks they need not apply. One family recounted being turned away at an apart-ment just a short while after they were told over the phone that it was available. Discrimination was also expressed in countless other ways, such as the white woman bus passenger putting her bus fare on the seat next to her to avoid having to touch the black hand of the Barbadian conductor. The receptionist at the store did not ask the Barbadian delivery man to sign for the heaters he had come to pick up because she assumed he could not write. The captain of the cricket team at the college in Birmingham that John Wickham attended automatically as-sumed that John would be a good bowler because he was tall and black.

Even after living many years abroad, and successfully adjusting to English or North American society, the orientation of the migrants was always to the Caribbean. Most friendships were with other islanders. Many tried to visit Bar-bados despite costly airfares, which cut into hard earned savings. Most sent re-mittances home to help support parents and other relatives. Even those who had been abroad for decades with no prospect of returning home still identified strongly with the homeland. They retained what observers call an "ideology of re-turn" (King 1978; Gmelch 1980). Their identification with the Caribbean and lack of interest in assimilating were encouraged by the white host societies, who kept the colored immigrants at arms' length. In England, the migrants were re-minded in countless ways that while the country welcomed their labor, at least as long as there were plenty of jobs to go around, it was not willing to extend to them the privileges of full citizenship. This was a shock for migrants who believed they were going to the "mother country," to a society they assumed would treat them as equals, on the basis of merit rather than color (Foner 1978: 41). Encounters with racism also diminished the migrants' respect for whites and further decreased their interest in identifying with the larger society.[8] What the migrants had learned and experienced overseas was not only important to their adjustment to life in the host societies, but it also influenced their decision to return and their readjustment in Barbados.

Returning Home

Returning to Barbados from the UK, U.S., or Canada is to move from a highly developed to a lesser developed economy and nation. Structurally, the move is similar to that of Mediterranean migrants returning home from Northern Europe, or Puerto Ricans and Mexicans returning from the U.S. to their homelands. Often return migration for Barbadians also means moving from an urban area (e.g., London or New York) to a small town or village at home.

For the returnees, coming home is the natural completion of the migration cycle. As noted earlier, at the time they left Barbados, most only planned to stay away long enough to save money to buy a house and perhaps a car, and to see something of the world. Roy Campbell's observation was typical, "On the way over to England my thinking was that I'd be away no more than five years. I had a goal of saving a certain amount of money and then coming back to Barbados and getting a little home." Yet, most overseas Barbadians never manage to return home, at least not permanently. Some cannot afford the passage or plane ticket back. Others who have not bettered themselves economically are disinclined to return because they will lose face.[9] Student emigrants are expected to come home with a diploma, while working emigrants are expected to have at least enough money to buy a home of their own. The very successful may not return home because it would mean giving up well-salaried positions and a standard of living that cannot easily be equaled in Barbados. To return home, the migrants must believe they can attain a reasonably comfortable standard of living in Barbados. Not surprisingly, the state of the home economy, employment opportunities, and exchange rates can all significantly influence the flow of return migrants in all countries.[10] Over the past few decades Barbados has seen a higher rate of return than any of its neighboring islands because of its stronger economy, high per capita income, and the availability of most modern amenities.[11]

During a holiday visit, migrants realize that it is possible to have the material comforts of abroad, while in other respects a more fulfilling life at home.[12] It is then that they see how much Barbados has prospered during their absence, and, importantly, that black Barbadians and not just the white elite, are benefiting from the new prosperity. They notice the increasing number of high quality wall houses, and new roads, restaurants, and recreational facilities—much of it associated with growth of tourism. Those who left Barbados in the 1950s and 1960s see that during their absence the country truly became independent, that the people who now run the island are black, and that large numbers of blacks have entered the middle class. Exalted by sunny blue skies, warm air, inviting sea, easygoing pace of life, and friendliness of their village neighbors, they seriously begin to consider a new life at home. Since it is usually Christmas or summer holidays when they visit, the atmosphere is especially festive and their relatives are in good cheer. They are eager to please, driving the migrants here and there to see sights and old friends.

Not surprisingly, during such a visit or immediately upon their return to Britain or North America, while memories are still fresh, migrants often reach a final decision to return for good. They make plans—setting a date, buying a land to build a house, and opening a Barbadian bank account. One woman, who wanted the family to stay in England, recalled how her husband brushed aside her reservations and instead only talked about "How beautiful Barbados was, that the country was doing much better." Many migrants later report, however, that perceptions of home acquired during these short holiday visits can be deceptive.

While migrants are drawn home primarily by what life in Barbados promises, they must also be somewhat discontented with their lives abroad, even if it is only the vague feeling that something is missing. People who are entirely satisfied with their lives rarely uproot themselves. Unemployment, racial tension, and personal problems push people home. Jobs for young West Indians in England are so scarce that, in an ironic reversal of their own parents' emigration, some who were born and raised in England are now leaving to seek their fortune in the Caribbean (Western 1992).

Some return migration is precipitated by personal crisis: breakup of a marriage, death of a spouse, trouble with children, or ill health. A hotel maid in an English resort town, who returned after a divorce, said, "After my husband left, it was just me and kids in the house, and that's not good for anybody. I was lonely and bored. We needed more relatives around." A worker in the London Post Office returned when he injured his back and could no longer deliver mail; a construction worker in Toronto came home after suffering a stroke; a mechanic in Brooklyn brought his family back when his mother, at home in Barbados, developed cancer. In Britain, doctors often advise West Indians with serious health problems, especially mental disorders, to re-emigrate. The change of scene and climate may be good for the patient, but it also helps to reduce the burden on the National Health Service.

Migrant parents are often disappointed in the education their children receive abroad, especially in inner city schools. In Britain many West Indian children drop out of school and a disproportionate number of those that remain perform at or near the bottom of every category of academic skill. Many Barbadian parents, who value education and proudly tell you that Barbados has one of the world's highest literacy rates, believe that their children will do better in Barbadian schools.

Despite such complaints, most migrants who return home go primarily because of their attachment to the land of their birth.[13] As one elderly man, chewing a stick of sugar cane, said, "The money [in Canada] was good and the people treated me with fairness, but in the end I wanted to be home with my own people, in my own land." A woman who had graduated from Colgate University and had worked as a housing research analyst in Washington, D.C. returned to Barbados to teach high school because "Barbados is still a developing country, and I felt that any contribution that I make in my lifetime I want to make here."[14]

Adjusting to Home

Returning is seldom as easy as a migrant expects. In my survey, 53 percent of the respondents were so dissatisfied during their first year at home that they believed they would have been happier abroad. Friendships did not materialize as hoped. Relatives and friends from their youth often proved, at closer quarters, narrow and greedy. Neighbors who had appeared affable or chummy during return holiday visits when presents were distributed, became distant or disinterested once the migrants returned. One woman observed about the people in her village:

The people say that I don't want friends, they say I don't want to share. Them that do the talking [gossiping] are the same ones that I brought goods for. I give them rice, I give them coffee, I give them dinner plates. I give all around and I try to keep friendship with them. They took my things, but then they cut me up.

Another woman said, "It makes you wonder if people really care about you, or if they just want the things that you can give them."

Sometimes old friends that the migrants had most looked forward to seeing and to recapturing the lost memories of their youth with were themselves gone. One man, disappointed to find that most his former friends had emigrated, said he did not know the younger crowd of men at the rum shop or any of the children. A stranger in his own village, he wondered aloud if he had made the right decision in returning to Barbados after more than twenty years away.

In their interactions with villagers and fellow workers, returnees often conclude that Barbadians who have never lived abroad are provincial and narrow-minded, an attitude which only makes it more difficult for them to establish friendships. One woman whispered to me, as though she were afraid of being overheard:

I have no good friends who have never been away. There are very few here I would want to call friends . . . their outlook on life is so small, so tiny, it's like they have blinkers on, like they're always going down a one-way street.

A man who had spent twenty-three years in England complained that the Barbadian women he met were boring and that he could not make conversation with them, "They sit there like great lumps of pudding with nothing at all to say."

Some returnees feel they no longer share the same interests as their neighbors. They say their own interests are more cosmopolitan and transcend the local community and the island. Returnees living in villages often complain that their neighbors are gossipy and preoccupied with the affairs of others. Having grown accustomed to the anonymity of big city life, they feel a loss of privacy as their every action and even their new possessions come under public scrutiny. In the words of one woman, "People go out of their way to make gossip. You can't lead your own life here. It's so small and everybody knows everybody. It's terrible." This same woman confided to me that she and her husband had made a mistake resettling in the village. "Maybe it wouldn't be so bad," she said, "if we had moved to Bridgetown."

Moreover, many sense that the villagers who stayed behind are jealous of their prosperity: large houses and new cars, and children's higher education. Some villagers diminish the migrants' accomplishments and elevated status by saying that money is easy to earn abroad and that anyone who goes away can come back rich. One prosperous family I know well, rather than being credited with having worked hard, was rumored to have received a "blessing" or to have won a lottery. Villagers rarely came to their shop, lest they add to the family's wealth. Said the disgruntled shopkeeper, who was considering re-emigrating to Canada:

Even the people from our church don't shop here. They don't want us to have their business, except for an occasional small thing when they run out and don't want to go into town. You can't win. If you come back with money, they are jealous. If you come back with nothing, they ridicule you. . . . When I was a poor shopkeeper, before I first left Barbados, we had more friends than we have today. Then we were all at the same level.[15]

On the other hand, returnees are sometimes insensitive. They may strain relationships with friends and neighbors by their frequent comparisons of Barbados to the society from which they have returned. Some talk too much about the metropolitan society and their experiences there when instead they would be better off trying to find common ground with people at home.

A common irritation to all migrants returning from the industrialized world is the slow pace of life at home. It is difficult to get things done.[16] Barbadian returnees report being frustrated at the delays in getting servicemen to make repairs, in getting a telephone installed, in clearing an overseas parcel at the local post office, and in having to wait in line while sales clerks chat with other customers. Having grown accustomed to the punctuality of Britons or North Americans, they are impatient and frustrated by its absence at home. "If people agree to meet you at eight o'clock," said Roy Campbell, "they don't turn up until eight-thirty or maybe even nine o'clock, and they don't say they are sorry for being late." Esther Griffith felt there were only two speeds in Barbados, "slow and dead stop."

Returnee retirees living on pensions often find the cost of living at home higher than they anticipated. Those whose savings are being eroded by the high cost of goods and energy often speak of little else—canned fruit is four times what they paid abroad, milk and eggs twice, water and electricity three times, and so forth. The cost of living becomes an obsession. A retired welder, who thought the $3600 he had saved while in England was "a fortune," found, "The cost of things like lumber and masonry for my house so high that my money disappeared fast. I could not even hold onto my passage money to England in case I ever wanted to go back." Many returnees, however, reduce their household expenses by producing some of their own food with kitchen gardens, fruit trees, and by raising sheep, goats, and chickens. One man who working as a waiter earns half as much in Barbados as he did at the same job in Toronto motioned to his backyard, "In Toronto I lived ten floors up in an apartment. Here I can go out in the yard and pick a coconut, a lime, or a banana, and I raise my own animals. In Canada I had to buy all that stuff."

For women, returning home can present special problems. Most held wage paying jobs while abroad; now at home they have difficulty finding work.[17] Faced with accepting low wages or early retirement, some become self-employed. One sews uniforms for hotel staff, another sells soft drinks from her house, and a third keeps the books for the family bus operation. Overseas, wage work helped these and other women gain a measure of independence. Having money of their own, if not outright control of their paychecks, enhanced their status and strengthened their claims for respect in relations with their husbands.[18] Listening to women returnees describe the mind-numbing tasks and daily repetition of the work they did in the sweatshops of London and New York makes it easy to underestimate the importance of work to these women. In middle class America these jobs are seen as menial, and even demeaning. Typically, my field school students in Barbados see the alternatives for the returnee women—being a homemaker in Barbados, tending a vegetable garden, having fresh air and open spaces—as a much better way of life. But this perception is not always shared by returnee women, who prior to their emigration had never earned a weekly paycheck nor enjoyed the autonomy, stimulation, and status that goes with having a full-time job. For them wage work, menial or not, is an improvement over life without a paycheck.

In the villages, some returnee women find there are not enough to things to do; some especially miss shopping. While living abroad they enjoyed browsing and looking for bargains in the large, department stores, and they liked the wide range of foodstuffs available in the supermarkets. In Barbados, most retail stores are small, the range of goods limited, and the prices higher. Many women have lost a favorite pastime.

For women who came back to Barbados without their grown children, the most serious source of unhappiness is often the separation. Ann Bovell speaks for many women when she confided at the end of one interview, "To tell the truth, I feel real bad me being here and the kids being over there (England)." Another woman's response to being cut off from her children has been to work even harder, rising before dawn to sew hotel uniforms in order to earn enough money to travel overseas each year to visit her four offspring in Canada, England, and Belgium. Parents hope that their children whom they raised overseas will someday move to Barbados, but few ever do.

Listening to returnees' woes begs the question: why do so many migrants who are familiar with Barbados and visited the island several times before their actual return home have difficulty readjusting? As one local who had never been away said, "You'd think they'd know what they do be getting into." The answer is best found in the changes that have occurred in the migrants themselves during their time abroad and, to a lesser degree, the changes that have taken place in the homeland during their absence. Migrants often do not realize how much their attitudes have been altered by their experiences in the metropolitan society until they come home. While abroad they only see themselves in opposition to mainstream English or North Americans, and they tend to think of themselves, and the other Barbadian emigrants they live among, as being no different from people back home. Only when they return to Barbados and try to resume relationships with old friends and relatives do they first see the differences. Returnees see the changes as their having become more "broadminded." Indeed most have become less ethnocentric: they are no longer convinced that the Barbadian or West Indian way of life is necessarily the only right way. And they are less inclined to do something simply because of tradition. They have seen alternatives and some are better than the customs at home. Hence, when they know a better way they sometimes become impatient with the time honored Barbadian traditions.

Many come back with a changed attitude towards work. Many say they learned the value of hard work, or how to work more efficiently. An architect who returned from Toronto said, "I now recognize that it takes work to be successful. I didn't really understand that before." A female office worker who had lived in Brooklyn for thirty-seven years said, "I learned that money doesn't grow on trees, that even in America you have to work hard to make money. Everyone should go away and see for themselves, it would be good for Barbados." They also come back with a clearer idea of what they want in life. As one middle-aged man explained the change he saw in himself:

I'm not interested in hanging around the way I did before I left. I want to go forward, to make something of myself. A lot of people here don't want a lot. As long as they have a roof over their head, own their own home, they're happy.

Meanwhile, Barbados is not the same place the migrants left a decade or two before. Although most welcome the new prosperity, the tripling of the number of cars since 1970 has snarled traffic, crime and drug use have increased, the development of hotels for tourists has driven up land prices on the coast so that there is no opportunity of buying a house near the sea, and young Barbadians are less courteous than they were a generation ago. These changes do not fit the image of Barbados that many migrants have retained from their youth, images that brief vacations at home had not corrected. In short, the cause of dissatisfaction among many migrants is the lack of fit between what they expected to find at home and what they experience. The most disgruntled are those who were most unrealistic about what Barbados could provide them. Their discontent is caused less by the actual social, economic, and environmental conditions at home than by their own expectations.

With the passage of time, however, most returnees' dreams and fantasies fade and they learn to cope with the inefficiency and petty annoyances. Gradually expectations about what can be accomplished in a day's work are lowered, and the slow pace of Barbadian life is no longer an irritant. Many also cope by occasionally leaving the island, whether on business, to visit relatives, or just for a holiday on a cheap charter package to Miami. Whatever the reason, a trip to an American or British city can satisfy their appetites for the things they miss in Barbados, whether it be good movies, particular cuisines, or discount merchandise. Being abroad again also serves to remind them of the drawbacks of life in the metropolitan society—the impersonality, not feeling safe on the streets at night, racial prejudice, and the rat race—and that in turn makes them appreciate Barbados and enables them to accept island life more easily.

While returnees complain about Barbados and experience some difficulty readjusting, most do adapt. After a year or two most are satisfied to be home. The figure of 53 percent who are dissatisfied during their first year at home, cited earlier, drops to 17 percent who are still dissatisfied at the end of their third year at home.

Local Perceptions of Returnees

Let us briefly turn to what Barbadians who have never lived abroad think of returnees. Do they look up to them? Do they see them as role models? Most Bajans readily agree that returnees have been changed by their overseas experiences. They say that returnees are more "broadminded" than Bajans who have never left the island. The term broadminded is such a common response that it seems almost a cliché. When pressed to explain exactly what they mean by it, people usually say something about the returnees having had more experience or having a greater knowledge of people and of the world. Another widespread perception is that returnees are harder working and more goal oriented. "When they come back here they know what they want from life and they go forward," one man remarked, "In that score you have to give them full credit, because they apply themselves diligently." When asked directly, most Barbadians also concede that returnees are less tolerant of racism and sexism and more willing to support unpopular causes, such as putting protection of the environment before business interests.

But Barbadians are also critical of returnees, particularly of those who do not make enough effort to assimilate back into society, or who think they are superior to their non-migrant countrymen simply because they have lived abroad. One of my neighbors in the village of Josey Hill said, "They feel that because they've been overseas in a big country and you ain't been nowhere that they are better than you." Another man said:

They think because you were here in Barbados all the time that you didn't learn anything, while they being abroad learned all about life. Some of them, because they've been in a big country come back down here to this small country and they think they is the world.

Several villagers related incidents to me in which a returnee tried to appear worldly by pretending to have forgotten or never to have known some local custom:

Sometimes they try to play the stranger. Like if you have a breadfruit in your hand, they might ask you, "Is that a breadfruit?" Now, you know they haven't forgotten what a breadfruit is.

Speech and dress are also mentioned as ways in which returnees stand out. Many have an English or North American accent when they return. And as one villager explained, "They try to put their words in the proper places, they try to raise their language up." If the returnee's accent is pronounced, locals may suspect it is intentionally put on, "You find that lots of them pick up a foreign accent whether it's genuine or not. It's something they put on to let you know that they've been somewhere."

Locals say that migrants who have been away for a short period, say three or four years, often have stronger accents than those who have been away much longer. The explanation given is that locals are more likely to forget that a person who was away for only a short period had in fact lived abroad, whereas no one forgets the experience of the man or woman who was away many years. About the latter, one woman said, "They don't need to remind people by talking like they've just left England. You know they have been away."

Some returnees are also said to stand out because of their clothes. "You can tell them by the way they dress. They wear stockings and sweaters and clothes like they were still living in a cold country. I always wonder how they manage underneath all them clothes, it must be so hot," said one villager. Elderly Barbadians recall that in the past the attire of returnees stood out even more than it does today. When Barbados was poorer and the island had less contact with the outside world, those migrants who came home were often a spectacle and the object of much attention. Speaking of the 1950s, one man recalled:

Them back from England would wear these three-piece suits and stockings, and they'd all come back with a watch. Even if it was a really cheap watch they'd want you to see it. If you hadn't noticed it, they'd pick up their wrist and look at the watch and say, "Gee, it's already two-thirty!" That was just to draw your attention to it, because having that watch was a great achievement.

Today most Barbadians deny being impressed by speech or dress of returnees, although their large houses and cars are a different matter.

Locals also believe that Barbadians who have been away are less religious when they come back. They are also said to have become less strict with their children. "They no longer flog their children to put them right," said one man, "They think that talking to the child, more than whipping it, is the better way. But I don't see their kids turning out any the better."

Nothing annoys Barbadians as much as hearing returnees complain about their country. This is often done in the context of comparing Barbados with the country the migrant has returned from. Barbados invariably comes out short in such comparisons. Locals say they do not want to hear how expensive the vegetables are in Barbados, that the cashiers are slow and discourteous, or that medical service is not what it is in Britain or Canada. They have heard it all before and do not want to hear it again. One woman told me about two migrants back from England that she overheard on the local bus, "They were laughing at our buses. Making fun of our buses, about how much better the buses were in England and that the roads there don't have no holes in it. It's not fair to stack up Barbados against a big country like England."

Some Impacts of Return Migration

Because most migrants move between areas of uneven development—usually from poorer to richer countries—migration has become linked to issues of national development.[19] One question governments and anthropologists alike are now asking is whether returnees have any impact on economic development when they return home. Do they bring back new ideas and attitudes that might rub off on local people? Do they bring back work skills or invest their overseas savings in ways that contribute to their society's development? Or in returning home do they merely add to the island's overcrowding and the pressure on its scarce resources?

Early on, many social scientists took the latter view, that returnees played a minimal role at best in introducing modern ideas (e.g., Dahya 1973; Rhoades 1978; and Rubenstein 1983). They found that returnees rarely invested their repatriated earnings in new enterprises that created jobs or benefited the region. Writing about the Mediterranean, King concluded, "The notion that returnees help in the development of their home country is falsely utopian" (King 1978: 17). For the English-speaking Caribbean, Rubenstein suggested that return migration and remittances actually added to the "deterioration of already trouble-ridden economies" (1983: 298). In a review of the literature, Kearney (1986: 246) concluded that, "few migrants learn any new skills, or if they do, rarely put them to use in the home community." However these conclusions are largely drawn from research conducted among migrants who returned to rural areas, where agrarian economies provided little opportunity for them to make use of the skills and training they acquired in urban-industrial settings abroad.

The Barbadian experience paints a different picture. About half of the migrants I surveyed believed they had initiated at least one constructive change in their work places based on knowledge they had acquired overseas. Those who were college educated or received technical training abroad were twice as likely as the non-trained workers to believe they had been innovators.

In some fields, new innovations were directly attributed to the influence of return migrants. An American-trained accountant, for example, introduced the electronic processing of financial accounts to a Bridgetown firm. A Minister of Health, who had spent many years in New York, introduced halfway houses for the mentally incapacitated who could care for themselves. A movement to dein-stitutionalize childcare in Barbados came from returnees working in the Ministry of Social Services who had become familiar with new approaches while working in Canada. Important innovations in computers, medicine, and engineering were also attributed to the influence of returnees.[20]

Opportunities for migrants to apply their foreign experience are greater in pri-vate sector jobs than in the public sector (Gmelch 1987). Foreign work experience, in fact, is considered important by many in the Bridgetown business community. An owner of a retail sales firm said he preferred to hire returnees because of their wider experience. Perhaps with some exaggeration, one businessman claimed, "There is nobody in business in Barbados who is moving up who has not been away."

There is less room for innovation in government. Barbados' civil service, es-tablished by the British and modeled after their own system, is hierarchical and rigid. Its bureaucrats, say many Barbadians, are primarily interested in defending their own positions. Unlike the business community, where the pressure of com-petition forces people to be at least minimally open to new ideas, there is no such need in the civil service. One civil servant who had returned from England talked about his superiors who had not been away:

Because you've been away and maybe know more about something, they feel threatened. They don't want to admit that maybe you have the answer, especially when you've only been on the job half as long.

The resistance to the foreign ideas of returnees is by no means restricted to gov-ernment bureaucrats. Barbados is a conservative society where people are slow to accept change, especially foreign ideas brought back by their own countrymen. "When proposing some change to my parishioners," said an Anglican rector, "I have to be very careful not to let them think I learned it in England." Another man said of returnees:

They have the same ideas as North Americans who live here. The difference is that people will listen to what the foreigner has to say, but not to their own kind. They'll say, "Who the hell is he to tell us what to do. He's only a Barbadian like us."

Sometimes innovations are resisted because they require extra work, something many Barbadians admit they are not prepared to do. Said one woman who re-turned from England with a Ph.D. in education, "Most Bajans are happy with the status quo, they take the path of least resistance. Don't ask them to change if it's going to mean more effort." In fact, she gave up trying to convince her teacher colleagues to hold "parent-teacher nights," modeled after those she'd seen in Canadian and British schools. "The teachers were somewhat open to the idea until they realized it was going to mean more work."

However, in occupations where there are many return migrants, they may col-lectively have an impact. This was the case with nurses at one hospital, who by strength in number modernized some procedures and upgraded their positions. In the words of one:

If you try to change things, there is opposition. But there are certain standards in the hospital and one is that they have meetings, and nurses are allowed to give their opinions. Since a lot of us have worked or were trained overseas, some things we say are heard.

Because of jealousy and resistance to new ideas, the influence of returnees at the local level is much less than it could be. Some of Valenza Griffith's ideas were rejected by her fellow nurses:

The standard of nursing in England is completely different. . . . Up there you are exposed to more equipment and teaching than here, and you have more different kinds of cases there. But you can't apply what you learned up there without being criticized. They'd [fellow nurses] soon tell you should've stayed up there.

A teacher recalled the way her colleagues would "push up their faces" at her suggestions.

Outside the workplace, the influence of migrants as purveyors of new ideas is especially difficult to measure or pin down. For example, there is no evidence of returnees having influenced the attitudes of locals towards racism. Yet, I am certain that it occurs. While some migrants may not say much about their encounters with racism overseas, others freely recount their experiences to neighbors and friends. Specifically they relate the stereotyped remarks they have overheard white Britons and Americans make about black people as being dirty, ignorant, loud, lazy, living off the backs of taxpayers, and eating smelly food. Anthropologists Connie Sutton and Susan Makiesky-Barrow (1975) believe that in the two Barbadian villages they studied, return migrants had a significant influence in awakening the racial and political consciousness of villagers who had not been away. It was largely from migrants that villagers learned how black people were regarded in predominantly white Britain and North America. It is not that Barbadians had never known racism for there is ample white bias in Barbados, rather they had long assumed that the prejudice of their own whites was a perversion of the true metropolitan culture and that whites in England or North America somehow were different. By living abroad, the migrants had learned a different reality, which they communicate in various ways to Barbadians at home. Sutton and Makiesky-Barrow (1975: 124) considered the returnees' influence in raising racial consciousness to be greater than that of either the Barbadian middle-class or student radicals. They also noted that while the media keep Barbadians abreast of happenings in the outside world, it is often the returnee who interprets the news from overseas for the villager, and in the course of doing so shapes public opinion.

Technology is probably the easiest place to look for evidence of the influence of returnees, as items of material culture are more easily transferred from one culture to another than are ideas. In an earlier period, Richardson (1985) notes that Barbadians returning from work on the Panama Canal introduced window

screens (which keep out disease bearing mosquitos). But today's returnees introduce little more than the peculiar use of wallpaper, wall-to-wall carpeting and
drapes, none of which are suited to a tropical climate. On the positive side, returnees who have become accustomed to new products and technology abroad
are quicker to adopt new ideas and goods when they appear in Barbados.

One problem with assessing the influence of returnees in the larger community
is trying to disentangle their role as agents of culture change from other external
influences on Barbadian society. Barbadians today have much contact with the
outside world through movies, foreign television programming, tourists, and
travel. In the realm of material culture, there is little that migrants can introduce
that locals have not already seen on TV or while visiting relatives abroad.

But returnees have a clear impact in another way. After years of hard work,
most emigrants arrive home with a sizable amount of capital from savings and
from the sale of overseas assets: house, car, and furniture. Most use their savings
to purchase housing or to improve the home or property they already own.[21] Returnee housing is invariably of high quality; most buy or build substantial and
high status wall houses, rather than the more common wood houses in which
many had grown up. In the villages, large, solidly constructed and brightly
painted returnee housing often sets a standard to which others aspire.

Most returnees also buy a car. Successful migrants are expected to buy a car in
Barbados or bring one home when they return. Car ownership is an important
status symbol among middle-class Barbadians, who shun public transportation.
But buying an automobile does not benefit the island's economy since all are
manufactured outside Barbados. The potential balance of payment benefits of
the returnees' repatriated earnings are canceled when the money is spent on im-
ported items (Rubenstein 1983: 298). Worse yet, car ownership adds to air and
noise pollution, and severe congestion in Barbados urban areas.

Anthropologists in other settings have argued that it would be far better if return migrants invested their savings in business enterprises that create new jobs
and capital rather than on housing and automobiles.[22] And it is largely the returnees' failure to do so that leads some scholars to conclude that returnees have
little or no impact on their homelands. Only one in seven Barbadian returnees in
the survey had invested their savings in a business.

Yet, while Barbadian returnees admittedly spend their repatriated savings
mostly on consumption—on housing, furnishings for their homes, and automobiles—these consumables do raise their living standard and their social status,
which was their reason for emigrating in the first place. It seems unreasonable to
expect them to invest their savings in a business before providing for their own
shelter. Often the problem is not the returnees' investment priorities, but simply
not having enough capital. Many more returnees would start businesses if they
had enough money remaining after taking care of their housing needs. And some
returnees, if they are financially successful at home, will later start up businesses
of their own. It was nearly twenty years before Richard Goddard, who returned
from Canada, finally had enough capital to buy a sugar estate, which he then di-

versified into different crops and livestock. His estate is now a small but important part of the national effort to find alternatives to growing sugar.

Conclusions

Since the bulk of postwar English speaking Caribbean migrants emigrated to North America and Britain, the skills and cultural knowledge with which they return are Western ones. Hence, in the Caribbean context "development" means becoming Western. At the national level, progress or development becomes a measure of the country's proximity to the institutions and values of British and North American society (Thomas-Hope 1985). The ethnocentrism inherent in this position is unfortunate, but in assessing the impact of migrants returning from Western metropoles it is difficult to avoid. The problem (suppressing an indigenous culture at the hands of Westernization) is mitigated, however, by the fact that Barbados is not a traditional non-Western society. The aboriginal Arawak and Carib inhabitants of Barbados were gone by the time of British settlement in the 1600s, and from that time until 1966 the island was a colony of Britain.

Furthermore, both black and white Barbadians have always been oriented toward Britain and more recently North America, and still look to these nations for their social and economic goals. In short, in the minds of most Barbadians the transfer of culture and capital from the metropolitan countries to their island nation does represent development.

With regard to labor and capital, the return of migrants to their homelands is also beneficial to the host countries. It is in the interests of the UK, U.S., and Canada to have migrant laborers go home as they age and become less productive and as their children begin to take spaces in the schools and universities. When migrants return home, Barbados, as other developing countries, bears the cost of the returnees' retirement. As capitalist economies mature and their populations age, temporary labor migration becomes preferred over permanent immigration (Kearney 1986: 344). It is not surprising that most industrial countries in the post World War II era preferred *guest* worker programs to permanent immigration.

Finally, it is also legitimate to ask what would have happened to Barbados had these migrants, and the many more who permanently remain abroad, not left their island. Young, healthy, and ambitious at the time of their emigration, we do not know how they would have changed their society had they stayed behind. Nor can we be sure how Barbados would have responded to and been changed by the increased unemployment and pressures on scarce resources that would have likely resulted.

Notes

Introduction: An Ethnography of Return

1. Indeed, fear of persecution or danger upon return is intrinsic to the very notion of a refugee as currently defined by international law (UNHCR 1999).

2. The UNHCR estimated that in 1998 alone there were 3.5 million returnees out of a total of 22.5 million refugees and internally displaced who fell under their jurisdiction (UNHCR 1999), Table 2, Persons of Concern to UNHCR at 1 Jan. 1998. Yet these numbers apply only to those who are officially designated as "refugees" by the UN and other international organizations, and therefore account for only a portion of returnees worldwide.

3. As early as 1885, Ravenstein in the *Laws of Migration* observed that the data for estimating the number of counter-stream migrants were scarce (cited in Sills 2000/2001).

4. These statistics differed greatly by area of origin. Only 3.5% of Asian immigrants had returned in that time-frame, whereas for South America, the rate was 24.8% (Borjas and Bratsberg 1996: 170).

5. In fact, it is fear of these political consequences that is often the stumbling block that prevents return in the first place. A striking contemporary example is that of the Palestinians and Israel. The Palestinians' emphasis on their right of return to the towns and homes from which they were displaced is met by the Israeli government's fear that such returns would change the demographic balance, and even lead to an end of a separate Jewish state.

6. There is not full agreement on the meaning of "diaspora." Safran says that diasporic peoples are "expatriate minority communities" who retain a memory of their homeland and who have settled in more than one place (Safran 1991: 83). Others equate diaspora with enforced dispersion and exile and as in the case of the biblical Jews (see Van Hear 1998 for a useful summary of the changing meanings of the term).

7. These returns may be spontaneous (organized by refugees and migrants themselves) or may be assisted by international organizations and nongovernmental organizations through "Go and See Visits."

8. These figures come from the International Organization for Migration Cross-Border Program Between Bosnia Herzegovina and Croatia (see IOM 2001). The actual number of "Go and See Visits" for that time was 7,296.

9. Although not a case of provisional return, the same notion of return as a legitimation of the home community can be seen in John Demos's famous study of French, Indian, and British relationships in early eighteenth-century New England. Some British captives decided to remain with their French or Indian captors and to assimilate into these communities, despite the chance to go home. Among British settlers, this refusal was viewed as rejecting redemption from their home communities and created great uneasiness, while the "return" of captives was viewed as a confirmation of the Puritan way of life and as both physical and spiritual salvation for the former captives (see Demos 1994).

10. For instance, Russell King defines "repatriation" as "involuntary and forced . . . by political authority or by some natural or personal disaster" (2000: 8).

Chapter 1. Illusions of Home in the Story of a Rwandan Refugee's Return

1. "L'autre rive: Chronique d'un réfugié ordinaire d'Afrique" (Katihabwa 1994), unpublished manuscript; page numbers from Janzen and Janzen (2000).

2. This is a pseudonym of his own choosing, as the narrative reveals later.

3. The Mennonite Central Committee was one of several hundred NGOs to work in the Great Lakes region in the months and years after the genocide and war in Rwanda. An international team made up of Zairians, French, American, and other African workers concentrated on postwar food production in Rwanda in the form of seed distribution, in the administration of four small refugee camps southwest of Bukavu, and in food distribution and reconciliation work in Burundi. Reinhild Zauenhoven Janzen and the author joined the MCC team for a short term from November 1994 to January 1995.

4. Despite this designation of "ex," units of the former Rwandan army continue through at least early 2002 to fight in the Congo war, allied with the Congolese National Army against the Rwandan Patriotic Army and their Congolese rebel surrogates.

5. The Rwandan Patriotic Army (RPF) was the military wing of the Tutsi-led force that emerged in Uganda and contributed significantly to the Ugandan army under President Museveni.

6. Zaire and Congo are used in hyphenated form or interchangeably. The name Zaire was synonymous with Mobutu. When the country was taken over by the Alliance forces under Kabila, it was renamed the Democratic Republic of Congo, its name before Mobutu's coup in 1965.

7. This line of analysis was developed in my lecture "Deciphering the Voices of Genocide Accounts in Rwanda" (Janzen 2000).

8. For examples of these radiant voices, see Janzen and Janzen (2000: 79, 85–89).

9. Category 1, meriting the death sentence, were those identified as "planners and organizers of the genocide." Category 2, not meriting the death sentence, to be handled case by case, were those who participated in actions that resulted in the deaths of individuals, or sexual crimes; Category 3 were those guilty of serious assault against persons; Category 4 were crimes against property. See Janzen and Janzen (2000: 216–17).

10. Interviews, Bujumbura, January 1995.

11. These experiences are reflected in Liisa Malkki's (1995a) study of Burundian Hutu exiles in Tanzania whose alienation from power goes hand in hand with a hardened mythic image of the other, and an ideological fueling of the intention of reclaiming home through violence.

Chapter 2. Contemplating Repatriation to Eritrea

1. Canada, the United States, and Sweden did not distinguish between Ethiopian and Eritrean refugees admitted for resettlement. Between 1980 and 1992, 9,262 "Ethiopians" were admitted to Sweden as refugees (Statens Invandrverket, personal communication, October 1995). In the United States in 1979–1987, African admissions (almost totally "Ethiopian") totaled 17,228 persons and Ethiopians comprised 2.7 percent of refugee admissions in 1983–1992 (U.S. Office of Refugee Resettlement 1993:18). In Canada the total number of Ethiopian refugees admissions in 1983–92 was 11,949, 5.5 percent of total refugee admissions (Immigration Statistics Division, Employment and Immigration Canada, cited in Moussa 1993: App. 3).

2. See Cichon (1986) for study of Eritreans in the U.S. In Canada 74 percent of the Ethiopian refugee population had attended high school (Moussa 1993: App. 3–6.) The men in this study averaged 11.26 years of education at a time when fewer than 1 percent

of their age cohorts in Ethiopia/Eritrea finished elementary school. Their educational range was from 0 years (nonliterate in their native language) to university completion. The educational level of women in Ethiopia and Eritrea was considerably lower than that of men but also ranged from nonliterate to university education. The Eritreans in Sweden had all completed high school. All spoke Swedish and most English.

3. Because the governments of resettlement did not distinguish between Ethiopian and Eritrean refugees, it is not possible to determine the sex ratio. In two studies of "Ethiopian" refugees resettled in the U.S., approximately 80 percent were single men (Cichon 1986; McSpadden 1989). In the United States in 1992, approximately 67 percent were men with a median age of 23.8 years. In Canada 67 percent of the Ethiopian refugee admissions for 1983–92 were male. Between 1982 and 1990 the age range at the time of landing was predominately 20–29 (McSpadden and Moussa 1993: 208).

4. Research with women in Toronto, Canada, was carried out by Helene Moussa.

5. For example, in the capital, Asmara, there are approximately 450,000 persons but only 53,000 houses.

6. See Van Hear (1998: 40–57) for a nuanced exploration of force and choice in both economic and forced migration.

7. All the names have been changed.

8. The importance of education to the Eritreans reflects a cultural tradition. At that time the literacy rate was about 10 percent. During the early 1960s when these refugees would have been of school age, less than 1 percent of the elementary-aged children completed school! In addition, during the Italian occupation of Eritrea prior to World War II, children were limited to four years of education. See Legum (1976: 63) and Levine (1965: 193).

9. For example, before independence women could not inherit or own land. They could not initiate divorce. An Eritrean saying cited by Matsuoka and Sorenson (1999: 228) demonstrates the devalued position of women, "Just as there is no donkey with horns, so there is no woman with a brain."

10. Eritreans in Sweden frequently contacted Eritrean government offices for guidelines for investment. Because of the newness of the restrictions it is often unclear what is required.

11. This recently promulgated regulation, predictably unsettling to the Eritreans in Sweden who were in the midst of plans to purchase land in Eritrea, was a major topic within their interviews.

12. These concepts are explored more fully in Moussa (1993) see also CIMADE (1981); COLAT (1981); da Rocha (1982); Fasic (1981); Vasquez (1981).

Chapter 3. Filipena Depictions of Migrant Life for Their Kin at Home

1. As of 1999, the Philippine government estimated that there were 3.5 million Filipinos working abroad, living in 120 countries and remitting $7 billion per year. See *Migration News* (1999b).

2. The notion of overseas Filipinos operating as "spectral presences" who hover on the edges of the Philippine nation-state's consciousness is elaborated by Vicente L. Rafael (1997).

3. According to International Labor Organization estimates, one third to one half of the Filipina domestic workers arrive in Hong Kong with college degrees (Choo 1996: 5). Almost all have at least a high school education, since a high school diploma is a requirement at most recruitment agencies. Until recently, even high schools in remote rural areas taught most of the curriculum in English rather than the local language. Thus, the vast majority of Filipinas in Hong Kong could use English as the language they had in com-

mon with their employers, unlike many of their counterparts from Thailand, Indonesia and other countries where English was less widely learned.

4. Yung (1996a). It is impossible to conceal the name of this group's chair, since she has been a district-level politician and regularly speaks and writes to the press. Any description of the Employers' Association would also identify her to many people residing in Hong Kong. Thus, she is quoted here as a public figure. Yung, during a 1996 interview at the elementary school where she is both vice principal and a teacher, was far less strident in person than in her letters to the media. She said immediately that it was "of course, the migrants who should be protected. Their conditions shouldn't be less than local workers." However, she soon turned the conversation to the myriad complaints of employers about the difficulties they had with the Filipina workers they had hired. There was, for example, the domestic worker who told her employer, "I can't touch water," and "asked to be terminated"; another who "threatened the employer that she'd commit suicide if she had to pay for the telephone"; a third who said that "if she had to face the [household's] children again, she'd have a nervous breakdown." The employers of these women, she reported, had done everything they could to be accommodating but had been left in a "no-win situation" in which they had lost money and considerable time.

5. Yung (1996b); *South China Morning Post*. See also *Migration News* (1999b).

6. I thank Wu Ka-ming for pointing this out.

7. For some, the signs (in a building housing affluent local Chinese as well as expatriates) were an ironic replay of the racist intent that had led to signs reputedly reading "Dogs and Chinese Not Admitted" at the entrance to the Bund or Westerners' Garden in Shanghai's International Settlement in the early 1900s. However, for a nuanced discussion of the actual regulations and the class and national prejudices that were evidenced, see Bickers and Wasserstrom (1995).

8. In one neighborhood where a center was proposed, some apartment owners expressed fears that the rental values of their apartments might diminish. When a center was finally established elsewhere, regulations were extensive. Everyone entering the school was warned not to smoke or create litter and told to register and show a special admission permit. In addition, only the school's hall, playground and a set of washrooms were left open. To satisfy the PTA, which was still worried that the place would "turn out to be a mess," a cleaning team had to be employed. See Wan (1994: 18).

9. See, too, Constable (1997b).

10. Others noted that there were many employers in Hong Kong who underpaid or otherwise mistreated their domestic workers and suggested that those who were dissatisfied should cook their own meals, do their own housework and look after their own children. See Hopper (1996); Daldry (1996), *South China Morning Post* April 8 1996 letters column. It was also observed that the public discussions of the rights and protections to be afforded the domestic workers were misdirected (as one letter writer to an English-language newspaper commented), given the "unremitting stream of racial discrimination" to which the local Chinese had been subjected during 150 years of colonial rule. See Yuen (1996).

11. See Cheung (1995). See also *South China Morning Post* (1995).

12. I thank Filomeno Aguilar for emphasizing this to me.

Chapter 4. Viet Kieu on a Fast Track Back?

An earlier version of this paper was presented at the 96th Annual Meeting of the American Anthropological Association, Washington, D.C., November 19, 1997. Charles Keyes, Ellen Oxfeld, Donald Long, and the study participants provided many helpful comments and advice on several versions of this paper. I especially benefited from Keyes's discussion of social memory and Oxfeld's and an anonymous reviewer's ideas about kinship and the local population's reactions to their returning kin. The eleven participants and several other colleagues in Vietnam provided insights and suggestions from their own experience and research on various drafts of this paper.

1. The most common revisionist argument was that, even though the United States had lost the war, its capitalist market system was winning the peace.

2. The lampoons revealed American pretensions of "winning the peace" while making the Vietnamese acutely aware of the stakes in opening up their society to Western influence.

3. This account reflects the experiences of the Vietnamese as a diaspora community. There is little discussion of her life in the U.S., and her focus is on reestablishing kinship ties and raising assistance for Vietnam.

4. I also conducted more informal interviews with Viet Kieu returning from Australia, New Zealand, and other European countries and eventually hope to follow up the interviews over time.

5. The interviews ranged from two to five hours; most lasted two and a half. All were conducted individually, except one that was held with a brother and sister together in their home. I taped the interviews in office conference rooms, homes, cafe bars, and restaurants and took extensive field notes. Several people suggested meeting in cafes and restaurants because they wanted to speak frankly away possible government listening devices. One person initially feared to be interviewed but later granted my request. All asked that their identity not be revealed, and some were concerned about being identified through their narratives. Because the interviews contained sensitive political material, I offered to share my analysis with all the participants and most commented (orally or in writing) on a first draft of this chapter. During the interviews, people sometimes turned off the tape recorder when discussing a personally or politically sensitive topic. I excluded these particular details in the analysis except indirectly in formulating insights or generalizations about the material. These various concerns and precautions suggested the ambiguous status Viet Kieu had in Vietnamese society and I later realized how much we monitored our responses and reactions at the time.

Nine interviews were held in English and two in French. All interviewees were fluent in English or French although one was more fluent in German. Interviewees often used common Vietnamese terms or expressions, but for most, English or French was their daily language of communication (even though they lived in Vietnam). Those who remained several more years, however, increasingly spoke Vietnamese as their daily language at home and at work.

6. These interviews, as Lipson and Omidian (1996: 3) observe with Afghan Americans in Northern California, read like chapters in a book, where each one referred to one before it. Connections with past narratives were very apparent and provided a common reference to the narratives, which were sometimes being refuted or rewritten about the Vietnamese refugee experience.

7. However, in returning to Hanoi (rather than Saigon), Ha realized retrospectively that her parents experienced two traumatic and disruptive moves in their lives—first from the north in 1954 and then from Saigon in 1975.

8. For a longer discussion of intergenerational issues around contraception in Southeast Asian refugee families in the U.S., see Long (1997).

9. For discussion of the new effects of the transition to a market economy, see Gibney (1995).

10. Subsequent to the time of writing, she has persuaded her husband to relocate his medical practice to Vietnam.

11. Interestingly, the nation of Vietnam has developed a complex narrative that goes beyond a particular cultural signification but also signifies a historical period (in the dominant literature), a type of war, and most recently a set of artistic images and imagination (see Bhabha 1990).

Chapter 5. Chinese Villagers and the Moral Dilemmas of Return Visits

Middlebury College generously supported this research during a sabbatical year in 1995–96. While in China, I benefited immensely from an affiliation with the Guangzhou Academy of Social Sciences. I am grateful to both institutions for their support and assistance. Without the introductions and advice of Li Jufang, I would have been unable to make the connections that enabled me to conduct research in Moonshadow Pond. My largest debt is to the residents of Moonshadow Pond, who opened their lives to me and never tired of answering my questions.

1. The Hakka are a linguistic and cultural group among the Han Chinese who are found in greatest numbers in southeast China, especially in Guangdong Province. The term "Hakka" is actually Cantonese for the word "guest" (*kejia* in Mandarin), and it refers to the notion that the Hakka are thought to have migrated to Guangdong Province and other areas of Southeast China from the north. While the Hakka may have been historically viewed as "guest people" by the predominantly Cantonese population of Guangdong Province, they constitute the vast majority of residents in Mei County, where I did my fieldwork. Indeed, Mei County is considered a center of Hakka culture. For more on Hakka ethnic identity see Constable (1996b) and Leong (1997).

2. Godley's (1989) article on the role of returned overseas Chinese in post-1949 China is an exception to this. An excellent summary of the changing role and status of returnees in the People's Republic, the article broadly focuses on the country as a whole, and thus, is not an ethnographic study.

3. Transliterations of Chinese terms in this chapter are provided in Mandarin pinyin. Due to my considerably greater facility in Mandarin as opposed to Hakka, most of my interviews were conducted in Mandarin. All these terms were denoted by the same set of characters in the written Chinese script in both Mandarin and Hakka, and as such there is no diminution of their meaning by providing their Mandarin versions.

4. On New Year's eve, the patrilineal family should be together—this includes parents, unmarried daughters, sons and their spouses, and so on down the patrilineal line. Married daughters generally return, with their husbands and children, to their natal homes on the second day of the New Year's festivities.

5. Interestingly, this same problem occurs in the Eritrean context among potential returnees (see McSpadden, this volume).

6. See Lozada (2001) for an interesting account of how state structures are supported by the practitioners of a transnational religion in a Catholic village in Mei Xian. In this case, state cadres are well represented at important Catholic ceremonies, such as the opening of a new church in the village. Further, the very process of gaining legitimacy in the eyes of the state by gaining official recognition also adds to state legitimacy.

7. The recent return of Governor Gary Locke (Washington state) to his ancestors' village in China is quite interesting in this regard. Locke is a fifth generation American who returned to his ancestral village this past October. After visiting his ancestors' graves, he was treated to an overwhelming reception and parade. The villagers who were interviewed obviously took great pride in his achievements, and pointed out that wherever he went he would always be "one of us" (Zimmerman).

Chapter 6. Changing Filipina Identities and Ambivalent Returns

I am grateful to Ellen Oxfeld, Lucia McSpadden, and Lynellen Long for organizing the American Anthropological Association panel at which the paper was first presented. I am also to grateful to Nancy Abelmann, Joseph Alter, Richard Fox, George Fouron, Elissa Helms, Satsuki Kawano, Jane Margold, Abby Margolis, and Nobue Suzuki for their comments and suggestions. Heartfelt thanks goes to Cynthia Tellez, Irma Laguindam, the volunteers and clients at the Mission for Filipino Migrant Workers, and the domestic workers in Hong Kong who shared their stories with me. The Asian Studies Center and China Program at the University of Pittsburgh provided funds that made the research possible. An earlier version of this chapter appeared as "At Home But Not at Home: Filipina Narratives of Ambivalent Returns" *Cultural Anthropology* 14, 2 (1999): 203–28.

Chapter 7. Returning German Jews and Questions of Identity

An earlier version of this chapter was published under the title, "Identity, Exile and Division: Disjunctures of Culture, Nationality, and Citizenship in German-Jewish Selfhood in East and West Berlin," in *Jews, Germans, Memory: Reconstructions of Jewish Life in Germany,* ed. Michael Bodeman (Ann Arbor: University of Michigan Press, 1996), 131–62. Much of this chapter is drawn from my introductory essay in John Borneman and Jeffrey Peck (1995). *Sojourners: The Return of German-Jews and the Question of Identity* (Lincoln: University of Nebraska Press). All translations of the cited interviews are mine. Reprinted by permission.

1. I am undoubtedly giving Marx a one-sidedly favorable reading here. For a more critical reading, see Sander Gilman's careful reading of this essay along with Marx's later rewriting in *The Holy Family.* Gilman argues that Marx's hatred for what he called the "Sabbath Jew" and the "finance Jew," along with his virulent attacks on Lasalle, were the result of "his antithetical self-image: thus his confusion and the vehemence of his own rhetoric when confronted by the contradictory aspects of that "Jew" which he sees within himself" (1986: 208).

2. Schmitt's discussion of the shifting nature of the political, and his criticism of liberalism's dangerous tendency to depoliticize and negate what is essentially political, are extremely important insights. I disagree with Schmitt, however, with regard to where the authority to decide on the exception should reside. Although Schmitt questions the reduction of politics to state doctrine, and thereby questions the sovereignty of the state, he also argues that the state should be the ultimate arbiter. However, by "state" he does not mean the liberal idea of state as opposed to society, which he criticizes for simply reversing the Hegelian idea of state as "a realm of morality and objective reason" (1976: 77). Rather, he defines the state as founded in a historically determined and contested "political." It follows from this empirically valid claim that states are one of many instances of authority in a competition over definitions. Therefore, the state has no a priori grounds to justify its claim to ultimate moral authority (Borneman 1992: 1–36, 74–118).

Chapter 8. Repatriation and Social Class in Nicaragua

This chapter grew out of a paper proposed for the 1997 American Anthropological Association Annual Meeting, as well as a paper delivered at the 14th International Congress of Anthropological and Ethnological Sciences in July, 1998. Materials for this chapter were derived from the author's fieldwork in Nicaragua from October 1985, to May 1987, and an additional visit in July 1990, after national elections had replaced the Sandinista-led government. The author also spent several months in Honduras in 1985, 1988, and 1990, including repeated visits to Nicaraguan refugee camps in southern Honduras. Additional sources include personal communications from colleagues and informants in Nicaragua and Honduras, and interviews conducted in both countries by Lucy Edwards, the author's wife, to whom he is grateful.

1. Refugees are here distinguished from internally displaced persons. While many people may be internally displaced within the boundaries of their home country for a variety of reasons—war, natural disaster, and development projects—refugees are outside their home country.

2. Sandinista policy toward Nicaragua's peasants was motivated, in part, by historical ties created during the 1920s and 1930s when peasants provided crucial support to the struggle of Augusto Cesar Sandino and his guerrilla forces. Sandino's failed struggle against dictatorship and foreign domination became a primary historical and cultural source of Sandinista discourse. Peasants also provided crucial support in the successful uprising against Somoza led by the Sandinista Front.

3. Under the Reagan Doctrine, U.S. military advisers trained Nicaraguan resistance forces in the tactics of "low-intensity conflict," which included psychological operations to undermine civilian morale, community spirit, and cooperation, and to further a sense of insecurity or unpredictability among the Nicaraguan civilian population, especially in more remote rural areas.

4. The majority of Nicaraguan peasant refugees went to Honduras, while a smaller number fled to Costa Rica. For a descriptive analysis of Nicaraguan refugee camp life in Costa Rica see Pacheco (1989). For a discussion of Costa Rican policy toward Nicaraguan refugees, see Ramirez (1989).

Chapter 9. Refugee Returns to Sarajevo and Their Challenge to Contemporary Narratives of Mobility

1. This widespread interpretation of repatriation discourse gradually has taken on the character of a myth. The involvement of UNHCR and host country government organizations in post-repatriation processes of reintegration indicates an increasing awareness in the international refugee regime that the problems of refugees do not automatically end when they have crossed the border into their countries of origin, and that repatriation needs to be supported economically and socially.

2. This sense of alienation is echoed by those refugee academics who themselves have written about return (Habib 1996; Zarzosa 1998).

3. Under the umbrella of temporary protection, the legal rights and living conditions of the Bosnian refugees differed markedly between host countries, from the policy of "non-integration" in Denmark (Grünenberg 1997; Schwartz 1998; Stefansson 1997) to more inclusive policies in other Western European countries (Koser and Black 1999a; van Selm-Thorburn 1998).

4. The findings here are based upon a total of nine months of fieldwork carried out in 1999 and again in 2001. The bulk of the research took place in Sarajevo, and therefore readers must keep in mind that the arguments put forward in the article apply to that particular location, and not necessarily to other parts of BiH. The main informants are repatriated refugees from a range of different host countries, both in the former Yugoslavia (Serbia, Montenegro and Croatia), in Western Europe (Germany, Austria, Switzerland, the Scandinavian countries, Great Britain, Italy, and Spain), in North America (the United States and Canada) and in other parts of the world (Australia, Israel and Turkey). Informants also included people who stayed behind during the conflict, IDPs, visiting refugees as well as representatives from international and local organizations.

5. For the purposes of this article I restrict the use of the term "livelihood" to material and economic conditions (and the expectations about these), taking on explorations of social relations and cultural affinity separately.

6. For example, returnees from Denmark have the right to economic assistance for each member of the family repatriating; transportation of personal belongings; economic support for technical equipment; and lately elderly refugees have been entitled to a so-called monthly reintegration payment for five years; and refugees going back to minority areas have the opportunity of support for having their house reconstructed.

7. It is important to point out that although the distinction between returnees and stayees on the face of it seems rather clear-cut, on closer inspection returnee and stayee are not neat opposites but relative and context-dependent categories. For example, some refugees left BiH quite late in the war; other refugees returned to the home country early, some even during the war. Likewise, IDPs, normally subsumed into the "stayee" category, have not stayed geographically put but have moved within the country.

8. Sandzak is a region situated on both sides of the border between Serbia and Montenegro, populated mostly by Muslims. During recent years significant numbers of people from Sandzak have settled down in Sarajevo.

9. Members of the Bosnian refugee diaspora express themselves in similar terms (for explorations of longings for "normal life" among Bosnians in Scandinavia see for example Eastmond 1998; Stefansson 1997; Ålund 1998).

Chapter 10. The Making of a Good Citizen in an Ethiopian Returnee Settlement

1. For a discussion of proactive approaches to the study of repatriation, see Hammond 1999.

2. At the same time, another 200,000 Eritreans also fled to the Sudan for the same reasons.

3. The camp was situated only a few meters from the border and was thus vulnerable to attack. In addition, the water supply was not sufficient to provide for all camp residents.

4. See Hendrie (1989, 1996) for an account of the repatriation of some refugees from Saffawa in 1985–87.

5. Ada Bai residents told me that the leaders had actually been representatives of the Tigrayan People's Liberation Front (TPLF), but because the TPLF was not supposed to have an official presence in the camps, they associated themselves with the humanitarian branch of the armed movement, REST.

6. Translated from the Tigrinya by the author, with assistance from Abebe Bekele.

7. Humera is a lowland area 640 meters above sea level, with temperatures ranging from 40–47 degrees centigrade. Unlike most of the rest of Tigray, which has two rainy seasons, it has only one rainy season, from June to September.

8. Clapham, for instance, reports that sesame exports which amounted to 84,600 metric tons in 1974 (the second largest exporter in the world), dropped to only 3,400 metric tons by 1982, after which time Ethiopia effectively ceased to be a sesame exporter and much of the state farm was abandoned (1988: 184–85).

9. REST *Six Month Report*, December 1993.

10. A well-built house typically lasts for five to ten years with only minor renovation at the end of each rainy season.

11. Land distribution was to be made on the following scale:

1–2 people:	1 hectare	(2.5 acres)
2–4 people:	2 hectares	(5 acres)
5 + people	3 hectares	(7.5 acres)

12. Unlike in the highlands, where farmers plow with oxen, the softer soil and hotter conditions make donkey traction appropriate. Donkeys are also considerably cheaper than (often half the price of) oxen.

13. A *baito* is a local governing council, found throughout Tigray.

14. Public meeting in Ada Bai, June 28, 1994.

15. I have examined the politics of the land distribution elsewhere. See Hammond (1994).

16. Hiwot had agreed to provide tractor plowing at 132–136 birr (approx. U.S.$ 27 at 1994 prices) per hour (approximately 2 hectares). This was said to be lower than the market rate of 150 birr per hour, although some farmers told me that they could find tractors to plow for 100 birr/hour. All of these estimates were significantly higher than the 1993 plowing rate of 80 birr per hour.

17. Bruce, Hoben, and Dessalegn (1992: 28).

18. The militia was a voluntary force made up of some of the most respected members of the community, most of whom had served with the TPLF during the war. They carried rifles and kalashnikov machine guns more as a sign of their status as militia members than out of any real or perceived threat that would merit their use.

19. Ethiopian Orthodox churches typically have several priests. The Abune Aregawi church at Ada Bai was the only church in the community and was said to have thirty priests associated with it.

Chapter 11. West Indian Migrants and Their Rediscovery of Barbados

1. Results of the survey research can be found in G. Gmelch (1987).

2. Some of the life histories were published by G. Gmelch (1992).

3. For more discussion see Holmes (1998).

4. Among the surveyed return migrants (n=135), those who went abroad to work were away an average of 15.3 years, and those who went to study were away an average of 9.7 years, before resettling in Barbados.

5. Most took up residence in inner city areas. West Indians in both Britain and the United States tend to be clustered in the inner city. As Cerri Peach (1968:85) notes of British cities, the older, more dilapidated, and therefore less costly housing is found near the urban center. Not surprisingly, as British towns evolve the newer and more desirable housing is built farther from the center.

6. Ibid., 53; see also, Holmes (1998), and Western, (1992).

7. See Chamberlain (1997) for good discussion of migrant family life.

8. The situation was somewhat different for Barbadians and other West Indians in the United States where there was already a large American black population; hence the West Indian immigrants settled in neighborhoods that were predominantly black. White Americans, knowing perhaps even less about the Caribbean origins of the migrants than was the case in Britain, merely lumped them in with American blacks. Their status as immigrants was invisible. By being treated as black Americans, argues Connie Sutton, the West Indians have been discouraged from assimilating: the immigrants see that the group they are being identified with "possess the lowest incomes and the highest school drop out and unemployment rates." Sutton (1987: 21).

9. I have heard Barbadians tell stories about migrants who came home and discovered that their wives or families had frittered away the remittances they had sent home. These frustrated and unhappy migrants, often with nothing to show for the years of effort and saving, often re-emigrated.

10. For more detailed discussions of the influence of macro-economic conditions on return flows in other settings see Paine (1974) Rhoades (1978) and Piore (1979).

11. For discussion of the economic conditions that encouraged an increase in return migration to Barados, see Worrell (1987).

12. Similarly, many of the returnees interviewed in earlier studies in Ireland and Newfoundland also said that favorable experiences during a holiday visit home was the impetus for them to return permanently (G. Gmelch 1983: 52).

13. The desire to return is usually stronger among men than women. In fact a number of the women I interviewed admitted that they had initially resisted their husbands' desires to come home.

14. For a detailed discussion of gender and the reasons for return migration, see Gmelch and Gmelch (1993).

15. This quotation was taken from an interview for a documentary video and therefore the wording is slightly different than the version that appears in the oral history in *Double Passage*.

16. For examples from other cultures, see Gmelch (1980).

17. The official unemployment rate in Barbados, which seldom drops below 25 percent, is two to three times the level of unemployment in the host societies.

18. Michael Whiteford's (1978) observations among Colombian migrant women, that migration is a "liberating process which results in a modicum of sexual equality," applies equally well to these Barbadians.

19. For an excellent review, see Kearney (1986).

20. For details see Gmelch (1987).

21. The preference to use one's savings to buy and improve housing has been widely described among returnees elsewhere. For a detailed discussion, see Rhoades, (1978) and for a review of similar cases see Gmelch (1980).

22. For good examples of this argument see Rhoades (1978) and King (1978).

Bibliography

Abbas, Ackbar
    1994   "Building on Disappearance: Hong Kong Architecture and the City." *Public Culture* 6: 441–59.
    1999   "Dialectics of Deception." *Public Culture* 11, 2: 347–64.

Abbay, Alemseged
    1998   *Identity Jilted, or Re-Imagining Identity? The Divergent Paths of the Eritrean and Tigrayan Nationalist Struggles.* Asnara: Red Sea Press.

Administration for Refugee and Returnee Affairs of the Transitional Government of Ethiopia (ARRA)
    1992   Proposal for the Repatriation of Ethiopian Refugees from the Sudan. Addis Ababa.

Aguilar, Filomeno
    1999   "Ritual Passage and the Reconstruction of Selfhood in International Labor Migration." *Sojourn* 14, 1: 98–130.

Ahmed, Leila
    1999   *A Border Passage: From Cairo to America—A Woman's Journey.* New York: Farrar, Straus and Giroux.

Akol, J. O.
    1994   "A Crisis of Expectation: Returning to Southern Sudan in the 1970s." In *When Refugees Go Home: African Experiences*, ed. Tim Allen and Hubert Morsink. 78–95. London: James Currey.

Aleinikoff, T. Alexander
    1995   "State-Centered Refugee Law: From Resettlement to Containment." In *Mistrusting Refugees*, ed. E. Valentine Daniel and John Christian Knudsen. Berkeley: University of California Press.

Allen, Tim, ed.
    1996   *In Search of Cool Ground: War, Flight and Homecoming in Northeast Africa.* Trenton, N.J.: Africa World Press.

Allen, Tim and Hubert Morsink
    1994a   "Introduction: When Refugees Go Home." In *When Refugees Go Home: African Experiences*, ed. Tim Allen and Hubert Morsink. London: James Currey.
    1994b   eds. *When Refugees Go Home: African Experiences.* London: James Currey. Trenton, N.J.: Africa World Press.

Al-Rasheed, Madawi
    1994   "The Myth of Return: Iraqi Arab and Assyrian Refugees in London." *Journal of Refugee Studies* 7, 2/3: 199–219.

Alund, Aleksandra, ed.
    1998   *Mot ett normalt liv: Bosniska flyktingar i Norden (Toward a Normal Life: Bosnian Refugees in the Nordic Countries).* Copenhagen: Nordisk Ministerråd.

Alvarez, Julia
   1992   *How the García Girls Lost Their Accents.* New York: Plume.
Amnesty International
   1997   a *An End to Silence.* New York: Amnesty International.
   1997   b *Hidden Violence.* New York: Amnesty International.
Anagnost, Ann
   1989   "Prosperity and Counterprosperity: The Moral Discourse on Wealth in Post-
           Mao China. In *Marxism and the Chinese Experience,* ed. Arif Dirlik and Maurice
           Meisner. Armonk, N.Y.: M.E. Sharpe.
Anderson, Bridget
   1993   *Britain's Secret Slaves: An Investigation into the Plight of Overseas Domestic Workers in the
           United Kingdom.* London: Anti-Slavery International.
Anonas, Michaela V.
   1995   "Surely, We Will Miss Hong Kong." *Tinig Filipino,* March 28.
Anwar, Muhammad
   1979   *The Myth of Return: Pakistanis in Britain.* London: Heinemann.
Appadurai, Arjun
   1990   "Disjuncture and Difference in the Global Cultural Economy." *Public Culture*
           2, 2: 1–24.
   1991   "Global Ethnoscapes: Notes and Queries for a Transnational Anthropology."
           In *Recapturing Anthropology: Working in the Present,* ed. Richard G. Fox. 191–210.
           Santa Fe, N.M.: School of American Research Press.
   1996   *Modernity at Large: Global Dimensions of Globalization.* Minneapolis: University of
           Minnesota Press.
Arellano, Teddy P.
   1992   "Statue Square a 'Home Away from Home.'" *South China Morning Post,* Letters
           to the Editor, October 14.
Barker, Martin
   1981   *The New Racism: Conservatives and the Ideology of the Tribe.* London: Junction
           Books.
Barrow, Christine
   1997   "Migration from a Barbados Village: Effects on Family Life." *New Community*
           5, 4: 381–91.
Barry, Ellen
   1997   "Go East, Young Man." *Boston Phoenix,* October 9–16.
Barth, Fredrik
   1969   *Ethnic Groups and Boundaries: The Social Organization of Culture Difference.* Boston:
           Little, Brown.
Basch, Linda
   1987   "The Politics of Caribbeanization: Vincentians and Grenadians in New
           York." In *Caribbean Life in New York City: Sociocultural Dimensions,* ed. Constance
           R. Sutton and Elsa M. Chaney. 160–81. New York: Center for Migration
           Studies.
Basch, Linda, Nina Glick Schiller, and Cristina Szanton Blanc
   1994   *Nations Unbound: Transnational Projects, Postcolonial Predicaments, and Deterritorialized
           Nation-States.* Amsterdam: Gordon and Breach.
Bascom, Johnathan
   1994   "The Dynamics of Refugee Repatriation: The Case of Refugees in Eastern
           Sudan." In *Population Migration and the Changing World Order,* ed. W. T. S. Gould
           and Alan M. Findlay. 225–48. Chichester: John Wiley.
Battistella, Graziano and Anthony Paganoni, eds.
   1996   *Asian Women in Migration.* Quezon City: Scalabrini Migration Center.

Beckles, Hilary McD.
   1990   *A History of Barbados: From Amerindian Settlement to Nation-State.* Cambridge: Cambridge University Press.

Bedana, Alejandro
   1991   *Una tragedia campesina: testimonios de la Resistencia.* Managua: Editora de Arte.

Beigel, Greta
   1953   *Recent Events in Eastern Germany.* New York: Institute of Jewish Affairs.

Bennett, Milton
   1991   "Towards Ethnorelativism: A Developmental Model of Intercultural Sensitivity." In *Education for the Intercultural Experience,* ed. R. Michael Paige. 21–72. Yarmouth, Maine: Intercultural Press.

Benz, Wolfgang
   1991   "Der Schwierige Status der judischen Minderheit in Deutschland nach 1945." In *Zwischen Antisemitismus und Philosemitismus: Juden in de Bundesrepublic,* ed. Wolfgang Benz. 9–23. Berlin: Metropol.

Berger, Peter L., Brigitte Berger, and Hansfried Kellner
   1973   *The Homeless Mind: Modernization and Consciousness.* New York: Random House.

Berry, John
   1992   "Acculturation and Adaptation in a New Society." *International Migration Review* 30: 69–85.

Bhabha, Homi
   1990   "Introduction. In *Nation and Narration,* ed. Homi Bhabha. 1–7. New York: Routledge.

Bickers, Robert and Jeffrey N. Wasserstrom
   1995   "Shanghai's 'Dogs and Chinese Not Admitted'." *China Quarterly* 142: 444–66.

Binh, Tri
   1997   "Hong Kong Airport Poster Leads Viet Kieu Architect to Restoring the Ha Noi Opera House." *Viet Nam News,* October 5, 1ff.

Bisharat, George E.
   1997   "Exile to Compatriot: Transformations in the Social Identity of Palestinian Refugees in the West Bank." In *Culture, Power, Place: Explorations in Critical Anthropology,* ed. Akhil Gupta and James Ferguson. Durham, N.C.: Duke University Press.

Black, Richard and Khalid Koser, eds.
   1999   *The End of the Refugee Cycle? Refugee Repatriation and Reconstruction.* New York: Berghahn.

Black, Richard, Khalid Koser, and Martha Walsh
   1997   *Conditions for the Return of Displaced Persons from the European Union.* Brighton: University of Sussex, Sussex Centre for Migration Research.

Bodemann, Y. Michael
   1983   "Opfer zu Komplizen gemacht? Der judisch-deutsche Bruch und die verlorene Identitat Anmerkungen zu einer Ruckkehr in die Bundesrepublik." *Die Zeit* 1 (December 30): 28.
   1993   "Jews in West Germany." Speech delivered at Cornell University.

Böhning, W. R.
   1972   *The Migration of Workers in the United Kingdom and the European Community.* London: Oxford University Press.

Borjas, George and Bernt Bratsberg
   1996   "Who Leaves? The Outmigration of the Foreign-Born." *Review of Economics and Statistics* 78, 1: 165–76.

Borneman, John
   1992   *Belonging in the Two Berlins: Kin, State, Nation.* Cambridge: Cambridge University Press.

1996   "Education After the Cold War: Remembrance, Repetition, and Rightwing Violence." In *Cultural Authority in Contemporary Germany: Intellectual Responsibility Between State Security Surveillance and Media Society,* ed. Michael Geyer and Robert von Hallberg. Chicago: University of Chicago Press.

Borneman, John and Jeffrey Peck
1995   *Sojourners: The Return of German Jews and the Question of Identity.* Lincoln: University of Nebraska Press.

Bovenkerk, Frank
1974   *The Sociology of Return Migration: A Bibliographic Essay.* The Hague: Martinus Nijhoff.

Breckenridge, Carol and Arjun Appadurai
1989   "Editors' Comment." *Public Culture* 2, 1: i–iv.

Brettell, Caroline
2000   "Theorizing Migration in Anthropology: The Social Construction of Networks, Identities, Communities, and Globalscapes." In *Migration Theory: Talking Across Disciplines,* ed. Caroline Brettell and James Hollifield. 97–135. New York: Routledge.

Bringa, Tone
1995   *Being Muslim the Bosnian Way: Identity in a Central Bosnian Village.* Princeton, N.J.: Princeton University Press.

Brubaker, Roger
1992   *Citizenship and Nationhood in France and Germany.* Cambridge: Cambridge University Press.

Bruce, John
1974   "Land Reform Planning and Indigenous Communal Tenures: A Case Study of the Tenure 'Chiguraf-Gwoses' in Tigray, Ethiopia." Ph.D. dissertation, University of Wisconsin-Madison.

Bruce, John, Allan Hoben, and Dessalegn Rahmato
1992   "After the Derg: An Assessment of Rural Land Tenure Issues in Ethiopia." Draft report submitted for discussion at the Workshop on Rural Land Tenure Issues in Ethiopia, August 27–29, Addis Ababa.

Bruner, Edward M.
1986   "Ethnography as Narrative." In *The Anthropology of Experience,* ed. Victor Turner and Edward M. Bruner. Urbana: University of Illinois Press.

Bryce-Laport, Roy S. and Delores M. Mortimer, eds.
1976   *Caribbean Immigration to the United States.* Occasional Papers 1. Washington, D.C.: Research Institute on Immigration Studies, Smithsonian Institution.

Buaken, Manuel
1948   *I Have Lived with the American People.* Caldwell, Ida.: Caxton Printers.

Buijs, Gina
1993   "Introduction." In *Migrant Women: Crossing Boundaries and Changing Identities,* ed. Gina Buijs. 1–20. Oxford: Berg.

Cantril, Albert Hadley
1965   *The Pattern of Human Concerns.* New Brunswick, N.J.: Rutgers University Press.

Cantril, Albert Hadley and Charles W. Roll, Jr.
1971   *The Hopes and Fears of the American People.* New York: Universe Books.

Carling, Jørgen
2002   "Migration in the Age of Involuntary Immobility: Theoretical Reflections and Cape Verdean Experiences." *Journal of Ethnic and Migration Studies* 28, 1: 5–42.

Carnegie, Charles V., ed.
1982   "Strategic Flexibility in the West Indies: A Social Psychology of Caribbean Migration." *Caribbean Review* 2, 1: 10–13, 54.

Carsten, Janet
    1995   "The Politics of Forgetting: Migration, Kinship and Memory on the Periphery of the Southeast Asian State." *Journal of the Royal Anthropological Instiutute* n.s. 1: 317–35.

Castles, Stephen and Godula Kosack
    1973   *Immigrant Workers and Class Structure in Western Europe.* London: Oxford University Press.

Cayog, Precy R.
    1996   "Behind the Gleaming Lights." *Tinig Filipino,* March, 22.

Centers for Disease Control (CDC)
    1992   "Famine-Affected, Refugee, and Displaced Populations: Recommendations for Public health Issues." *Morbidity and Mortality Weekly Review* 41, no. RR-13 (Internet version).

Central American Historical Institute
    1984   "Nicaragua's Agrarian Reform." *Central American Historical Institute Update* 3, 2 (January 13).

Cerase, Francesco
    1974   "Expectations and Reality: A Case Study of Return Migration from the United States to Southern Italy." *International Migration Review* 8, 2: 245–62.

Chamberlain, Mary
    1997   *Narratives of Exile and Return.* New York: St. Martin's Press.

Chambers, Iain
    1994   *Migrancy, Culture, Identity.* London: Routledge.

Chaney, Elsa M.
    1987   "The Context of Caribbean Migration." In *Caribbean Life in New York City: Sociocultural Dimensions,* ed. Constance R. Sutton and Elsa M. Chaney. 3–14. New York: Center for Migration Studies of New York.

Chen Ta
    1940   *Emigrant Communities in South China: A Study of Overseas Chinese Migration and Its Influence on Standards of Living and Social Change.* Ed. Bruno Lasker. New York: Institute of Pacific Relations.

Cheng, Shu-ju Ada
    1996   "Migrant Women Domestic Workers in Hong Kong, Singapore and Taiwan: A Comparative Analysis." In *Asian Women in Migration,* ed. Graziano Battistella and Anthony Paganoni. 109–22. Quezon City: Scalabrini Migration Center.

Cheung, A.
    1995   "Worse if Workers Are Legal." *South China Morning Post,* October 30.

Chimni, B. S.
    1999   "From Resettlement to Involuntary Repatriation: Towards a Critical History of Durable Solutions to Refugee Problems." New Issues in Refugee Research Working Paper 2. Centre for Documentation and Research. Geneva: UNHCR.

Ching, Frank
    1999   "A Shadow over Hong Kong." *Far Eastern Economic Review,* July 15.

Choo, Kristin
    1996   "Maid in Hong Kong." *Chicago Tribune,* June 30.

Chow, Rey
    1992   "Between Colonizers: Hong Kong's Postcolonial Self-Writing in the 1990s." *Diaspora* 2, 2: 150–70.

Cichon, Donald J., Elzbieta Gozdziak, and Jane Grover
    1986   *The Economic and Social Adjustment of Non-Southeast Asian Refugees.* 2 vols. Falls Church, Va.: Research Management Corporation.

Clapham, Christopher
   1988   *Transformation and Continuity in Revolutionary Ethiopia*. Cambridge: Cambridge
              University Press.
Clark, Michael
   1991   "Remembering Vietnam." In *The Vietnam War and American Culture*, ed. John
              Carlos Rowe and Rick Berg. 177–207. New York: Columbia University Press.
Clay, Jason W. and Bonnie K. Holcomb
   1986   *Politics and the Ethiopian Famine, 1984–1985*. Cambridge, Mass.: Cultural Sur-
              vival.
Clay, Jason W., Sandra Steingraber, and Peter Niggli
   1988   *The Spoils of Famine: Ethiopian Famine Policy and Peasant Agriculture*. Cambridge,
              Mass.: Cultural Survival.
Clifford, James
   1988   *The Predicament of Culture: Twentieth-Century Ethnography, Literature, and Art*. Cam-
              bridge, Mass.: Harvard University Press.
   1992   "Travelling Cultures." In *Cultural Studies*, ed. Lawrence Grossberg, Cary Nel-
              son, and Paula Treichler. New York: Routledge. 96–116.
   1994   "Diasporas." *Cultural Anthropology* 9, 3: 302–38.
Cohen, Robin
   1997   *Global Diasporas: An Introduction*. Seattle: University of Washington Press.
Colectivo Latinamericana de Trabajo Psicosocial (COLAT)
   1981   "Towards a Libertarian Therapy for Latin American Exiles." In *Mental Health
              and Exile: Papers Arising from a Seminar on Mental Health and Latin American Exiles.*
              10–13. London: World University Press Service.
Coles, Gervase
   1985   "Voluntary Repatriation: A Background Study." Unpublished paper.
Comité intermouvement d'aide aux déplacés et aux réfugiés (CIMADE)
   1981   "The Influence of Political Repression and Exile on Children." In *Mental
              Health and Exile: Papers Arising from a Seminar on Mental Health and Latin American
              Exiles.* 22–34. London: World University Service.
Commission for Real Property Claims of Displaced Persons and Refugees (CRPC) and
   UNHCR
   1997   "Return, Relocation, and Property Rights: A Discussion Paper." Sarajevo:
              CRPC/UNHCR.
Constable, Nicole
   1996a   "Jealousy, Chastity, and Abuse: Chinese Maids and Foreign Helpers in Hong
              Kong." *Modern China* 22, 4: 448–79.
   1996b   "Still Guest People: The Reproduction of Hakka Identity in Calcutta, India."
              In *Guest People: Hakka Identity in China and Abroad*, ed. Nicole Constable. Seattle:
              University of Washington Press.
   1997a   *Maid to Order in Hong Kong: Stories of Filipina Workers*. Ithaca, N.Y.: Cornell Uni-
              versity Press.
   1997b   "Sexuality and Discipline Among Filipina Domestic Workers in Hong Kong."
              American Ethnologist 24, 3: 539–58.
   1999   "At Home But Not at Home: Filipina Narratives of Ambivalent Returns."
              Cultural Anthropology 14, 2: 203–28.
   2000   "Public Spaces and Private Homes: Negotiating Filipina Domestic Worker
              Identities in Hong Kong." In *Home and Hegemony: Domestic Service and Identity Pol-
              itics in South and Southeast Asia*, ed. Kathleen M. Adams and Sara Dickey.
              121–48. Ann Arbor: University of Michigan Press.
Cornish, Flora, Karl Peltzer, and Malcolm MacLachlan
   1999   "Returning Strangers: The Children of Malawian Refugees Come 'Home'?"
              Journal of Refugee Studies 12, 3: 264–83.

Cumper, George E.
1957   "Working Class Emigration from Barbados to the U.K." *Social and Economic Studies* 6, 1: 76–83.
Cuny, Frederick C., Barry N. Stein, and Pat Reed
1992   *Repatriation During Conflict in Africa and Asia.* Dallas: Centre for the Study of Societies in Crisis.
Curtin, Philip D.
1984   *Cross Cultural Trade in World History.* Cambridge: Cambridge University Press.
Da Rocha Lima, Valentina
1982   "Women in Exile: Becoming Feminists." *International Journal of Oral History* 5, 6: 81–99.
Daily Yomiuri
1997   "H. K. Extravaganza Draws Filipino Workers." *Daily Yomiuri* On-Line, <www.yomiuri.co.jp/newsj/0630dy10.htm> June 28.
Dahya, Badr
1973   "Pakistanis in Britain: Transients or Settlers." *Race* 14, 3: 241–77.
Daldry, Emma Jane
1995   "Complaints About Filipinas Not On." *Eastern Express,* October 21–22.
Dann, Graham
1984   *The Quality of Life in Barbados.* London: Macmillan.
Davison, Robert Barry
1962   *West Indian Migrants: Social and Economic Effects of Migration from the West Indies.* London: Oxford University Press.
De Waal, Alex
1991   *Evil Days: 30 Years of War and Famine in Ethiopia.* London: Africa Watch.
Delauze, Gilles and Felix Guattari
1988   *A Thousand Plateaus: Capitalism and Schizophrenia.* London: Athlone.
Demos, John
1994   *The Unredeemed Captive: A Family Story from Early America.* New York: Knopf.
Dilling, Yvonne
1989   *In Search of Refuge.* Scottsdale, Pa.: Herald Press.
Diner, Dan
1986   "Negative Symbiose: Deutsche und Juden nach Auschwitz." *Babylon* 1: 9–20.
Dirks, Nicholas B.
1994   "Ritual and Resistance: Subversion as a Social Fact," In *Culture/Power/History: A Reader in Contemporary Social Theory,* ed. Nicholas B. Dirks, Geoff Eley, and Sherry B. Ortner. 483–503. Princeton, N.J.: Princeton University Press.
Domínguez, Virginia R.
1975   *From Neighbor to Stranger: The Dilemma of Caribbean Peoples in the United States.* New Haven, Conn.: Antilles Research Program, Yale University.
Duara, Prasenjit
1997   "Nationalists Among Transnationals: Overseas Chinese and the Idea of China, 1900–1911." In *Ungrounded Empires: The Cultural Politics of Modern Chinese Transnationalism,* ed. Donald Nonini and Aihwa Ong. New York: Routledge.
Dumont, Jean-Paul
2000   "Always Home, Never Home: Visayan Helpers and Identities." In *Home and Hegemony: Domestic Service and Identity Politics in South and Southeast Asia,* ed. Kathleen M. Adams and Sara Dickey. 119–36. Ann Arbor: University of Michigan Press.
Dung, Cao Ly
1996   "Generation X-Patriate." *Vietnam Economic Times* 22 (February): 20–21.

Dustman, Christian
  2001   "Children and Return Migration." www.ucl.ac.uk/uctbbb21/abstract/dy-nast.htm.
Eastmond, Marita
  1997   *The Dilemmas of Exile: Chilean Refugees in the U.S.A.* Gothenburg Studies in Social Anthropology 13. Gothenburg: Acta Universitatis Gothoburgensis.
  1998   "Nationalist Discourses and the Construction of Difference: Bosnian Muslim Refugees in Sweden." *Journal of Refugee Studies* 11, 2: 161–81.
Eastmond, Marita and Joakim Öjenda
  1999   "Revisiting a 'Repatriation Success': The Case of Cambodia." In *The End of the Refugee Cycle? Refugee Repatriation and Reconstruction,* ed. Richard Black and Khalid Koser. New York: Berghahn.
Eich, Dieter and Carlos Rincon
  1984   *The Contras: Interviews with Anti-Sandinistas.* San Francisco: Synthesis Publications.
Elmusa, Sharif
  1995   "When the Wellsprings of Identity Dry Up: Reflections on Fawaz Turki's *Exile's Return.*" *Journal of Palestine Studies* 2, 1: 96–102.
  2000   "The Massacre of Refugees in the Congo: A Case of Negative Externalities, UN Peacekeeping Failure, and International Law." *Journal of Modern African Studies* 38, 2: 163–202.
Engelhardt, Manfred
  1991   Interview with Hilde Eisler. *Deutsche Lebensläufe: Gesprache.* Berlin: Aufbau Verlag. 27–48.
Erikson, Erik H.
  1975   "On the Nature of Psycho-Historical Evidence." In *Life History and the Historical Moment.* 113–68. New York: Norton.
Fabian, Johannes
  1983   *Time and the Other: How Anthropology Makes Its Object.* New York: Columbia University Press.
Feld, Steven and Keith H. Basso
  1996   "Introduction." In *Senses of Place,* ed. Steven Feld and Keith Basso. 3–13. Santa Fe, N.M.: School of American Research Press.
Ferris, Elizabeth
  1987   *The Central American Refugee.* New York: Praeger.
FitzGerald, Frances
  1973   *Fire in the Lake: The Vietnamese and the Americans in Vietnam.* New York: Random House.
Fitzherbert, Katrin
  1967   *West Indian Children in London.* Occasional Papers on Social Administration 19. London: Bell.
Foner, Nancy
  1978   *Jamaica Farewell: Jamaican Migrants in London.* Berkeley: University of California Press.
  1979   "West Indians in New York City and London: A Comparative Analysis." *International Migration Review* 13, 2: 284–97.
Frucht, Richard
  1968   "Emigration, Remittances, and Social Change: Aspects of the Social Field in Nevis, West Indies." *Anthropologica* 10: 193–208.
Fundación de Ayuda Social de las Iglesias Cristianas (FASIC)
  1981   "A Social-Psychological Study of 25 Returning Families." In *Mental Health and*

Exile: Papers Arising from a Seminar on Mental Health and Latin American Exiles. 35–40. London: World University Press.

Gamboa, Veronica P.
1996   "It's Our Day! It's Our Day!" *Tinig Filipino,* January, 22.

Gaw, Kenneth
1991   *Superior Servants: The Legendary Amahs of the Far East.* Singapore: Oxford University Press.

Gay, Peter
1978   *Freud, Jews, and Other Germans: Masters and Victims in Modernist Culture.* New York: Oxford University Press.

Gay, Ruth
1992   "What I Learned About German Jews." *American Scholar* 54: 467–84.

Gebremedhin, Naigzy
1995   "Environmental Aspects of Resettlements." Paper presented at Government of Eritrea workshop on the PROFERI Phase 1 Operational Plan, Asmara, Eritrea, May 19–20.

General Accounting Office (GAO)
1991   Nicaraguan Resistance: Programs for Repatriation and Resettlement. GA1.13 NSIAD 91–234. Washington, D.C.: General Accounting Office.

Georges, Eugenia
1992   "Gender, Class, and Migration in the Dominican Republic: Women's Experiences in a Transnational Community." In *Towards a Transnational Perspective on Migration: Race, Class, Ethnicity, and Nationalism Reconsidered,* ed. Nina Glick-Schiller, Linda Basch, and Cristina Blanc-Szanton. 81–99. Annals of the New York Academy of Sciences 645. New York: New York Academy of Sciences.

German Development Institute (GDI)
1995   "Promoting the Reintegration of Former Female and Male Combatants in Eritrea: Possible Contributions of Development Co-operation to the Reintegration Programme." Final Report to Government of Eritrea. Asmara, Eritrea, April.

Ghosh, Amitav
1988   *The Shadow Lines.* New York: Viking.

Ghosh, Bimal
2000   *Return Migration: Journey of Hope or Despair.* Geneva: United Nations and International Organization for Migration.

Gibney, Frank
1995   "Vietnam: Back in Business." *Time,* April 24, 34–39.

Giddens, Anthony
1990   *The Consequences of Modernity.* Stanford, Calif.: Stanford University Press.

Giles, Winona, Helene Moussa, and Penny Van Esterik, eds.
1996   *Development and Diaspora: Gender and the Refugee Experience.* Dundas, Ont.: Artemis Enterprises.

Gilman, Sander
1986   *Jewish Self-Hatred: Anti-Semitism and the Hidden Language of the Jews.* Baltimore: John Hopkins University Press.
1991   *The Jew's Body.* New York: Routledge.

Giorgis, Tedla W.
1984   "Cross-Cultural Counselling of Ethiopian Refugees." Paper prepared for the Ethiopian Community Development Council Workshop on Refugee Mental Health, San Francisco, June.

Glass, Ruth
1960   *Newcomers: The West Indians in London.* London: Allen and Unwin.

Glick-Schiller, Nina, Linda Basch, and Cristina Blanc-Szanton
  1992a   "Transnationalism: A New Framework for Understanding Migration." In *Towards a Transnational Perspective on Migration: Race, Class, Ethnicity, and Nationalism Reconsidered*, ed. Nina Glick-Schiller, Linda Basch, and Cristina Blanc-Szanton. 1–24. Annals of the New York Academy of Sciences 645 New York: New York Academy of Sciences.
  1992b   eds. *Towards a Transnational Perspective on Migration: Race, Class, Ethnicity, and Nationalism Reconsidered.* New York: New York Academy of Sciences.
Gmelch, George
  1980   "Return Migration." *Annual Review of Anthropology* 9: 135–59.
  1983   "Who Returns and Why: Return Migration Behavior in Two Atlantic Societies." *Human Organization* 42, 1: 46–54.
  1987   "Work, Innovation, and Investment: The Impact of Return Migrants in Barbados." *Human Organization* 46, 2: 131–40.
  1992   *Double Passage: The Lives of Caribbean Migrants Abroad and Back Home.* Ann Arbor: University of Michigan Press.
Gmelch, George and Sharon Bohn Gmelch
  1993   "Gender and Migration: The Readjustment of Women Migrants in Barbados, Ireland and Newfoundland." *Human Organization* 54, 4: 470–73.
  1994   *The Parish Behind God's Back: The Changing Culture of Rural Barbados.* Ann Arbor: University of Michigan Press.
Godley, Michael
  1989   "The Sojourners: Returned Overseas Chinese in the People's Republic of China." *Pacific Affairs* 62, 3 (Fall): 330–52.
Goldberg, David P.
  1972   *The Detection of Psychiatric Illness by Questionnaire.* London: Oxford University Press.
Gómez-Pe–a, Guillermo
  1998   "1995–*Terreno Peligroso*/Danger Zone: Cultural Relations Between Chicanos and Mexicans at the end of the Century." In *Borderless Borders: U.S. Latinos, Latin Americans, and the Paradox of Interdependence*, ed. Frank Bonilla, Edwin Melendez, Rebecca Morales, and Maria de los Angeles Torres. 131–37. Philadelphia: Temple University Press.
Gorostiaga, Xabier
  1991   "Obstacles to Political Consensus in Nicaragua." Paper presented at Seminar on Nicaragua's Search for Democratic Consensus. Woodrow Wilson Center, Washington, D.C.
Government of Eritrea
  1996   *Draft Constitution English Version.* Asmara, Eritrea: Constitutional Commission of Eritrea. July.
Graham, Mark and Shahram Khosravi
  1997   "Home Is Where You Make It: Repatriation and Diaspora Culture Among Iranians in Sweden." *Journal of Refugee Studies* 10, 2: 115–33.
Grosfoguel, Ramon
  1995   "Depeasantization and Agrarian Decline in the Caribbean." In *Food and Agrarian Orders in the World Economy*, ed. Philip McMichael, 33–254. Westport, Conn.: Praeger.
Grünenberg, Kristina
  1997   " 'Det tomme rum?' Midlertidighed, flygtningelandsbyer og bosniske krigsflygtninge i Danmark" (" 'The Empty Space?' Temporality, Refugee Villages and Bosnian War Refugees in Denmark"). MA thesis, Institute of Anthropology, University of Copenhagen.

Gupta, Akhil and James Ferguson
  1992   "Beyond 'Culture': Space, Identity, and the Politics of Difference." *Cultural Anthropology* 7, 1: 6–23.
Habib, Laila
  1996   "The Search for Home." *Journal of Refugee Studies* 9, 1: 96–102.
Hackett, Beatrice
  1997   "Politics, Economics and Growing Older for German Refugees and Expellees of 1945." Paper prepared for panel "Coming Home? Immigrants, Refugees and Those Who Stayed Behind," Annual Meeting of the American Anthropological Association, November 1997, Washington, D.C.
Haitian Refugee Center v Civilletti
  1980   503 E. Supp. 442 (1980), U.S. Circuit Court, Miami.
Hammer, Manfried and Julius Schoeps, eds.
  1988   *Juden in Berlin, 1671–1945: Ein Lesebuch.* Berlin: Nicolai.
Hammond, Laura
  1994   "Returnees, Local Farmers and Big Business: The Politics of Land Allocation in Humera, Ethiopia." In *Land Tenure and Land Policy in Ethiopia After the Derg: Proceedings of the Second Workshop of the Land Tenure Project,* ed. Dessalegn Rahmato. 248–63. Working Papers on Ethiopian Development 8. Dragvoll: University of Trondheim Centre for Environment and Development.
  1995a   "Preliminary Findings of Household Economic Survey, Ada Bai Returnee Settlement, Humera, Ethiopia." Report ubmitted to the UN Emergencies Unit for Ethiopia, Addis Ababa.
  1995b   "Household Economic Survey, Ada Bai Returnee Settlement, Humera, Ethiopia." Report submitted to the UN Emergencies Unit for Ethiopia, Addis Ababa.
  1999   "Examining the Discourse of Repatriation: Toward More Proactive Theory of Return Migration." In *The End of the Refugee Cycle? Refugee Repatriation and Reconstruction,* ed. Richard Black and Khalid Koser. New York: Berghahn.
  2001   "This Place Will Become Home: Emplacement and Community formation in a Tigrayan Returnee Settlement, Northwest Ethiopia." Ph.D. dissertation, University of Wisconsin, Madison.
Hannerz, Ulf
  1992   *Cultural Complexity: Studies in the Social Organization of Meaning.* New York: Columbia University Press.
Hansen, Art
  1991   "Some Insights on African Refugees." In *Selected Papers on Refugee Issues,* ed. Pamela A. DeVoe, 100–110. Washington D.C.: American Anthropological Association.
Harrell-Bond, Barbara Elizabeth
  1986   *Imposing Aid: Emergency Assistance to Refugees.* Oxford: Oxford University Press.
  1989   "Repatriation: Under What Conditions Is It the Most Desirable Solution?" *African Studies Review* 32, 1: 41–69.
Harvey, David
  1989   *The Condition of Postmodernity: An enquiry into the Origins of Cultural Change.* Oxford: Blackwell. Cambridge, Mass.: Blackwell, 1990.
Hayslip, Le Ly with Jay Wurts
  1989   *When Heaven and Earth Changed Places: A Vietnam Woman's Journey from War to Peace.* New York: Penguin.
Hendrie, Barbara
  1989   "Cross Border Relief Operations in Eritrea and Tigray." *Disasters* 13, 4: 351–60.

1996   "Assisting Refugees in the Context of Warfare: Some Issues Arising from the Tigrayan Refugee Repatriation, Sudan to Ethiopia, 1985–7." In *In Search of Cool Ground: War, Flight, and Homecoming in Northeast Africa*, ed. Tim Allen. 35–43. Trenton, N.J.: Africa World Press.

Herrera-Sobek, Maria
1998   "The Corrido as Hypertext: Undocumented Mexican Immigrant films and the Mexican/chicano Ballad." In *Culture Across Borders: Mexican Immigration and Popular Culture*, ed. David R. Maciel and Maria Herrera-Sobek. 227–58. Tucson: University of Arizona Press.

Hill, Donald R.
1977   *The Impact of Migration on the Metropolitan and Folk Society of Carriacou, Grenada.* Anthropological Papers of the American Museum of Natural History 54, 2. New York: American Museum of Natural History.

Hinds, Donald
1966   *Journey to an Illusion: The West Indian in Britain.* London: Heinemann.

Hiro, Dilip
1971   *Black British, White British.* London: Eyre and Spotiswood.

Hirsch, Eric and Michael O'Hanlon
1995   *The Anthropology of Landscape: Perspectives on Place and Space.* New York: Oxford University Press.

Hirschon, Renée
1989   *Heirs of the Greek Catastrophe: The Social Life of Asia Minor Refugees in Piraeus.* Oxford: Clarendon Press.

Hoben, Allan
1973   *Land Tenure Among the Amhara of Ethiopia.* Berkeley: University of California Press.

Hobsbawm, Eric J.
1990   *Nations and Nationalism Since 1780: Programme, Myth, Reality.* Cambridge: Cambridge University Press.

Hobsbawm, Eric J. and Terence O. Ranger
1992   *The Invention of Tradition.* Cambridge: Cambridge University Press.

Holmes, Colin
1988   *John Bull's Island: Immigration and British Society, 1871–1971.* London: Macmillan.

Hopper, Mark
1996   "Easy Solution." *South China Morning Post*, letters column, April 8.

Hsing, You-tien
1997   "Building *Guanxi* Across the Straits: Taiwanese Capital and Local Chinese Bureaucrats." In *Ungrounded Empires: The Cultural Politics of Modern Chinese Transnationalism,* ed. Aihwa Ong and Donald Macon Nonini. New York: Routledge.

Hsu, Madeline
1996   "Living Abroad and Faring Well: Migration and Transnationalism in Taishan County, Guangdong, 1904–1939." Ph.D. Dissertation, Yale University.

Human Rights Watch
1995   *Rwanda: The Crisis Continues.* New York: Human Rights Watch, April.
1997   *What Kabila Is Hiding: Civilian Killings and Impunity in the Congo.* New York: Human Rights Watch, October.

Huseby-Darvas, Eva
1997   "'A Turk in My Bed? The Predicament of Repatriation Among Refugees from the Former Yugoslavia Living in Ethnically Mixed Marriages." Paper prepared for panel "Coming Home? Immigrants, Refugees, and Those Who

Stayed Behind," Annual Meeting of the American Anthropological Association, November 1997, Washington, D.C.

Indra, Doreen
1999   *Engendering Forced Migration: Theory and Practice.* New York: Berghahn Press.

International Crisis Group (ICG)
1998   *Rebuilding a Multi-Ethnic Sarajevo: A Strategy for Promoting the Return of Minorities to the Bosnian Capital.* ICG Balkans Report 30. Brussels: ICG.
1999   *Is Dayton Failing? Bosnia Four Years After the Peace Agreement.* ICG Balkans Report 80. Brussels: ICG.

International Organization for Migration (IOM)
2001   "Report to Donors on Refugee Returns." Unpublished.

Jacobmeyer, Wolfgang
1983   "Judische Uberlebende als 'Displaced Persons.'" *Geschichte und Gesellschaft* 9: 421–52.

Jamieson, Neil L.
1993   *Understanding Vietnam.* Berkeley: University of California Press.

Jansen, Stef
1998   "Homeless at Home: Narrations of Post-Yugoslav Identities." In *Migrants of Identity: Perceptions of Home in a World of Movement,* ed. Nigel Rapport and Andrew Dawson. New York: Berg.

Janzen, John
1999   "Text and Context in the Anthropology of War and Trauma: The African Great Lakes Region, 1993–95." *Suomen Anthropologi* 4: 37–57.
2000   "Deciphering the Voices of Genocide Accounts in Rwanda." Department of Anthropology International Health Series lecture, Case Western Reserve University, February 17.

Janzen, John and Reinhild Kauenhoven Janzen
2000   *Do I Still Have a Life? Voices from the Aftermath of War in Rwanda and Burundi.* Publications in Anthropology 20. Lawrence: University of Kansas.

Javate de Dios, Aurora
1996/7   "The Feminization of Migrant Labor: Its Implications for NGOS." *Philippine Women's Forum* 7: 4–13.

Jen, Gish
1991   *Typical American.* New York: Penguin.

Kaimowitz, David
1984   "Nicaragua's Agrarian Reform: Six Years Later." In *Nicaragua: Unfinished Revolution,* ed. Peter Rosset and John Vandermeer, 390–92. New York: Grove Press.

Kang, K. Connie
1997   "Koreans Reflect Regretfully on L.A. They Left Behind." *Los Angeles Times,* Thursday, April 29.

Kaplan, Caren
1996   *Questions of Travel: Postmodern discourses of Displacement.* Durham, N.C.: Duke University Press.

Katihabwa, Sebastien
1994   "L'autre rive: chronique d'un refugie ordinaire d'Afrique." Bujumbura. Unpublished manuscript.

Kearney, Michael
1986   "From the Invisible Hand to the Visible Feet." *Annual Review of Anthropology* 13: 331–61.
1995   "The Local and the Global: The Anthropology of Globalization and Transnationalism." *Annual Review of Anthropology* 24: 547–65.

Kenny, Michael
  1986   "Twentieth Century Spanish Expatriate Ties with the Homeland: Remigration and Its Consequences." In *The Changing Faces of Rural Spain,* ed. Joseph B. Aceves and William A. Douglass. 97–121. New York: Schenkman.
Kibreab, Gaim
  1996a   *People on the Edge in the Horn.* Trenton, N.J.: Red Sea Press.
  1996b   *Ready, Willing . . . and Still Waiting: Eritrean Refugees in Sudan.* Uppsala: Life and Peace Institute.
  1999   "Revisiting the Debate on People, Place, Identity and Displacement." *Journal of Refugee Studies* 12, 4: 384–410.
King, Russell L.
  1978   "Return Migration: Review of Some Cases from Southern Europe." *Mediterranean Studies* 1, 2: 3–30.
  1986   "Return Migration and Regional Economic Development: An Overview." In *Return Migration and Regional Economic Problems,* ed. Russell L. King. London: Croom Helm.
  2000   "Generalizations from the History of Return Migration." In *Return Migration: Journey of Hope or Despair?,* ed. Bimal Ghosh. 7–55. Geneva: United Nations and IOM.
King, Russell L. and Alan Strachan
  1980   "The Effects of Return Migration on a Gozitan Village." *Human Organization* 39: 175–79.
Kingston, Maxine Hong
  1989a   *The Woman Warrior: Memoirs of a Girlhood Among the Ghosts.* New York: Vintage/Random House.
  1989b   *China Men.* New York: Vintage/Random House.
Kipnis, Andrew
  1997   *Producing Guanxi: Sentiment, Self, and Subculture in a North China Village.* Durham, N.C.: Duke University Press.
Kirchner, Peter
  1991   "Die judische Minderheit in der Bundesrepublik." In *Zwischen Antisemitismus und Philosemitismus: Juden in de Bundesrepublik,* ed. Wolfgang Benz. 29–38. Berlin: Metropol Verlag.
Knudsen, John Chr.
  1995   "When Trust Is on Trial: Negotiating Refugee Narratives." In *Mistrusting Refugees,* ed. E. Valentine Daniel and John Chr. Knudsen. 13–35. Berkeley: University of California Press.
Kondo, Dorinne
  1990   *Crafting Selves: Power, Gender, and Discourses of Identity in a Japanese Workplace.* Chicago: University of Chicago Press.
Korsmoe, Sam
  1996   "Coming Home." *Vietnam Economic Times* 22 (February): 16–19.
Koser, Khalid
  2000   "Return, Readmission, and Reintegration: Changing Agendas, Policy Frameworks, and Operational Programmes." In *Return Migration: Journey of Hope or Despair?,* ed. Bimal Ghosh. 57–99. Geneva: United Nations and IOM.
Koser, Khalid and Richard Black
  1999a   "Limits to Harmonization: The 'Temporary Protection' of Refugees in the European Union." *International Migration* 37, 3: 521–41.
  1999b   "The End of the Refugee Cycle? In *The End of the Refugee Cycle? Refugee Repatriation and Reconstruction,* ed. Richard Black and Khalid Koser. 2–17. New York: Berghahn.

Kubát, Daniel, ed.
1981   *The Politics of Return: International Return Migration in Europe, Proceedings of the First European Conference on International Return Migration (Rome, November 11–14, 1981).* New York: Center for Migration Studies.

Kusterer, Karin and Edita Dugalić
1998   *Tilbage til Bosnien: Edita vender hjem* (orig: *kommst du mit nach Bosnien?*). Aarhus: CDR Forlag.

Lavie, Smadar and Ted Swedenburg
1996   "Introduction." In *Displacement, Diaspora, and Geographies of Identity,* ed. Smadar Lavie and Ted Swedenburg. 1–25. Durham, N.C.: Duke University Press.

Legum, Colin
1976   *Ethiopia: The Fall of Haile Selassie's Empire.* New York: Africana Publishing Co.

Leong, Sow-Theng
1997   *Migration and Ethnicity in Chinese History: Hakkas, Pengmin, and Their Neighbors,* ed. Tim Wright. Stanford, Calif.: Stanford University Press.

Lever-Tracy, Constance, David Ip, and Noel Tracy
1996a   *The Chinese Diaspora and Mainland China: An Emerging Economic Synergy.* New York: St. Martin's Press.
1996b   "Diaspora Capitalism and the Homeland:Australian Chinese Networks into China." *Diaspora* 5: 239–73.

Levine, Donald N.
1965   *Wax and Gold: Traditions and Innovations in Ethiopian Culture.* Chicago: University of Chicago Press.

Levy, Andre
1997   "To Morocco and Back: Tourism and Pilgrimage Among Moroccan-Born Israelis." In *Grasping Land: Space and Place in Contemporary Israeli Discourse and Experience,* ed. Eyal Ben-Ari and Yoram Bilu. Albany, N.Y.: SUNY Press.

Levy, Reynold
1999   Letter from the President of the Inernational Rescue Committee. June.

Lipson, Juliene G. and Patricia Omidian
1996   "Health and the Transnational Connection: Afghan Refugees in the United States." In *Selected Papers on Refugee Issues* 4, ed. Ann M. Rynearson and James Phillips. 2–17. Arlington, Va.: American Anthropological Association.

Liu, Xin
1997   "Space, Mobility and Flexibility: Chinese Villagers and Scholars Negotiatie Power at Home and Abroad." In *Ungrounded Empires: The Cultural Politics of Modern Chinese Transnationalism,* ed. Donald Nonini and Aihwa Ong. New York: Routledge.

Ljunggren, Borje
1997   *Vietnam: Reform and Transformation.* Stockholm: Center for Pacific Asia Studies.

Long, Lynellyn D.
1993   *Ban Vinai: The Refugee Camp.* New York: Columbia University Press
1997   "Refugee Women, Violence, and HIV." In *Sexual Cultures and Migration in the Era of AIDS,* ed. Gilbert Herdt. 87–106. Oxford: Clarendon Press.
2000   "Mobility in a Mobile World: A Social Policy Perspective." *Selected Papers on Refugee Issues* 7. Arlington, Va.: American Anthropological Association.

Lozada, Eriberto
2001   *God Aboveground: Catholicism and Transnationalism in a Chinese Village.* Stanford, Calif.: Stanford University Press.

Luize, Wilhelm and Richard Hopfner
1965   *Berlin ABC.* Berlin: Presse- und Informationsamtes des Landes Berlin.

Macek, Ivana
   2000   *War Within: Everyday Life in Sarajevo Under Siege.* Uppsala Studies in Cultural An-
             thropology 29. Uppsala: Acta Universitatis Upsaliensis.
Madamba, Vady
   1993   "On Friday Afternoon in Statue Square." *Diwaliwan* 1 (February): 56.
Makiesky-Barrow, Susan
   1976   "Class, Culture and Politics in a Barbadian Community." Ph.D. dissertation,
             Brandeis University.
Malengreau, Guy
   1949   *Vers un paysannat indigène.* Brussels: Georges van Campenhout.
Malkki, Liisa H.
   1990   "Context and Consciousness: Local Conditions for the Production of Histor-
             ical and National Thought Among Hutu Refugees in Tanzania." In *National-
             ist Ideologies and the Production of National Cultures,* ed. Richard Gabriel Fox.
             Washington, D.C.: American Anthropological Association.
   1992a   "National Geographic: The Rooting of Peoples and the Territorialization of
             National Identity Among Scholars and Refugees." *Cultural Anthropology* 7, 1:
             24–43.
   1995a   *Purity and Exile: Violence, Memory, and National Cosmology Among Hutu Refugees in
             Tanzania.* Chicago: University of Chicago Press.
   1995b   "Refugees and Exile: From 'Refugee Studies' to the National Order of
             Things." *Annual Review of Anthropology,* vol. 24, ed. William H. Durham, E.
             Valentine Daniel, and Bambi Schieffelin. 495–523. Palo Alto, Calif.: Annual
             Reviews.
   1997   "National Geographic: The Rooting of Peoples and the Territorialization of
             National Identity Among Scholars and Refugees." In *Culture, Power, Place: Ex-
             plorations in Critical Anthropology,* ed. Akhil Gupta and James Ferguson. 52–77.
             Durham, N.C.: Duke University Press.
Manguera, Joyce R.
   1996   "The Spell of the Year 1997." *Tinig Filipino,* March 22.
Manila Chronicle
   1997a   "HK Maids Divided on Handover." June 27, 1, 8.
   1997b   "FVR Confident RP-HK Ties Will Continue." June 30, 1, 8.
   1997c   "Kaibigan Poses Challenge to Gov't." July 3, 5.
Margold, Jane A.
   1995   "Narratives of Masculinity and Transnational Migration: FilipinoWorkers in
             the Middle East." In *Bewitching Women, Pious Men: Gender and Body Politics in
             Southeast Asia,* ed. Aihwa Ong and Michael Peletz. 274–98. Berkeley: Univer-
             sity of California Press.
Marshall, Don D.
   1982   "The History of Caribbean Migrations: The Case of the West Indies."
             Caribbean Review 11, 1: 6–9, 52.
Massey, Douglas S.
   1987   "Understanding Mexican Migration to the United States." *American Journal of
             Sociology* 92, 6: 1372–1403.
Massey, Douglas S., Rafael Alarcon, Jorge Durand, and Humberto Gonzàlez
   1987   *Return to Aztlan: The Social Process of International Migration from Western Mexico.*
             Berkeley: University of California Press.
Matsuoka, Atsuko and John Sorenson
   1999   "Eritrean Canadian Refugee Households as Sites of Gender Renegotiation."
             In *Engendering Forced Migration: Theory and Practice,* ed. Doreen Indra. 218–41.
             New York: Berghahn.

McCann, James C.
1990   "A Dura Revolution and Frontier Agriculture in Northwest Ethiopia, 1898–1920." *Journal of African History* 31: 121–34.
McClintock, Anne, Aamir Mufti, and Ella Shohat, eds.
1997   *Dangerous Liaisons: Gender, Nation, and Postcolonial Perspectives.* Minneapolis: University of Minnesota Press.
McSpadden, Lucia Ann
1987   "Ethiopian Refugee Resettlement in the Western United States: Social Context and Psychological Well-Being." *International Migration Review* 21, 3: 796–819.
1989   "Ethiopian Refugee Resettlement in the Western United States: Social Context and Psychological Well-Being." Ph.D. dissertation, University of Utah.
1991   "Cross-Cultural Understandings of Independence and Dependence: Conflict in the Resettlement of Single Ethiopian Males." *Refuge* 10, 4: 21–25.
1993   "Resettlement for Status Quo or Status Mobility: Ethiopian and Eritrean Refugees in the Western United States," In *Refugee Empowerment and Organizational Change: A Systems Perspective,* ed. Peter W. Van Arsdale. 63–81. Arlington, Va.: American Anthropological Association.
1999   "Negotiating Masculinity in the Reconstruction of Social Place: Eritrean and Ethiopian Refugees in the United States and Sweden." In *Engendering Forced Migration: Theory and Practice,* ed. Doreen Indra. 242–60. New York: Berghahn.
McSpadden, Lucia Ann and Helena Moussa
1994   "I Have a Name: The Gender Dynamics in Asylum and in Resettlement of Ethiopian and Eritrean Refugees in North America." *Journal of Refugee Studies* 6, 3: 203–25.
1996   " 'Returning Home?' The Decision-Making Processes of Eritrean Women and Men." In *Development and Diaspora: Gender and the Refugee Experience,* ed. Winona Giles, Helene Moussa, and Penny Van Esterik. Dundas, Ont.: Artemis Enterprises.
Mendoza, Maria Cristy D.
1996   "Farewell, Hong Kong." *Tinig Filipino,* February 26.
Mehreteab, Amanuel
1995   "The Anvil of Peace." *Eritrea Profile,* January 7, 5.
Migration News
1999a   "Hong Kong: Maids." 6, 1. January. <http://migration.ucdavis.edu>.
1999b   "Philipines: Celebrate Migrants." 6, 10. October. <http://migration.ucdavis.edu>.
Mintz, Sidney
1974   "The Rural Proletariat and the Problem of Rural Proletarian Consciousness." *Journal of Peasant Studies* 1: 291–325.
Montes, Segundo
1989   *Refugiados y repatriados: El Salvador y Honduras.* San Salvador: Departamento de Sociologia y Ciencias Politicas, Universidad Autonoma Jose Simon Canas.
Mooney, Brian C.
1997   "Lately, Irish Eyes Turning Homeward." *Boston Globe,* March 17.
Moore, Sally Falk
1994   "The Ethnography of the Present and the Analysis of the Process." In *Assessing Cultural Anthropology,* ed. Robert Borofsky. 362–75. New York: McGraw-Hill.
Mosse, George
1985   *German Jews Beyond Judaism.* Bloomington: Indiana University Press.
Moussa, Helene
1992   "Caught Between Two Worlds: Eritrean Women Refugees and Voluntary

Repatriation." Paper presented at the Development After Disaster Horn of Africa Conference, University of Manitoba, May 29–30.

1993   *Storm and Sanctuary: The Journey of Ethiopian and Eritrean Women Refugees.* Dundas, Ont.: Artemis Enterprises.

Mukherjee, Bharati
1989   *Jasmine.* New York: Fawcett Crest.

Mukherjee, Bharati and Clark Blaise
1995   *Days and Nights in Calcutta.* St. Paul, Minn.: Hungry Mind Press.

Mydans, Seth
2000   "Clinton in Vietnam: The Overview." *New York Times,* A1.

Nandy, Ashis
1995   *The Savage Freud and Other Essays on Possible and Retrievable Selves.* Princeton, N.J.: Princeton University Press.

Narayan, R. K.
1967   *The Vendor of Sweets.* New York: Penguin.

Newbury, David
1998   "Understanding Genocide." *African Studies Review* 41, 1 (April): 73–98.

Nonini, Donald and Aihwa Ong
1997a   eds. *Ungrounded Empires: The Cultural Politics of Modern Chinese Transnationalism.* New York: Routledge.
1997b   "Towards A Cultural Politics of Diaspora and Transtionalism." In *Ungrounded Empires: The Cultural Politics of Modern Chinese Transnationalism,* ed. Donald Nonini and Aihwa Ong. New York: Routledge.

Olwig, Karen Fog
1998   "Contested Homes: Home-Making and the Making of Anthropology." In *Migrants of Identity: Perceptions of Home in a World of Movement,* ed. Nigel Rapport and Andrew Dawson, 225–36. New York: Berg.

Olwig, Karen Fog and Ninna Nyberg Sørensen
2002   "Mobile Livelihoods: Making a Living in the World." In *Work and Migration: Life and Livelihoods in a Globalizing World,* ed. Ninna Nyberg Sørensen and Karen Fog Olwig. New York: Routledge.

Ondaatje, Michael
1982   *Running in the Family.* New York: Vintage Books.

O'Neill, Marnie
1993   "Club Bans Maids." *Hong Kong Standard,* April 8.

Ong, Aihwa
1993   "On the Edge of Empires: Flexible Citizenship Among Chinese in Diaspora." *Positions* 1, 3: 745–78.
1999   *Flexible Citizenship: The Cultural Logics of Transnationality.* Durham, N.C.: Duke University Press.

Ostow, Robin
1989   *Jews in Contemporary East Germany: The Children of Moses in the Land of Marx.* New York: St. Martin's Press.
1990   "The Shaping of Jewish Identity in the German Democratic Republic, 1949–1989." *Critical Sociology* 17, 3: 47–59.

Oxfeld, Ellen
1993   *Blood, Sweat, and Mahjong: Family and Enterprise in an Overseas Chinese Community.* Ithaca, N.Y.: Cornell University Press.

Pacheco, Gilda
1989   *Nicaraguan Refugees in Costa Rica: Adjustment to Camp Life.* Washington, D.C.: Center for Immigration Policy and Refugee Assistance, Georgetown University.

Paine, Suzanne
1974   *Exporting Workers: The Turkish Case.* London: Cambridge University Press.
Parker, Kenneth
1993   "Home Is Where the Heart . . . Lies." *Transition* 59: 65–77.
Pastor, Robert A., ed.
1985   *Migration and Development in the Caribbean: The Unexplored Connection.* Boulder, Colo.: Westview Press.
Paterniti, Michael
1997   "Saigon: The Sequel." *New York Times Magazine,* January 12, 22ff.
Patterson, Sheila
1965   *Dark Strangers: A Study of West Indians in London.* Harmondsworth: Penguin.
1969   *Immigration and Race Relations in Britain, 1960–1967.* London: Oxford University Press.
Peach, Ceri
1968   *West Indian Migration to Britain: A Social Geography.* London: Oxford University Press.
Peck, Abraham J.
1991   "Zero Hour and the Development of Jewish Life In Germany After 1945." In *A Pariah People?* New York: American Jewish Archives.
Phillips, James
1994a   "Central American Refugees as Agents of Social Change." Paper presented at the Annual Meeting of the Society for Applied Anthropology, Cancun, Mexico.
1994b   "Nicaragua's Peasants and the Search for Peace." *Human Peace* (International Union of Anthropological and Ethnological Sciences) 10, 2 (Winter): 11–16.
1994c   "Salvadorans and Nicaraguans in Honduras: A Comparative Analysis of Community-Building, Repatriation, and the Formation of Refugee Identity." In *Selected Papers on Refugee Issues,* vol. 3, ed. Amy Zaharlick and Jeffrey Mac-Donald, 98–118. Arlington, Va.: American Anthropological Association.
1998   "Anthropology and Forcibly Displaced Peoples: A Critical Review." Paper presented at the Fourteenth International Congress of Anthropological and Ethnological Sciences, Williamsburg, Virginia.
Philpott, Stuart B.
1973   *West Indian Migration: The Montserrat Case.* New York: Humanities Press.
Pilkington, Hilary and Moya Flynn
1999   "From 'Refugee' to 'Repatriate': Russian Repatriation Discourse in the Making." In *The End of the Refugee Cycle? Refugee Repatriation and Reconstruction,* ed. Richard Black and Khalid Koser. New York: Berghahn.
Piore, Michael
1979   *Birds of Passage: Migrant Labor in Industrial Societies.* Cambridge: Cambridge University Press.
Planco, Nenita C.
1992   "No More Blue Christmases." In *Sa Pagyuko Ng Kawayan: Short Stories,* ed. Linda R. Layosa and Laura P. Luminarias. 81–87. Hong Kong: Tinig Filipino.
Pool, David
1997   *Eritrea: Towards Unity in Diversity.* London: Minority Rights Group International.
Portes, Alejandro and Rubén G. Rumbaut
1990   *Immigrant America: A Portrait.* Berkeley: University of California Press.
Povrzanovic, Maja
1998   "Practice and Discourse About Practice: Returning Home to the Croatian Danube Basin. *Anthropology of East Europe Review* 16, 1: 69–75.

Quesada Aldana, Sergio
　1998　　"The Socio-Cultural Impact of Dam Building in Mexico." Paper presented at
　　　　　the Fourteenth International Congress of Anthropological and Ethnological
　　　　　Sciences, Williamsburg, Virginia.
Rafael, Vicente
　1997　　"'Your Grief Is Our Gossip': Overseas Filipinos and Other Spectral Pres-
　　　　　ences." *Public Culture* 9: 267–91.
Ragus, Evangeline C.
　1992　　"My Beloved Home." In *Sa Pagyuko Ng Kawayan: Poems,* ed. Linda R. Layosa
　　　　　and Laura P. Luminarias. 57–58. Hong Kong: Tinig Filipino.
Ramírez Boza, Mario A.
　1989　　*Refugee Policy Changes: The Case of Nicaraguans in Costa Rica.* Washington, D.C.:
　　　　　Center for Immigration Policy and Refugee Assistance, Georgetown University.
Rapport, Nigel and Andrew Dawson
　1998a　　"Home and Movement: A Polemic." In *Migrants of Identity: Perceptions of Home
　　　　　in a World of Movement,* ed. Nigel Rapport and Andrew Dawson. New York:
　　　　　Berg.
　1998b　　"The Topic and the Book." In *Migrants of Identity: Perceptions of Home in a World
　　　　　of Movement,* ed. Nigel Rapport and Andrew Dawson.
Ray, Kakoli
　2000　　"Repatriation and De-territorialization: Meskhetian Turks' Conception of
　　　　　Home." *Journal of Refugee Studies* 13, 4: 391–414. New York: Berg.
Rex, John and Sally Tomlinson
　1979　　*Colonial Immigrants in a British City: A Class Analysis.* London: Routledge and
　　　　　Kegan Paul.
Rhoades, Robert Edward
　1978　　"Intra-European Return Migration and Rural Development: Lessons from
　　　　　the Spanish Case." *Human Organization* 37, 2: 136–47.
Richardson, Bonham C.
　1983　　*Caribbean Migrants: Environment and Human Survival on St. Kitts and Nevis.*
　　　　　Knoxville: University of Tennessee Press.
　1985　　*Panama Money in Barbados, 1900–1920.* Knoxville: University of Tennessee
　　　　　Press.
Richarz, Monika
　1988　　"Juden in der BRD und DDR seit 1945." In *Judisches Leben in Deutschland seit
　　　　　1945,* ed. Micha Brumlik, Doron Kiesel, Cilly Kugelmann, and Julius
　　　　　Schoeps. Frankfurt am Main: Athenaum.
Rodman, Margaret C.
　1992　　"Empowering Place: Multilocality and Multivocality." *American Anthropologist*
　　　　　94, 3:640–56.
Rouse, Roger
　1991　　"Mexican Migration and the Social Space of Postmodernism." *Diaspora* 1, 11:
　　　　　8–23.
Rubenstein, Hymie
　1983　　"Remittances and Rural Underdevelopment in the English-Speaking
　　　　　Caribbean." *Human Organization* 42, 4: 295–306.
　1986　　*Coping with Poverty: Adaptive Strategies in a Caribbean Village.* Boulder, Colo.: West-
　　　　　view Press.
Rubinstein, Danny
　1991　　*The People of Nowhere: The Palestinian Vision of Home.* New York: Random
　　　　　House.

Rushdie, Salman
1991   *Imaginary Homelands: Essays and Criticism 1981–1991.* London: Granta Books.
Safran, William
1991   "Diasporas in Modern Societies: Myths of Homeland and Return." *Diaspora* 1, 1: 83–99.
Said, Edward
1987   "Reflections on Exile." *Granta* 13 (Autumn): 157–72.
1992   "Reflections on Exile." In *Out There: Marginalization and Contemporary Cultures,* ed. Russell Ferguson et al. Cambridge, Mass.: MIT Press.
1994   "Return to Palestine-Israel." In *The Politics of Dispossession: The Struggle for Palestinian Self-Determination,* ed. Edward Said. New York: Pantheon.
1998   "The Treason of the Intellectuals." *Al-Ahram Weekly* 435, June 24–30.
1999   *Out of Place: A Memoir.* New York: Knopf.
Saloutos, Teodor
1956   *They Remember America: The Story of the Repatriated Greek Americans.* Berkeley: University of California Press.
Scharlin, Craig and Lilia V. Villenueva
1992   *Philip Vera Cruz: A Personal History of Filipino Immigrants and the Farmworkers Movement.* Los Angeles: UCLA Labor Center, Institute of Industrial Relations and UCLA Asian American Studies Center.
Schiller, Nina Glick, Linda Basch, and Christina Blanc-Szanton, eds.
1992   *Towards a Transnational Perspective on Migration: Race, Class, Ethnicity, and Nationalism Reconsidered.* Annals of the New York Academy of Sciences 645. New York: New York Academy of Sciences.
Schmitt, Carl
1976   *The Concept of the Political.* Trans. George Schwab. New Brunswick, N.J.: Rutgers University Press.
Schwartz, Jonathan M., ed.
1998   *Et midlertidigt liv: Bosniske flygtninge i de nordiske lande (A Temporary Life: Bosnian Refugees in the Nordic Countries).* Copenhagen: Nordic Council of Ministers.
Sepulveda, Danielle C.
1995   "Challenging the Assumptions of Repatriation." *Courier* 150: 83–85.
Serematakis, C. Nadia
1996   *The Senses Still: Perception and Memory as Material Culture in Modernity.* Chicago: University of Chicago Press.
Shami, Seteney
1996   "Transnationalism and Refugee Studies: Rethinking Forced Migration and Identity in the Middle East." *Journal of Refugee Studies* 9, 1: 3–26.
Shank, Robert
1994   "Returnee Agricultural Crop and Land Assessment." Report for UN Emergencies Unit for Ethiopia, Addis Ababa.
Shipler, David K.
1997   "Robert McNamera and the Ghosts of Vietnam." *New York Times Magazine,* August 10, 30ff.
Siegel, James T.
1969   *The Rope of God.* Berkeley: University of California Press.
Sills, Stephen
2000/   "Return Migration." <www.public.asu.edu/liulang/return%20migration
2001   .htm>.
Simon, David and Rosemary Preston
1992   "Return to the Promised Land: The Repatriation and Resettlement of Namibian Refugees, 1989–1990." In *Geography and Refugees: Patterns and*

Processes of Change, ed. Richard Black and Vaughn Robinson. 47–63. London: Belhaven Press.

Skeldon, Ronald
1995 "The Last Half Century of Chinese Overseas (1945–1994): Comparative Perspectives." *International Migration Review* 9, 2 (Summer): 576–79.
1997 *Migration and Development: A Global Perspective.* Longman: Harlow.

Slyomovics, Susan
1998 *The Object of Memory: Arab and Jew Narrate the Palestinian Village.* Philadelphia: University of Pennsylvania Press.

Smith, Graham
1999 "Transnational Politics and the Politics of the Russian Diaspora." *Ethnic and Racial Studies* 22, 3: 500–523.

Smith, Michael Peter
1994 "Can You Imagine? Transnational Migration and the Globalization of Grassroots Politics." *Social Text* 39: 15–33.

Sontag, Susan
1989 *On Photography.* New York: Anchor Books.

South China Morning Post
1995 "Illegal Maids 'Threat'." October 2, 5.
1996 "Cardinal Sin Praises Honesty of Filipino Workers." April 8.

Stack, Carol
1996 *Call to Home: African Americans Reclaim the Rural South.* New York: Basic Books.

Stafford, Charles
2000 *Separation and Reunion in Modern China.* Cambridge: Cambridge University Press.

Stalker, Peter
2001 *The No-Nonsense guide to International Migration.* London: Verso.

Stefansson, Anders H.
1997 "Repatrieringens nostalgi: Forestillinger om hjem, hjemland og tilbagevenden blandt bosniske flygtninge i Danmark" ("The Nostalgia of Repatriation: Imaginations of Home, Homeland and Return among Bosnian Refugees in Denmark" (Nordic Comparative Studies on the Reception of Refugees from a Repatriation Perspective). MA thesis, Institute of Anthropology, University of Copenhagen.
2000 "Det fremmede hjem: Bosniske flygtninges illusioner om hjemlandet" ("The Strange Home: Bosnian Refugees' Illusions About the Homeland." *Tidsskriftet Antropologi* 41: 47–61.

Stepputat, Finn
1993 "National Conflict and Repatriation: An Analysis of Relief, Power, and Reconciliation." CDR Project Proposal 93.4. Copenhagen: Centre for Development Research. October.
1994 "Repatriation and the Politics of Space: The Mayan Diaspora and Return Movement." *Journal of Refugee Studies* 7, 2/3: 175–85.
1999 "Repatriation and Everyday Forms of State Formation in Guatemala." In *The End of the Refugee Cycle? Refugee Repatriation and Reconstruction,* ed. Richard Black and Khalid Koser. 210–26. New York: Berghahn Books.

Stewart, Edward C. and Milton J. Bennett
1991 *American Cultural Patterns: A Cross-Cultural Perspective.* Yarmouth, Maine: Intercultural Press.

Stolcke, Verena
1995 "Talking Culture: New Boundaries, New Rhetorics of Exclusion in Europe." *Current Anthropology* 36, 1: 1–24.

Stoeltje, Beverly
    1996   "The Snake Charmer Queen: Ritual, Competition, and Signification in American Festival." In *Beauty Queens on the Global Stage: Gender, Contrasts, and Power*, ed. Colleen Ballerino, Richard Wilk Cohen, and Beverly Stoeltje. 13–30. New York: Routledge.

Sutton, Constance R.
    1987   "The Caribbeanization of New York." In *Caribbean Life in New York City: Sociocultural Dimensions*, ed. Constance R. Sutton and Elsa M. Chaney. New York: Center for Migration Studies.

Sutton, Constance R. and Susan Makiesky-Barrow
    1975   "Migration and West Indian Racial and Political Consciousness." In *Migration and Development: Implications for Ethnic Identity and Political Conflict*, ed. Helen I. Safa and Brian M. Du Toit. 113–44. The Hague: Mouton.

Tadiar, Neferti Xina X
    1997   "Domestic Bodies of the Philippines." *Sojourn* 12, 2: 153–91.

Taylor, Clark
    1999   *Return of Guatemala's Refugees: Reweaving the Torn*. Philadelphia: Temple University Press.

Tebeje, Ainalem
    1989   *Cultural Interaction of Canadian and Ethiopian Newcomers in Canada*. Ottawa: Employment and Immigration Canada.

Thomas-Hope, E.
    1985   "Return Migration and Implications for Caribbean Development." In *Migration and Development in the Caribbean: The Unexplored Connection*, ed. Robert A. Pastor. 157–73. Boulder, Colo.: Westview Press.
    1986   "Transients and Settlers: Varieties of Caribbean Migrants and the Socio-Economic Implications of Their Return." *International Migration* 24: 559–70.

Tinig Filipino
    1995   "Are You Preparing for Your Future?" March: 36.

Tollefson, James W.
    1989   *Alien Winds: The Reeducation of America's Indochinese Refugees*. New York: Praeger.

Torrefranca, Maria Sheila D.
    1992   "The Great Divide." In *Sa Pagyuko Ng Kawayan: Short Stories*, ed. Linda R. Layosa and Laura P. Luminarias. 31–40. Hong Kong: Tinig Filipino.

Tran, Thanh Van
    1987   "Ethnic Community and Supports and Psychological Well-Being of Vietnamese Refugees." *International Migration Review* 21, 3: 833–44.

Trinh, T. Minh-Ha
    1991   *When the Moon Waxes Red: Representation, Gender, and Cultural Politics*. New York: Routledge.

Tsuda, Takeyuki
    2000   "Migration and Alienation: Japanese-Brazilian Return Migrants and the Search for Homeland Abroad." Working Paper 24. Center for Comparative Immigration Studies, University of California-San Diego.

Turki, Fawaz
    1994   *Exile's Return: The Making of a Palestinian American*. New York: Free Press.

United Nations Development Programme (UNDP)
    2000   *Human Development Report, Bosnia and Herzegovina: Youth*. Sarajevo: Independent Bureau for Humanitarian Issues/UNDP.

United Nations High Commissioner on Refugees (UNHCR)
    1996   *Handbook—Voluntary Repatriation: International Protection*. Geneva: UNHCR.

1999   UNHCR and Refugees: UNHCR by Numbers. <www.unhcr.ch/unan-dref/numbers/table2.htm>.
2003   Statistics Package, February 2003.
United Nations Research Institute for Social Development (UNRISD)
1996   WSP Research Update 2. Geneva: War-Torn Societies Project. August.
U.S. Office of Refugee Resettlement
1993   *Statistics of Refugee Admissions.* Washington, D.C.: U.S. Government Printing Office.
Useem, Joh, Ruth Hill Useem, and John Donoghue
1963   "Men in the Middle of the Third Culture: The Roles of American and Non-Western People in Cross Cultural Administration." *Human Organization* 22, 3: 169–79.
Van Arsdale, Peter W., ed.
1991   *Refugee Empowerment and Organizational Change: A Systems Perspective.* Arlington, Va.: American Anthropological Association.
van de Port, Mattijs
1998   *Gypsies, Wars and Other Instances of the Wild: Civilisation and Its Discontents in a Serbian Town.* Amsterdam: Amsterdam University Press.
Van Hear, Nicholas
1994   "The Socio-Economic Impact of the Involuntary Mass Return to Yemen in 1990." *Journal of Refugee Studies* 7, 1: 18–38.
1998   *New Diasporas: The Mass Exodus, Dispersal and Regrouping of Migrant Communities.* London: UCL Press.
van Selm-Thorburn, Joanne
1998   *Refugee Protection in Europe: Lessons of the Yugoslav Crisis.* The Hague: Martinus Nijhoff.
Vasquez, Ana
1981   "Adolescents from the Southern Cone of Latin America in Exile: Some Psychological Problems." In *Mental Health and Exile: Papers Arising from a Seminar on Mental Health and Latin American Exiles.* 22–34. London: World University Press.
Verdery, Katherine
1998   "Transnationism, nationalism, Citizenship, and Property: Eastern Europe Since 1989." *American Ethnologist* 25, 2: 291–306.
Viet Nam News
1997   "Visiting Viet Kieu Granted Special Privileges in VN." September 23, 1ff.
Vlastos, Stephen
1990   "Revisionist Vietnam History." In *The Vietnam War and American Culture,* ed. John Carlos Rowe and Rick Berg. 52–74. New York: Columbia University Press.
Voutira, Effie
1991   "Pontic Greeks Today: Migrants or Refugees?" *Journal of Refugee Studies* 4, 4: 400–420.
Wan, Apple
1994   "'Quiet'First Day at Maid Centre." *Hong Kong Standard,* December 5.
Wang, Gungwu
1985   "South China Perspectives on Overseas Chinese." *Australian Journal of Chinese Affairs* 13 (January): 69–84.
1990   *China and the Overseas Chinese.* Singapore: Times Academic Press.
Warner, Daniel
1994   "Voluntary Repatriation and the Meaning of Return to Home: A Critique of Liberal Mathematics." *Journal of Refugee Studies* 7, 2/3: 160–74.

Watson, James L.
  1975   *Emigration and the Chinese Lineage: The Mans in Hong Kong and London.* Berkeley: University of California Press.
  1977   ed. *Between Two Cultures: Migrants and Minorities in Britain.* Oxford: Blackwell.
  1997   *Golden Arches East: McDonald's in East Asia.* Stanford, Calif.: Stanford University Press.
Western, John
  1992   *A Passage to England: Barbadian Londoners Speak of Home.* Minneapolis: Univesity of Minnesota Press.
White, Jenny
  1997   "Turks in the New Germany." *American Anthropologist* 99, 4: 754–69.
Whiteford, Michael B.
  1978   "Women, Migration and Social Change: A Colombian Case Study." *International Migration Review* 12, 2 (Summer): 236–47.
Wicker, Hans-Rudolf
  2000   "From Complex Culture to Cultural Complexity." In *Debating Cultural Hybridity: Multi-Cultural Identities and the Politics of Anti-Racism,* ed. Pnina Werbner and Tariq Modood. London: Zed Books.
Wiltshire, Rosina
  1992   "Implications of Transnational Migration for Nationalism: The Caribbean Example." In *Towards a Transnational Perspective on Migration: Race, Class, Ethnicity, and Nationalism Reconsidered,* ed. Nina Glick Schiller, Linda Basch, and Christina Blanc-Szanton. 175–87. Annals of the New York Academy of Sciences 645. New York: New York Academy of Sciences.
Wolf, Eric R.
  1969   *Peasant Wars of the Twentieth Century.* New York: Harper and Row.
Wolfe, Tom
  1940   *You Can't Go Home Again.* New York: Harper.
Wood, Charles H. and Terry L. McCoy
  1985   "Migration, Remittances, and Development: A Study of {West Indian} Caribbean Cane Cutters in Florida." *International Migration Review* 19, 2: 251–77.
Woon, Yuen-Fong
  1984   "An Emigrant Community in the Ssu-yi Area, Southeastern China, 1885–1949: A Study in Social Change." *Modern Asian Studies* 18, 2: 273–306.
  1989   "Social Change and Continuity in South China: Overseas Chinese and the Guan lineage of Kaiping County, 1949–87." *China Quarterly* 118 (June): 324–44.
Worrell, Delisle
  1987   *Small Island Economies: Structure and Performance in the English-Speaking Caribbean Since 1970.* New York: Praeger.
Wyman, Mark
  1993   *Round-Trip to America: The Immigrants Return to Europe, 1880–1930.* Ithaca, N.Y.: Cornell University Press.
Yahil, Chaim
  1971   "Berlin: Contemporary Period." In *Encyclopedia Judaica,* vol. 4. New York: Macmillan.
Yan, Yunxiang
  1996   *The Flow of Gifts: Reciprocity and Social Networks in a Chinese Village.* Stanford, Calif.: Stanford University Press.
  1998   "The Culture of *Guanxi* in a North China Village." *China Journal* 35: 1–26.

Yang, Mayfair
  1994   *Gifts, Favors, and Banquets: The Art of Social Relationships in China.* Ithaca, N.Y.: Cornell University Press.
  1999   "Mass Media and Transnational Subjectivity in Shanghai: Notes on (Re)Cosmopolitanism in a Chinese Metropolis." In *Ungrounded Empires: The Cultural Politics of Modern Chinese Transnationalism.* New York: Routledge.
Yuen, K. C.
  1996   "Racism Accusations Aimed at Wrong Quarter." *South China Morning Post,* March 26.
Yung, Betty Ma Shan Yee
  1996a   "Maids Do Not Need Protection." *South China Morning Post* letters column, March 23.
  1996b   "Falsely Accused Employers Are Sitting Ducks." *South China Morning Post* letters column, May 10.
Zarzosa, Helia Lopez
  1998   "Internal Exile, Exile and Return: A Gendered View." *Journal of Refugee Studies* 11, 2: 189–98.
Zetter, Roger
  1988   "Refugees, Repatriation, and Root Causes." *Journal of Refugee Studies* 1, 2: 99–106.
  1994   "The Greek-Cypriot Refugees: Perceptions of Return Under Conditions of Protracted Exile." *International Migration Review* 28, 2: 307–22.
  1999   "Reconceptualizing the Myth of Return: Continuity and Transition Amongst the Greek-Cypriot Refugees of 1974." *Journal of Refugee Studies* 12, 1: 1–22.
Zimmerman, Rachel
  1997   "Chinese Village Swells with Pride as Washington Governor Seeks His Roots on a Pilgrimage." *New York Times,* October 12, A1.

Contributors

John Borneman, Professor of Anthropology at Princeton University, has conducted fieldwork in Germany and Central Europe and written widely on kinship, sexuality, nationality, and political form. Currently, he is engaged in research in Lebanon and Syria. His recent publications include *Settling Accounts: Violence, Justice, and Accountability in Postsocialist States* and *Death of the Father: An Anthropology of the End in Political Authority.* Researching the returns of German Jews allowed Borneman to examine the intricacies of recreating a national identity that had been badly damaged.

Nicole Constable, Professor of Anthropology and Research Professor at the University Center of International Studies at the University of Pittsburgh, has conducted research on Hakka Chinese identity, Filipina overseas domestic workers, and correspondence marriages of Filipinas and Chinese women with American men. She is author of *Christian Souls and Chinese Spirits, Maid to Order in Hong Kong,* and *Romance on a Global Stage.* Constable undertook the present study to understand why so many of the Hong Kong Filipina domestic workers expressed ambivalence about returning home.

George Gmelch, Professor of Anthropology at Union College, has done extensive research in Ireland, England, Alaska, and the Caribbean as well as brief studies in Japan and Austria. Some of his publications are *The Irish Tinkers, Double Passage: Caribbean Migrants Abroad and Back Home, The Parish Behind God's Back* (with Sharon Gmelch), *In the Ballpark: The Working Lives of Baseball People,* and *Inside Pitch: Life in Professional Baseball.* Gmelch's long-term interest in returns initially began in Ireland where he was intrigued by the stories people told of what it was like to come home after spending many years abroad.

Laura Hammond, who teaches in the Department of International Development, Community and Environment at Clark University, lived in the Horn of Africa in 1993–2000. She has conducted research in Ethiopia, Eritrea, and Somalia/Somaliland on forced migration, food security, and conflict. She first began studying returns when the war ended and the refugees started coming home. She continues to focus on return movements throughout the Horn of Africa.

John M. Janzen, Professor of Anthropology and Director of the African Studies Center at the University of Kansas, Lawrence, has conducted research on African and Western traditions of health and healing in sub-Saharan Africa. In recent years, he has extended this research to investigate African healing traditions in war and social displacement. His recent publications are: *Do I Still Have a Life? Voices from the Aftermath of War in Rwanda and Burundi*, coauthored with Reinhild Kauenhoven Janzen, and *The Social Fabric of Health: An Introduction to Medical Anthropology*. Research and relief work in the African Great Lakes region in 1994–95 brought Janzen face-to-face with refugees from Rwanda, Burundi, and Congo, some of whom sought permanent exile and others who succeeded in returning home.

Lynellyn D. Long was Chief of Mission for the International Organization for Migration in Bosnia-Herzegovina (2000–2002) and the Population Council's Country Representative in Hanoi, Vietnam (1996–2000). She has conducted refugee and migration studies in Thailand, Vietnam, Sudan, Malawi, Kenya, Macedonia, and Bosnia-Herzegovina and recently completed research and programs to address forced labor migration and trafficking through Central and Eastern Europe. Her books include *Ban Vinai: The Refugee Camp* and *Women's Experiences with HIV/AIDS: An International Perspective* (edited with Maxine Ankrah). After living many years outside the United States, she was interested in knowing how other people imagined home, why they chose to return, and how they fared.

Jane A. Margold teaches in the Anthropology Department at Sonoma State University, and has conducted research on migration, especially forms of forced or coerced migration, such as human trafficking. As one of the founding members of the Bay Area Anti-Trafficking Task Force, she works as an activist to end forced labor and sexual trafficking practices. She has published extensively on labor, migration, the Philippines and Hong Kong in *Urban Anthropology, Critique of Anthropology, Journal of Historical Sociology*, and *Bulletin of Concerned Asian Scholars*. In her studies of Filipino migrations, Margold observed that migrants of every era have gone home, whether on the physical or imaginary plane, and given the centrality of the image of return, she welcomed the opportunity to examine this phenomena among Hong Kong bound migrants.

Lucia Ann McSpadden, Senior Research Fellow of the Life and Peace Institute, carried out fieldwork in the Horn of Africa on the repatriation of Eritrean refugees and longitudinal research on the psychological and economic status of resettled Ethiopian and Eritrean refugees in North America. Her current research is on the roles nongovernmental organizations play in refugee repatriation. Her numerous publications include books and articles on refugees, repatriation, women and violence, and peace building and reconciliation. She is also a Fellow of the American Anthropological Association and Society of Applied Anthropology. She observed that the issue of whether of not to return was a consistent concern of Eritrean refugees shaping their idea of their future, no matter where they were in their overall journey.

Ellen Oxfeld, Professor of Anthropology at Middlebury College, has conducted fieldwork among Hakka Chinese in Calcutta, India, Mei Xian, China, and Toronto, Canada. She has written on family strategies, ethnic identity, economic culture, and notions of personhood in the Chinese diaspora, and on ritual, political authority, moral systems, and kinship in contemporary rural China. She is the author of *Blood, Sweat, and Mahjong: Family and Enterprise in an Overseas Chinese Community.* She is presently writing an ethnography of moral and social conflicts in a Chinese village. For her, seeing literally the same people she had known in Toronto and Calcutta from the different vantage point of their village relatives in China inspired her to study their return.

James Phillips, Adjunct Professor of Anthropology at Southern Oregon University, has done research in peasant and plantation communities, urban neighborhoods and shantytowns, and refugee resettlements in Latin America and the Caribbean for thirty years. As a professor at several universities, researcher, and policy analyst for private international development and nongovernmental organizations, he has focused on issues related to refugees, development, and social and political change in (post)colonial societies. He has recently completed *A Short History of Tolerance in the State of Jefferson* and is currently working on a book about society and culture in the Caribbean. He was impressed that Salvadoran and Nicaraguan refugees in Honduras returned home under very different conditions and processes but in both cases became change agents in their own societies.

Anders H. Stefansson, Research Fellow at the Institute of Anthropology, University of Copenhagen, has conducted research among Bosnian refugees in Denmark and on processes of reconstruction and refugee reintegration in postwar Sarajevo. His forthcoming dissertation is entitled, " 'Under My Own Sky?' The Cultural Dynamics of Refugee Return and Reintegration in Post-War Sarajevo." His own interest in refugee (re)integration grew out of an earlier study he conducted of how Bosnian refugees in Denmark imagined home and return.

Index

abuse: of Ethiopian refugees, 190; of Filipina workers, 54; NGOs against, 54, 55, 56; of women, 54, 113, 190

ACNUR (Alto Comisionado de las Naciones Unidas para los refugiados; = UNHCR), 153; Nicaraguan refugee statistics by, 159–60, 162, 163; relief provided by, 165–66; repatriation involvement of, 160, 162, 163, 164–65. *See also* UNHCR

Ada Bai: farming in, 192–98; housing in, 193–94, 202; meaning of, 193; population increase in, 198; religion in, 201, 234n19; resettlement in, 188, 192–96; stabilization of, 203; war effects on, 189, 203–4. *See also* Ethiopia

ADFLC (Alliance of Democratic Forces for the Liberation of Congo-Zaire), 20, 31

Advocate, 206

Africa. *See* Eritrea; Ethiopia; Rwanda; Zaire

Aguilar, Filomeno, 50–51, 228n12

alienation: Bosnian, 178–80, 182–83; research, 172–73, 232n2; Viet Kieu, 77–78, 86. *See also* racism

Alliance of Democratic Forces for the Liberation of Congo-Zaire. *See* ADFLC

Amah Drama, 55–56

Amerasians, 71

American Jewish Committee, 148

amnesia, structural or genealogical, 50

Anagnost, Ann, 99

ancestors, Chinese connection to, 98–99

Anonas, Michaela V., 106

Aquino, Corazon, 61

Arellano, Teddy P., 107

Asian Currency Crisis, 66, 83

assimilation: Filipina, 46–47; German Jewish, 140, 146; Viet Kieu, 65, 71, 72, 87–89

autobiographies: Filipina, 49, 51–52, 57–62, 109–21; German Jewish, 127–29; Rwandan, 19–33; Viet Kieu, 69–70

Baker, Abu, 39

ban-mui ("Philippine girl"), 53, 55

Banyamulenge fighters, 20, 30

Barbados, 206–23; adaptation to, 213–17; Canada resettlement from, 207; cultural differences in, 217–19; descendants of, 208; economy of, 211–12, 216, 219–23, 234n10; education of, 212, 220; emigration from, history of, 207–8; employment for migrants from, 206, 209, 212, 215, 220–21, 234n17; expectations of migrants from, 211, 213–14; expectations of villagers from, 217–19; family relationships for migrants from, 209–10; geography of, 208; housing in, 222, 235n22; identity of, 215–16; kinship re-establishment in, 213–14; language adjustments for, 218; modernization of, 219–23; Panama resettlement from, 207–8, 221–22; population growth in, 206, 207; privacy in, 213–14; racism against, 210–11, 221, 234n8; reasons for leaving, 208–9; repatriation to, 211–13; social status of emigrants from, 213–15, 217–19, 221; United Kingdom resettlement from, 207, 208–9; United States resettlement from, 206, 234n8; women from, 215, 234n18

Barth, Fredrik, 89

Bedana, Alejandro, 158

Bekele, Abebe, 233n6

Benario, Ruth, 130–31, 134–35, 140–41

Bennett, Milton, 46

Berger, Goetz, 131–32, 136, 142–43

Berlin Wall, fall of, 171

Bernardo, Virginia, 111
BiH. *See* Bosnia-Herzegovina
Bodemann, Y. Michal, 139
border crossings, 152–53, 157–58
Borjas, George, 2
Borneman, John, 231
Bosnia-Herzegovina (BiH): alienation in, 178–80, 182–83; cultural differences in, 180–82; deaths in, 178; diaspora, 179, 233n9; economy of, 176–78; emotions of, 178–80, 182–83; employment in, 176–77; Federation, 175; financing renovation of, 176; government of, 174–75; independence of, 174–75; provisional return to, 9; racism in, 176–77; refugees in Denmark, 232nn3, 6; refugees in Germany, 179, 183; refugees in Norway, 184; repatriation to, 174–75; Republika Srpska, 175, 177; return to, 1–2, 170–71, 176–78, 182–84; returnees versus stayees of, 178–80, 232n7; Socialist Republic, 176; volunteers versus expellees in, 175; war in, 174–75, 176, 178
Bosnjak (Bosnian Muslim): cultural differences of, 180–81; resettlement of, 177
Bovell, Ann, 215
Bovell, Norman, 209, 210
Bratsberg, Bernt, 2
Bruce, John, 196
Bugingo, refugee testimony of, 7, 19–25
Burundi, war in, 20

Campbell, Roy, 211, 214
Canada: Barbadian resettlement to, 207; educational opportunities in, 226–27n2; Eritrean refugees in, 34, 226–27nn1–3
career opportunities. *See* employment
Caribbean. *See* Barbados
Carsten, Janet, 50, 62
Central America. *See* Honduras; Nicaragua
Chambers, Iain, 170
children, 53, 115, 120–21, 133, 209–10, 218; education of, 40–41, 77, 212, 228n8; separation from, 115, 209–10, 215
China: ancestral ties to, 98–99; communism in, 93–94, 100; diaspora terms in, 92, 93; economic change in, 91, 99; emotional ties to, 95; employment in, 91, 99; ethnographies of, 91–92; expectations of villagers in, 92, 95–96, 98–103; family responsibilities in, 95–97, 98–101, 103; Filipinas in Hong Kong versus people of, 105–6; financing renovation of, 95; Hong Kong versus, 92–93; migration to and from, 93–94;

moral dilemmas of return visits to, 90–103; political change in, 91, 93–94; returnees as foreigners, 101–2; returnees as kin, 97–101; rituals of, 97, 230n4; social status in, 91, 99–100, 102. *See also* Hong Kong
Chow, Rey, 105
Cichon, Donald J., 226n2
circular migration, 2, 153
citizenship: Eritrean refugee, 45–46; German Jewish, 130, 134, 137, 138–39, 143; marriage for, 133–34; Viet Kieu, change in, 83–86, 88–89
civil war: in Ethiopia, 204; in Nicaragua, 150, 151, 152, 156–57, 158–59
Clapham, Christopher, 233n8
class. *See* social status
clear cutting, 194–96, 198
Clifford, James, 104, 109
Cold War: migration after, 148
Commission for Refugees (COR), Sudan, 190–91
Commonwealth Immigration Act, 207
communication: blocked, 160; cultural differences in, 82; homeland, 49; repatriation, 29–30
communism: in China, 93–94, 100; in Germany, 127–49; in Nicaragua, 158; in Vietnam, 74, 87
CONARE. *See* Honduran National Refugee Commission
concentration camps: death in, 136; escape from, 132; unification from, 147–48
Congo. *See* Zaire
Congo war, 19–20, 226n4
Congolese National Army, RPF versus, 226n5
Constable, Nicole, 53, 55, 60
contra (counterrevolution). *See* Nicaraguan Resistance
COR. *See* Commission for Refugees
Costa Rica, refugee camps in, 232n4
cotton production, 193
Court, Margaret, 29
Cramer, Ernst, 131–32, 135, 141–42
Croatia, 1–2, 7, 9
cultural differences: in Barbados, 217–19; in BiH, 180–82; in communication, 82; in marriages, 110; peasants roles in mending, 167. *See also* "deculturation"
cultural fundamentalism, 171

Dalpasen, Cresencia, 111
Dayton Peace Agreement (DPA), 174, 175
deaths: of Bosnians, 178; of Ethiopians, 189–90;

of family upon return, 118–19; of German Jews, 128–29, 136; of Nicaraguans, 159, 162; sentencing, Organic Law for, 32, 226n9

"deculturation," 32, 110

Demos, John, 225n9

Deng Xiaoping, 100

Denmark, BiH refugees in, 232nn3, 6

depeasantization, 154–55, 168

the Derg, 191, 193

diaspora, 4; Bosnians, 179, 233n9; Chinese, terms for, 92, 93; complications of, 49–50; defined, 49, 225n6; Filipina, terms used by, 107; Jews, 225n6; literature, 5, 35; recording experiences of, 51–52

discrimination. See racism

Doi Moi (renovation), 11, 12, 69, 87

domestic workers. See Filipinas

DPA. See Dayton Peace Agreement

economy: of Barbados, 211–12, 216, 219–23, 234n10; of BiH, 176–78; of China, 91, 99; of Eritrea, 35; of Ethiopia, 203–4; farming effects on, 166–68; of Nicaragua, 158–59, 161, 166–68; return effects on, 3, 12, 14, 219–23; of Sarajevo, 176; of Vietnam, 67, 69–70, 81, 83, 87–88

education, 40–41, 77, 212, 228n8; of Barbadians, 212, 220,; of Eritreans, 8, 38–41, 226n2; of Filipinas, 53, 227n3; in homelands, 7; of men, 39–40, 227n3; of Sarajevans, 181–82; in United Kingdom, 212; of Viet Kieu, 74, 77–78; of women, 40–41, 227n2, 228n9

Edwards, Lucy, 231

Eisler, Hilde, 133–34, 136–37, 143–45

El Paraiso, refugee camps in, 160

El Salvador, refugees from, 153

"emotional-moral profiles," 25

emotions: of Bosnians, 178–80, 182–83; of Chinese, 95; of Viet Kieu, 75, 79, 80

employment: of Barbadians, 206, 209, 212, 215, 220–21, 234n17; in BiH, 176–77; in China, 91, 99; domestic, 50–51, 53–56, 228nn4–8; employer-employee relationships, 115–16; of Eritreans, 35, 36–38, 42–43; of Filipinas in Hong Kong, 50–51, 53–56, 104–5, 114, 228nn4–8; laws, 54; of men, 42–43, 207; in Nicaragua, 158; in Sudan, 191; in United Kingdom, 207; of Viet Kieu, 67–68, 70–71, 82–83, 85; of women, 43, 50, 53–56, 207, 215

Engelhardt, Manfred, 144

English fluency: of Filipinas, 53, 227n3; of Viet Kieu, 72, 76, 77, 229n5

environmental degradation, regulations against, 198

EPLF. See Eritrean People's Liberation Front

EPRDF. See Ethiopian People's Revolutionary Democratic Front

Eritrea: Canada migration from, 34, 226nn1–3; citizenship for refugees of, 45–46; divorce rate in, 45; economic context of return to, 35; education in, 38–41, 226n2, 228n8; employment for people of, 35, 36–38, 42–43; Ethiopian distinction from, 36, 226n1, 227n3; family responsibilities for people of, 41–42; feminism introduced to, 44; housing in, 35, 228n5; imagined return to, 7; independence of, 35; interview methods for people of, 48; landowners of, 42; liberation of, 35, 36–37, 203–4; political context of return to, 35; racism against people of, 36; reconstruction of, 35; refugees from, 34, 226nn1–3; repatriation to, 34–48; return to, determinants of, 38; social status of, 36–37, 39–40; to Sudan, 34; Sweden migration to, 34, 36, 226nn1–2; United States migration from, 34, 36, 226nn1–3

Eritrean People's Liberation Front (EPLF), 35, 43

Esquipulas Two peace accord, 164

Ethiopia: abuse of refugees from, 190; civil war in, 204; community leadership in, 198–200, 203–5; deaths of refugees from, 189–90; economy of, 203–4; environmental degradation in, regulations against, 198; Eritrean distinction from, 36, 226n1, 227n3; Eritrean liberation from, 35, 36–37, 203–4; farming in, 192–98; financing renovation of, 197; government of, 191–92, 195, 196–97; land allocation in, 196–200; land owning in, 192–201; land shortage in, 196–98; land voting in, 200–201; Marxism in, 191; military draft in, 204; politics in, 201–2; repatriation to, 191–92; return to, 187–205; sesame exports from, 193, 233n8; social construction of, 201–2; Sudan refuge from, 188–91; UNHCR aid for refugees from, 190, 197; war in, 35, 36–37, 203–4

Ethiopian People's Revolutionary Democratic Front (EPRDF), 191

ethnography: of China, 91–92; of Filipinas, 108–9; of return, 1–15

ex-FAR. See Rwandan Armed Forces

exiles: from Germany, 128–29; from Latin

exiles: (*continued*)
America, 46; from Philippines, 108–9; from Rwanda, 21–29
expectations: of Barbadian migrants, 211, 213–14, 217–19; from Chinese villagers, 92, 95–96, 98–103; of Viet Kieu, 69–70

family relationships: for Barbadians, 209–10; for Filipinas, 115, 118–19, 120, 121–22, 123; for Viet Kieu, 79–81, 84–85
family responsibilities: for Chinese, 95–97, 98–101, 103; for Eritreans, 41–42; for Filipinas, 50–51, 111, 118–19, 227n1; for Viet Kieu, 71. *See also* remittances
fan ke (foreign guests), 92, 101
FAR. *See* Rwandan Armed Forces
farming: in Ada Bai, 192–98; clearing land for, 194–96, 198; commercial, 197–98; community, 198–200; economy rebuilding on, 166–68; in Ethiopia, 192–98; globalization versus, 155, 156; *gudgele* system for, 195, 199; in Humera, 193, 196, 197–98, 233n7; in Nicaragua, 155, 156, 166–68; shortages of land for, 196–98
fascism: elimination of, 147–48. *See also* Nazis
Federal Republic of Germany (FRD), Jewish citizenship in, 130, 138–39
feminism, Eritreans and, 44. *See also* women
Filipinas: abuse of, 54; assimilation of, 46–47; autobiographies of, 49, 51–52, 57–62, 109–21; Chinese in Hong Kong versus, 105–6; diaspora terms of, 107; education of, 53, 227n3; employment of, 50–51, 53–56, 104–5, 114, 228nn4–8; English fluency of, 53, 227n3; ethnographies of, 108–9; exile of, 108–9; family relationships for, 115, 118–19, 120, 121–22, 123; family responsibilities for, 50–51, 111, 118–19, 227n1; homesickness among, 107, 117; in Hong Kong, 8, 49–62, 104–24; identity of, 46–47, 109–21; marriages, 110, 112–13; OCWs, 105–6, 123, 124; performance of, 57–59; racism against, 53, 56, 228n8; social status of, 56, 104–5, 123–24
financing: for BiH renovation, 176; for China renovation, 95; for Ethiopia renovation, 197; for repatriation, 43
France: evacuation of government, 74; Viet Kieu in, 69–70, 74, 81, 86
FRD. *See* Federal Republic of Germany

Galinski, Heinz, 139
Gaw, Kenneth, 55

GDR. *See* German Democratic Republic
Gemeinde (Jewish community), 137, 140
genders: imagined return among, 8–9; inequality of, 43–45. *See also* men; women
generation gaps: Viet Kieu, 80–81
genocide: in Germany, 128–29; in Rwanda, 21–27
German Democratic Republic (GDR), Jewish citizenship in, 130, 134, 137, 138–39, 143
German Jews: assimilation, 140, 146; autobiographies of, 127–29; citizenship of, 130, 134, 137, 138–39, 143; deaths of, 128–29; exile of, 128–29; housing for, 137–38; identity of, 127–30, 133, 140–45, 146–47, 231n1; political stances of, 129, 130, 133–34, 142, 148; racism against, 132–34; religious suppression of, 135, 138; repatriation of, 12, 127–49; return decisions of, 134–37; social status of, 131; in United States, 131–32
Germany: Allied division of, 137; Bosnian refugees in, 179, 183; communism in, 127–49; genocide in, 128–29; Hallstein Doctrine, 139; Israeli relations with, 147, 148; Marxism in, 142, 143, 231n1; migration from, 8, 10; Viet Kieu in, 76, 77, 85
gift-giving. *See* family responsibilities; financing; remittances
Gilman, Sander, 231n1
globalization: depeasantization caused by, 154, 155; farming versus, 155, 156; returns affected by, 3
"Go and See Visits," 9, 225nn7–8
Goddard, Richard, 222–23
Godley, Michael, 230n2
gongde (beneficent works), 95
Gorostiaga, Xabier, 166–67
government: of BiH, 174–75; of Eritrea, 43; of Ethiopia, 191–92, 195, 196–97; of France, Viet Kieu under, 74; of Honduras, 162–63; of Hong Kong, 53; of Israel, 3; of Nicaragua, 155–56, 158–59, 162–64, 231n2; repatriation viewed by, 162–63; state, 14, 231n2; tracking return by, 2. *See also* politics
Gozdziak, Elzbieta, 226n2
Greene, Graham, 67
Griffith, Esther, 214
Griffith, Valenza, 209, 221
Grosfoguel, Ramon, 154
Grover, Jane, 226–27n2
Guangdong Province. *See* China
Guatemala, repatriation to, 13

gudgele system (farming groups), 195, 199
Gulf War: repatriation during, 11
gungyahn (servant/worker), 53

Haiti, hearings for refugees, 151
haiwai qiaobao (overseas compatriots), 92
Hakka, 91, 230n1
Hallstein Doctrine, 139
Hammond, Laura, 12
Hanoi, Viet Kieu in, 67, 70
Hanoi Opera House restoration, 70
Hayslip, Le Ly, 69–70
Hinds, Eric, 206
Hitler, Adolf, 131, 132, 140, 141
Hiwot Mechanization Company, 194, 196, 233n16
Ho Trieu Tri, 70
Hoben, Allan, 196
Hollingsworth, 206
Holocaust, 147–48
The Holy Family (Marx), 231n1
home: image of, 32; imagined, 33
homecoming, 9–11, 172–74
homelands: communication with, 49; defamiliarization with, 49, 172; defined, 5; educational opportunities in, 7; meaning of, 106, 107–8; poem about, 107. *See also* kinship
homelessness, 173, 184–85
homesickness, among Filipinas, 107, 117
Honduran National Refugee Commission (CONARE), 160, 163
Honduras: communication control from, 160, 161; government of, 162–63; peace in, 163–64; refugee camps in, 7, 153, 157, 159–62; refugee repatriation from, 162–63; return from, 155–56, 163–64
Hong Kong: China versus, 92–93; Chinese versus Filipina workers in, 105–6; Employers of Overseas Domestic Helpers Association, 54; employment in, 50–51, 53–56, 104–5, 115, 228nn4–8; Filipinas in, 8, 49–62, 104–24; government, 53; labor laws in, 54; migration to, 52–56; Special Administrative Region, 52–53
housing: in Ada Bai, 193–94, 202, 233n10; in Barbados, 222, 235n22; in Eritrea, 35, 228n5; for German Jews, 137–38; new housing for returnees, 12
huaqiao (overseas Chinese), 92, 93, 96, 97–102
Humera, farming in, 193, 196, 197–98, 233n7
Hutu. *See* Rwanda

ICP. *See* International Communist Party
identity: of Barbadians, 215–16; of Filipinas,

46–47, 109–21; of German Jews, 127–30, 133, 140–45, 146–47, 231n1; mistaken, 81; of Nicaraguans, 157–58; of refugees, 46–47, 151–52; after repatriation, 172–74; of Viet Kieu, 72, 81, 87–89
IDPs. *See* internally displaced persons
ILO. *See* International Labor Organization
Imaginary Homelands (Rushdie), 108
immigrants: children of, 53, 115, 120–21, 133, 209–10, 218; refugees versus, 36; restriction on, 93, 207
Immigration and Naturalization Service (INS), 2
imprisonment. *See* concentration camps; refugee camps
INS. *See* Immigration and Naturalization Service
internally displaced persons (IDPs), 174–75, 180, 232n7
International Communist Party (ICP), 68
International Labor Organization (ILO), 227n3
International Organization for Migration (IOM), 225n8
interracial marriages, 7, 82, 84–85
Israel: German relations with, 147, 148; Jews in, 3, 9–10; Palestinians returning to, 10; political consequences of Palestinian return to, 225n5

Janzen, Reinhil Zauenhoven, 226n3
Jerusalem, return to, 10
Jews: diasporic, 225n6; Israeli, 3, 9–10. *See also* German Jews
Jewish Agency, 129

Katihabwa, Sabastien, 19, 32–33
Kearney, Michael, 219
Keyes, Charles, 228
Kibreab, Gaim, 197, 198
King, Russell L., 219, 225n10
kinship: Barbadian reestablishment of, 213–14; of Chinese villagers with returnees, 92, 97–101; "downward looking" system of, 50; photographs for, 49, 51–52, 57–62; Viet Kieu reestablishment of, 83–86
Klein, Albert, 136
Kondo, Dorinne, 114

land owning: by Eritreans, 42; by returned Ethiopians, 192–201, 233n11; by Nicaraguans, 167–68; in refugee camps, 190; by vote, 200–201; by women, 196
language adjustments: for Barbadians, 218; for Filipinas, 53, 227n3; for Viet Kieu, 72, 76, 77, 229n5

laws, labor, 54
Laws of Migration (Ravenstein), 225n3
Lenin, Vladimir, 143
Levinson, Nathan, 138
literature: diaspora, 5, 35; migration, 5–6, 109; transnationalist, 6, 172
Locke, Gary, 230n7
Long, Donald, 228
Long, Lynellyn, 230

MacNamara, Robert, 66–67
mahjeh (big sister), 54
Makiesky-Barrow, Susan, 221
Malkki, Liisa, 29, 46, 151, 187, 226n11
Mao Zedong, 91
marriage: abuse in, 113; for citizenship, 133–34; between classes, 90; cultural differences in, 110; Filipina, 110, 112–13; interracial, 7, 82, 84–85; transnational, 43–45, 110, 112–13, 209–10; Viet Kieu, 71, 84–85
Marx, Karl, 142, 143, 231n1
Marxism: in Ethiopia, 191; in Germany, 142, 143, 231n1
Matsuoka, Atsuko, 44, 228n9
Mazzini formula, 146
MCC. *See* Mennonite Central Committee
McSpadden, Lucia Ann, 48, 230
Mei County. *See* China
memoirs, 10
memorabilia of host country, 51, 58, 60
memories: of family in homeland, 92, 101; of Holocaust, 147–48; of host society, 60; of homeland, 1, 7, 108; of trauma, 8; of Vietnam, 72–75, 81, 88
men: education of, 39–40, 227n3; emigration of Chinese, 93–94; emigration of Filipino, 123; employment of, 42–43, 207; return viewed by, 212–13, 234n13
Meneses, Vida Luz, 150, 169
Mengistu, Haile Mariam, 191
Mennonite Central Committee (MCC), 226n3
Mexico: depeasantization in, 154; deportation to, 11; NAFTA plans for, 154; return to, 2
Meyer, Julius, 138
migration: from Barbados, 207–8; from China, 93–94; circular, 2, 153; after Cold War, 148; from Germany, 8, 10; to Hong Kong, 52–56; literature, 5–6, 109; from United States, 2–3; after World War II, 8, 127–49, 207
Migration News, 227n1
military draft: in Ethiopia, 204; in Nicaragua, 157, 159, 163

Mintz, Sidney, 154
Miskito Indians, 159, 160, 163
mobility, conceptualization of, 184–86
Mobutu. *See* Zaire
Montes, Segundo, 153
Moonshadow Pond, China. *See* China
Mosse, George, 148–49
Moussa, Helene, 36, 40, 44, 48, 228nn4, 12
muijai (little maid or younger sister), 53–54
multiculturalism. *See* cultural differences
Muslim. *See* Bosnjak (Bosnian Muslim)
"My Beloved Home" (poem), 107–8
"mytho-histories," 29

NAFTA (North American Free Trade Agreement), 154
natural disasters, in Nicaragua, 150, 151
Nazis, 132, 133, 135, 137, 146
New York Times, 66, 67
Newbury, David, 25
NGOs (nongovernmental organizations): labor abuse counteracted by, 54, 55, 56; refugee relief from, 190
Nicaragua: civil war in, 150, 151, 152, 156–57, 158–59; communism in, 158; deaths of refugees from, 159, 162; economy of, 158–59, 161, 166–68; employment in, 158; farming structure in, 155, 156, 166–68; government in, 155–56, 158–59, 162–64, 231n2; identity of people from, 157–58; imagined return to, 7; land owning in, 167–68; military draft in, 157, 159, 163; natural disasters in, 150, 151; peace in, 163–64, 167–68; politics in, 152, 155–56; reasons for leaving, class differences in, 158–59; refugees from, 150–53, 159–60, 231n1; repatriation to, 160–68; social status of people from, 14, 157–62; UNHCR relief for, 165–66. *See also* peasants; Somoza dictatorship
Nicaraguan Resistance: attack by, 158–59; demobilization of, 162, 164; formation of, 155; function of, 160, 161; peace agreement with, 164, 165; recruitment of, 157, 163; repatriation of, 164–66; training of, 160, 231n3; United States support for, 157–58, 160, 165, 231n3
nongovernmental organizations. *See* NGOs
North American Free Trade Agreement. *See* NAFTA
Norway, Bosnian refugees in, 184

OCWs. *See* Overseas Contract Workers
ODP. *See* Orderly Departure Program

Ogata, Sagako, 27, 29
Operation Wetback, 11
Orderly Departure Program (ODP), 68
"An Ordinary African Refugee" (Katihabwa), 32–33
orejas (spies), 160
Organic Law (1996), 32, 226n9
Organization of African Unity (OAU), 151
"The Other Shore: Chronicle of an Ordinary African Refugee" (Katihabwa), 19, 32
Overseas Contract Workers (OCWs), Filipina, 105–6, 123, 124
Oxfeld, Ellen, 228, 230

Pacheco, Gilda, 232n4
Palestinians, return to Israel, 10, 225n5
Panama, Barbadian emigration to, 207–8, 221–22
Parker, Kenneth, 108
Patek, Martin, 144
Peach, Ceri, 208–9
peasants, Nicaraguan: becoming refugees, 153–55; class differences between wealthy and, 157–62; cultural development by, 167; defined, 153; displacement of, 155–56, 158–59; economic development by, 166–68; repatriation viewed by, 161
Peck, Jeffrey, 128, 144–45, 231
Peterson, Pete, 67
Philippines. *See* Filipinas
photographs: for imagined return, 8; for kinship, 49, 51–52, 57–62
politics, 3, 225n5; of BiH, 174–75; of China, 91, 93–94; of Eritrea, 35, 43; of Ethiopia, 201–2; of Germanic Jews, 129, 130, 133–34, 142, 148; of Nicaragua, 152, 155–56; of religion, 201; of Sudan, 190–91; of Vietnam, 12, 68, 69–70, 83–84, 87–88
privacy, loss of, 213–14
proletarianization, 154, 156
property, 6. *See also* housing; land owning
Puerto Rico, return to, 2, 206

Qing dynasty, emigration laws of, 93
Quesada Aldana, Sergio, 154

racism: against Barbadians, 210–11, 221, 234n8; against Bosnians, 176–77; against Eritreans, 36; against Filipinas, 53, 56, 228n7; against German Jews, 132–34; against Viet Kieu, 79
RAF. *See* Rwandan Armed Forces
Rafael, Vicente L., 227n1

Ragus, Evangeline C., 107–8
Rahmato, Dessalegn, 196
Ramírez Boza, Mario A., 232n4
Rawayan River, Ethiopia, 193
Reagan Doctrine, Nicaraguan Resistance training under, 231–32n3
Red Cross, 165
refugee camps: in Costa Rica, 232n4; in El Paraiso, 160; in Honduras, 7, 153, 157, 159–62; in Serbia, 7; in Sudan, 189–91; in Tanzania, 8; in Zaire, 7, 19–20, 30–32
refugees: court hearings for, 151; departure by sea, 75; from El Salvador, 153; from Eritrea, 34, 226nn1–2; experience process of, 152; from Haiti, 151; identity of, 46–47, 151–52; immigrants versus, 36; from Nicaragua, 150–51, 159–60, 231n1; peasants becoming, 153–55; from Rwanda, 19–33; social status change of, 151–53; studies of, 6, 154; Viet Kieu, 75–77; from Yugoslavia, 171
Relief Society of Tigray. *See* REST
religion: conversion of, 77, 139; politics in, 201; support from, 77; suppression of, 135, 138, 143, 231n1; tolerance promoted through, 167; transnationalism in, 230n6
repatriation, 11–13; ACNUR attitude toward, 160, 162, 163; to Barbados, 211–13; to BiH, 174–75; communication, 29–30; defined, 153, 225n10; to Eritrea, 34–48; to Ethiopia, 191–92; financing for, 43; forced, 11–12; of German Jews, 12, 127–49; government attitudes toward, 162–63; to Guatemala, 13; Gulf War, 11; identity after, 172–74; to Nicaragua, 160–68; of Nicaraguan Resistance, 164–66; peasant attitudes toward, 161–62; research, 172–74, 187–88, 219; to Sarajevo, 12, 13, 170–86; social effects of, 12–13, 24–25, 34, 150–69; UNHCR attitude toward, 160, 162, 163, 171, 232n1; of Viet Kieu, 12; voluntary, 171, 175
Republika Srpska (SP), 175, 177
REST (Relief Society of Tigray), 189, 197, 204, 233n5
return: ambivalence on, 109–21; concept of, 3–4; defined, 4–5, 153; economic effects of, 3, 12, 14, 219–23; ethnography of, 1–15; globalization affecting, 3; imagined, 7–9; increase in, 1–2, 225n2; inevitability of, 72–73, 212–13; in literature, 5–7; men's view of, 212–13, 234n13; moral dilemmas of, 90–104; planning for, 2, 72–73; political consequences of, 3, 225n5; provisional,

return: (*continued*)
9–11; state policies for, 14, 231n2; repatriated, 11-13; statistics, 1, 2, 4, 171, 174, 207,
225n2; terrorist threats and, 3; tracking, 2;
virtual, 4; women's view of, 109, 213,
234n13. *See also* repatriation
Rex, John, 209
Richardson, Bonham C., 221–22
remittances, 2, 14, 42, 52, 61, 90-91, 93, 109,
114. *See also* family responsibilities; financ-
ing
riots, 2
rituals: Chinese, 97, 230n4; Viet Kieu, 83
Rivera, Brooklyn, 160
Rouse, Roger, 120
RPF. *See* Rwandan Patriotic Front
Rubenstein, Hymie, 219
Rushdie, Salman, 108
Russia, imagined return to, 1
Rwanda: exile from, 21–29; imagined return to,
7; MCC in, 226n3; return to, 19–33;
UNHCR in, 26, 28; Zaire versus, 20, 30
Rwandan Armed Forces (RAF or FAR): in
Congo war, 19–20; training, 22–24
Rwandan Patriotic Front (RPF), 20, 23, 24, 27,
226nn4–5

Safran, William, 109
Said, Edward, 15, 108, 124
"Saigon: The Sequel," 66
Sandinista rue, 155–56, 158–59, 163, 164,
166–67, 231n2
Sandino, Augusto Cesar, 231n2
Sandzak, 232n8
Sapoa Peace Accord, 165
Sarajevo: cultured versus uncultured people in,
181–82; economy of, 176; education system
in, 181–82; ethnic minorities in, 180–81;
population decrease in, 178; repatriation to,
12, 13, 170–86; social status in, 178,
181–82. *See also* Bosnia-Herzegovina
Schmitt, Carl, 145, 231n2
SED. *See* Socialist Unity Party
Selassie, Haile, 193
Serbia, refugee camps in, 7
Serematakis, C. Nadia, 58
sesame exports, 193, 197, 203–4, 233n8
Sin, Jaime, 61
social status: of Barbadians, 213–15, 217–19,
221; of Chinese, 91, 99–100, 102; of Eritreans, 36–37, 39–40; of Filipinas, 56,
104–5, 123–24; of German Jews, 131; of
marriages, "bad class," 90; of Nicaraguans,

14, 157–62; of peasants, 153–55; of
refugees, change in, 151–53; repatriation effects on, 12–13, 24–25, 34, 150–69; of
Sarajevans, 181–82; of Viet Kieu, 71, 72,
77; of women, 60–61, 123–24
Socialist Federal Republic of Yugoslavia. *See* Yu-
goslavia
Socialist Unity Party (SED), Jewish citizenship
in, 130
*Sojourners: The Return of German-Jews and the Ques-
tion of Identity* (Borneman and Peck), 231
Somoza dictatorship, 155, 156, 162, 231n2. *See
also* Nicaragua
Sorenson, John, 44, 228n9
sorghum production, 197, 203
South China Morning Post, 228n10
SP. *See* Republika Srpska
Stack, Carol, 104, 123
Stafford, Charles, 97
Stalin, Josef, 140, 141, 143
Sudan: conditions of refugee camps in, 189–90;
COR, 190–91; employment in, 191; Er-
itrean asylum in, 34; Ethiopian asylum in,
188–91; politics of confinement in, 190–91;
Saffawa camp in, 190–91; Wad Kowli camp
in, 189–90
sugar production, 208, 222–23
Sutton, Connie, 221, 234n8
Sweden: educational opportunities in, 227n2;
Eritrean refugees in, 34, 36, 226nn1–2

Tadiar, Neferti Xina X., 60
"Taglish," 107
Tanzania, refugee camps in, 8
terrorist threats, return affected by, 3
Tet holiday, 83
Thornhill, Rose, 209
Tigray Region. *See* Ethiopia
Tigrayan People's Liberation Front (TPLF): land
shareholders of, 197; rebel coalitions of,
191, 199; refugee relief from, 189, 204,
233n5
Tinig Filipino, 105, 106, 112
Tomlinson, Sally, 209
TPLF. *See* Tigrayan People's Liberation Front
transnationalism, 3; in literature, 6, 172; in mar-
riage, 43–45, 110, 112, 209–10; in religion,
230n6
Trinidad: emigration to, 208; return to, 206
Tutsi. *See* Rwanda

UNHCR (United Nations High Commissioner
for Refugees): Bosnian refugee relief by,

174; Ethiopian refugee relief by, 190, 197; Nicaraguan refugee relief by, 165–66; repatriation viewed by, 160, 162, 163, 171, 232n1; return statistics by, 1, 225n2; Rwandan refugee relief by, 26, 28

United Kingdom: Barbadian emigration to, 207, 208–9; education in, 212; employment in, 207

United Nations High Commissioner for Refugees. *See* UNHCR

United Nations Research Institute for Social Development. *See* UNRISD

United States: Barbadians in, 206, 234n8; court hearings in, 151; Eritrean refugees in, 34, 36, 226–27nn1–3; German Jews in, 131–32; migration from, 2–3, 10; Nicaraguan Resistance support by, 156–57, 160, 163, 165, 231n3; Viet Kieu in, 75–77, 79, 86

Universal Declaration of Human Rights (1948), 151

UNRISD (United Nations Research Institute for Social Development), 35

Viet Kieu: alienation of, 77–78, 86; assimilation of, 65, 71, 72, 87–89; autobiographies, 69–70; bribery by, 81–82; categorizing, 65–69; citizenship change in, 83–86, 88–89; education of, 65, 74, 77–78; emotions of, 75, 79, 81; employment of, 67–68, 70–71, 82–83, 85; English fluency of, 65, 72, 76, 77, 229n5; expectations of, 69–70; family relationships for, 79–81, 84–85; family responsibilities for, 71; in France, 69–70, 74, 81, 86; generation gaps of, 80–81; in Germany, 76, 77, 85; in Hanoi, 67, 70; identity of, 72, 81, 87–89; kinship re-establishment of, 83–86; marriages, 71, 84–85; memories, 73–75; privileged return for, 15; provisional return for, 10; racism against, 79; refugees, 75–77; repatriation of, 12; return experiences of, common, 72; return statistics of, 67; rituals, 83; social status of, 71, 72, 77; in United States, 75–77, 79, 86; Vietnamese relations with, 81–83, 87–89

Vietnam: communism in, 74, 87; Congressional visits to, 66–67; economic changes in, 67, 69–70, 81, 83, 87–88; memories of, 73–75, 81; political system of, 12, 68, 69–70, 83–84, 87–88; Viet Kieu relations with, 81–83, 87–89

Vietnam Economic Times, 67, 68

Vietnamese Communist Party, 67

virtual returns, 4

Volksdeutsche (Germans by blood), 140, 146

voluntary repatriation, 171, 175

Wang Gungwu, 93

War-Torn Societies project, 35

Wendezeit, 128

West German Basic Law (1949), 146

West Indies. *See* Barbados

Whiteford, Michael, 234n18

Wickham, John, 210

Wir für Uns, 138

women: abuse of, 54, 190; Barbadian, 215, 234n18; education of, 40–41, 227n2, 228n9; employment of, 43, 50, 53–56, 207, 215; Ethiopian, 190; imagined return among, 8–9; land ownership by, 196; relationships for, 115, 120, 121–22, 123, 209; return viewed by, 109, 213, 234n13; social status of, 44–45, 60–61, 123–24. *See also* Filipinas

Woon, Yuen-Fong, 93

Woreda Office of Agriculture, 196–97

World Jewish Congress, 129

World Zionist Organization, 129

World War II: migration after, 8, 127–49, 207; refugees defined after, 151

Wyman, Mark, 2

Yugoslavia: BiH independence from, 174–75; imagined return to, 7; refugees from, 171

Yung, Betty Ma Shan Yee, 228nn4–5

Zaire: genocide in, 21–27; refugee camps in, 7, 19–20, 30–32; Rwanda versus, 20, 30

Zetter, Roger, 46

ziji ren (persons in the same circle), 9

Acknowledgments

First and foremost we acknowledge many returnee friends and colleagues whose insights and ideas have inspired this work. We wish them all safe and enriching returns.

We would like to thank three anonymous reviewers for their thoughtful suggestions for revisions of both the work as a whole and of the individual chapters. In addition, we thank Cliff Hackett for helping us remember Bea's ideas and insights in this volume. We much appreciate Rada Radosevic and Nidia Casati for their help in finding relevant data on Bosnian returns and for their insights and observations on one of the major return programs of contemporary times, and we appreciate Kyle Thompson's help in the final editing of this volume. We also thank the institutions that encouraged and supported our work: International Organization for Migration, Population Council, and Middlebury College. And we acknowledge our editor Peter Agree, who supported the idea of this volume from its inception and who helped us overcome the perils of edited volumes.

Finally, we acknowledge Frank Nicosia, Dennis Long, and our parents, whose impatience hastened the process and who know that returns are a valuable part of any journey.

A special memory and thanks go to Emil Oxfeld, who believed in this volume and would have liked to have seen it.